collections on the Crusades. Phillips is the co-editor of the academic journal *Crusades* and writes regularly for *BBC History* and *History Today*. He has made numerous radio and television appearances, including *Boris Johnson and the Dream of Rome* (BBC2); *The Crusades* (with Rageh Omaar) in the *Christianity* series on Channel 4, and *The Crescent and the Cross* (History Channel).

JONATHAN PHILLIPS

Holy Warriors

A Modern History of the Crusades

VINTAGE BOOKS
London

Published by Vintage 2010

10 9

Copyright © Jonathan Phillips 2009

Jonathan Phillips has asserted his right under the Copyright, Designs
and Patents Act 1988 to be identified as the author of this work

First published in Great Britain in 2009 by
The Bodley Head

Vintage
Random House, 20 Vauxhall Bridge Road,
London SW1V 2SA

www.vintage-books.co.uk

Addresses for companies within The Random House Group Limited
can be found at: www.randomhouse.co.uk/offices.htm

The Random House Group Limited Reg. No. 954009

A CIP catalogue record for this book
is available from the British Library

ISBN 9781845950781

Penguin Random House is committed to a sustainable future for
our business, our readers and our planet. This book is made from
Forest Stewardship Council® certified paper.

Printed and bound in Great Britain by Clays Ltd, St Ives plc

For my parents

Contents

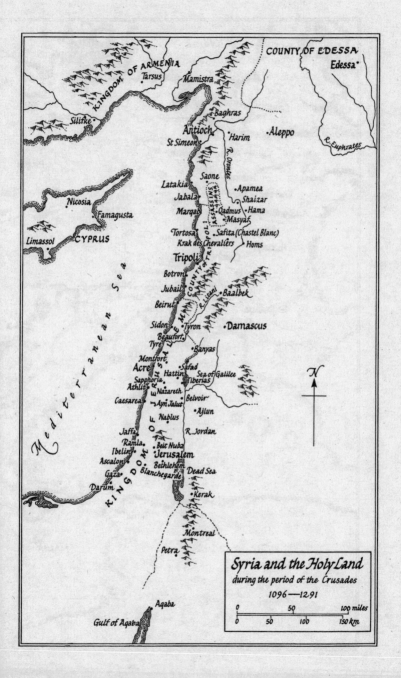

Syria and the Holy Land
during the period of the Crusades
1096—1291

Europe and the Near East

N

0   100   200   300 miles
0   100   200   300   400   500 km

Black Sea

grade

R. Danube
Nicopolis   Varna

ovo

Adrianople   Constantinople

hessalonica   Nicaea

Aegean
Sea   Konya

EUBOEA   Chios   Ephesus   Aleppo

Athens   Antalya   Antioch

ethoni   Rhodes   CYPRUS   Damascus

CRETE   Acre

e   a   n   S   e   a   Jerusalem

Damietta   Kerak

Alexandria

Cairo

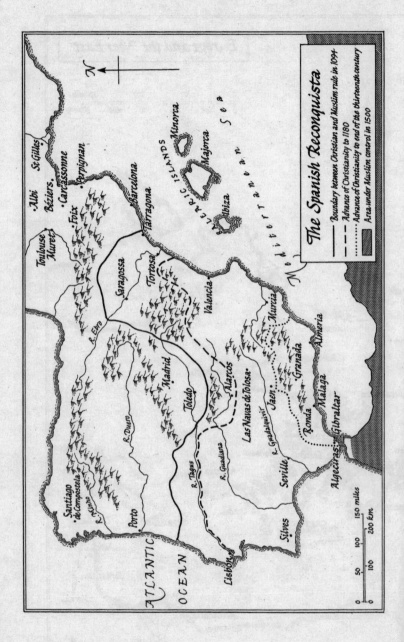

The Spanish Reconquista

—— Boundary between Christian and Muslim rule in 1094
– – – Advance of Christianity to 1180
······· Advance of Christianity to end of the thirteenth century
▨ Area under Muslim control in 1500

N

ATLANTIC OCEAN

Mediterranean Sea

BALEARIC ISLANDS

Santiago de Compostela
R. Minho
Porto
R. Duero
R. Tagus
Lisbon
R. Guadiana
Silves
Seville
R. Guadalquivir
Algeciras
Gibraltar
Ronda
Málaga
Granada
Almería
Jaén
Las Navas de Tolosa
Murcia
Alarcos
Valencia
Toledo
Madrid
R. Ebro
Saragossa
Tortosa
Tarragona
Barcelona
Perpignan
Foix
Carcassonne
Béziers
Albi
St Gilles
Toulouse
Muret
Minorca
Majorca
Ibiza

0   50   100   150 miles
0   100   200 km

The Wider Baltic Region

North Sea

NORWAY

SWEDEN

FINLAND

N

L. Ladoga

Gulf of Finland

Uppsala

Baltic Sea

GOTLAND

L. Peipus

Novgorod

RUSSIA

Pskov

Gulf of Riga

LETIGALLIA

SCANIA

Riga

R. Düna

DENMARK

Roskilde

SAMOGITIA

Vilnius

Bosau

RÜGEN

Danzig

Lübeck

Demmin

POMERANIA

Marienburg

Tannenberg

LITHUANIA

Hamburg

Dobin

Stettin

PRUSSIA

Bremen

Havelberg

R. Oder

R. Vistula

Magdeburg

SAXONY

POLAND

R. Elbe

0   100   200 miles
0   100   200   300 km

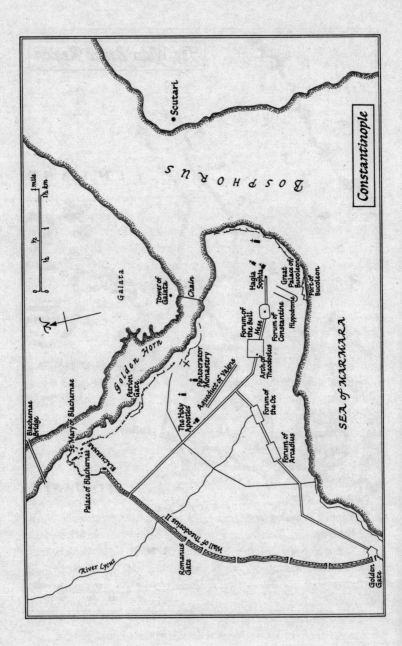

Constantinople

Scutari

BOSPHORUS

Galata

Tower of Galata

Chain

Golden Horn

Hagia Sophia

Great Palace of Bucoleon

Port of Bucoleon

Forum of the Bull

Mese

Hippodrome

Forum of Constantine

Arch of Theodosius

Pantocrazor Monastery

Aqueduct of Valens

Petrion Gate

The Holy Apostles

Forum of the Ox

SEA OF MARMARA

Blachernae Bridge

St Mary of Blachernae

Palace of Blachernae

BLACHERNAE

Forum of Arcadius

Wall of Theodosius II

River Lycus

Romanus Gate

Golden Gate

N

0   ½   1   1 mile

0   ½   1   1½ km

Acknowledgements

In the course of writing this book a great many people have offered invaluable advice and support, as well as providing me with opportunities to visit, to discuss and to learn about some of the people and places covered here. I would like to thank: William Purkis, Francis Robinson, Jonathan Harris, Matthew Bennett, Natasha Hodgson, Peter Jackson, Osman Latiff, Justin Champion, Paul Sturtevant, Andrew Taylor, Andy Hershey, Dimitri Collingridge, David Jeffcock and Will Lane. The good-natured enthusiasm and culinary skills of the students on the University of London MA in Crusader Studies have also been vital. I am very grateful to Catherine Clarke for her positive and clear-sighted guidance and to all the team at Felicity Bryan for their hard work; my thanks also to Fletcher and Co. in New York. Will Sulkin has shown immense faith in this project and provided crucial conceptual input and editorial advice; David Milner has been an excellent and observant editor and the help of Tim Bartlett and Kay Peddle has been much appreciated. My thanks, again, to Emmett Sullivan for his photographic expertise. The emotional and practical kindnesses of many others has been essential and I am hugely thankful to Alex and Ruth Windscheffel, Eileen Moore, Kate and Andrew Golding, Amanda and Lenny Goodrich, Lisa Drage, Sharon-Lee Broomfield, the Chappell family, Roger and Leila Moore, and particularly Anne Meyer and Sir Idris Pearce, and Sophie and John Wallace. My greatest debts are to my parents for providing me with such wholehearted support throughout my life; thanks also to my dad for his interest and research at such a difficult time for him; to my sons who both make me so proud: Tom for his ever-sharp observations and humour and Marcus for his happy enthusiasm. Finally, to my wonderful wife, Niki, for her patience, belief and love without which I could not be.

Introduction

Christianity versus Islam; crusade against jihad. Blood and dust; withering, shimmering heat; the ring and scrape of metal on metal: some of the sights, sounds and sensations we imagine to represent the age of the crusades, an epic clash between two of the world's great religions and a struggle in which men and women fought and died for their faith. Yet this familiar tale does not tell the complete story. This book, which is aimed squarely at the general reader or those looking for an overview of the subject, will, of course, explore this conflict of ideas, belief and culture. But it will also show the myriad contradictions and the diversity of holy war: friendships and alliances between Christians and Muslims; triumphs of diplomacy rather than the sword; the launch of crusades against Christians, and calls for jihads against Muslims. Taken as a whole, this rich, multifaceted relationship has the capacity to produce a more evocative and insightful account than the usual tales of Christian–Muslim bloodshed alone.

Large sections of this book are character-driven. Like many readers, I suspect, the irresistible allure of one of history's great double acts, Richard the Lionheart and Saladin, drew me into the subject as a student and from this developed an interest in the motives and the ideologies of the protagonists. Evidence from contemporary writings, such as chronicles, songs, sermons, travel diaries, letters, financial accounts and peace treaties, along with visual material from art, architecture and archaeology, provides a profusion of voices and images that enables us to reconstruct the age of the crusades. Although there is a narrative thread here, this is not a detailed, chronological history of the subject: that is one purview of the academic textbook.

I have chosen to bring to life a variety of figures and events outside of those well known to a general audience. It remains essential to describe the unexpected victory of the First Crusade; the titanic tussle between Richard the Lionheart and Saladin; the breathtaking naivety of the Children's Crusade, and the brutal and crafty suppression of the Knights Templar, but the lives of others can illuminate the age of the crusades just as well: soon after the First Crusade, for example, a fiery jihad preacher, al-Sulami, exhorted the citizens of Damascus to holy war but his message was decades ahead of mainstream opinion and his early audiences numbered only a handful of people; Queen Melisende of Jerusalem was an intimidating and astute politician who dominated the kingdom of Jerusalem during the mid-twelfth century – yet the idea of a woman ruling the most war-torn area of Christendom seems inherently counter-intuitive. Frederick II of Germany was an Arabic-speaking Holy Roman Emperor who retook Jerusalem in 1229 without striking a blow, but at the same time he was under a ban of excommunication from the pope; during the late fourteenth century, Henry Bolingbroke (many years before he became the paranoid and brutal King Henry IV of England), behaved as a pilgrim and holy warrior, intent upon creating a chivalric reputation for himself in northern Europe and the Holy Land.

The motives of crusaders have long intrigued historians and, self-evidently, faith lies at the heart of holy war. From a modern-day western perspective, extreme religious fervour is often synonymous with the fanaticism of minorities, but in the Europe of the central Middle Ages crusading was regarded as virtuous and positive. It was a society saturated with religious belief in which faith provided the template and the boundaries for almost every aspect of behaviour and where recognition of divine will and fear of the afterlife were universal. The fight against the enemies of God offered people a way to evade the torments of hell and this is one reason why crusading became a fundamental feature of medieval life. Everyone from emperors, kings and queens, bishops, dukes and knights, down to peasants and prostitutes, took part in crusades; they were, in the twelfth and thirteenth centuries at least, a totally mainstream activity, accepted and endorsed by an entire culture and not, as later became the case, simply the preserve of the noble elite.

But religion was not the sole driving force for crusaders. Part of the fascination with the crusading age, and one theme in this book, is to see how other ideas, such as the lure of land and money, a sense of honour and family tradition, a desire for adventure, and the obligation of service, all sat alongside – and sometimes smothered – religion. Given the impossibility of ascribing precise motives to any individual from this distance in time we have to weigh the available evidence and point to trends and probabilities. The actions of most crusaders were shaped by multiple, overlapping reasons, and behaviour that may seem contradictory to us was not always viewed as such. When, therefore, crusaders from the mercantile powerhouse of Genoa defeated Muslims and, at the same time, secured a profit for their city, they interpreted their success as a sign of divine approval. In other words, in these circumstances, they comfortably assimilated a close link between money and holy war. Likewise, there was a complex relationship between chivalry and crusading. By the mid-thirteenth century the knightly code had become the quintessential basis of noble life and the pursuance of fame and heroic deeds was – *if* performed in God's name – the pinnacle of chivalric achievement rather than, as it can appear to us, purely an exercise in ego-building. Economic motives and military excess could, in some cases, dominate or distract crusading expeditions and, on occasion, this provoked intense criticism. The question of motivation shimmers and shifts across time and space, and trying to trace it is part of the challenge and the excitement of this subject.

I have tried to offer comparable insight into the motives of the Islamic world. To some extent, linguistic restrictions hamper this but an increasing amount of material has been translated from Arabic and the sources and characters that I have chosen to highlight the Muslim perspective are especially rich. Similar themes concerning changes in motive over time, or identifying a complex interplay of motives – most obviously seen in the case of Saladin – will be explored.

The chronological and geographical scope of this book reflects a modern academic consensus on the duration and the extent of crusading.[1] In the decades after the conquest of Jerusalem in 1099 crusading diversified to encompass expeditions in Iberia, the Baltic, North Africa, as well as campaigns against enemies of the Church within Europe, such as the Cathars of southern France, along with political opponents of the papacy, including Emperor Frederick II of Germany. This conceptual flexibility helped to extend the appeal of crusading both geographically and intellectually; it also enabled the idea to remain 'live' and relevant for centuries after the end of Christian control over the Holy Land in 1291. Eventually, of course, crusading did decline, and into the seventeenth century it was widely regarded as a distant and barbaric concept of little value at all. This came to change during the nineteenth century, a situation prompted by the emergence of European overseas empires, particularly in the eastern Mediterranean. Thus, in sharp contrast to the decline and dismissal of crusading during the Age of Enlightenment, the relentless ambition of imperialism and colonialism, coupled with the cultural phenomena of Romanticism and orientalism, overlapped and combined to produce a dramatic revival in imagery and ideas descended from crusading. How far this derivation was accurate is something further to ponder. The momentum and diversity of the 'crusading' theme carried on into World War I, especially with the British involvement in Palestine; and then, with a more sinister aspect, into the alliance between General Franco and the Catholic Church in Spain during the civil war and beyond. As a historian of the twelfth century, tracing the centuries-long legacy of crusading has been a hugely exciting and enjoyable experience and my debt to scholars of later periods such as Housley, Christiansen, Knobler, Siberry, Riley-Smith and Bar-Yosef is considerable. My synthesis has also tried to pull in work beyond these studies – hence, for example, the discussions of nineteenth-century Italy and General Franco.

The sheer flexibility of crusading imagery in the language and culture of the West is remarkable. At one end of the spectrum lie, for example, the comic-fiction heroes Batman and Robin, 'those relentless crusaders for law and order'; or the legendary time-travelling television character Dr Who, described by one of its actors as 'an intergalactic crusader'.[2] 'Crusades' – or an appeal for a good cause – have been launched for entirely worthy, secular reasons: former US president Bill Clinton made a widely reported call for a crusade to reverse the epidemic of obesity in 2005 and 2006; crusades for fair play in sport or to end hospital waiting lists are also familiar to us. In some quarters, however, metaphor can creep dangerously close to reality and politicians have learnt to be wary of the word. In early 2007, during his last months as prime minister, Tony Blair was asked on the BBC Radio 4 *Today* programme if he saw himself as 'a crusader' for social reform. Deftly, but determinedly, Blair avoided taking the bait and simply stated that he was concerned to improve social justice; given the issue of his own spirituality and Britain's controversial involvement in Iraq it was vital for him to sidestep any notion of accepting the label 'crusader', whatever the context.

The closest – and most uncomfortable – overlap between crusading metaphor and reality was in September 2001 as President George W. Bush spoke of the continued efforts to find the associates of those responsible for the horrific attacks of 9/11: 'this crusade . . . this war on terror is going to take a while'. Listening to his comments two thoughts came to mind: first, a feeling of real anxiety at the backlash an American president's use of the word 'crusade' was likely to produce; secondly, I started to wonder why, exactly, had he used it in the first instance? What images was he trying to conjure up? After all, other than the First Crusade's capture of Jerusalem in 1099, the vast majority of crusading expeditions, to the Holy Land at least, had failed – often pretty ignominiously. Why, then, over 900 years after it was first conceived did an idea from late eleventh-century Europe resonate so powerfully across the modern world? Trying to answer these questions was one prompt for me to begin this book.

I wrote a short piece for the *Independent* newspaper that outlined a perception in the Islamic world that linked medieval crusades – Christians invading Muslim lands and killing their inhabitants – with modern western involvement in places such as Egypt, Palestine and Iraq where this contemporary activity was portrayed as a continuation of the crusader wars of the past.[3] Whether such a direct connection is at all accurate has become almost irrelevant – it is accepted as a truism, albeit one that rests on a fascinating trail of evidence derived from European sources and also sustained in, and generated by, the Islamic world itself. Historians such as Sivan and Hillenbrand have considered this issue with real insight and my debt to their efforts is evident below, although an emphasis on the neglected legacy of folk-lore and a brief consideration of the writings of individuals such as President Nasser and President Carter are paths of my own making.[4]

Drawing together the extraordinarily diverse legacy of crusading in the Christian West, and then tracking the ebb and flow of jihad in the Muslim world, brings one back to the war of words and deeds between President Bush and Osama Bin Laden, an exchange from the modern age, yet one with the deepest and most twisted of roots.

The First Stages of Christian–Muslim Conflict

It is convenient to brand Pope Urban II's call for the First Crusade in November 1095 as the starting point of the conflict that echoes down to us today. In many respects, however, this is wrong because the two faiths had already been in opposition for centuries and, while it is easy to see crusade and jihad as two sides of the same coin, separate strands of holy war had grown into being long before Urban's speech at Clermont.

As we shall see below, Christian thinkers used Roman theories of a 'just war' as a basis for their own concept of holy war, and this would be refined further to formulate the crusade. Yet Christianity was not the only belief system to have ideas of holy warfare, and in the early seventh century another faith emerged with its own brand of religious conflict: Islam. The Prophet Muhammad's teachings spread at bewildering speed and within years of his death in 632 his adherents had seized the Arabian peninsula and Jerusalem. From the very beginning this new religion enshrined a duty of holy war on its followers and also fused (theoretically, at least) religious and political authority in the office of the caliphate, Muhammad's successors as the spiritual head of Islam. By 711 Muslim forces had swept through North Africa and cascaded across the Straits of Gibraltar into Christian Spain. Only twenty-one years later their progress was halted by a defeat at Tours in central France and they retired southwards to consolidate their rule over the Iberian peninsula. The thought of central and southern France under Islamic rule is quite an eye-opener to a modern audience, although militarily it was, seemingly, a step too far for the invaders. One reason why Islam expanded so rapidly was that 'Peoples of the Book', that is Christians and Jews were, in recognition of the shared heritage of their faiths (Christ, for example, is a prophet in Islam and is a prominent figure in the Koran), treated with tolerance and not compelled to convert. Thus, as long as these subject peoples, known as *dhimmi*, paid the appropriate tax they could continue to practise their religion and this, in turn, meant less resentment, more assimilation and often, eventually, conversion.

In 832 the Muslims seized Sicily from the Byzantines (who were Orthodox Christians) and in 846 they even raided Rome itself; in broad

terms, however, the ninth and the tenth centuries can be described as
a period of consolidation, rather than expansion. In the years just
before the crusades the Seljuk Turks emerged as the main power in
the Muslim world. These nomadic tribesmen from central Asia had
embraced and energised Sunni Islam in the late tenth century. At the
Battle of Manzikert in 1071 they crushed the Byzantine army and then
swept through Asia Minor to bring themselves within range of
Constantinople itself. This threat prompted appeals to the Catholic
West for help and eventually provided one of the triggers for the First
Crusade.[5]

The Europe which spawned the First Crusade was chiefly characterised by endemic violence and, in obvious contradiction, profound
religious belief. After the collapse of the Carolingian empire in the
ninth century the region was plagued by a lack of central authority.
Counts, castellans and knights competed with one another for power
at a local or regional level, and in a landscape wearied by frequent
failures of the harvest, armed knights ravaged neighbourhoods, stole
cattle and property and even attacked churches and monasteries. With
royal power in France, for example, best described as vestigial (the
king wielded almost no practical authority thirty miles outside of
Paris), the scope for social disorder and personal advance was immense.
The vast majority of this fragmented, localised society lived in the
countryside. Urban centres were small and underdeveloped (Paris and
London had perhaps 30,000 inhabitants); long-distance travel was difficult because roads were narrow and often impassable in winter,
although the river networks offered some help to traders. Religion
was the solitary idea to bind this patchwork society together and in
the latter half of the eleventh century a dynamic group of clerics
seized control of the Catholic Church and began to drive forward an
agenda of Christian renewal. Prior to this, the papacy had been a
divided, introspective institution, but the reformers' energy generated
a sharp increase in papal authority. For the first time in centuries
the successor of St Peter began to shape the religious and political
behaviour of the Catholic West; notable amongst his concerns were
the sin-drenched knightly classes.

In practical terms, the Catholic Church required allies to protect
and advance its position; unlike the position in the Islamic world,
Church and State were separate entities. While the secular powers

directed European warfare the language and symbolism of holy war
had been evident in struggles against the pagan Vikings, for example;
or in papal support for William the Conqueror's invasion of England
in 1066. But these were not yet crusades: that is, *papally* authorised
holy wars across, or outside, the boundaries of Christendom.
Nonetheless, the Church started to try to steer the noble classes, and
a series of initiatives known as the Peace of God and the Truce of
God were designed to curtail attacks on the more vulnerable sections
of society. The papacy began to work more closely with lay powers
and in 1053 Pope Leo IX gave limited spiritual rewards to warriors who
helped him defend his lands in Italy. Around the same time territories on the edge of Christian Europe became more aggressive and
outward-looking and started to pick away at the frontiers of Islam. In
the 1060s the Normans of southern Italy attacked Sicily (with papal
endorsement); in 1074 Pope Gregory VII tried (unsuccessfully) to
organise an army to face the Muslims of the eastern Mediterranean
and in 1089 Pope Urban II offered spiritual rewards to knights who
fought the Spanish Muslims at Tarragona. This growing co-operation
between the papacy and the secular powers was a vital prerequisite
for crusading. Although the First Crusade did not represent the starting
point of conflict between Christians and Muslims, papal initiation of
warfare on this scale was new, and the offer of spiritual rewards to
the participants represented a further advance. The crusade was forged
in this crucible of knightly violence, territorial expansion, growing
papal power and the need for salvation. Christian warfare with Islam
had acquired a new intellectual and theological basis; and this,
combined with an unprecedented popular appeal, gave the conflict an
incalculably sharper edge and provided a rationale that would last for
centuries.

I

'Deus vult!': The First Crusade and the Capture of Jerusalem, 1095–1099

"'A grave report has come from the lands around Jerusalem . . . that a race absolutely alien to God . . . has invaded the land of the Christians . . . They have either razed the churches of God to the ground or enslaved them to their own rites . . . They cut open the navels of those whom they choose to torment . . . drag them around and flog them before killing them as they lie on the ground with all their entrails out . . . What can I say of the appalling violation of women? On whom does the task lie of avenging this, if not on you? . . . Take the road to the Holy Sepulchre, rescue that land and rule over it yourselves, for that land, as scripture says *floweth with milk and honey* . . . Take this road for the remission of your sins, assured of the unfading glory of the kingdom of heaven." When Pope Urban had said these things . . . everyone shouted in unison: *"Deus vult! Deus vult!"*, "God wills it! God wills it!"'[1]

In this vivid – and hugely exaggerated – language, as reported by Robert of Rheims, Pope Urban II launched the First Crusade at Clermont in central France in November 1095. Four years later, having endured a journey of astounding hardship, the self-proclaimed 'knights of Christ' arrived at Jerusalem. On 15 July 1099 the crusaders stormed the walls and put its defenders to the sword to reclaim Christ's city from Islam.

Pope Urban II and the Call to Crusade

While, 900 years later, a distant descendant of Pope Urban's creation continues to cast its shadow on Christian–Muslim relations across the world, it is an irony that crusading was primarily intended to remedy problems within western Europe. As the head of the Catholic Church, Urban was responsible for the spiritual well-being of everyone in Latin Christendom. Yet Europe was beset by a variety of evils: violence and lawlessness were rife and Emperor Henry IV of Germany, the most powerful secular ruler, was, at times, an excommunicate, cast out of the Church because he had challenged papal authority.[2] In Urban's mind, the fundamental cause of such chaos was a diminution of faith; it was his role to restore peace and stability. If this was to be achieved spiritual concern would have to be blended with canny political calculation; perhaps to a modern audience the second of these elements sits a little uneasily on a man in his position, but to Urban the two were indivisible; as pope he did everything that was necessary to further God's work.

It was Urban's genius that he conceived of a plan that offered benefits to the pope *and* to all of his flock. Perhaps he achieved this partly because of his family background: he was from the county of Champagne in northern France and was a man of noble blood. The combination of this high-born lineage and a successful career in the Church gave him a direct insight into the hopes and fears of the knightly classes and this, in part, explains why crusading satisfied the aspirations of so many. He linked several ingredients familiar to medieval society, such as pilgrimage and the idea of a holy war against the enemies of God, with an unprecedented offer of salvation, a combination almost guaranteed to enthuse the warriors of western Europe.

To persuade people – in any age – to leave their homes and loved ones, and to venture into the unknown it is usually necessary to convince them that the cause is worthwhile. As many modern conflicts reveal, propaganda can play a vital part in a build-up to war. Pope Urban II's address at Clermont used highly inflammatory images to provoke moral outrage in his audience. The Muslims were described in language that emphasised their 'otherness' and their barbarity towards innocent Christians. In reality, while it is true that pilgrims were occasionally maltreated, it was also the case that there had been no systematic persecution of Christians by the Muslims of the Holy Land for decades. Yet Urban's impassioned rhetoric demanded a response from the knights of France. He called for vengeance, a concept that was second nature to knights accustomed to correcting an injustice through force, supported by the weight of moral right.

Through references to authorities on Church law, such as St Augustine, Urban and his circle of advisers constructed a case whereby violence could, in certain circumstances, be seen as a morally positive act.[3] This required a just cause – usually it was a reaction to the aggression of another party, in this case the alleged atrocities committed by the Muslims. It needed proper authority to proclaim the war; and also right intention – that is, pure motives in a conflict of proportional, but not excessive, force. To these 'just war' principles, crusading added the taking of a vow and an association with pilgrimage. Thus, because it was judged to be morally positive the crusade became an act of penance that merited a spiritual reward. Earlier attempts to restrict the violence that plagued eleventh-century Europe included the Peace of God movement in which the Church forbade fighting for a specific period of time under pain of ecclesiastical penalties. At Clermont, however, Urban urged the knights of France to cease their private wars and to begin a battle worthy of their noble status; to fight for God was to take service with the ultimate Lord, and to win forgiveness for their wicked lives was a prize immeasurably greater than any earthly riches could offer.[4]

Without doubt the violent warriors of the West had committed many acts displeasing to God and here Urban offered them a chance to avoid a terrible fate. Practically every church in the land had a sculpture or a fresco of hell: savage devils gouged out the eyes of screaming sinners; others were skinned or tortured with spears and pitchforks; impaled humans were roasted for eternity.[5] The message from the Church was terrifyingly simple: there was no avoiding the consequences of sin; a knight, therefore, needed an escape route from Satan's fires. These same frescoes also showed heaven – a place of peace, tranquillity and everlasting safety. Making pilgrimages and giving donations to monastic houses could help to avoid hell, but Urban brilliantly presented what one contemporary described as 'a new way to attain salvation'.[6] The pope judged – correctly – that the crusade would be a sufficiently arduous experience to deserve the remission of all penance; in effect it would wipe the slate clean and all the vicious, violent misdeeds of the medieval warrior – or anyone who took part – would be cleared. As far as the knightly classes were concerned, the neatest aspect of all was that they could continue fighting – only now their energies were directed towards the enemies of God, rather than their fellow Christians. Thus, the cause in which they fought meant the Church now blessed their activities, rather than condemned them.

Those who wished to take part in the crusade had to make a public statement of their commitment in the form of a vow and being marked with the sign of the cross. Often amidst hugely emotional scenes, enthusiastic recruits would surge forwards and demand to have a cloth cross pinned to their shoulder, desperate to bear the symbol that represented Christ's sacrifice and their own imitation of his suffering. Preachers adopted the words of Christ himself: 'If any man will come after me, let him deny himself, and take up his cross and follow me.' If a crusader deserted his vows then he deserved eternal opprobrium; Urban 'commanded that . . . he should forever be regarded as an outlaw, unless he came to his senses and undertook to complete whatever of his obligation was left undone'.[7] As an aside, the crusade also had the effect, temporarily at least, of bringing huge numbers of people under the control of the Church. Once again, we can see how Urban had found a way to enhance the standing of the papacy while offering something attractive to others.

The call to free the Holy Sepulchre and the Christians of the East was shaped in a familiar form; namely, a pilgrimage. This was a fundamental feature of medieval life; the notion of turning to a saint for help was an everyday experience and people sought the assistance of these heavenly beings in health, harvests, fertility, protection and forgiveness for sins. The presence of a saint was manifested by relics, parts of a saint's body, or objects associated with his or her life, that were believed to retain their holy power and to offer a conduit to divine help. The veneration of relics often required a journey and some saints became associated with particular causes: St Leonard of Noblat, for example, was the patron saint of prisoners. People in captivity prayed to him and when their incarceration ended they made a pilgrimage to Noblat (in central France) and, as a mark of gratitude, placed their chains on the church altar. While many pilgrimages were simply processions or visits to local churches, longer journeys to important shrines, such as that of St James at Santiago de Compostela in north-western Spain, grew in popularity during the eleventh century. The ultimate pilgrimage destination was the Holy Land – the place where Christ had lived and died. Because He had ascended to heaven there was no body to venerate and so the focus was on places touched by His presence and His death, most particularly His tomb, the Holy Sepulchre in Jerusalem. The Holy Land, and this particular site above all, became the principal goal of the First Crusade. For the crusaders, a journey there deserved the greatest reward of all – the remission of all sins. This was integral to the hearts and minds of medieval man and the notion of regaining Christ's land for Christianity lay at the core of Urban's appeal.

Even though the papacy advanced spiritual motives as the prime reason for the crusade it is clear that more worldly factors also played their part. Robert of Rheims' account (written *c*.1106–7) of Urban's speech pointed this up when he claimed the pope spoke of a land of milk and honey – an alluring prospect for people troubled by poor harvests and in search of a change from the drudgery of village life. While the desire to liberate Christ's city had to be paramount – otherwise God would not favour the expedition – some crusaders would need to remain in the Levant to hold the territory; there was very little point in taking Jerusalem if everyone then returned home. The First Crusade was in part, therefore, a war of Christian colonisation, as well as Christian liberation. For those prepared to take a chance it offered a new life. However, as it turned out, while huge numbers were willing to become crusaders, relatively few people chose to stay in the East afterwards. If the hope of plunder and riches helped to draw people towards this great adventure, in the event, the acquisition of wealth proved far harder than it had appeared beforehand.

Notwithstanding Urban's desire to restore the spiritual well-being of western Europe it was an external trigger that prompted him to launch the crusade. In March 1095 envoys arrived from Emperor Alexius of Constantinople to appeal for help against the Muslims of Asia Minor. Alexius ruled the Byzantine Empire, the successor to the old Roman Empire, and had, until recent years, controlled territories that stretched across Asia Minor to Antioch in northern Syria, as well as modern-day Greece, Bulgaria and Albania. By 1095, much of Asia Minor had been lost, although ongoing troubles within the Muslim world gave him an opportunity to fight back.[8] For many years he had sent requests for groups of well-armed knights to help his cause and there was, by now, a strong tradition of western mercenaries serving

in the imperial army. In 1095, however, Alexius, understandably, failed
to anticipate that Pope Urban would use this opportunity to make a
far wider appeal to the people of Latin Christendom and launch the
crusade.[9] Pope Urban himself also had an agenda with regard to
Alexius. In 1054, disputes over doctrinal matters and, more pertinently,
the relative authority of the pope to the patriarch of Constantinople
had provoked a schism between the Catholics and the Orthodox
Church: a situation that still exists today. In spite of this split, the two
camps maintained contact and Urban saw the crusade as an opportunity to foster better relations – although from his perspective Rome
was the senior partner because the Catholics were the people offering
help to their Orthodox brothers. In fact, Urban cast himself in the
role of a father to his 'son' the Byzantine emperor, and saw Rome
as a mother to Constantinople.

Recruitment, Pogroms and Preparations for the Crusade

Urban and his circle considered how best to broadcast the crusade
appeal. In an era before mass communications it was vital to make
as big a visual impact as possible. This meant staging numerous public
ceremonies: the Council of Clermont was carefully publicised with
invitations sent to churchmen across France, Spain and parts of
Germany. Urban chose Clermont for its central location and the
meeting attracted thirteen archbishops, eighty bishops and cardinals
and over ninety abbots. For about a fortnight the pope laid down a
legislative programme for the spiritual recovery of Christendom. On
the penultimate day he unveiled the centrepiece of his agenda: the
crusade. Urban knew that his own presence was crucial and to this
end he then embarked upon a huge tour that took him hundreds of
miles northwards to Le Mans and Angers, down to Bordeaux, Toulouse
and Montpelier in the south.[10] This was no casually arranged ramble,
however; no pope had been north of the Alps for fifty years. Even in
today's Internet age the appearance of a celebrity – be it at a
supermarket opening or a major political rally – attracts crowds of
people eager to see or hear a famous individual for themselves. The
arrival of such a powerful figure was bound to excite attention and
Urban did his utmost to exploit this. Time and again, for example, at

Saint-Gilles, Le Puy, Chaise-Dieu, Limoges, Tours and Poitiers, the pope would appear on the feast day of the local saint, or else he would consecrate a new building or attend an important festival. In other words, he was careful to choose an opportunity which allowed him to address the biggest crowd possible. The arrival of the papal entourage was a truly splendid sight; the wealth and splendour of Pope Urban and his court were dominated by the successor of St Peter who wore a conical white cap with a circlet of gold and gems around the base.

It was not just through his personal appearances that Urban recruited crusaders. The audience at Clermont carried the call back to their homes and, even though the response to his speech had been rapturous, the pope had little sense of the extraordinary zeal with which his words would be taken up. News of the expedition surged across Europe and saturated the Latin West with crusading fervour. The pope's appeal to the knights of France soon spread to encompass parts of Spain and Germany as well.

One immediate, if undesired, side effect was a series of attacks against the Jews.[11] The rabble-rousing sermons of a preacher named Folkmar incited audiences to turn against the non-Christians in their midst. Jewish communities had peacefully existed in western Europe for many centuries. Folkmar took Urban's theme of alien peoples and, instead of directing Christian violence towards the Muslims, he chose to emphasise the Jews' history as the killers of Christ and to suggest that they therefore deserved punishment. One contemporary Hebrew source wrote: 'the princes and nobles and common folk in France took counsel and set plans to rise up like eagles and to battle and to clear the way for journeying to Jerusalem, the holy city, and for reaching the sepulchre of the crucified, a trampled corpse who cannot profit and who cannot save for he is worthless. They said to one another: "Behold we travel to a distant land to do battle with the kings of that land. We take our souls in our hands in order to kill and to subjugate all those kingdoms which do not believe in the crucified. How much more so should we kill and subjugate the Jews who killed and cruci-fied Him."'[12] Of comparable importance was the Jews' wealth – many people owed them money (secured by the sin of usury – the charging of interest on loans), and the crusaders needed large sums of cash to set out. In spite of enjoying the nominal protection of local bishops, in the late spring of 1096 the Jewish quarters in Cologne, Speyer Mainz and Worms were besieged and stormed. The army of Count Emicho of Leiningen was especially culpable. He was described as a wicked man: 'our chief persecutor. He had no mercy on the elderly, on young men and young women, on infants and sucklings, nor on the ill. He made the people of the Lord like dust to be trampled. Their young men he put to the sword and their pregnant women he ripped open.'[13] The Christian chronicler Albert of Aachen suggested that there was an effort to convert the Jews – often forcibly.[14] Hebrew sources echo this in reporting the crusaders' attitude: 'Let us take vengeance first upon them. Let us wipe them out as a nation; Israel's name will be mentioned no more. Or else let them be like us and acknowledge the child born of menstruation.'[15] Beyond these terrible episodes in the Rhineland, however, the attacks were limited; this was not a Europe-wide or systematic persecution of the Jews. The ecclesiastical author-ities tried to calm matters; the Bible forbade the killing of Jews. The need to prevent major civil unrest was another reason to bring these events to a close; the Jews' payment of bribes to local bishops also helped and order was duly restored.

Crusaders from the Rhineland – often known as the Peasants' Crusade – set out for the East as early as the spring of 1096, led by the charismatic preacher, Peter the Hermit. Historians have shown that this group included a number of nobles and it is no longer, as previously thought, regarded as an army made up of rustics; it has now been renamed the People's Crusade. These adventurers reached Constantinople in August 1096 where their dismal levels of discipline horrified Alexius. The emperor took harsh measures to preserve the safety of his city while the fear and animosity generated by this group contributed much towards subsequent tensions between the crusaders and the Greeks. Alexius persuaded the Rhinelanders to cross the Bosphorus into Asia Minor and then he abandoned them, providing little support in terms of guides or supplies. Within a few weeks the crusaders encountered the armies of Kilij Arslan, the Seljuk Turkish sultan of Asia Minor. In October 1096 his forces slaughtered the vast majority of the Christians, although Peter the Hermit managed to escape. As Albert of Aachen observed, it was just punishment for the crusaders' ill-treatment of the Jews. This was scarcely an auspicious start to the First Crusade.[16]

While these events unfolded in the East, the main armies began to finalise their preparations. The first good harvest in years seemed to signify divine approval and across Europe people raised money for their great adventure. Many individuals have left traces of their preparations in charters – documents that detail the sale or mortgage of their lands and the acquisition of money and provisions. In subsequent centuries material of this sort becomes bland and formulaic, an efficient record of the practical details of a transaction. Back in the late eleventh century, however, such bureaucratic conformity was blissfully ill-developed and charters often contained long and elaborate stories that explained why an individual had taken a particular course of action. This material can give a vivid insight into the mindset of the contemporary nobility, not least because the charters were made prior to the expedition's departure and are not clouded by the knowledge of its subsequent success.[17] A document of the castellan Nivelo of Fréteval related: 'Whenever the impulse of warlike fierceness roused me, I would gather about myself a band of mounted men and a crowd of followers. I would descend upon the village and freely give the goods of the men of St Père of Chartres to my knights for food. Now, therefore, I am going as a pilgrim to Jerusalem, which is still in bondage with her sons, to secure the divine pardon that I seek for my misdeeds.'[18] We can see in this the violence and chaos so troublesome to Pope Urban; in this instance a church had been targeted for the knightly depredations. Yet with the call for the crusade, Nivelo saw a chance to redeem himself and to make good his sins as a pilgrim warrior fighting to liberate Jerusalem. The fusion of pilgrimage and holy war is neatly displayed in a Provençal charter for Guy and Geoffrey of Signes, who took the cross 'on the one hand for the grace of pilgrimage and on the other, under the protection of God, to wipe out the defilement of the pagans and the immoderate madness through which innumerable Christians have already been oppressed, made captive and killed with barbaric fury.'[19]

Who were the First Crusaders?

In the autumn of 1096 the main crusading armies set out on the 3,000-mile journey from northern Europe to Jerusalem. It has been estimated that about 60,000 people took part in the expedition. The population of western Europe may have been around 20 million; self-evidently the vast majority of people stayed at home; if, however, one considers ties of family, friendship and trade then the crusade touched the lives of millions. Fulcher of Chartres wrote: 'whoever heard of such a mixture of languages in one army since there were French, Flemings, Frisians, Gauls, Allobroges [Savoyards], Lotharingians, Allemani [southern German and Swiss], Bavarians, Normans, English, Scots, Aquitainians, Italians, Danes, Apulians, Iberians and Bretons.'[20] While recent episodes such as the Norman Conquest of England in 1066 gave some indication of the resources required for a large military campaign, the crusade was on a far greater scale. It has been estimated that the expedition cost four times a knight's annual income and so loans, gifts and mortgages were essential.[21] Families gave what they could; often they had to support more than one individual because brothers, or fathers and sons went together. Gifts of horses and mules were particularly welcome, as were precious stones, gold and silverware. The currency of the time was of such a small denomination that it was utterly impractical to try to carry the necessary cash, otherwise the crusader army would have consisted of countless treasure-carrying carts. While we know that at least seven different currencies (coins from Lucca, Chartres, Le Mans, Melgueil, Le Puy, Valence and Poitou) were in circulation amongst the Provençal contingent alone, the better option was to take precious objects to trade with local money-changers en route.[22] Yet Urban's offer of salvation struck a deep chord with the wider populace – who would not want to have all their sins wiped clean? Thus, men and women, young and old, the poor and the infirm joined the expedition as pilgrims. Many were utterly unsuited to the rigours of the campaign and in the course of the crusade the majority of this anonymous mass perished through disease or starvation, or deserted.

Two particular groups were not represented on the crusade. One body of people who wished to take part were banned, namely monks. Their vows required them to remain in the cloister; they were to fight the Devil through prayer, rather than with the sword. As Urban wrote: 'we do not want those who have abandoned the world and vowed themselves to spiritual warfare either to bear arms or to go on this journey; we forbid them to go.'[23] The fact that Urban had to issue letters making such points explicit shows that many monks were attracted to the concept. Probably the most noticeable absentees from amongst the First Crusaders were kings. Monarchs could have provided an obvious focus of command and resource, yet none became involved. In large part, this was a matter of circumstance, although their absence undoubtedly suited Urban because it meant the papacy retained a dominant position in the campaign. King William Rufus of England was in perpetual conflict with his churchmen; Emperor Henry IV of Germany was never likely to participate on account of the long-running conflict between his empire and the papacy, while King Philip of France was also cast out of the Church, albeit for more carnal reasons. He had pursued a relationship with Bertrada of Anjou, who was already married to Count Fulk IV of Anjou ('le Réchin' – Fulk 'the Repulsive', a name acquired because of his hideously deformed feet). Clearly this was a situation the Church could not sanction. Philip refused to end the affair (he too was already married) and he was duly excommunicated; it would be unacceptable for the 'Knights of Christ' to be headed by an adulterer.

Without the presence of kings it was left to members of the senior nobility to provide leadership, and five individuals stand out particularly. Godfrey of Bouillon ruled the duchy of Lorraine, a region on the border between France and Germany, although it was to the ruler of the latter that he owed obedience.[24] Godfrey was a deeply religious man who, contrary to Urban's strictures, brought a group of monks with him to provide spiritual support. He was also a fearless soldier, famed for his ability in single combat. Generous, gracious and affable, this tall, bearded man was a model holy warrior. His younger brother Baldwin began his career as a cleric but he set aside his habit and became a soldier. Also tall, with brown hair and a beard, he was serious in dress and speech; those who did not know him well took him to be a bishop. Baldwin was married to an Englishwoman, Gothehilde, who accompanied him on the campaign. He was a fine horseman and fighter, although as events reveal, he had a harsh, pragmatic streak too. Count Stephen of Blois was a charming, well-educated man who wrote poetry and sent back letters to his wife Adela, a daughter of William the Conqueror.[25] He was an individual of high standing and at one point seems to have been made commander of the army, although as we will see, this was not a task he carried out with any distinction or dignity. Count Raymond of Saint-Gilles was an Occitan-speaking noble whose territory was based around Toulouse in southern France.[26] He was an older man, in his sixties at the time of the crusade, who had committed himself to support Pope Urban's appeal prior to the Council of Clermont. Raymond actually sold his lands in Europe as a sign that he was wholehearted in his wish to forge a new life in the Holy Land or die in the attempt. He was a strong-willed, pious individual, although rather arrogant and overbearing in his manner; in fact, his lack of diplomatic skills ultimately cost him the throne of Jerusalem. Finally, there was Bohemond of Taranto, arguably the most controversial figure on the crusade.[27] He was a Norman-Sicilian whose father had already passed over him in his choice of successor; he was in consequence not especially wealthy, but possessed a fierce determination to advance his standing. Bohemond was a formidable warrior, tall, fair-haired and blue-eyed; clean-shaven unlike most of his colleagues, he had the bravery required of a champion of Christ. As a Norman-Sicilian he was a traditional enemy of the Byzantines and had taken part in an unsuccessful invasion of the empire in the 1080s.

As the crusaders set out in late 1096, chroniclers recorded the tearful scenes of departure. Fulcher of Chartres wrote of the overwhelming emotional turmoil at this traumatic moment: 'Oh what grief there was! What sighs, what weeping, what lamentation among friends when husband left his wife so dear to him, his children, his possessions however great, his father, his mother, brothers and many other relatives! But . . . none flinched from going because for love of God they were leaving . . . firmly convinced that they would receive a hundredfold what the Lord promised to those who loved Him. Then husband told wife the time he expected to return, assuring her that if by God's grace he survived he would come back home to her. He commended her to the Lord, kissed her lingeringly, and promised her as she wept that he would return. She, though, fearing that she would never see him again, could not stand but swooned to the ground, mourning her loved one whom she was losing in this life as if he were already dead. He departed . . . with firm resolution.'[28] Onward, Christian Soldiers.

The Early Stages of the Crusade: From Constantinople into Asia Minor

The various contingents of crusaders planned to rendezvous at Constantinople. Some marched through Italy and then sailed from Brindisi across to the western edge of the Byzantine Empire in Dalmatia. Others followed the old pilgrim roads through Hungary and entered Alexius' lands from the north. The crusaders' stay at Constantinople was to be fraught with tensions; as we saw above, the behaviour of the People's Crusade had alarmed the Greeks and the arrival of the main armies provoked deeply conflicting emotions. It must be remembered that the emperor had requested a few hundred knights to enter his service; what he got was tens of thousands of holy warriors, intent on passing through his lands towards Jerusalem and, numbered amongst them, some of his greatest enemies. More significantly, there was a massive philosophical gulf between the Greeks and the crusaders. To the Byzantines, holy war – be it crusade or jihad – was abhorrent. They fought for the empire; the emperor was the leader of Christ's people but they expected no spiritual rewards for their endeavours. They were immensely suspicious of the crusaders' professed motives and suspected that the wish for land and money was the real reason for their presence.[29] The crusaders felt that, as fellow Christians, the Byzantines should provide them with food. When this failed to appear they felt entitled to seek supplies; however, the line between foraging and ravaging was an easy one to cross. Alexius dispatched his own troops to shadow the crusaders. Sometimes this ensured peace, on other occasions there was conflict; the papal legate Bishop Adhémar of Le Puy was beaten up and nearly killed in one exchange in the Balkans.[30]

Alexius was determined to turn the crusade to his advantage and any help that he provided was to come at a price. His daughter Anna Comnena was in Constantinople when the crusaders arrived and, fifty years later, she wrote *The Alexiad*, an account of her father's life. Notwithstanding this time lapse, she neatly summarised his methods: he 'used every means possible, physical and psychological, to hurry [the crusaders] to cross the straits [the Bosphorus].'[31] The Byzantines were masters of ceremony and display and they employed their most

potent advantage – the city of Constantinople itself – to great effect.[32]
Its sheer size amazed the crusaders: the population of Paris at this
time was approximately 30,000; Constantinople's was around 350,000.
The city was shaped like a colossal triangle – the Bosphorus and the
Golden Horn provided protection on two sides; on the third the mighty
double-layered Theodosian walls, built in the sixth century to keep
out the barbarian hordes, stretched for three and a half miles between
the two waterways. The 'queen of cities', as the Byzantines described
their capital, was a place of wealth and splendour far beyond the experiences of the vast majority of the westerners. Hundreds of churches
lay filled with relics of unimaginable beauty and value, while at the
heart of the city lay the magnificent cathedral of the Hagia Sophia
(Holy Wisdom), far bigger than any building in the West. Covered
with the most stunning mosaics, its interior walls were cloaked in
multi-coloured marble. The Greeks offered the nobles and churchmen
guided tours of the holy sites and then entertained them in the vast
and opulent imperial palaces. Alexius himself played the part of the
all-powerful ruler to the full. Godfrey of Bouillon and his men were
received by the emperor who was 'seated, as was his custom, looking
powerful on the throne of his sovereignty, not getting up to offer
kisses [of welcome] to the duke or anyone'.[33] It was entirely plain
which was the superior force.

Alexius insisted that the senior nobles should hand back any lands
that had formerly been in the possession of the Greeks. In effect, this
meant the bulk of Asia Minor and Antioch. The latter had been under
Byzantine control until 1085 and was one of the five patriarchal
seats of the Christian Church. To the Greeks, Constantinople was the
home of Christianity and a far more important city than Jerusalem.
That the crusaders wished to recover it was of limited interest to
them. The emperor also demanded a form of vassalage; the crusaders
were to swear peace and mutual friendship – in other words, to behave
themselves – and in return they would receive imperial support and
advice, although Alexius would not journey to Jerusalem in person.
Some nobles were reluctant to give oaths to a non-Catholic ruler; a
few evaded the situation by traversing the Bosphorus immediately and
others, such as Raymond of Saint-Gilles, attempted to resist or to
negotiate down the level of allegiance required. The majority, however,
acquiesced. For those who conceded gracefully there were advantages:

Godfrey of Bouillon was given a mound of gold and silver, as well as purple silks and fine horses; even the Greeks' old enemy, Bohemond of Taranto, was persuaded to conform and after taking his oath he was rewarded with the contents of a room so full of riches that he could barely enter.[34]

By the middle of 1097 the armies of the First Crusade were ready to move into Muslim lands. By sheer coincidence – and there is absolutely no evidence that this was planned – the crusaders chose to enter the Muslim world at a moment when it was particularly weak.[35] There was, and remains, the basic division in the Islamic faith between the Sunni and the Shi'a. The former were in control of Asia Minor, Syria and the lands of Persia to the east; their spiritual leader was the caliph of Baghdad. The Fatimid dynasty was Shi'a and they ruled Egypt from Cairo, the base of their caliphate. Such was the level of bitterness between Sunni and Shi'a that they were prepared to ally with the crusaders against one another rather than form a united front against the invading Christians. This situation was compounded by a catastrophic period of upheaval during the mid-1090s when caliphs and viziers from both camps died with alarming regularity – often in the most dubious circumstances. The later Muslim writer, Ibn Taghribirdi, wrote of 1094: 'this year is called the year of death of caliphs and commanders.'[36] In Asia Minor the demise of the powerful Seljuk sultan, Malikshah, created a power vacuum which meant that the crusaders did not encounter a major international power, but only smaller lordships more concerned with defeating each other than confronting the Christians. Little help came from the leadership of Islam. The caliph of Baghdad showed negligible interest in events on the western periphery of his lands and largely ignored appeals for help. Unsurprisingly, of course, given the unprecedented nature of the Christian invasion, most Muslims failed to recognise that this was a war of religious colonisation. They perceived it as another raid from Byzantium, rather than a war of conquest and settlement, and this misunderstanding also helps to explain the lack of concerted resistance to the crusaders. With the benefit of hindsight, knowing just how marginal the crusaders' survival actually was, had they faced a more formidable leader, such as Malikshah, it is doubtful whether they would have even managed to cross Asia Minor.

The city of Nicaea (modern Iznik), about 120 miles into Asia Minor, was the first settlement to be attacked by the crusaders. By June 1097 they were joined by their Greek allies and the Muslims soon had to surrender. This marked the only real co-operation between the two Christian groups. Later the same month came the first serious test of the crusaders' strength. While the Greeks had warned them of Muslim tactics, little, it seems, had prepared them for the intensity of the onslaught. Seljuk armies were based around cavalry, most of whom were lightly armoured, highly skilled archers. They would gallop to within 50–60 metres of the crusaders, release a hail of arrows and then retreat. Fulcher of Chartres, an eyewitness, wrote 'The Turks were howling like wolves and furiously shooting a cloud of arrows. We were stunned by this . . . to all of us such warfare was unknown.'[37] As the crusader army pushed across Asia Minor it was Bohemond's men who became the focus of special attention. After an exhausting day of skirmishing on the march he was forced to halt and sent urgent entreaties for help to Godfrey and Raymond. The anonymous writer of the *Gesta Francorum*, an eyewitness to these events, lauded Bohemond's men for their fortitude in withstanding the ferocity of the Seljuk assaults. He also made a point of praising the role of women in the army: 'they were of great help to us that day, for they brought water for the men to drink and gallantly encouraged those who were fighting and defending them.'[38] Godfrey and Raymond arrived at speed by the following morning and after an epic six-hour struggle (known as the Battle of Dorylaeum), the combined strength of the crusaders prevailed. As the *Gesta Francorum* commented, 'If God had not been with us in this battle and sent the other army quickly, none of us would have escaped.'[39]

The march through Asia Minor tested the crusaders' physical and mental resolve; most of the knights' fine warhorses died and the greatest warriors of the age were reduced to riding oxen, while goats, sheep and even dogs carried the baggage. In the late summer of 1097 the crusader army began to divide up. Baldwin of Boulogne headed east towards Edessa (modern Sanliurfa), a fertile region astride the River Euphrates in the south-east of modern Turkey. Edessa was an important site in early Church history because it was the first city to formally adopt Christianity and was the burial place of the apostles Thomas and Thaddeus.[40] At the time of the First Crusade it was ruled by Christian Armenians who welcomed the westerners' support against the Muslims who surrounded their lands. At first, relations between the two parties were good: the local ruler, Thoros, adopted Baldwin as his son in a strange ritual where the two men stripped to the waist and embraced while a large white shirt was placed over both of them. In fact, Thoros was not especially popular with his people and he was soon torn to pieces by a mob, which left Baldwin to take control for himself. Notwithstanding Edessa's Christian past, this was an act of brazen territorial acquisition by Baldwin, largely disconnected from the spiritual concerns at the heart of Urban's appeal.

The Siege of Antioch: The Crusaders' Greatest Test

The majority of the army struggled grimly onwards, impelled by the lure of Jerusalem. By October 1097 they reached Antioch in northern Syria (although today just inside Turkey and called Antakya). It was here that the pivotal battles of the crusade were fought; the holy warriors' faith and fortitude were challenged as never before. It would take almost ten months to break the defenders' resistance, a period of extraordinary suffering and hardship on both sides, yet one that was fundamental to the crusaders' success. Modern Antioch, bisected by the Orontes, is a rather nondescript city that covers a fraction of the area of its late classical heyday, yet the shattered remains of its medieval citadel still crown the vertiginous 1,600-feet ridge that looms over the site. Walls and towers cling to the steep sides of this great rock, but on the plain below the formidable ring of double walls that once confronted the crusaders has now almost gone. The size of the city and the scale of its fortifications meant that it was impossible to blockade effectively; in any case, the defenders had prepared well. As the harsh Syrian winter drew on it was the Franks (as they were generically known in both the Christian and Muslim worlds) who began to struggle. On occasion, supplies arrived at the nearby port of Saint-Simeon, courtesy of the Greeks, but the presence of such a large army inevitably began to denude the locality of food. The crusaders were forced to make increasingly distant and dangerous foraging trips and the price of basic commodities soared. Only 1,000 horses had survived and the cold and rain caused tents and equipment to rot. Pestilence broke out and thousands of crusaders died or deserted; a steady stream of people left the expedition – perhaps those driven predominantly by material desires believed their hopes to be lost and gave up. Outside Antioch the crusaders constructed their own fortifications and made sporadic assaults on the city, but the campaign appeared to have stalled. The siege dragged on into the spring of 1098 with sallies, bombardment, engagement and counter-engagement. In June, however, the crusaders made a breakthrough. As we saw earlier, Bohemond was a man without lands and the chance to carve out a principality based upon such a splendid city was too good to miss. Unknown to his colleagues, Bohemond had contacted a renegade Armenian inside Antioch who was prepared to betray the city to the crusaders. With pressure for progress at a peak Bohemond made a proposition to the other leaders: if he could get the Christians into the city, they should agree that he could keep it. At first the others refused – they argued that everyone had toiled in front of its walls and that all should share its spoils. News of the imminent arrival of a large Muslim relief force from Mosul focussed the minds of the nobles, however; Bohemond's colleagues consented on condition that if Alexius came to help, the city would be given to him as they had promised.[41]

Just before dawn on 3 June 1098, a rope was lowered from one of the towers on the southern wall of the city. Before the first fingers of light crept over the citadel the crusaders clambered up ladders and began to take control of the walls; soon a gate was opened and the holy warriors flooded in. While they began to massacre the inhabitants and to seize as much booty as they could, the majority of the defenders simply withdrew to the safety of the citadel. In other words, the crusaders had taken only the outer shell of Antioch. Within days, the army from Mosul appeared and the westerners became pincered between the Muslims in the citadel and those outside the city: the besiegers had become the besieged. Christian morale plummeted and the crusaders experienced terrible privations. Food was in desperately short supply. The Gesta Francorum recorded: 'These blasphemous enemies of God kept us so closely shut up in the city of Antioch that many of us died of hunger . . . So terrible was the famine that men boiled and ate the leaves of figs, vines, thistles and all kinds of trees. Others stewed the dried skins of horses, camels, asses, oxen or buffaloes, which they ate. These and many other troubles and anxieties . . . we suffered for the Name of Christ and to set free the road to the Holy

Sepulchre.'[42] More men deserted, including Stephen of Blois. These individuals became known as the 'rope-dancers of Antioch', a derogatory term deriding them for their cowardice. Yet Stephen's actions had a further consequence because in his retreat across Asia Minor he encountered Alexius, belatedly coming to assist his allies. Unsurprisingly, the news that the Franks were doomed caused him to turn back; there was no point in carrying on to Antioch if, by the time he arrived, the crusaders had been defeated. Of course, events turned out differently and, regardless of Alexius' apparent good faith, his decision to retreat allowed Bohemond to claim the Byzantines reneged on their promise to provide military support and that he was free from his oath to return former Greek lands to them.[43]

By late June the First Crusade was on the verge of collapse. It seemed that only a miracle could save the expedition and, in the heightened, desperate atmosphere of a failing holy war, that is exactly what happened. Peter Bartholomew, a pilgrim in Count Raymond's contingent, had a vision in which he claimed that St Andrew appeared to him and told him where to find the Holy Lance, the lance that had pierced Christ's side during the crucifixion.[44] As an object so intimately linked to Christ's last days on earth this was a relic of incalculable importance. A group of thirteen men gathered in the Church of St Peter in Antioch and all day they dug frantically at the specified place. By the early evening hope was beginning to fade, yet the men laboured away in the sputtering torchlight and then, finally, a spade struck wood; it was there! A miracle! The chronicler Raymond of Aguilers witnessed the discovery and was so overcome that he kissed the point of the lance even before it was removed from the ground. The news whipped through the Christian camp, energising and inspiring the common troops as never before. God had encouraged them to persist and they faced their opponents with renewed vigour. Some amongst the leadership were more sceptical, however. They saw the prestige that accrued to Count Raymond's men for having discovered the relic and wondered whether it was simply a ploy to enhance his position. At this stage, however, it was unwise to broadcast such concerns too loudly, largely because morale was so greatly enhanced. Adhémar of Le Puy proclaimed a three-day fast, ordered the women out of the camp and banned gambling and swearing in an effort to cleanse further the crusaders' morality as they prepared for battle.

On 28 June, in six contingents, the Christians lined up outside the city for a do-or-die confrontation. The priests put on their finest vestments and prayed to God to rescue them from evil: 'So we closed our ranks and, protected by the sign of the cross, marched into battle.'[45] By this time, after two years on campaign, the remaining knights were a tough, battle-hardened force; a loose analogy from the modern day might be a tour or competition in which an international sports team draws players from different club sides. In the course of the tour the players learn how to work with new colleagues to good effect and by the end of the competition they are, in theory, at a peak. The crusaders possessed a cohesion that troops gathered for specific campaigns usually lacked; this was long before the existence of standing armies who could practise tactics on a daily basis. The Muslims began with their customary bombardment of darts and arrows but the crusaders kept their discipline perfectly. It was during this engagement that many of the men saw further evidence of divine support. 'There also appeared from the mountains a countless host of men on white horses, whose banners were all white. When our men saw this they did not understand what was happening, or who these men might be, until they realised that this was the succour sent by Christ, and that the leaders were St George, St Mercurius and St Demetrius (this is quite true for many of our men saw it).'[46] Given the confusion of battle, the desperation of the troops, the extraordinary pitch of religious fervour – combined with a lack of food and drink – such apparently implausible events formed an integral part of the crusading experience and did much to inspire victory. The Christians executed a series of complex military manoeuvres and drove the Muslims from the field.[47]

Soon the defenders in the citadel realised that all was lost; they surrendered – Antioch was again in Christian hands. The crusaders were exhausted after their victory and settled down to recuperate. As often happens to those weakened by conflict and poor diet, disease struck hard. Thousands of men and women perished, almost certainly of typhoid. The most notable casualty was Adhémar of Le Puy.[48] His firmness and diplomatic skills had done much to keep tensions between the lay nobles at a manageable level, but with his demise the papal influence over the campaign waned and the squabbles between the senior warlords escalated.

The discovery of the Holy Lance had an interesting coda. As noted above, some suspected that Peter Bartholomew's 'discovery' had been rigged to enhance the authority of Raymond's Provençal forces. Rivals voiced their scepticism and Peter, by this time so convinced of his role as a divine agent, offered to be subjected to an ordeal: trial by fire. By the time of the First Crusade this practice was in decline because people increasingly doubted its veracity. The heat of the fire, for example, could be manipulated by the unscrupulous to affect the result; in a more spiritual sense, it was deemed insulting to demand that a miracle from God act in such a peremptory fashion.[49] Peter opted for one of the most rigorous forms of the ordeal ever recorded. After four days of fasting and spiritual preparations he was ready for his test. In front of a huge audience he carried the relic down a narrow gap between two walls of blazing olive branches, four feet high and thirteen feet long. Raymond of Aguilers was again an eyewitness and reported that Peter emerged unscathed and shouted 'God help us!' He was then borne to the ground by an ecstatic mob, determined to grab a piece of clothing from such a sanctified soul. In the course of this frenzy, Raymond claimed that Peter's backbone was broken and this caused his death. Others were more doubtful: Fulcher of Chartres wrote that the priest's skin was scorched and that he was so badly hurt that he perished from his burns: divine judgement on his fraudulent behaviour. The cult of the Holy Lance withered, but whatever the truth of its discovery it had done its work.[50]

In late 1098 the surviving crusaders began to advance south. In November they besieged the town of Ma'arrat an Nu'man. Once again, in the depths of winter, supplies were hard to find, and Fulcher of Chartres reported: 'our men suffered from excess hunger. I shudder to say that many of our men, terribly tormented by the madness of starvation, cut pieces of flesh from the buttocks of Saracens lying there dead. These pieces they cooked and ate, savagely devouring the flesh while it was insufficiently roasted.' Such an act has understandably disgusted generations, although a sense that this was done as a sign of the crusaders' hatred of the Muslims should be uncoupled from the simple, harsh realities of warfare. (In more recent times, for example, cannibalism has been well documented amongst early settlers in nineteenth-century Tasmania or in the terrible conditions during the Russian Revolution. During the winter of 1921 in the Volga district people refused to bury their dead relatives and insisted on keeping them to eat; bands of cannibals and traders started to hunt children for food, parents killed babies to feed their other children and even doctors took to eating the remains of their patients.[51])

It was around this time that tensions became apparent between the rank and file and the leadership. The former, impelled by their desire to reach the Holy Sepulchre, fulfil their vows and return home, demanded to push on. The nobles, however, were too busy feuding with one another over who should lead the campaign and who might hold past and future conquests. In the end, people-power triumphed and pressure from the pilgrims forced the armies to move on, although Bohemond remained behind to consolidate his hold on Antioch. He firmly resisted calls from Alexius to hand the city over to the Greeks, which frustrated the emperor's design of re-establishing Byzantine influence in northern Syria and generated a tension that would scar relations between the Greeks and the Latin settlers for decades to come.

The Capture of Jerusalem – Triumph and Atrocity

In the meantime, the main crusading armies moved southwards with such speed that many towns were left unconquered in their wake. On 7 June 1099 they finally reached the goal of their three-year journey, Jerusalem, the place marked as the centre of the world on most medieval maps and the most important city in the Christian world. Many were moved to tears. Bohemond's nephew, Tancred, saw the city from the Mount of Olives and sank to his knees saying that he would willingly give his life for the opportunity to kiss the Holy Sepulchre.[52]

By now the crusader force had dwindled to around 1,300 knights and 12,500 footmen. They faced unfamiliar opponents because in August 1098 the Fatimid Egyptians had seized the city from their Sunni Muslim rivals. A strong garrison, including 400 elite warriors, was well prepared: the Eastern Christians who lived in Jerusalem were expelled to avoid possible betrayal, the local wells were poisoned and the cisterns inside the city filled to the brim. The walls that encircle Jerusalem today date, for the most part, from the Ottoman period, but their foundations, course and scale are a close match to those of the late eleventh century.

They stretch for about two and a half miles in circumference and are complemented by a moat to the north, the natural defences of the Valley of Jehoshaphat to the east and the Kidron Valley to the south. The crusaders made a loose encirclement of the city but concentrated their troops in two particular sections. Raymond of Saint-Gilles went to the south-western corner, while the remainder of the men under Godfrey and Tancred went to the north-western district. Early attacks foundered; the defences (a double wall to the north) were too high and the crusaders lacked the wood to build ladders. Tancred himself solved the problem. It seems that he was afflicted with terrible diarrhoea; he slunk away to a remote spot to seek relief only to discover a cave filled with beams of timber – a truly divine intervention. The arrival of more wood, plus tools and nails from a Genoese supply ship, was a further boost. The crusaders spent the next few weeks engaged in the construction of two mighty siege towers, several catapults and a ram. At the height of summer, water supply remained a problem; some were forced to travel six miles to find refreshment and even then it was said to have been filled with leeches. Meanwhile the men laboured hard. Pride of place went to the two huge towers, each about fifty feet tall and built on wheeled platforms to enable them to move up to the city walls. Animal hides and branches provided a level of protection for the men inside. A mighty battering ram was another essential weapon, a huge beam tipped with a lethal metal head designed to smash through the lower walls. Those within the city prepared their own defences: catapults were set up and parts of the fortifications disappeared under a mattress-type padding to try to absorb the impact of crusader artillery.

As the struggle approached its climax, the level of antipathy between the Christians and the Muslims intensified. An Egyptian spy was captured and then catapulted back towards his co-religionists; the defenders responded by spitting and urinating on crosses. The crusaders decided to fortify themselves spiritually as well. One man had a vision of the dead papal legate, Adhémar of Le Puy, who advised the holy warriors to stage a special penitential procession to the Mount of Olives, the place where Christ ascended into heaven. Afraid to ignore the direction of such a respected figure, the leadership decided to follow this instruction. Barefoot and bearing crosses and relics, the clergy headed a snake of crusaders down the Valley of Jehoshaphat and then up to the sacred place, praying, chanting and invoking God's favour.[53]

By now, with food and water in short supply and the prospect of Egyptian reinforcements imminent, religious devotion became coloured with the growing need for a quick breakthrough. Raymond's tower exerted pressure to the south-west and kept large numbers of defenders occupied. On the other hand, the siege tower to the north-west of the city seemed to be achieving very little. Muslim resistance was strong and the defenders had prudently gathered where the crusaders posed their greatest threat. On the night of 13 July, however, Godfrey showed his military genius; he had seen another area of the wall that was weaker, less well defended and offered a flatter approach for the siege tower. The duke ordered his siege machine to be broken up into its constituent parts and then, under cover of darkness, laboriously moved over a mile to the east and reassembled.

A little detective work can reconcile eyewitness descriptions with the present-day topography to identify a short stretch (sixty metres) of fortifications, between the second tower east of Herod's Gate and the next larger salient beyond it. Today, opposite the Rockefeller Museum, it is possible to stand among the overgrown thorn bushes in the ditch and to look up at the walls above. Notwithstanding the grind of modern traffic passing close by it is a deeply sobering experience to pause in the shadows at the foot of these fortifications and to imagine the brutal, desperate struggle that took place on the very same spot on 14 and 15 July 1099.

Godfrey's decision to change the focus of the attack was an inspired one as well as a remarkable physical feat. At dawn, the crusaders launched their onslaught, desperate to capitalise on their advantage. First of all, they brought a huge battering ram to bear on the outer wall in order to create a breach for the tower. An eyewitness described the intensity of the fighting around it: 'The hellish din of battle broke loose; from all parts stones . . . flew through the air, and arrows pelted like rain. But God's servants, resolute in their faith, regardless of the outcome of death or immediate vengeance on the pagans, endured this patiently . . . Defenders rained down upon the Christians stones, arrows, flaming wood and straw, and threw mallets of wood wrapped with ignited pitch, wax, sulphur, tow and rags on the machines. The deeds performed in the day-long battle were so marvellous that we doubt that history recorded any greater.'[54] After hours of fighting the crusaders' muscle power thrust the metal-tipped monster through the stonework to make the first breach. As the day ended they were now poised for the final assault; the battle for Jerusalem was at a pivotal juncture; as one contemporary wrote: 'With the coming of night, fear settled on the two groups . . . alertness, labour and sleepless anxiety prevailed in both camps, and on our side confident hope, on theirs, gnawing dismay.'[55]

At daybreak, the struggle began again. Godfrey himself commanded the battle from inside the great siege tower and the unwieldy device was heaved through a lethal storm of rocks and flames to within a few feet of the curtain wall. One stone decapitated a man who stood next to the duke, but Godfrey fought on undaunted. The tower was about six feet above the defences and this differential proved crucial because the men on the top storey could pin down the defenders. The Muslims even deployed a form of Greek fire – a naphtha-based substance that could not be extinguished by water. Fortunately local Christians had warned the crusaders about this and a store of vinegar was on hand to quell the flames. Nonetheless, the Muslims' stubborn resistance started to sap both the morale and the energy of the Christians; many of their siege weapons had been shattered and they had taken heavy casualties. Around midday, however, a crusader archer began to shoot blazing arrows into the Saracens opposite the siege tower. The fire raged with particular intensity – perhaps it had ignited some of the Muslims' own inflammable weapons – and the defenders had to flee from the walls. Here was the crusaders' opportunity: hurriedly, Godfrey ordered the siege tower's drawbridge to be lowered and it swung onto the walls. Two brothers, Ludolf and Englebert of Tournai, are named as the first men to leap onto the ramparts. With this breach made, ladders were laid against the walls and Godfrey's men poured into the north of the city.[56] Raymond had made little headway to the south-west but as news of the breakthrough spread, Muslim resistance quickly collapsed.

The combined tensions of the three-year march, the terrible suffering at the siege of Antioch and the fierce fight outside Jerusalem, compounded by their uncompromising religious fervour, contributed to the crusaders unleashing savagery and slaughter on an appalling scale. They had liberated the holy city, now they sought to purge it of unbelievers. 'Some of the pagans were mercifully beheaded, others pierced by arrows plunged from towers, and yet others, tortured for a long time, were burned to death in searing flames. Piles of heads, hands and feet lay in the houses and streets, and indeed there was a running to and fro of men and knights over the corpses.'[57] A group of Muslims on the roof of a building, wrongly identified by the crusaders as the Temple of Solomon, surrendered only to be killed soon afterwards. Women and children were not spared in this brutal orgy of destruction. The crusaders 'seized infants by the soles of their feet from their mothers' laps or their cradles and dashed them against walls or broke their necks; they were slaughtering some with weapons [others] with stones; they were sparing absolutely no gentile of any place or kind.'[58] The horror of these events has left an indelible stain on Muslim–Christian relations down the centuries.

The crusaders also seized huge amounts of booty: gold, silver, precious stones and horses. Men took property for themselves; if a crusader entered and stayed in a house, he was entitled to keep it. Some even slit open the stomachs of Muslims they suspected had swallowed valuables in an attempt to conceal them from the crusaders. 'No one has ever seen or heard of such a slaughter of the pagans, for they were burned on pyres like pyramids', an eyewitness reported.[59] Yet, amidst this almost incomprehensible violence, the crusaders' thoughts turned to devotion. One later writer vividly evoked this combination of religious zeal and extreme brutality, a blend that does not sit well with our own sensibilities:

> It was impossible to look on the vast numbers of the slain without horror; everywhere lay the fragments of human bodies. Still more dreadful was it to gaze upon the victors themselves, dripping with blood from head to foot . . . Then, clad in fresh garments with clean hands and bare feet, in humility they began to make the rounds of the venerable places which the Saviour had deigned to sanctify and make glorious with His bodily presence . . . with particular veneration they approached the church of the Passion and Resurrection of the Lord . . . It was a source of spiritual joy to witness the pious devotion . . . with which the pilgrims drew near to the holy places, the exultation of heart and happiness of spirit with which they kissed the memorials of the Lord's sojourn on earth.[60]

Three weeks later, at the Battle of Ascalon, the crusaders defeated a large Egyptian army to seal the campaign's success; the Holy Land was in Christian hands. The conquest of Jerusalem was an astonishing achievement: 'The Lord has certainly renewed His miracles of old' was one analysis.[61] The crusaders seized the spoils of war – they had, after all, incurred huge expenses in the course of their journey, and many needed money to return home. For those who had driven themselves on to Jerusalem, there is little doubt that religious motives were at the heart of their experience: 'The children of the Apostles freed the city for God and the Fathers', as one contemporary stated.[62] Their growing military cohesion and the divisions within the Muslim world both contributed to their victory, but piety was their ultimate motive. It is one of history's ironies, however, that Pope Urban did not live to learn of the crusade's success: he died in July 1099.

Godfrey's actions during the siege, along with Raymond's abrasive personality, led to the former being elected to rule this new land. Such was Godfrey's piety, however, that he declined a crown, not wishing to be a king in the land of the Lord; instead he took the more modest title Advocate of the Holy Sepulchre.[63] In the autumn of 1099 many crusaders prepared to leave for the West, exhausted but exultant. These men returned as heroes, celebrated in verse and chronicles and feted for their achievements: models for future generations to emulate.[64] Perhaps only 300 knights remained in the nascent Christian state of Jerusalem – a figure that entirely demolishes the old charge that most crusaders were simply in search of new lands; for the majority at least, their dearest wish was a safe voyage back to their families and loved ones. In the Muslim world there was, in some quarters at least, shock and outrage at these events. Yet neither the caliph, nor the Seljuk sultan, dispatched an army to take on the new arrivals. Such neglect was vital to the Frankish settlers because it allowed them a breathing space to consolidate their conquest and to establish Catholic rule in the Holy Land and a presence that would endure for almost 200 years.

2

'May God's curse be upon them!': Relations Between Muslims and Franks in the Levant, 1099–1187

In the decade after the capture of Jerusalem the Franks set up four states in the Levant: the kingdom of Jerusalem; the county of Tripoli (roughly equivalent in area to the modern Lebanon), the principality of Antioch (coastal Syria) and, inland, astride the River Euphrates, the county of Edessa. The religious and ethnic mix of these regions was bewildering: Armenians, Greek Orthodox, Maronites, Jacobites, Nestorians, Sunni Muslims, Shi'a Muslims, splinters within the Shi'a such as the Nizari (known as the Assassins), as well as the Jews and the Zoroastrians. The fact that the Franks imposed their authority on such a polyglot society was one of their most remarkable – and often ignored – achievements. The early years of the Latin East were marked by a series of sieges and battles as the newcomers sought to carve out their territories but, by 1109, with a couple of exceptions on the coast (Tyre did not fall until 1124 and Ascalon in 1153), they had established the full extent of their lands. A detailed narrative of these conquests is the purview of textbooks and, in most cases, gives the Frankish perspective; the writings of three contemporary Muslim writers will give us an alternative viewpoint. They may not provide a complete picture of the period – and they certainly contain comparable levels of bias and prejudice against their opponents – but they can offer a thought-provoking insight into the impact of the Christian invasions and a glimpse of the priorities and concerns of the Muslim population. Our three sources are Ali ibn Tahir al-Sulami, an irate Damascene preacher; Usama ibn Munqidh, a melancholy old poet and warrior; and Ibn Jubayr, a perspicacious Spanish Muslim who visited the Levant in the course of a penitential pilgrimage.

The Impact of the First Crusade and the Idea of Jihad

The caliph of Baghdad offered little assistance or direction to the Syrian Muslims at the time of the First Crusade and this lack of leadership provoked outrage amongst those directly affected by the Christian invasion and sparked angry protests in verse (the conventional medium for such communication at the time):

> The unbelief of the infidels has declared it lawful to inflict harm on
>   Islam, causing prolonged lamentation for the faith.
> What is right is null and void and what is forbidden is [now] made licit.
> The sword is cutting and blood is spilt.
> How many Muslim men have become booty?
> And how many Muslim women's inviolability has been plundered?
> How many a mosque have they made into a church!
> The cross has been set up in the *mihrab* [prayer niche].
> The blood of the pig is suitable for it.
> Korans have been burned under the guise of incense.
> Do you not owe an obligation to God and Islam,
> Defending thereby young men and old?
> Respond to God: woe on you! Respond![1]

In time, jihad became the driving force of Islam's response to the events of 1099. Jihad means 'struggle' and, as we shall see, it has numerous parallels with the concept of a crusade; there is, however, a fundamental difference in their origins. The crusade was invented by Pope Urban II in 1095, but the jihad was a part of the Islamic faith from its foundation in the seventh century. The notion of holy war is found in both the Koran and the Hadith, the sayings of Muhammad, and they both stress the virtues and celestial rewards of the jihad.[2] One Hadith, for example, states that 'The Gates of Paradise are under the shadow of the swords' – a sentiment comparable to the crusading idea of a holy warrior finding a place in heaven.

The jihad itself has two elements, the 'greater' and the 'lesser' jihad. The former (*al-jihad al-akbar*) is the struggle against an individual's lower self; it is a personal fight against immorality and sin. This is of paramount spiritual value, and seen by many as a necessary precursor to the lesser jihad (al-jihad al-asghar). The latter is a perpetual obligation on all Muslims to strive to extend the House of Islam (Dar al-Islam) until all mankind accepts the faith or submits to Muslim government. Non-Muslims within the House of Islam must be protected – unless they are polytheists – and should follow formally recognised religions such as Christianity and Judaism; these people must, however, pay a tax. Land outside the House of Islam is the House of War (Dar al-Harb) and there exists a permanent state of hostility between the two houses until the former is triumphant. Truces of up to ten years could be permitted.

Al-Sulami's Call to Arms: A Revival of Jihad?

Within this basic framework, however, some flexibility is possible. First, safe-conducts enable trade and diplomacy to take place between Muslim and non-Muslim regions. Secondly, in the centuries before the crusades, political reality caused theorists to evolve an intermediate area between the House of War and the House of Islam: the House of Peace (Dar al-Sulh). This reflected a period of stability across Islamic lands that, at that time, stretched from Spain to central Asia. This is not to say that the concept of jihad disappeared entirely; in the mid-tenth century there was a period of holy war against the Byzantines in Asia Minor and numerous holy warriors (ghazis) flocked to join the fighting. By the time of the crusades, however, there is little evidence of the sermons and propaganda intended to incite Muslims to perform their religious duty: faction and disunity were rife; perfect conditions for the ideologically driven westerners to force their way to Jerusalem.

With no direction from their spiritual head in Baghdad the secular leaders of the Near East showed little enthusiasm for jihad. The crusaders, of course, represented a fusion of secular and spiritual interests and therein lay one of their great strengths. But in the Islamic world it took decades for this combination to form a shared agenda that would inspire Muslims to cohere in sufficient numbers to expel the Christians. It would be wrong to say that no one invoked the idea of jihad against the Franks immediately after the First Crusade, and amongst those who tried to stir his people was the Damascene legist al-Sulami who preached around 1105–6. Parts of his treatise *Kitab al-Jihad* (*The Book of Holy War*) survive to give a razor-sharp image of the religious classes' perception of recent events; the text is no less interesting for its similarities with crusader writings.[3]

Al-Sulami often spoke from the elaborately carved pulpit (*minbar*) in the Great Umayyad Mosque in Damascus, a magnificent building that remains one of the splendours of medieval Islam. He used Hadith to remind people that the holy war was the duty of all Muslims; he then offered an acute overview of the problems of the Islamic world. To him, the failure to prosecute the jihad was one cause of the present situation; it was a disgrace that such a state of affairs had been allowed to develop and now God punished such laziness and dereliction of duty through the break-up of the Muslim world. Al-Sulami also showed an awareness of the wider world when he (correctly) reminded his audience that the Christians had already captured Sicily and parts of Spain. Now, al-Sulami argued, the Christians perceived the divisions amongst the Levantine Muslims and set out eastwards with Jerusalem as 'their dearest wish': an accurate appraisal of the crusaders' primary target. He was also perceptive enough to describe the westerners as fighting a jihad themselves; in other words, he understood that religion was the crusaders' dominant motive.

His speech was directed at the ruling military classes, the sultans: those men with a responsibility to protect and defend the people. He lambasted them for their inactivity: 'drive away insignificant things and sluggishness and go to fight the jihad with your wealth and your-selves.' He regarded their present moral laxity as the cause of the crusader invasion: 'the Franks acted as they did because of the Muslims' blame of God . . . He warned you with a punishment the like of which He did not warn you with before . . . If only you would desist from sin! Otherwise He will make you fall into the hands of your enemy . . . May God hasten your waking up from the sleep of neglect . . .'[4]

His appeal for action was couched in remarkably similar terms to contemporary calls for the crusade; in fact, it may be only a slight exaggeration to suggest that the removal of the word jihad and the modification of names would allow this to pass off as a crusade sermon. Al-Sulami's emphasis on the duty to act, the defensive nature of the warfare, the need to protect one's co-religionists, the divine opportunity granted by God, the prospect of heavenly rewards, and the terrible consequences of lax behaviour were all concepts used by Christian preachers. There was, however, no question of one set of ideas feeding the other; the texts simply display the shared principles of a monotheistic faith working through the concept of a holy war to arrive at many of the same interpretations and justifications for such actions. Al-Sulami wrote:

> Prepare, God have mercy on you, to strive hard at the imposition of this jihad and the obligation to defend your religion and brotherhood with aid and support. Take as your booty an expedition that God, who is exalted, has arranged for you without great effort. You will gain from it a finest winner [God] and a glory which . . . [will] remain on you for many ages to come. Beware with all watchfulness that you avoid disgracing yourselves or you will arrive at a fire with flames, which God, who is exalted, has made an evil place and your worst final destiny.[5]

One distinctive feature of the Islamic approach emerges: in direct contrast to Pope Urban II's words at the Council of Clermont where he warned the crusaders to act out of devotion alone, rather than striving for honour or glory, there was an offer of both secular and spiritual rewards: 'God and his Prophet promised to whomever fought the jihad in His cause to gain their [enemies'] wealth, women and lands'; a more realistic approach, perhaps.[6]

Al-Sulami chose to interpret the arrival of the crusaders as a divine challenge to the ruling classes and a task they had been specially chosen to face: 'Know that God, who is praised, only sent this enemy to you as a trial, to test your steadfastness with it. He, who blesses and is exalted, said: "Let us test you so that We will know those of you who fight hard and are steadfast."'[7] The notion of a test was frequently used by Christian preachers, as was al-Sulami's next suggestion – the need for a moral regeneration to provide the proper preparation for holy war.[8] In both cases, spiritual purity, or 'right intention' was requisite: 'Give precedence to jihad of yourselves over jihad of your enemies, for if you yourselves are among your enemies . . . Make right what is between you and your Creator, and what is wrong with your [current] state of being will be made right for you . . .'

Towards the close of his tract, al-Sulami called for a restoration of unity in the Muslim world and repeated his injunctions directed at the region's leadership to fulfil their Koranic responsibilities to guide the people and to guard the faith. He was well aware that the fragmented condition of the Islamic Near East had aided the crusaders' cause. Al-Sulami was not entirely pessimistic, however; he made a terse and accurate critique of the Franks' position at the time (c.1105–6) and mentioned 'the paucity of their horses and equipment and the far distance of their reinforcements and support'. These were, of course, perpetual difficulties for the settlers and proved core reasons for their eventual defeat.

Again in his closing comments the writer castigated his audience; he complained of the shame in delaying opposition to the Franks and the disgrace in fearing them. In spite of the power of this call to jihad the most telling indicator of its failure to resonate with the people of Damascus was the size of al-Sulami's audiences – on one occasion just six people attended. Divisions amongst the warlords of the Muslim Near East were so profound that it was decades before the religious classes could exert sufficient influence on the ruling elites to make the jihad the primary rallying call against the Christian colonists. As we shall see, it was Imad ad-Din Zengi's capture of Edessa in 1144 that marked the first major advance for the counter-crusade, and it was his devout and powerful son, Nur ad-Din (1118–74), who brought faith and fighting together to pose an even greater test to the crusaders.

Usama ibn Munqidh: Observer of Men and Beasts

Our next guide to twelfth-century Islam led a truly remarkable life: Usama ibn Munqidh was born on 4 July 1095, just four months before Urban II launched the First Crusade, and he died aged ninety-three on 17 November 1188, a little over a year after Saladin's reconquest of Jerusalem.[9] He lived through a vast spectrum of events that encompassed Muslim defeat and revival, warfare amongst his co-religionists and conflict with the Franks. His family held the fortress of Shaizar, a castle that still clings to a spine of rock overlooking the River Orontes in central Syria. The Banu Munqidh were one of the numerous small lordships that emerged from the chaotic events in the late eleventh-century Muslim Near East and, as such, Usama's people had to navigate between the competing pressures of the incoming crusaders and the larger local power centres of Aleppo, Hama and Damascus. They also had to deal with less predictable forces such as the Assassins, a group

who lived within ten miles of Shaizar and whose uncompromising nego-
tiating techniques brought them notoriety across the medieval world.[10]

Usama's father, Murshid, was a man of immense piety who
combined an enthusiasm for the hunt with intensive study of the
Koran. He created more than forty copies of the text himself and
composed commentaries on its meaning and style. He managed to
conduct his two passions simultaneously, as Usama recounted: 'On
the day he went forth to the mountain to hunt partridge, while he
was on the way there, yet still distant from it, he would tell us, "Go,
split up. Any of you who still hasn't done his recitation should now
go and do it." For we, his children, had memorised the Koran. And
so we would then disperse and recite the Koran until he arrived at
the hunting spot and ordered someone to summon us. He would then
ask us how much we had recited. Once we had informed him, he
would say, "Me, I've recited one hundred verses", or something close.
My father (may God have mercy on him) could recite the Koran just
like it was when it was first revealed.'[11]

Murshid was not, however, interested in heading the family and
when he stood aside for his younger brother, the tensions generated
amongst the Banu Munqidh clan led to Usama leaving home in June
1131: a moment of profound sadness for him and, in several senses, an
event from which he never recovered. Throughout the remainder of
his adult life he hoped to return to Shaizar and become its lord, yet
this never happened. He began a career that took him across the courts
of the Muslim Near East and brought him service with a cosmopolitan series of rulers: at Hama he worked for the brutal Zengi (with
whom he stayed until 1138), then to Unur of Damascus (1138–44), the
Fatimid court in Cairo (1144–54), then back to Damascus and Nur ad-
Din (1154–64), next to the remote Upper Tigris city of Diyar Bakr
(1164–74) and finally to Damascus a third time under the patronage of
Saladin (1174–88). He was not, however, employed solely as a military
man, and it was his celebrated reputation as an individual of learning
and culture (*adab*) that enabled him to attract such a powerful and
varied range of employers and to criss-cross the Sunni–Shi'a divide.
Adab required good manners, great prowess as a writer and orator
and the ability to memorise a huge store of verse; at its most developed Usama's task was to provide an intellectual focus to a court, as
well as a sense of refinement. Usama even wrote a manual of ideal

male conduct, *The Kernels of Refinement*, which stressed ideas of honour and military strength. Skill as a hunter, a pastime that interested him enormously, was also helpful. Finally, it was desirable to be thin and handsome: needless to say, gifts possessed by Usama himself.[12]

Usama was a prolific writer and gained a great reputation in his own lifetime as a poet. Poetry was probably the most important method of communication in medieval Islam and was used to entertain, to impress, and to propagandise the jihad.[13] Poetry was also employed to conduct affairs of state and when, on behalf of Nur ad-Din of Damascus, Usama conducted lengthy diplomatic negotiations with the vizier of Egypt, they were in verse.

Amongst the many items in Usama's *oeuvre* was a hugely popular collection of poetry; Saladin himself kept a copy with him. He also composed works on sleep and revelatory dreams; women; a history of recent events; a *Counsel to Shepherds*; an anthology of *Dwellings and Abodes* (an analysis of the erotic prelude, a genre of classical Arabic literature); a study of especially ornate poetry, *The Creator of High Style*, and finally, a book on the lore of the stick, *The Book of the Staff*.[14] The last of these was written around 1171–2 and was a collection of verse and prose incidents connected with the symbol of Usama's old age – his walking stick. Some were tales of famous sticks, such as that of Moses; some told of his own experiences (a few involving the Franks); others were designed simply to amuse. In one incident, a man complained to his local *qadi* (judge) that his wife had beaten him with a stick so fiercely that it broke. The *qadi* looked sad, which prompted the man to say that there was nothing to worry about – she had done this from her evil nature and lack of education. But the *qadi* responded 'I would not grieve, even if she killed you. My only worry is that she may think that all men are like you.'[15]

His best-known book in modern times is his *Kitab al-I'tibar*, the *Book of Contemplation* – partly because it contains so many lively anecdotes and partly because it has been translated from Arabic. As the title suggests, it was not a narrative history but principally a work of instruction. Through the *Book of Contemplation* we can glimpse much of Usama's view of the world and his thoughts on the Franks. In the broadest sense he reflected the widely shared feeling of Muslim cultural superiority over the Christians. The latter were brave – in the way that animals could be brave – but lacked modesty and sophistication.

'Glory be to the Creator, the Maker! Indeed, when a person relates matters concerning the Franks, he *should* give glory to God and sanctify Him! For he will see them to be mere beasts possessing no other virtues but courage and fighting, just as beasts have only the virtues of strength and the ability to carry loads.'[16] The latter years of Usama's career overlapped with the efflorescence of the jihad under Nur ad-Din and Saladin, yet his writings lack a sustained polemical thrust against the Christians, perhaps an indication that the author's own concerns and personality were largely secular in nature.

Usama grew up with many indigenous Christians in the vicinity – in fact, at Shaizar in 1114 the Banu Munqidh menfolk joined the local Christian villagers in their Easter celebration. Yet he obviously disapproved of their morals, as shown in this tale told to him by a bath-keeper: 'I once opened a bath in al-Ma'arra to earn my living. Once, one of their knights came in. Now, they don't take to people wearing a towel about their waist in the bath, so this knight stretched out his hand, pulled off my towel from my waist and threw it down. He looked at me – I had recently shaved my pubic hair . . . Then he moved in closer to me. He then stretched his hand over my groin, saying, "By the truth of my religion, do that for me too." He then lay down on his back: he had it thick as a beard in that place. So I shaved him and he passed his hand over it and, finding it smooth to the touch, said: "Salim, by the truth of your religion, do it to Madame!" . . . meaning his wife. The attendant brought her . . . She lay down on her back and the knight said, "Do her like you did me!" So I shaved her hair there as her husband stood watching me. He then thanked me and paid me my due for the service. Now, consider this great contradiction! They have no sense of propriety or honour, yet they have great courage. Yet what is courage but a product of honour and disdain for ill repute.'[17]

Understandably Usama found Christian theology to be deficient and, on many occasions, he ends an anecdote with an almost reflexive imprecation: 'May God curse them!' In spite of this stereotypical invective, his writings reveal that he had much to do with the Frankish elite, particularly during his service to Unur of Damascus around 1140. As well as giving us colourful information about Usama's career and personality, these episodes may reveal some pertinent features of Frankish rule and Christian–Muslim relations.

In the course of one embassy to Jerusalem, Usama was permitted to visit the Temple complex of the holy city. This contains the Dome of the Rock and, more importantly, the al-Aqsa Mosque which is the place the Prophet lead the other prophets in prayer during his Night Journey from Mecca to Jerusalem.[18] During his stay Usama observed the difference between those Franks settled in the Levant and their co-religionists who had just arrived from the West: 'Anyone who is recently arrived from the Frankish lands is rougher in character than those who have become acclimatised and have frequented the company of Muslims. Here is an instance of their rough character (may God abominate them!) Whenever I went to visit the holy sites in Jerusalem, I would go to the al-Aqsa Mosque . . . where the Templars, who are my friends, were. They would clear out that little mosque so that I could pray in it. One day, I went into the little mosque, recited the opening formula "God is great" and stood up in prayer. At this one of the Franks rushed at me and grabbed me and turned my face towards the east saying, "Pray like *this*." A group of Templars hurried towards him, took hold of the Frank and took him away from me. I then returned to my prayers. The Frank, that very same one, took advantage of their inattention and returned, rushing upon me . . . So the Templars came in again, grabbed him and threw him out. They apologised to me, saying, "This man is a stranger, just arrived from the Frankish lands . . . he has never before seen anyone who did not pray towards the east." "I think I have prayed quite enough," I said and left. I used to marvel at that devil, the change of his expression, the way he trembled and what he must have made of seeing someone praying towards Mecca.'[19] This dramatic vignette shows the sharp contrast between those accustomed to dealing with Muslims on a daily basis, both as inhabitants of their own lands and as political neighbours, and the new arrival, stirred up by the inflammatory rhetoric of crusade preachers and lacking any sense of tolerance towards his religious opponents. The story also demonstrates the diplomatic courtesies extended to a high-level ambassador and proves that even in Jerusalem itself, during the mid-twelfth century at least, a Muslim was permitted private prayer. Perhaps the most surprising remark in his testimony was the description of the Templars as Usama's friends. As we will see below, these men were usually the most implacable opponents of Islam, sworn to its destruction, yet in this case they evidently felt it appropriate to protect Usama.

Friendship could find a basis in the shared interests of an equestrian elite. Usama and the Frankish knights were both products of a culture in which the horse was a status symbol, an essential companion in battle and on the hunt. While each could admire the other's bravery in warfare, they might also, in the case of the hunt, enjoy a pastime together. In the early 1140s Usama was in the company of Unur of Damascus when the Muslim ruler went hunting with King Fulk of Jerusalem – another great devotee of the chase – on lands near Acre. Unur was quite taken with a large falcon that had been trained to bring down cranes and even to attack gazelles; he asked the king if he could have the falcon and Fulk duly obliged. Such diplomatic niceties helped to seal an alliance between Damascus and Jerusalem when both parties feared the growing power of Zengi, *atabeg* of both Aleppo and Mosul, and deemed it prudent to make such a deal: just one of many examples of a Christian–Muslim pact.[20] Given the basic parameters of the Crusades, on the surface at least, arrangements of this sort seem unlikely, but the day-to-day realities of living in close proximity to each other meant that such relationships – be they personal, like Usama's, or political, as in this case – were not impossible. The zeal of the First Crusaders, wading through Jerusalem in the blood of their enemies, had become tempered by basic practicalities and the settlers' lack of numbers. We can see a recognition of this from a Christian perspective too; Fulcher of Chartres, a First Crusader who chose to remain in the Levant, wrote a famous assessment of the inhabitants of the Frankish lands around 1120: 'We who were once Occidentals have now become Orientals . . . He who was of Rheims or Chartres has now become a citizen of Tyre or Antioch. We have already forgotten the places of our birth; already these are unknown to many of us or not mentioned any more. Some already possess homes or households by inheritance. Some have taken wives not only of their own people, but Syrians, Armenians, or even Saracens who have achieved the grace of baptism. Words of different languages have become the common property known to each nationality, and mutual faith unites those who are ignorant of their descent . . . He who was born a stranger is now as one born here; he who was born an alien has become a native.'[21] Thus, the Franks had become 'easternised' and acculturated to their new surroundings, the local people and their practices. It would be a grave exaggeration to claim that anything approaching a 'rainbow nation' had emerged, but indications of assimilation and interaction do exist and suggest a fuller picture and more nuanced version of the standard 'Christian fights Muslim' dichotomy.

Usama himself was obsessed with hunting. The land near his native Shaizar was a mix of woods and marsh, home to gazelles, boar, hares and, most challenging of all, lions. It may be no coincidence that Usama actually means 'lion' and his *Kitab al-I'tibar* is packed with stories about his adventures. Pride of place is held by his single-handed killings of the beast; he claimed that he had more experience with lions and knowledge about fighting them than any other person. He told of a hunt with his father: 'I mounted my horse with my spear by my side and charged at the lion. The lion faced me and let out a roar. My horse reared and my spear, because of its weight, fell out of my hand. The lion chased me for a good stretch, then turned back to the foot of the hill and stood there. It was one of the biggest lions I had ever seen, like the arch of a bridge, and ravenous. Every time we approached it, it would come down from the hill and chase after the horses . . . I saw it leap onto the haunches of the horse belonging to an attendant of my uncle, tearing the man's clothing and leggings with its claws. Then it returned to the hill. There was thus no way of getting at the lion until I climbed above it on the slope of the hill and rushed my horse down upon it and thrust my spear at it, piercing it. I left the spear sticking in its side. The lion then rolled over onto the slope of the hill with the spear still in it. The lion died . . .' Usama was so devoted to the hunt that he even imported dogs and falcons from Byzantium.[22]

The finer points of warfare were also of interest to Usama. His terse assessment of Frankish strategy reflected their need to preserve men and horses: 'The Franks (God curse them) are of all men the most cautious in war.'[23] This was also a strategy born out of bitter experience. On several occasions the Christians' excitement caused them to chase Muslim forces, apparently fleeing in disarray, only for the 'defeated' enemy to turn, encircle their pursuers and slaughter them. On a personal level Usama was keen to inform his audience about his own heroic achievements and to pass on tips; the list of 'my favourite lance thrusts' is – to a non-expert – perhaps a little self-referential, but it shows one measure of esteem amongst the military classes of the Muslim Near East.[24]

Usama was also a keen recorder of medical practice. Sometimes he used his observations to ridicule the barbaric Franks – although it is striking that he often followed a ghastly or risible example of ill-treatment with something more sober or practical; in other words, he wrote in a series of antitheses that should not be broken up.[25] Usama reported that a Frankish physician intervened in the treatment of a knight with an abscess on his leg and a woman afflicted with 'imbecility'. He asked the knight, "'Which would you like better: living with one leg or dying with both?" "Living with one leg," replied the knight. The physician then said: "Bring me a strong knight and a sharp axe." The physician laid the leg of the patient on a block of wood . . . and [the knight] struck him – I'm telling you I watched him do it – with one blow, but it didn't chop the leg all the way off. So he struck him a second time, but the marrow flowed out of the leg and he died instantly. He then examined the woman and said: "This woman, there is a demon inside her head that has possessed her. Shave off her hair." So they shaved her head. The woman then returned to eating their usual diet – garlic and mustard. As a result her dryness of humours ["imbecility"] increased. So the physician said, "That demon has entered further into her head." So he took a razor and made a cut in her head in the shape of a cross. He then peeled back the skin so that the skull was exposed and rubbed it with salt. The woman died instantaneously.'[26] Easy as it is to mock these episodes they were followed by two stories of successful treatments: first, for the healing of wounds using vinegar; second for dealing with sores caused by scrofula, using a Frankish recipe.[27] In fact, the physician who told Usama of these excruciating treatments was an Eastern Christian himself; indeed, it was often the indigenous Christians, along with Jews and Muslims, who had the most advanced medical knowledge of the day. The works of the great classical author Galen had survived in Arabic, rather than Latin, and formed a basis for much contemporary treatment. It was undoubtedly true that, initially at least, the Franks lagged behind the locals; indeed, they often employed them at their own courts. Yet the newcomers began to assimilate eastern practices with their own techniques and in the case of the great hospital of the Knights of St John in Jerusalem (which could accommodate up to 2,000 people in extreme emergencies), there was a marked improvement in the standards of medical practice which, in turn, found their way back to Europe.[28]

By the mid-1170s Usama had joined Saladin's service and the poet's son, Murhaf, became a close companion of the sultan and joined him on campaign. His aging father was, initially at least, very well treated. The sultan showed him great generosity and Usama, in return, wrote in praise of his military strength, his achievements as the champion of Sunni orthodoxy and his benevolence: 'the sultan of Islam and the Muslims! Unifier of the creed of faith by his light, subjugator of the worshippers of the cross by his might, raiser of the banner of justice and right. The reviver of the dynasty of the Commander of the Faithful.'[29]

Saladin sought Usama's advice on warfare and, of course, *adab*. It is an interesting thought that some of the sultan's famously courteous behaviour could have been learned from the well-travelled poet of Shaizar. Usama's work was popular at court and he regaled gatherings of the ruling household with his compositions. It was in this period that Usama wrote his major poetry anthology – *The Kernels of Refinement* – and the *Book of Contemplation*.[30] Yet all was not well. If one reached the age of forty, then one was esteemed in the Islamic world, but by this time Usama was into his eighties. He felt that he had overstayed his time: 'my life has been so prolonged that the revolving days have taken from me all the objects of pleasure.' He continued:

> Even as I write, my lines seem troubled
> Like the writing of one with hands terror-stricken, palsied
> I wonder at this feebleness in my hands as they lift up a pen
> When previously they had shattered spears in the hearts of lions.
> If I walk, it is with cane in hand, bemired
> Are my legs as if I waded through a mud-soaked plain . . .
> Destiny has forsaken me, leaving me like
> An exhausted pack-camel abandoned in the wastes . . .
> A journey is coming, and its time is nigh.[31]

In his final years Usama seems to have been sidelined from the court and was confined to his own house, reduced to looking back at his exciting youth and lamenting his decline. He acknowledged that God had spared him on countless occasions but now he prepared to meet his destiny. Examples of divine power suffused his writings. God intervened to save a person from death because it was not his or her time to die. God determined the destiny of all and there was no way to avoid one's fate – Usama finally met his end in Damascus in November 1188.

Ibn Jubayr: A Spanish Pilgrim in the Lands of Saladin and the Crusaders

Just a few years before Usama's death another celebrated poet of the Islamic world had passed through Damascus. Ibn Jubayr's legacy offers a fascinating blend of religious devotion and sharply observed travelogue, the product of his pilgrimage to Mecca.[32] His homelands were in Muslim-controlled Andalusia, but he left the great court of Granada in February 1183 and over the next two and a quarter years he passed through Ceuta in North Africa, then Sardinia, Alexandria, Cairo, down the Nile to the Red Sea, across to Mecca and Medina, over the Arabian Desert to Baghdad, up the Tigris to Mosul, over to Aleppo in northern Syria and on to Damascus. He then stayed for thirty-two days in the kingdom of Jerusalem where he sought and secured passage home on a Genoese ship. This sailed via the Greek Islands towards Sicily, but was shipwrecked outside Messina. Ibn Jubayr and his fellow passengers survived and he was able to complete his journey home on another vessel.

One attraction of his book is its candid style: Ibn Jubayr was highly critical of numerous aspects of the Islamic Near East and scorned many of its rulers – the notable exception being Saladin whom he regarded as a man of many splendid virtues. To read a Muslim visitor's view of the Frankish East would be of interest in its own right but the fact that Ibn Jubayr was present in late 1184, just as the Latin kingdom of Jerusalem was in the throes of an internal political crisis and facing immense pressure from the ascendant power of Saladin, makes it especially compelling. Ibn Jubayr's book became widely admired in the Muslim world and it was copied and incorporated into the work of many later writers. They also praised his other compositions in poetry and prose; one wrote: 'His reputation was immense, his good deeds many, and his fame widespread; and the incomparable story of his journey is everywhere related.'[33]

Ibn Jubayr's original career was as an administrator. One day in

1182 he was summoned by his master, the governor of Granada, who wished to dictate a letter to him. The governor offered him a glass of wine, but Ibn Jubayr followed the example of the Prophet and refused alcohol. His master was infuriated and roared: 'By Allah! You will drink seven glasses!' Ibn Jubayr protested in vain, but fearful of the governor's rage he swallowed the forbidden liquid. Seeing his secretary's acute distress the governor was overcome with remorse and called for some gold dinars. Seven times he filled Ibn Jubayr's goblet with the coins and then tipped them into his gown. In spite of the fact that he had been coerced into the shameful act, the secretary resolved to use the money to make a penitential pilgrimage to Mecca to expiate his sins. As a devout Muslim Ibn Jubayr would have made this journey once in his lifetime in any case; this traumatic incident provided him with the motive and the means to accomplish it.[34]

There is much in Ibn Jubayr's writing that has the feel of an enthusiastic tourist, albeit a deeply religious one. He loathed sea travel and found parts of the land journey arduous as well; his description of luxury camel transport is heartfelt: 'The best and most comfortable camel litters used are the *shaqadif*, and the best of those are made in the Yemen, for the travelling seats are covered with leather and are roomy. Two of them are bound together by stout ropes and put across the camel. They have supports at each corner, and on those rest a canopy. The traveller and his companion in counterpoise will thus be veiled from the blaze of the midday heat and may sit reclining and at ease beneath its covering. With his companion he may partake of food and the like, or read, when he wishes, the Koran or some other book; and who so deems it lawful to play chess may, if he wish, play his companion, for diversion and to relieve the spirit.'[35] On the other hand, his comments on the heat of the Arabian peninsula convey a tone of grim suffering: 'We had lived between air that melts the body and water that turns the stomach from appetite for food.'[36]

Ibn Jubayr provides a remarkably detailed description of Mecca and its environs. He took part in numerous processions and religious events and visited countless mosques, shrines, tombs and colleges while fulfilling his spiritual obligations. Throughout these episodes one senses his devotion and can share in his pride when, for example, in the house of the Prophet's birth he was able to press his cheek onto the marble basin that marked the place of nativity.[37]

While he marvelled at the heartlands of Islam, he cared little for some of its inhabitants: 'This is the country of Islam most deserving a *hisbah* [flogging] and in this case the scourge employed should be the sword.'[38] While it is true that Saladin, temporarily at least, managed to bring a semblance of political unity to the Muslim Near East, Ibn Jubayr's comments indicate that there remained – then as now – a huge degree of sectarian tension: 'The greater number of the people of these Hejaz and other lands are sectarians and schismatics [Shi'ites] who have no religion and have split into diverse schools of thought.'[39] He also felt that women were poorly treated in Mecca: 'On the whole, in comparison with the men they are wretched and cheated. They see the venerated house and may not enter it, they gaze upon the blessed Stone, but cannot touch it, and their lot is wholly one of staring and feeling the sadness that moves and holds them . . . May God, by His grace and favour, advantage them for their sincere intentions and their faith.'[40]

Ibn Jubayr was unimpressed by Baghdad, a huge city, some sections of which were in ruins. He regarded its citizens as vain and exploitative, although he admired the beauty of the women and praised the quality of the preachers and clerics. Next he travelled north-west and in the course of his journey saw flaming bitumen pits, evidence of the presence of oil in the region. It seems that he felt more comfortable in Syria, both emotionally and physically. Damascus was easily his favourite city: 'the Paradise of the Orient' as he described it.[41] Ibn Jubayr offers a vivid description of the Great Umayyad Mosque with its refulgent gold and green mosaics depicting buildings and plants (Islamic art should not represent humans). Even today, these entrancing works, in restored form, decorate the front of the main prayer hall. He climbed onto the great dome above the hall and marvelled at its technological sophistication, and he venerated a definitive recension of the Koran, owned by the 'Uthman, the third caliph of Islam and a companion of Muhammad, and sent by him to Syria.'[42]

It was in Damascus that Ibn Jubayr came into close contact with members of Saladin's court. His treatment of Saladin is, of itself, highly interesting. He was not, of course, in the sultan's employ, unlike several other contemporary writers, such as Beha ad-Din ibn Shaddad or Imad ad-Din. The author was an outsider who had no prior obligation either to praise or to condemn the man. In the event, his opinion was overwhelmingly positive. The sultan was a gift from God, a right-eous man and Ibn Jubayr praised him for 'his zeal in waging holy war against the enemies of God'.[43] Saladin was energetic: never retiring to a place of rest, always ready to make his saddle his council chamber. Ibn Jubayr did not meet him in person because the sultan was besieging Kerak while the author was in Damascus; he did, however, talk to a jurist and a gathering of learned men about their leader.[44] Notwithstanding his primary purpose as a travel writer Ibn Jubayr was pleased to set out stories regarding the sultan's virtues and he provided episodes that demonstrated his magnanimity, his generosity, his impartiality and his belief in the importance of law and justice. 'May God, by His favour, grant that Islam and the Muslims may long enjoy his preservation of them.'[45] Ibn Jubayr was also careful to note that the setting of the tale concerning generosity was a poetry symposium, a matter close to the author's heart and, of course, an indication of the sultan's cultivation and interest in *adab*. These posi-tive aspects of Saladin's rule and personality are familiar to us from the writings of other Muslim commentators and also from western sources, such as the Old French Continuation of Archbishop William of Tyre, the most important historian of the Frankish East. But Ibn Jubayr helps to confirm, if further evidence was needed, the reality of such character traits.[46]

After leaving Damascus, Ibn Jubayr travelled into the kingdom of Jerusalem where he encountered a few surprises. As we shall see, in the mid-1180s Saladin launched ever more serious attacks on the Franks; indeed, as Ibn Jubayr departed from Damascus he met a returning raiding party that carried money, furniture, cattle and huge numbers of Christian prisoners for the slave markets. This was the jihad in action and the author abandons his usual equanimity and launches into a tirade against the Franks. Of Queen Sibylla of Jerusalem he wrote: 'at this place [Tibnin], customs dues are levied on the cara-vans. It belongs to the sow known as Queen who is the mother of the pig who is the lord of Acre – may God destroy it.'[47] Yet, much to the author's amazement, in spite of these ferocious cultural and reli-gious confrontations, trade and pilgrimage continued. 'One of the most astonishing things that is talked of is that though the fires of discord burn between the two parties, Muslim and Christian, two armies of them may meet and dispose themselves in battle array, and

yet Christian and Muslim travellers will come and go between them
without interference . . . The Christians impose a tax on the Muslims
in their land which gives them full security; and likewise the Christian
merchants pay a tax upon their goods in Muslim lands . . . The soldiers
engage themselves in war, while the people are at peace and the world
goes to him who conquers. Such is the usage in war of the people in
these lands . . . The state of these countries in this regard is truly more
astonishing than our story can convey. May God by His favour exalt
the word of Islam.'[48]

Most disturbing to him was the Franks' treatment of Muslims within
their lands and the attitude of those Muslims who lived under Christian
rule. As he moved towards the port of Acre, 'our way lay through
continuous farms and ordered settlements whose inhabitants were all
Muslims, living comfortably with the Franks. God protect us from
such temptation. They surrender half their crops to the Franks at
harvest time, and pay as well a poll tax for each person. Other than
that they are not interfered with, save a light tax on the fruits of trees
. . . their hearts have been seduced, for they observe how unlike them
in ease and comfort are their brethren in the Muslim regions . . . The
Muslim community bewails the injustice of a landlord of its own faith
and applauds the conduct of its opponent and enemy, the Frankish
landlord, and is accustomed to justice from him.'[49]

Ibn Jubayr could barely reconcile this state of affairs with the
contemporary strategic situation and he roundly condemned his co-
religionists. The Franks had generally treated Muslim farmers well
since the earliest years of the conquest – in large part, simply as a
matter of expediency. They had tried to persuade westerners to come
and settle in the Holy Land; agents toured Europe and offered advantageous deals on tax, ownership and status: in effect an appeal to 'Go
East, Young Man'. While these efforts had drawn some to a new life,
the majority of the population remained either indigenous Christian
or, in some districts such as that near Acre, Muslim. If the Franks had
slaughtered or purged these peoples there would have been no one to
farm the land and no one for them to tax; within months the economy
would have collapsed. In one instance we know that Tancred of Antioch
arranged for the wives of native labourers to return to their farms
(now under his control) from Aleppo, where they had fled for safety.
Had the Franks systematically abused their Muslim tenants there would

have been a real prospect of rebellion. In fact, as Ibn Jubayr's outraged description demonstrates, as landlords and farmers the Franks ruled the Levant successfully and, until the autumn of 1187 when Saladin's victory was certain, only one Muslim revolt was recorded.

Our guide described the city of Acre, one of the premier ports of the Frankish East, but at this time, a place of little distinction to him. Even allowing for Ibn Jubayr's bias the picture is not flattering: 'Its roads and streets are choked by the press of men, so that it is hard to put foot to ground. Unbelief and impiety burn there fiercely, and pigs [Christians] and crosses abound. It stinks and is filthy, being full of refuse and excrement.'[50] Amidst this olfactory assault, however, the writer noted that one part of the central mosque remained for use by Muslims. In order to keep some semblance of order, the Franks allowed individual prayer by Muslims throughout their lands. What was banned, however, was the *khutba*, the Friday prayer meetings – in other words, communal gatherings which could have provided a primary forum to preach and to stir up discontent. From Acre, Ibn Jubayr went north to Tyre, a place that he found cleaner and friendlier to Muslims. There he witnessed a Christian wedding and, in spite of his prejudices, he could not help but be drawn into the celebration. The rich detail with which he described the event brings the ceremony vividly before us: the noise, the colour, the sense of everyone sharing a joyous occasion, almost regardless of their faith. The author's attraction to the bride was a source of particular concern to him; one can feel his cultural and religious principles reassert themselves over his more earthly emotions; a victory for the greater jihad.

An alluring worldly spectacle deserving of record was a nuptial procession which we witnessed one day near the port in Tyre. All the Christians, men and women, had assembled and were formed in two lines at the bride's door. Trumpets, flutes, and all the musical instruments were played until she proudly emerged between two men who held her right and left as though they were her kindred. She was most elegantly garbed in a beautiful dress from which trailed, according to their traditional style, a long train of golden silk. On her head she wore a golden diadem covered by a net of woven gold, and on her breast was a like arrangement. Proud she was in her ornaments and dress, walking with little steps of half a span, like a dove or in the manner of a wisp of cloud.

God protect us from the seduction of the sight. Before her went Christian notables in their finest and most splendid clothing, their trains falling in behind them. Behind her were her peers and equals of the Christian women, parading in their richest apparel and proud of bearing in their superb ornaments. Leading them all were the musical instruments. The Muslims and other Christian onlookers formed two ranks along the route, and gazed upon them without reproof. So they passed along until they brought her to the house of the groom; and all that day they feasted. We thus were given the chance of seeing this alluring sight, from the seducement of which may God preserve us.[51]

When Ibn Jubayr arranged passage home he chose to board a Christian ship. This particular vessel was Genoese and it was from there, as well as Pisa and Venice, that the bulk of western European shipping originated. The three Italian cities were bitter rivals, both at home and abroad. Their commercial web stretched across Europe and the Middle East, from Iberia and the Balearics, to North Africa, Constantinople, Alexandria and the Holy Land. As Ibn Jubayr had observed, commerce rarely respected lines of religious demarcation, although outsiders were often picked upon at moments of extreme tension. The Italian traders played a crucial role in the subjugation of the coastal cities of Syria because without their ability to defeat Muslim shipping and to besiege and blockade settlements by sea, the Franks would have been unable to consolidate their hold on the Levant. Ongoing commercial traffic and, even more importantly, the transport of pilgrims, were both vital for the economy and, in the case of pilgrimage, fundamental to the *raison d'être* of the Christian presence in the region. This military assistance was not, however, given freely. The Italians were devout Catholics whose cities were full of churches and relics; they were, therefore, pleased to help recover Christ's patrimony. Yet they saw no contradiction between this and securing generous commercial privileges from the rulers of the Frankish East and continuing to pursue trade with the Islamic world.[52] For this very reason, Ibn Jubayr and fifty other Muslims were able to board ship at Tyre. The presence of Christian pilgrims on the same boat caused mild concern to our writer who commented, 'The Muslims secured places apart from the Franks. Some Christians called *bilghriyin* [pilgrims] came aboard. They had been on the pilgrimage to Jerusalem and were too numerous to count. May God in His grace and favour soon relieve us of their company and bring us to safety.'[53] The writer's journey home proved dramatic. He hated the sea, and quoted a poem to prove the point:

> The sea is bitter of taste, intractable:
> No need of it have I.
> Is it not water and we earth?
> Why then do we endure it?[54]

When the vessel ran aground in Messina harbour it was only through the generous intervention of King William II of Sicily that the passengers were saved. Ibn Jubayr finally reached Granada on 25 April 1185. He made one further journey to the Levant – between 1189 and 1191 – before settling in Alexandria, where he died in 1217.

By the time of Usama ibn Munqidh's demise in 1188, the jihad had reached its climax with Saladin's recovery of Jerusalem. Yet, strangely, neither Usama nor Ibn Jubayr made much reference to holy war in their writing. The former was certainly not a theologian, but a pious poet who performed all of his devotional obligations. Perhaps he had spent the most active decades of his career at a time of relative – and the word is used with caution – calm between the Frankish settlers and the Muslims. As he recognised, there was a possibility for a modus vivendi, but by his twilight years such days were passed and the ideas of al-Sulami – ironically the earliest of our sources here – had come to prevail. The Damascene cleric was no longer the lone voice, way ahead of his time; his message had become the clarion cry for his people. By the 1180s, the call for the jihad had taken firm root amongst the political elite of Muslim Syria and Egypt. The Islamic Near East had caught up with al-Sulami's stirring cry for action; the desire to remove the Franks was paramount. Yet even within this impassioned rhetoric, as Ibn Jubayr shows us, pilgrimage, a basic devotional act for both faiths, could continue as well. This blend of trust, admiration and occasional respect, alongside anger, hostility, disdain and suspicion makes relations between Christians and Muslims in this period so intriguing and so full of contradictions.

3

'A woman of unusual wisdom and discretion': Queen Melisende of Jerusalem

Within fifty years of its capture, Jerusalem, the most prestigious city in Christendom, was ruled by a woman. Queen Melisende's powerful and charismatic personality cast its influence across the Levant for over two decades – a remarkable achievement in the most war-torn environment in Christendom and in such a male-dominated age. Broadly speaking, medieval women were characterised as either sinful temptresses, heiresses to the legacy of Eve, or simply lacking the physical strength to govern. Biblical authority indicated women were subject to the authority of their husbands.[1] Melisende came to the throne of Jerusalem through a complex combination of personal determination and circumstance. At first glance, however, the possibility of any woman wielding authority in the Levant seems remote.

The Early Frankish Rulers of Jerusalem

As we have seen, the first Frankish ruler of Jerusalem, Godfrey of Bouillon, refused to call himself king in Christ's city and modestly took the title of Advocate of the Holy Sepulchre. He died just over a year later to be succeeded by his more pragmatic brother, Baldwin of Boulogne, who was crowned king in November 1100. Thus began the royal line, headed by one of the great warrior-leaders of the First Crusade. King Baldwin I had to expand and consolidate his lands in the face of fierce Muslim opposition. He also needed to establish a dynasty, his first wife having died during the terrible crossing of Asia Minor. And so, in 1098 he married the Armenian noblewoman, Arda, partly in an attempt to forge closer links with the indigenous Christians of northern Syria.[2] Arda travelled south to be installed as queen of

Jerusalem but within six years, Baldwin – whose wars had made him desperately short of cash – cast her aside to seek a wealthier bride. Arda fled to Constantinople where she is said to have lost her queenly dignity and become a common prostitute. Flagrantly ignoring the fact that Arda was still alive the king then married the wealthy, but late middle-aged, Adelaide of Sicily. Once he had spent all her money Baldwin callously repudiated this queen too and sent her home: apparently the king regarded women as useful sources of financial and political advancement but little else, and in not providing an heir, he had failed in the most vital responsibility of a medieval monarch.

At the time of his death Baldwin I's closest male relative had returned to Europe. By chance, however, the king's cousin, also named Baldwin – and, at that time, count of Edessa – was in Jerusalem. Rather than suffer a long interregnum the nobility agreed he should be crowned and his family soon came south to start a new life in the holy city.[3] Fourteen grim months as a captive of the Muslims in 1123–4 did little to deter Baldwin II from an aggressive military policy and he fought numerous campaigns across the Levant. His Armenian wife, Morphia, bore him four daughters – Melisende, Alice, Hodierna and Yveta – before she died in 1126. Once again there was no immediate male heir. Circumstances required that an outsider be brought in to marry the eldest princess and become king, although, as we shall see, first Baldwin, and then Melisende, were utterly determined to protect the standing of their own bloodline.[4] Transforming this desire into a reality lies at the heart of this episode and in the course of the struggle Melisende challenged and, in her lifetime at least, overturned women's conventional role as passive and politically inferior to men.

As (often) a child heiress, then a bride, a mother and finally a widow, women could carry or create the royal line of succession. For every ruling house the maintenance of a dynasty was a matter of the utmost priority; a woman could, therefore, through the various stages of her life, hold or transmit something of inestimable value.[5] By bearing children a woman could derive glory and hold a special place in a ruling family. To convert that into genuine day-to-day influence and to overcome the strictures of churchmen was, for the majority of medieval noblewomen and queens, impossible. Elsewhere in twelfth-century Europe, several women – such as Matilda of England – attempted to become rulers, but their efforts almost invariably failed and were not repeated for centuries. For Melisende the boundaries imposed by her sex were there to be broken.

The Death of King Baldwin II and the Succession of Fulk and Melisende

In August 1131 King Baldwin II marched into Jerusalem after settling a rebellion in northern Syria. Within a week of his return, however, the king was struck down by a serious illness and his condition rapidly deteriorated. Baldwin realised that his last days were at hand and he asked to be carried the 300 metres from the royal palace in the Temple of Solomon to the palace of the patriarch of Jerusalem in the Holy Sepulchre.

The head of the Catholic Church in Jerusalem occupied a series of spacious apartments connected to the uppermost part of the rotunda of the Holy Sepulchre. Baldwin could hardly be closer to the core of the Christian faith – the place where Jesus had been buried and had risen again. It was on a quest to free the Lord's tomb from Muslim hands that he had set out on the First Crusade and fought and suffered during the 3,000 long miles from his homeland in Boulogne to the holy city. Thirty-three years later he was one of the few surviving veterans of the crusade and it was wholly apposite that he chose to die at the place of greatest spiritual resonance for Christian pilgrims.

As his strength faded Baldwin summoned his eldest daughter, the slender, dark-haired Melisende, his son-in-law, Count Fulk V of Anjou, and their son, a two-year-old also named Baldwin. For Melisende it must have been an intensely poignant moment as she witnessed the loss of her remaining parent and the change in her status from princess to queen. Fulk had waited for this time since his arrival in the Holy Land three years earlier. The nobles of Jerusalem had unanimously chosen him to marry Melisende because he was a man of considerable military experience and the head of one of the most important families in western Europe. He was also known to the Franks from an earlier pilgrimage to the Levant when he stayed with the newly founded Order of Knights Templar. When Baldwin passed away, Fulk believed that he would become king of Jerusalem.

As his time drew near, Baldwin had one final, maverick decision to hand down. It was an act that would have profound consequences for Melisende, Fulk and the future of the kingdom of Jerusalem. Baldwin summoned the patriarch and various senior nobles to join his family at his bedside. In front of these witnesses the ailing monarch formally resigned the crown and then – and here lay the twist – he committed the kingdom *not* to Fulk alone, but to the care of Melisende and the infant Baldwin as well. In other words, he decreed that Jerusalem would be ruled by a triumvirate, not just by one man.

The majority of people in the room murmured their assent – for one individual, however, years of planning and anticipation were in utter ruins. As he heard the pronouncement Fulk must have felt shaken to the core – a mixture of horror and fury; yet at such a solemn moment he could hardly give vent to his true emotions. He had relinquished his position as count of Anjou in order to rule Jerusalem *in his own right*. He had not surrendered his old life in France to share power with anyone, not even his own wife. Now he had been cornered and confronted with – potentially – the demolition of his sole authority.[6]

As a piece of political drama this deathbed scene was an episode of the highest order. Who could resist the dying command of a hero of the First Crusade, the anointed king of Jerusalem? Baldwin had sent a startlingly clear signal that it was *his* bloodline – carried in the person of Melisende – and not Fulk's, that lay at the heart and soul of the kingdom. Baldwin did not, under any circumstances, wish to see the lands that he had fought so hard for, absorbed into Fulk's Angevin Empire. Yet it was precisely because Baldwin's line had to be transmitted through a woman, with all the disadvantages that this carried in medieval society, that he had needed to stage such a *coup de théâtre*. Fulk was important as a provider of military leadership and to father children, but Baldwin plainly wished to limit his influence and to ensure that Melisende held power as well. Much depended on how Melisende herself handled this legacy. Some women may have simply acquiesced to their husband's wishes – as the Church recommended they should – in which case Baldwin's decree would have become a hollow and worthless act. There were numerous cases of female regents being bullied aside by the political and military muscle of men who sought power for themselves. The dying king knew his daughter well, though; Melisende had the strength of character to uphold her position to the full and as the years unfolded her uncompromising political skills showed her father's faith in her to be entirely justified.

It is difficult not to feel some sympathy for Fulk. There was no record of any overt tension between Baldwin and his son-in-law in the three years before the king died; in fact, William of Tyre recorded quite the opposite. Fulk is reported to have 'devotedly fulfilled all the duties of a son . . . and in deference to the lord king he proved he was not lacking in those qualities which ordinarily win friends.'[7] Yet Orderic Vitalis, who wrote within a decade of these events, offered a different perspective and observed that Fulk had 'exercised authority undisturbed as [Baldwin's] son-in-law and heir throughout the realm during the [last] year of the old king's life.'[8] Fulk would have been able to stamp his influence on the royal household and the arrival of a number of Angevin newcomers may have perturbed Baldwin. While the presence of extra warriors was always welcome in the Holy Land, such men would need lands and titles for themselves – which could only come at the expense of the indigenous nobility: those who had grown strong in supporting King Baldwin. The invitation to Fulk was the first time that such a powerful western lord had been asked to settle in the Levant; almost certainly the king had underestimated the wider effects of his being there.

While the nobility of Jerusalem had universally endorsed the choice of Fulk as ruler, evidently they had now reconsidered; some may have feared that he would cast Melisende aside. After all, his father, Fulk le Réchin, had, in spite of his nickname, married four, possibly five times and Fulk himself had an adult son, Elias, from his first marriage. At the time of his father's negotiations to wed Melisende, Elias had been expected to succeed to the county of Perche in northern France, but had since been cheated out of this by his father-in-law. Could the next king of Jerusalem lever his own son into the line of succession in the East?

After Baldwin had revealed his final wishes he removed himself from any further controversy when he donned a monk's cowl and took vows of holy orders. Like many nobles of the time he chose to end his life as a cleric and forsook the secular world to be closer to God. On 21 August 1131 the king died. He was buried near his predecessors in the Church of the Holy Sepulchre at the foot of Mount Calvary, the place of Christ's crucifixion.

Within a month Fulk, Melisende and the young Baldwin were crowned. The coronations of Baldwin I and Baldwin II had taken place at the Church of the Holy Nativity in Bethlehem, but the 1131 ceremony was moved to the focal point of the kingdom, the Holy Sepulchre – an early indication that Fulk wanted to change direction. The court officials chose 14 September, the day of the Exaltation of the Holy Cross, a commemoration of the discovery of the relic of the True Cross, as an auspicious and appropriate day for the occasion.

The coronation was a great public event, designed to cement in the minds of everyone who witnessed it the beginning of a new period of divinely sanctioned rule. In a society without means of mass communication, such carefully staged displays were vital opportunities to reinforce notions of power and splendour. Detailed descriptions of thirteenth-century coronations allow us to reconstruct the events of 1131 with some confidence; we also have the evidence of an early twelfth-century coronation oath.[9] The minutely calculated ceremonial emphasised the royal dignity, the position of the senior nobility, especially the great officers of state, as well as the authority of the Church. Many parts of the ritual can be traced back to the settlers' homelands and dated from the age of Charlemagne, giving them further gravitas by the weight of tradition.

Once the coronation date had been announced the preparations began. The nobility of Jerusalem travelled to the capital to take part in the ceremony, as did representatives from Antioch, Tripoli and Edessa. Bishops, abbots and all the other churchmen of the realm also started to assemble. A more exotic touch was added by the presence of an embassy from Fatimid Egypt; serious political turmoil prompted the new vizier, Kutayfat, to seek a truce with the Christians and his envoys carried a beautiful gift, a carved ivory *tau* or staff, to advance their cause.[10] Most of the annual pilgrim visitors were still in the Holy Land and they must have been delighted to witness an event of such importance. As the great day approached, people were drawn towards the holy city to watch or take part in the coronation; Jerusalem must have been overflowing with visitors staying with friends, fellow religious groups or in the many hostels.

On 14 September Fulk and Melisende dressed in the royal palace, assisted, as ever, by their servants. They wore special robes, beautifully embroidered dalmatics – wide-sleeved tunics, open at the sides – and

stoles. The family assembled in the Temple complex at the entrance
to the royal palace where the marshal and the constable awaited them
with horses and the royal standard. This was a square of white cloth
with a cross at each corner and one in the centre to represent the
wounds of Christ. Fulk and Melisende mounted their horses, specially
caparisoned for the event, and the chamberlain pointed the way
forwards with the royal sword. Behind the couple came the seneschal
carrying the sceptre and the constable holding the standard. Given the
scale of the entourage it is likely that the procession went along Temple
Street, one of the wider thoroughfares of the city – perhaps seven
metres across, rather than the two to three metres of most byways.
Temple Street ascends gently uphill for about 300 metres until a small
dog-leg moves onto David Street. The way was thronged with cheering
spectators, crammed in doorways, leaning from windows, standing in
front of shops and up on the flat roofs of the houses. The route was
decorated with highly coloured banners and a swell of noise and anticipation rolled ahead of the approaching party. After another couple
of hundred metres the procession turned right onto Patriarch Street
and moved alongside the western wall of the Hospital of St John before
turning right into the courtyard in front of the Holy Sepulchre itself.
The street plan of this district of Jerusalem is barely changed today
and many of the buildings that rise either side of these roads are
crusader in origin. Almost claustrophobic, and often in heavy shadow
because of the narrow streets, the area has a truly medieval feel. The
absence of traffic, the bustle of people buying and selling; the slower,
less certain pace of strangers visiting holy sites; the smells of cooking
food and exotic spices, and the mounds of brightly coloured merchan-
dise provide the modern tourist with some echoes of the crusader age.

Fulk and Melisende dismounted at the courtyard of the Holy
Sepulchre. The constable handed the royal standard to the marshal
and took the horses' bridles. Standing in the doorway of the church,
waiting to welcome the royal couple, was Patriarch William I of
Jerusalem, accompanied by his senior churchmen and the Eastern
Christian religious hierarchy, all wearing their finest robes. The party
moved from daylight into the holy of holies, the candlelit rotunda
that contained Christ's tomb. The building in place today was (as we
will see later) the product of a reconstruction programme initiated
by Fulk and Melisende soon after their coronation, but in September

1131 the Sepulchre area was already laid out in a basic circular shape. As the candles flickered and incense wafted through the air, everyone knelt in worship and the patriarch led prayers for a successful reign. William then asked Fulk and Melisende to take the coronation oath. No previous rulers of Jerusalem had been designated joint monarchs in the way that Baldwin II had prescribed, but given Fulk and Melisende's status – and the events that followed – we should assume that they both took the same oath. The infant Baldwin must also have been present, but for obvious reasons only as a witness.

The text of the twelfth-century coronation oath has survived and in this case probably resembled these words: 'I, Melisende [or Fulk] promise, in the presence of God and his angels, from this day and henceforth, to conserve law, justice and peace for the Holy Church of God in Jerusalem and for my subjects.'[11] They also agreed to seek the advice of the best churchmen of the land where needed. After swearing the oaths the king and queen promised to maintain and defend the crown. William then kissed the couple, turned to the clerics, nobles and visitors who packed into the church and asked them to confirm that Fulk and Melisende were the lawful heirs to the throne. Three times he asked the question and on the third, a shout of 'Oill!' (Yes!) echoed around the building. A further acclamation came through the open doors of the church from those unable to squeeze inside, then everyone sang the hymn 'Te Deum laudamus'.

Another solemn procession then entered the rotunda. Senior nobles had taken the royal crowns out of the treasury of the Holy Sepulchre and carried them forwards. The king and queen sat in their choir stalls near the altar and Mass was said. William proclaimed a blessing and began to anoint them. This was one of the most crucial elements of the coronation ritual; the blessing of kings and queens with consecrated oil set them apart from all other laymen. Dukes and counts made oaths and received insignia, but royalty were the only secular people anointed in such a way. The patriarch, holding a horn that contained holy oil, dipped his fingers into it and then touched the head and shoulders of Fulk and Melisende. They now had divine sanction. Next Patriarch William moved on to the symbols of office; given that a joint coronation was unprecedented, either a duplicate of each object had to be found or, more likely, they were given to Fulk alone. A ring, to symbolise loyalty, was put on the king's finger and he was girded with a sword to indicate justice and the duty of defence. Then he was crowned, given a sceptre in his right hand to signify the punishment of sinners and an orb in his left to show dominion. At this point, Melisende must have been crowned queen.

The two monarchs turned to the senior churchmen present, said 'Long live the king/queen in prosperity' and kissed all of them before turning to their thrones. The Mass ended with Communion. The patriarch blessed the royal standard and gave it to the constable. One wonders what was running through the minds of Fulk and Melisende. In some ways, both must have felt elated by the sense of occasion, their being the centre of attention, the bellow of acclaim from the audience, the special ritual of anointing and the placing of the crowns upon their heads. Fulk must have been conscious of his elevation: from the ranks of the senior nobility as count of Anjou he had now reached the very top echelon, that exclusive level of royalty. Exactly how unwilling he was to share this with Melisende would soon become evident. Nothing from his experiences in western Europe would have prepared him for an equal division of authority with a woman; indeed he almost certainly believed that his wife should obey him in all things. The day secured Fulk's handhold on royal status, but he resolved to ignore the element of joint rule that lay at the heart of the ceremony and he began to exercise power in the way he felt to be appropriate and his due.

Melisende too had moved to the highest rank of secular life; perhaps she felt some trepidation – even as a joint ruler she was doing something almost unprecedented in living memory. The only comparable case had been that of Queen Urraca of Castile and León (1109–26) and she had used a male companion to help govern without a husband.[12] Whether Melisende knew much about Urraca's experiences is unclear. At the very least she could rely on a core group of her father's nobles with whom she had grown up and who were likely to be loyal to Baldwin's memory.

The king and queen stepped out from the Holy Sepulchre into the sharp light of day to receive the cheers of the crowds outside. They retraced their steps back to the Templum Domini (today the al-Aqsa Mosque) where they laid their crowns on the altar to commemorate the presentation of Jesus to Simeon in the temple. This was the last solemn act of the day. Now the nobility of Jerusalem served a splendid celebratory banquet – singing, storytelling and dancing rounded off

one of the landmark events in the history of Jerusalem: the inaugur-
ation of a new and experimental phase for the royal dynasty.

Murder and Treason: The Rebellion of Count Hugh of Jaffa

Within three years the royal marriage was in serious trouble and the
kingdom of Jerusalem on the verge of its gravest political crisis to
date. Two of the most influential men in the land, Count Hugh of
Jaffa and Roman of Le Puy, lord of Transjordan, conspired to challenge King Fulk. Their motivation was a combination of the personal
and the political, and represented the entwined interests of Queen
Melisende and the native nobility.[13]

Hugh was in the prime of life: about twenty-eight years old, he was
tall, handsome and a distinguished warrior. William of Tyre eulogised:
'In him the gifts of nature seemed to have met in lavish abundance;
without question, in respect to physical beauty and nobility of birth,
as well as experience in the art of war, he had no equal in the kingdom.'[14]
The count was the son of Hugh II of Le Puiset who had set out on
crusade in 1106–7. En route to the Levant his wife had given birth to
a son in Apulia. The boy had remained at the Sicilian court until he
came of age when he travelled to the Holy Land and sought his inheritance from King Baldwin II around 1120. He was related to the royal
house of Jerusalem through his father, and his family ties and career
made him a natural associate of Melisende. Soon after 1123 he married
Emma of Jaffa, the widow of Eustace Grenier (in his day the most
powerful landowner in the kingdom and a royal constable). Emma
must have been rather older than Hugh because she already had two
sons, Eustace, lord of Sidon, and Walter, lord of Caesarea, both of
whom were adults and important nobles in their own right.

During the early 1130s tensions began to simmer between the king
and Count Hugh. The count grew arrogant: he refused to obey royal
commands and started to drift towards open defiance of his monarch.
Hugh was an immensely influential noble in his own right and the
county of Jaffa was probably the wealthiest lordship in the kingdom
of Jerusalem. Charters indicate that he enjoyed the full trappings of
a royal household, including a chancellor and treasurer. His position

was unique in the kingdom: no one else possessed the title of count; in fact, the only other men in the entire Levant with such a rank were the count of Tripoli and the count of Edessa.

As the friction between the two men became increasingly overt Hugh began to formulate a strategy. Almost nine centuries later, the details of his conspiracy are elusive, but we are fortunate to have a charter from the principality of Antioch that yields dramatic evidence. A document dated July 1134 places Hugh in the court of Melisende's sister, Alice of Antioch.[15] The princess had already shown herself to be the most independently minded and rebellious individual in the Latin East by staging two uprisings against the king of Jerusalem. This being so, it is unlikely to have been a coincidence that the count travelled over 280 miles north to see her. He must have gone to sound her out and alert her to the likelihood of open confrontation. As the champion of Melisende's cause it is logical that he would want to enlist the help of the queen's sister.

As the political momentum behind Hugh and Melisende increased, another, more personal, aspect to the situation became apparent. Fulk began to suspect the count of being more than simply friendly towards the queen. Perhaps he felt insecure – he was an older, placid man who may have been threatened by the obvious familiarity between Melisende and her dashing contemporary. Some whispered – tantalisingly – that there was proof of a more intimate relationship, yet none of our sources offers details. In such circumstances it is hard to make a genuine assessment of the truth. Sexual innuendo was, and remains, one of the oldest and easiest ways to disparage an opponent's name, and if the gossip came from the royal camp it could have had a far wider impact. Such rumours obviously impugned the good name of the queen herself and if an open allegation of adultery were proven the legal process would be barbaric. The queen could undergo an ordeal by fire and if found guilty, according to laws laid down in the 1120 Concordat of Nablus, she would be punished by rhinotomy, the slitting or cutting off of her nose; Hugh would be castrated. Melisende might then share the fate of the lady of Banyas, a woman found guilty of adultery, although in this instance at the hands of her Muslim captors, and be sent to a convent. No medieval queen had been treated in such a way, but in the poisonous atmosphere of 1134 such an outcome was a theoretical possibility.

Unsurprisingly, when the matter of his wife's infidelity was coupled with the simmering political conflict, Fulk conceived 'an inexorable hatred' of Count Hugh. Charges of adultery reflected badly on the vitality of a king who seemed unable to preserve the sanctity of his marriage bed. Such an accusation would also damage the standing of the infant Baldwin, although, as we have seen, Elias, Fulk's grown son from his first marriage, was waiting in the wings. It would be too sensitive to air the accusations of adultery in a formal setting – if Fulk was to flush out the conspirators then the political route offered the best way forward.

At the suggestion of the king, and perhaps out of loyalty to his mother, Countess Emma of Jaffa, Walter of Caesarea brought the matter to a head. At an assembly of the royal court of Jerusalem Walter made the most sensational and inflammatory claim possible: that Hugh and certain companions had conspired to kill King Fulk.[16] The fact that Walter confronted his own stepfather added an extra sharpness to the situation. Regicide was extraordinarily rare: the sanctity of kingship meant that except in open battle – such as King Harold at Hastings in 1066 – slaughtering God's anointed representative was almost unheard of. The fact that the king's own wife and her alleged lover were behind such a move made this story even more incredible.

This was a moment of the highest tension: the king and the count faced each other across the royal court. The older man was trying to grasp the power he believed to be rightfully his, the other sought to preserve the status and dignity of the queen of Jerusalem. At the heart of this conflict was Melisende, the pivot around which the entire struggle turned. When he heard the accusation Hugh stood firm; he stated that he was innocent of this heinous charge. Proof may be difficult to provide, however. In the belief that he had allies amongst the native population the count turned to the court of his peers and said that he would submit to their judgement. The barons and leading churchmen of the land conferred. Could they condemn one of the most important nobles in Outremer, or should they join him, and break with tradition to defy the anointed king? In the early twelfth century an accuser and witnesses spoke to the court and then the nobility debated the outcome. The idea of a prosecution, a defence, and trial by jury were not invented in a form recognisable to us until the reign of King Henry II of England, forty years later. In the medieval mindset only God could know the truth. The court decreed the matter should be settled by single combat, as was the fashion in contemporary France and Germany, and a date for the trial was set. Hugh and Walter were to face each other, fully armed and mounted on horseback. They would charge at each other until one was unhorsed. The rider might be able to finish off his opponent at that point, or he could dismount and begin hand-to-hand fighting. Sometimes the struggle was so close that the men ended up wrestling unarmed. In one contest the winner secured victory by biting off his enemy's nose, in another by wrenching his opponent's testicles. The defeated man was usually slain.[17]

Hugh returned to his lands at Jaffa, but on the day designated for the ordeal he failed to attend. Some interpreted this as an admission of guilt and there was disquiet even amongst his own supporters. Walter was famous for his strength and perhaps Hugh feared his stepson's fighting skills. In any case, the High Court condemned Hugh's absence and he was found guilty of treason and his lands forfeit.[18] Had he fought and won, Fulk's position would have become untenable.

William of Tyre described Hugh's reaction to this news as a combination of panic and foolishness: on hearing the court's verdict Hugh sailed south forty miles from Jaffa to Muslim-held Ascalon. He asked the inhabitants for help against the king – something they readily agreed to. As we have seen, treaties between Christians and Muslims were a fact of life in the Levant; the difference here was the state of division amongst the Christians which made Hugh's presence of particular interest to the Ascalonites. The count argued that he had support within the kingdom and that he could offer – presumably relying on Melisende's agreement – something to the Muslims in return. We know that they already paid King Baldwin II an annual financial tribute, so a reduction, or even a termination, were the most likely bargaining chips available. An agreement was sealed with an exchange of hostages, again a common custom, and Hugh returned to Jaffa.[19]

The Ascalonites delighted in the dissension between the Christians and mounted raids into the kingdom up to Arsuf. The king was furious; the court proceedings had swung the balance of power in his direction, but this military threat had to be countered. He gathered all the troops he could and besieged Jaffa. The city lies on the coast and has a small port overlooked by a castle perched on a rocky outcrop.

At first, Hugh did not act alone. The treaty with Ascalon had not entirely alienated his supporters, but as the king's troops surrounded Jaffa some began to feel that his chances of success were fading. They tried to reason with him, but Hugh would not submit – he had, after all, been found guilty of a charge of high treason and must have anticipated a severe punishment. As the count persisted in his stance, more men began to slip away and, fearful of the consequences, offered their loyalty to the king.

The Muslim world looked on with pleasure. Ibn al-Qalanisi, a contemporary Damascene writer, gleefully observed: 'Reports were received that a dispute had arisen amongst the Franks – though a thing of this kind was not usual with them – and fighting had taken place in which a number of them were killed'.[20] As Fulk sat distracted outside Jaffa, Muslim troops captured the important city of Banyas in the north of the kingdom; the civil war was beginning to exact a severe cost on the Christians.

The deadlock at Jaffa had to be broken. If at all possible, the king needed to avoid a full-scale assault. It was essential to prevent the loss of any Christian knights, or the damage to Fulk's reputation in the Levant and across the Latin West would only worsen. Churchmen visited the king and cited the book of Matthew (12:25): 'Every kingdom divided against itself is brought to desolation; and every city or house divided against itself shall not stand.' Patriarch William led a delegation of nobles to mediate between the two sides. After several bitter meetings 'for the sake of harmony and the greater honour of the king', William of Tyre recorded that a compromise was reached.[21]

Hugh and his remaining associates were sentenced to three years' exile. After this, they could return without reproach, although in the interim the revenues from the count's estates would be used to pay his ongoing debts and borrowings. In the circumstances this was an astounding result. Hugh had been accused of plotting to murder the king and found guilty by the High Court. He had made a treaty with Muslims, exposed the kingdom of Jerusalem to danger and loss and openly defied the king at the gates of Jaffa. The death sentence seemed the only logical outcome – yet he had escaped with a ludicrously light punishment and, even more remarkably, he had not even been stripped of his lands. In three years he could come home to Jaffa and resume control of the most powerful lordship in the kingdom. Here – surely

– we can discern the influence of Melisende. As Hugh's most prominent ally and in her theoretical position as co-ruler, she must have
told Fulk that to execute the count would humiliate her and create a
deep and permanent division in the kingdom, starting in the royal
household. The magnanimous sentence may also show that Hugh's
grievances against Fulk had some substance; such a penalty implicitly
acknowledges that his case had merit. Hugh may have regarded himself
as innocent, but given the way in which events had played out, he
could still feel relieved at the outcome.

The matter was far from over, however. Hugh decided to pass his
exile in his childhood home of Sicily. The conflict had ended in late
1134 and he now needed to wait until the New Year for passage to the
West. Ships of the time were so primitive that the commercial fleets
of Genoa, Pisa and Venice only sailed the seas between March and
October for fear of the treacherous winter storms of the
Mediterranean.[22] Hugh was passing time at a shop in the Street of the
Furriers in the heart of Jerusalem. The cold winters of the Levant
meant the production of such warm clothing was essential and this
was one of many small, localised industries in this crowded district
of the old city.[23] Hugh was obviously familiar with one of the merchants
named Alfanus and he had settled down to play dice – a very common
pastime amongst medieval people. Hugh was enjoying himself and a
crowd gathered around to watch and to cheer at the players' changing
fortunes. As he hunched over the table to roll the bones the count
had no sense of danger at all. Suddenly, a knight from Brittany drew
his sword and launched a frenzied attack, stabbing and slashing at
Hugh again and again. The spectators screamed in horror, some drew
their own weapons and, as the count fell bleeding to the floor, rushed
forward to defend him. They jumped on the would-be assassin and
captured him.

News of the assault ran through the city like wildfire; people
huddled together to exchange stories and information. Who was the
assailant? How badly wounded was Hugh? Gradually a dark and insistent consensus emerged: King Fulk's hand must lie behind the deed.
In his anger against the man who may have sullied his marriage bed,
the man who had openly defied him, and whom he had been compelled
to treat so easily, people said that the king had commissioned the
unnamed Breton to murder his rival. Hugh's cause attracted a wave

of sympathy; no longer was he a treacherous outlaw. To the people of Jerusalem the atrocity showed that he was more sinned against than sinning and that their king was malicious and vindictive.

If he really was behind the plot Fulk cannot have anticipated such a public backlash in favour of the rebel. The king presumably wanted to eliminate the political and personal threat posed by Hugh; his demise would also send out a message that in spite of the compromise judgement, Fulk would punish any opponents, if necessary by means outside the due process of law. He knew that Melisende would be furious, but, given the poor state of their relationship at this time, he calculated that he could weather any storm from her and, deprived of her closest ally, that she would submit.

The king needed to act to quell the outcry. Fulk ordered the captive to be brought before the High Court, the body responsible for judging capital offences. Wisely, however, the monarch stayed away from the meeting. Given the plentiful number of witnesses there was no need for any formal hearing and the assailant did not deny the charge. By unanimous agreement the court sentenced the Breton to the mutilation of his members. Such a harsh punishment was intended to deter others from such foul acts. It meant the hacking off of the hands, the feet and the tongue. If the guilty party survived the blood loss and the likely infection he would be condemned to a life of utter misery, crawling around, begging outside churches, eating from the floor and facing almost certain death from exposure or starvation.

The court's decision was relayed to the king who asked that the man be permitted to keep his tongue. We shall never know whether Fulk engineered the plot, but if he erred in doing so he was astute enough to realise that if the man's tongue was severed it might look as though he were trying to silence him. The Breton was tortured to reveal whether he was acting at the king's behest, but even after the mutilation he maintained that he had been working on his own initiative and only anticipated a reward from Fulk thereafter. This confession did much to mollify the mood of the crowd and open hostility towards the king abated.[24]

Hugh slowly recovered from his injuries. We do not know where he was treated. Given the location of the attack it is probable that he was taken to the leading medical centre of the day, the Hospital of St John of Jerusalem, just 200 metres to the west of the Street of the

Furriers and directly south of the Holy Sepulchre itself. There had been a hospice in Jerusalem since the days of Muslim rule when a group of Amalfitan merchants ran some form of charitable foundation. After the Christian conquest the kings of Jerusalem eagerly supported the institution and the hospital acquired a Frankish character. In 1113 it secured papal recognition as a religious order and soon grew rapidly. It was open to everyone, regardless of status, race or religion, although the majority of its patients were the thousands of pilgrims who came to the Holy Land each year.

Hugh must have needed his wounds cleaning and stitching, after which he was looked after with a mixture of prayer – a vital component of medieval health provision – and close care. Each patient in the hospital had their own bed, sheets, a cloak, a woollen hat and boots for going to the latrines. A staff of four doctors did daily ward rounds, took the pulse and examined urine. Much of the treatment centred around good basic nourishment with sugar-based drinks (from sugar cane sent down from the county of Tripoli) and meat three times a week. Some medical practices seem strange to us; for example the meat of female cows was banned because it was deemed to promote mental instability; some patients were treated by the use of hot stones – known as lapidary – to bring out fevers. As a man of wealth Hugh may have been moved to the house of one of his supporters but the basic principles of health care would have remained the same.[25]

Once he had convalesced the count sailed to Apulia and began to serve out his exile. It seems that a combination of his failed revolt, the legacy of his injuries and his separation from Melisende broke Hugh's spirit. He was received with every sympathy by Roger II of Sicily, who generously gave him the county of Gargano, but months later he died without ever returning to the Holy Land.[26]

It was in the royal palace that the effects of the attempted murder were felt most profoundly: the botched assassination tipped the balance of power to the queen. Melisende felt outraged by the entire episode. The combination of her assertive personality and a sense of moral right precipitated a sea change in the running of both the household and the government of the entire kingdom. Whether the stories of her relationship with Hugh were true or not, she was incandescent at the damage to her integrity. Allies of the king, such as Rohard, lord of Nablus, who had spread rumours about Melisende's behaviour, were forced to remove themselves from the household – it was said, for their own safety. Fear of her anger caused these men to stay away from bigger assemblies, such as feast days or processions. Most pointedly, Fulk himself was completely shunned by Melisende, her kindred and her supporters. The royal marriage was, for the time being, dead. Melisende knew that her good name had been damaged by the public nature of the dispute and she was furious with the king for giving credence to such stories. Whether Hugh was her lover or not she cared deeply for him and when he was cast into exile she was grief-stricken for her absent companion. Interestingly, the Old French edition of William of Tyre's chronicle, written later in the twelfth century, stated that Hugh had died '*por li*' (for her), giving the count's actions a chivalric aspect. He had sacrificed his life for his lady.[27]

The Triumph of Melisende

As time went on the open hostility between the king and queen caused increasing concern. Close friends of the couple tried to mediate between the two camps, but Melisende was immovable; Fulk had to offer major compromises to restore a semblance of normality. In the end he managed to persuade her to forsake the open antipathy towards his friends and to permit them to attend public gatherings. William of Tyre tells us of the most crucial concessions made by the king: 'From that day forward, the king became so uxorious that, whereas he had formerly aroused her wrath, he now calmed it, and not even in unimportant cases did he take any measures without her knowledge and assistance.'[28]

Herein lies the heart of the matter. Running in tandem with the queen's close relationship with Count Hugh was the fundamental dispute over Fulk's governance of the kingdom. He had refused to accept King Baldwin II's deathbed deviation from the original agreement that he should rule in his own right – instead he had tried to forge a path of his own. Rather than exercising joint power with Melisende, he had ignored her. Furthermore, as Baldwin II anticipated, Fulk started to introduce his Angevin henchmen into positions of authority at the expense of the native nobility. He dismissed the royal chancellor and a royal viscount and replaced them with his own men.[29] In other words, a central aspect of the revolt of Hugh of Jaffa was the survival of the native nobility of Jerusalem, represented most dramatically in the person of Melisende herself. The contemporary Anglo-Norman writer, Orderic Vitalis, made this telling observation about Fulk's behaviour after his coronation:

> To begin with he acted without the foresight and shrewdness he should have shown, and changed governors and other dignitaries too quickly and thoughtlessly. As a new ruler he banished from his counsels the leading magnates who from the first had fought resolutely against the Turks and helped Godfrey and the two Baldwins to bring towns and fortresses under their rule, and replaced them with Angevin strangers and other raw newcomers to whom he gave his ear; turning out the veteran defenders, he gave the chief places in the counsels of the realm and the proprietorship of castles to new flatterers. Consequently great disaffection spread, and the stubbornness of the magnates was damnably roused against the man who changed officials so gauchely. For a long time, under the influence of the powers of evil, they turned their warlike skills, which they should have united to exercise against the heathen, to rend themselves. They even allied on both sides with the pagans against each other, with the result that they lost many thousands of men and a certain number of fortresses.[30]

Although Orderic wrote in northern Europe, his sources had, in outline, given a political narrative – excluding the details of any relationship between Hugh and Melisende – of the 1134 civil war, and provided a concise explanation as to why the uprising had taken place. In Damascus, Ibn al-Qalanisi also understood the problem: 'After Baldwin [II] there was none left amongst the Franks possessed of sound judgement and capacity to govern. The new king-count [Fulk] who came to them by sea from their country was not sound in his judgement, nor was he successful in his administration.'[31]

Fulk had tried to sideline his queen, but through her indomitable will and the resistance led by Count Hugh, Melisende preserved her rightful inheritance and the power of the nobility of Jerusalem. The way in which she gained the ascendancy and forced Fulk to make such huge concessions showed the authority of a woman with strong personality and true bloodline. Fulk had not suspected that Melisende would challenge him with such determination; to his mind a woman should follow the Church orthodoxy and submit to her husband. In dealing with the unknown he had been caught off guard and had behaved ponderously until brought to recognise the wider political reality. As William of Tyre stated, from that time onwards the king and the queen acted together – as Baldwin II had decreed. Charters that date from the period after the civil war demonstrate this. A gift to the Hospitallers in late 1136 was confirmed by Fulk 'with the assent of his wife Melisende', and another described an agreement made with 'the consent of Queen Melisende'.[32]

It was not just in the kingdom of Jerusalem that the effects of Fulk's loss of power were felt. Almost as soon as the situation in the south began to resolve itself, Princess Alice of Antioch rose in rebellion. The death of Prince Bohemond II in 1130 had brought turmoil to northern Syria. In 1134, for the third time in six years, Melisende's younger sister threw off the direction imposed by the king of Jerusalem and asserted her desire to rule the principality as regent for her little daughter Constance. In 1130, King Baldwin II had travelled north to impose order; two years later, Fulk did the same. On this latest occasion, however, Melisende continued to flex her political muscles. The king was prepared to remove Alice again, but Melisende countered him. She told him not to interfere in her sister's governance of Antioch and, constrained by his promises to the queen, Fulk meekly agreed. For a brief period in 1135–6, Alice – who remained unmarried – ruled as sovereign in the principality of Antioch while her sister seems to have been the dominant partner in the kingdom of Jerusalem – a time of genuine female ascendancy. King Baldwin II's eldest daughters were clearly a remarkable pair of women. To rule (or dominate) two territories at the same time in the macho, violent eastern Mediterranean was a spectacular achievement.[33]

The Melisende Psalter: Art, Politics and Reconciliation

There is a touching footnote to the dispute in Jerusalem because it seems that Fulk genuinely hoped to restore close personal relations with his wife. As well as making good his political failings the king commissioned a lavish and carefully chosen gift for her. Melisende's piety was well known and she was also recognised as a patroness of books.[34] Fulk thought hard about the most appropriate present he could give his wife and, to modern eyes at least, he certainly came up with a magnificent peace offering. The Melisende Psalter is an extraordinarily beautiful little book that survives today in the British Museum. It is only twenty-two centimetres tall and fourteen centimetres wide – roughly the size of a modern paperback – but it has a multicoloured silk spine and a dozen roundels, studded with turquoise, ruby and emerald stones that decorate the intricate ivory covers. Inside, it contains twenty-four full-page hand-coloured illuminations of scenes from the New Testament, a calendar of saints' days and observances, as well as prayers, many of which have highly decorated initial letters. The book is not explicitly addressed to the queen, but its contents and decorative themes make such an identification almost certain. The Latin text, for example, is written for a secular woman, rather than an abbess (such as her sister Yveta). There is a special focus on the veneration of the Virgin Mary and Mary Magdalen, suggestive of a connection to the nearby abbey of St Mary Jehoshaphat in Jerusalem, a house patronised by the queen and later her burial place. More obviously the calendar has two especially personalised entries amidst the daily list of general ecclesiastical commemorations. The twenty-first of August is highlighted as the date of King Baldwin II's death and 1 October as the passing of Queen Morphia. No other rulers of Jerusalem are mentioned, although the capture of the holy city on 15 July is noted. The inclusion of Melisende's parents is surely the most obvious sign that the book was for her. A more subtle indication that the gift came from Fulk – apart from the fact that it must have cost an enormous sum of money, perhaps only affordable by a king – is in the carving of a bird at the top of the back cover. It is labelled 'Herodius' – also known as 'fulica' in medieval bestiaries; in other words the bird is a falcon, and the name is a pun on Fulk.

The illustrations were produced in a workshop connected to the Church of the Holy Sepulchre and four different illuminators painted the pictures. Their work reflects a mixture of influences: English, French, Byzantine, Arabic and Levantine, and they created a genuinely unique synthesis of styles. The ivory covers are particularly striking and their images are a clear indication of the message Fulk wished to convey. The front cover shows stories of King David from the Old Testament in which he proves his strength and fitness to rule, his humility and his interest in harmony. In between the roundels is a battle between Virtues and Vices, the latter depicted as women with long, dishevelled hair, defeated by women with neat head coverings. The monarch on the back cover, placed under the falcon, and dressed in the manner of a king of Jerusalem – the Byzantine-style regalia of a crown and chlamys – is probably meant to represent Fulk. He carries out the six acts of mercy as specified in the book of Matthew, giving out food and drink, clothing, help to the sick, visiting prisoners and sheltering strangers. In between these roundels, Islamic-style birds and beasts fight. In essence, the covers show the restoration of a state of equilibrium and reveal a penitent king making good his misdeeds. The gift was meant to mark an end to the hostilities; it was a truly sumptuous book and the trouble taken over its subject matter and its production shows Fulk's desire to apologise to his wife. We do not know of Melisende's reaction when she was presented with the psalter; but we can judge some return to normality for the royal couple because in 1136 a second son, named Amalric, was born.

As the product of a mixed Frankish–Armenian marriage, Melisende represented a combination of different strands of Christianity and she displayed this broad cultural background in her enthusiastic support of the Catholic and Eastern Christian Churches. Women had played a crucial role in spiritual matters since the early days of Christianity and the patronage of religious institutions was a familiar way for medieval queens to exercise power. There is a neat contradiction here because in spite of the Church's portrayal of women as following the fallen Eve figure, many religious houses and senior churchmen looked to women in authority for advancement and often formed close relations with them. A deeply pious woman, Melisende gave many gifts to monasteries, encouraged the building and improvement of churches such as the Templum Domini or the Armenian cathedral of St James, and was known to welcome pilgrim visitors.[35] The queen also commissioned the huge fortified convent of St Lazarus at Bethany, east of Jerusalem, for her youngest sister, Yveta, to take charge of. She then donated to it a huge collection of gold, silver and jewelled religious objects.[36] Most importantly, perhaps, she oversaw the reconstruction of the spiritual heart of Christianity, the Church of the Holy Sepulchre.

Melisende's patronage went beyond religious buildings and she created a school of book-makers and miniature-painters, the style of which again reflected her mixed heritage. She also organised the construction of a vaulted complex of shops in Jerusalem, including the legendary (and still surviving) Street of Bad Cooking.[37]

In 1143 the royal couple were out riding near Acre when the king spied a hare and, with his customary enthusiasm for the hunt, he sped after the animal. As he urged his mount onwards the horse stumbled and Fulk was catapulted out of the saddle and landed on his head. Unconscious and bleeding from his nose and ears he lapsed into a coma, much to the horror of the men with him. Melisende soon arrived at the scene and became hysterical with grief and anxiety, screaming, crying and hugging her husband's inert form. Such intense grief seems to indicate that the marriage had, eventually, been a happy one. The king was carried back to Acre where he lingered for a couple of days, but his injuries proved fatal and he died on 10 November 1143. A funeral cortege soon wound its way towards Jerusalem where the clergy and population came out to meet their monarch. He was buried with his predecessors in the Church of the Holy Sepulchre at the foot of Mount Calvary.[38]

Melisende, Queen-Regnant of Jerusalem

Melisende was left as the queen-regnant for their young son, Baldwin III, but when he came of age she refused to step aside. To survive and prosper she needed a strategy. As a relatively young widow she was in a tantalising position – chaste yet fertile; she needed male allies, but she was unwilling to marry and risk creating factional strife. Almost inevitably, however, there were rumours of a lover. Abbot Bernard of Clairvaux, the greatest churchman of the age, learned of this situation and warned the queen to maintain the standing of a widow: 'I have heard certain evil reports of you, and although I do not completely believe them I am nevertheless sorry that your good name should be tarnished either by truth or falsehood. It is not beneath your dignity as a queen to be a widow . . . Before God as a widow, before men as a queen. Remember that you are a queen whose worthy and unworthy actions cannot be hidden under a bushel.'[39]

To modern eyes, the most obvious manifestation of power is in the political arena. The prime symbol of this in the medieval age was the sword, ceremonially bestowed upon a lord's son, and the representation of strength, virility and authority. Almost every royal seal depicts a king holding such a weapon. Women were almost always excluded from the battlefield and so this crucial aspect of medieval rule was denied to them. On the rare occasions that they ventured into battle they were usually condemned as 'savage' or 'delinquent', like prostitutes. It was for men alone to fight. This was a fundamental part of the framework in which Melisende had to work. For a woman to survive and to overcome the handicap of her sex she had to employ alternative strategies to succeed. One way of doing so – fighting aside – was to become, in effect, a temporary man. Displays of dignity, resolve and decisiveness were a vital aspect of the required performance. In 1143, Bernard of Clairvaux advised Melisende: 'The king, your husband, being dead, and the young king still unfit to discharge the affairs of the kingdom . . . the eyes of all will be on you, and on you alone the burden of the whole kingdom will rest. You must set your hand to great things and, although a woman, you must act as a man by doing all you have to do in a spirit prudent and strong. You must arrange all things prudently and discreetly so that all may judge you from your actions to be a king rather than a queen and so that the Gentiles [i.e. the Muslims] may have no occasion for saying: Where is the king of Jerusalem?'[40]

Even these actions were not necessarily sufficient. If a woman took on male attributes too fully, then she could be criticised. At one point in the struggle for power in England, Melisende's contemporary, Matilda, began to behave in a masculine way, only to be condemned by hostile writers for being unfeminine and having 'every trace of a woman's gentleness removed'.[41] A balance was needed: if women could overcome the demands of their bodies and show careful and strong political judgement, contemporaries felt it might be possible for them to rule successfully.

Yet the picture was more complicated still and power could take myriad other forms. There were many different ways, both public and private, for women to exert a profound impact on government, the household and cultural and religious life. It was in the household that a woman had the greatest opportunity to direct her husband, her children and her family. Medieval writers understood – and in the case of some churchmen, feared – the influence that could be gained through 'the embraces of love' as one author rather coyly expressed it. After Count Stephen of Blois deserted from the First Crusade, his wife Adela frequently encouraged him to return 'between conjugal caresses': a positive use of the bedchamber. On the other hand, some writers believed that the presence of women at court caused a loss of knightly virility and counselled against it.[42]

From Fulk's death in 1143 Melisende ruled Jerusalem, first in her own right, then gradually giving more of a role to her son, Baldwin III. She dealt adroitly with the fall of Edessa in 1144 and met the crowned heads of France and Germany as they came to the Holy Land in the Second Crusade in 1148 (see Chapter Four). She skilfully maintained this balancing act until 1151–2 when Baldwin began to demand to rule alone. A civil war broke out and Melisende was compelled to back down, although she maintained a position of great honour and influence until her declining years. It seems likely that she suffered some form of wasting illness and she also showed the first signs of Alzheimer's disease, being described as 'somewhat impaired in memory'.[43] She died in September 1161 with her two surviving sisters at her bedside, the family ties between this generation of the royal family holding close until the end. She was buried in the Church of the Virgin Mary in the valley of Jehoshaphat just outside the walls of Jerusalem where the site of her tomb remains visible today.[44]

A conventional contemporary assessment of Melisende would have depicted her as an ambitious, greedy woman who lusted after power for herself, who seduced men to achieve her own ends and lacked the strength to govern properly. In fact, such were her political skills and so great was the force of her personality that the majority of writers (even though they were mainly churchmen) viewed her positively – even allowing for their inbuilt bias against the 'evils' of women. William of Tyre described her as 'a woman of unusual wisdom and discretion', who had set out to 'emulate the magnificence of the greatest and noblest of princes and to show herself in no ways inferior to them'. She had succeeded and proven to be 'an equal to her ancestors': men such as Godfrey of Bouillon and King Baldwin I, the heroes of the First Crusade.[45] For a medieval queen to be placed in such exalted company shows what a remarkable individual she was.

4

The 'blessed generation': St Bernard of Clairvaux and the Second Crusade, 1145–1149

Abbot (later St) Bernard of Clairvaux can justifiably lay claim to being the most influential churchman in western Europe during the twelfth century. Father figure to kings, princes and popes, he acted as the self-appointed moral compass of the age. Bernard was responsible for the extraordinary rise of the Cistercian monks, he was a leading advocate of the Knights Templar and, in conjunction with Pope Eugenius III, he led the preaching of the Second Crusade. It was Bernard who convinced the knights of Christendom that they were a 'blessed generation', especially favoured by God with an opportunity to defeat the Muslims. Inspired by the abbot's preaching, huge armies marched to the Holy Land in 1147–8 but after a mere four days outside the walls of Damascus the crusaders were forced into a humiliating retreat: a catastrophic blow to Christian morale in both Europe and the Holy Land.[1]

Zengi and the Capture of Edessa

The Second Crusade was triggered by the loss of Edessa in north-eastern Syria in late 1144. Its conqueror, Zengi of Aleppo and Mosul, was an intelligent and ruthless individual, widely regarded as the most fearsome warrior of the period. The early stages of his career demonstrated the same self-serving tendencies displayed by many other Syrian warlords at the time; in fact, Zengi seemed to care little about his opponents' faith and he treated all his enemies with the same extraordinary levels of brutality – hardly material for a hero of the jihad. In 1139, for example, he promised the Muslims of Baalbek safe conduct if they surrendered, only to torture and crucify them after they submitted. He maintained a terrifying level of discipline throughout his army. Ibn al-Adim wrote: 'when he rode the troops used to walk behind him as if they were between two threads out of fear that they would trample on the crops . . . If anyone transgressed, he was cruci-fied. Zengi used to say: "It does not happen that there is more than one tyrant (meaning himself) at one time."' He was no less cruel to those in his entourage – emirs who displeased him were killed or banished and their sons castrated. One of his wives was divorced during a bout of drunkenness: Zengi sent her to the stables where he ordered the grooms to gang rape her while he looked on.[2]

In late 1144 Zengi turned his attention to the Frankish city of Edessa and when he learnt Count Joscelin was absent, Zengi saw a chance to pounce. He rushed his forces to the area and laid siege to the city. Edessa was a site with formidable defensive fortifications so to gain entry Zengi decided to construct a complex series of tunnels. By late December his labourers had burrowed deep under one of the walls. They packed the passage with inflammable material and set the wooden supports ablaze: as smoke billowed from the tunnel entrance the passageway collapsed. The walls above began to crack and then to tumble; once the dust had drifted away it was clear that the Muslim sappers had torn a deep gash in the Christians' defensive cordon. The Franks tried desperately to stave off the Muslim assault but to no avail, and Zengi's men began to slaughter the citizens and seize precious relics. The 'Elegy for the Fall of Edessa', written by a local Armenian Christian within two years of the siege, evoked a harrowing scene:

Like wolves among a flock of lambs [they] fell upon them in their midst.
They slaughtered indiscriminately, the martyrs let out streams of blood,
They massacred without compassion the young and the children.
They had no mercy on the grey hairs of the elderly or with the tender
    age of a child.[3]

This thunderous strike against the principal city of one of the Latin States fulfilled the hopes of jihad propagandists – at last the counter-crusade was underway. News of these events was greeted with horror and fear in Antioch and Jerusalem; relief armies were sent north but could do little. The gravity of the situation prompted an appeal to western Europe and the response to this has become known as the

Second Crusade. A series of small expeditions to the Holy Land had taken place in 1107–8, 1120–4 and 1128–9 and historians generally regard these as crusades because there is evidence (sometimes hazy, admittedly) of a call for help, a papal response and ceremonies to take the cross.[4] By virtue of its massive scale, however, the Second Crusade was markedly different from these lesser campaigns and, as the preaching effort gathered pace, it evolved into a bold and radical attempt to extend the frontiers of Christendom in three different directions: the Holy Land, the Baltic and the Iberian peninsula.

Pope Eugenius III and the Call for the Second Crusade

In the spring of 1145 messengers from the Frankish East told of the fall of Edessa: their targets were Pope Eugenius III, King Louis VII of France and King Conrad III of Germany. By December, Eugenius and Louis both expressed their desire for a new crusade. Eugenius published what is the earliest surviving papal bull to call for a crusade (the texts of Pope Urban II's appeals are not extant); it is known by its opening words *Quantum praedecessores* (How greatly our predecessors), a magisterial statement that became the benchmark for such appeals for decades to come. Carefully researched and skilfully crafted so as to convey its message to maximum effect, in essence *Quantum praedecessores* was a rousing challenge to the present generation to live up to the achievements of their illustrious forefathers on the First Crusade – a theme that played a central role in the attraction of the new expedition.[5]

In the five decades since the capture of Jerusalem the deeds of these men had been revered, repeated and embellished to become enshrined as a true manifestation of divine will and earthly heroism. The First Crusaders had accomplished something of incomparable pride to all Catholics and this, coupled with the polyglot nature of the force, meant that chroniclers across Christendom recorded their triumph. No previous event had provoked such an efflorescence of historical writing; within years of the fall of Jerusalem several narratives had memorialised the deeds of the holy warriors, a trend that continued for decades afterwards. William of Malmesbury, an Anglo-Norman author who composed *The Deeds of the Kings of England* in the 1120s, conveys the feeling well:

leaders of high renown, to whose praises posterity, if it judge aright, will assign no limits; heroes who from the cold of uttermost Europe plunged into the intolerable heat of the East, careless of their own lives, if only they could bring help to Christendom in its hour of trial ... Let poets with their eulogies now give place, and fabled history no longer laud the heroes of Antiquity. Nothing be compared with their glory has ever been begotten by any age. Such valour as the Ancients had vanished after their death into dust and ashes in the grave, for it was spent on the mirage of worldly splendour rather than on the solid aim of some good purpose; while of these brave heroes of ours, men will enjoy the benefit and tell the proud story, as long as the round world endures and the holy Church of Christ flourishes.[6]

Given limited levels of literacy, verse accounts of the crusade must have done much to sustain the legacy of 1099 as well. Written forms of the *Chanson d'Antioche* and the *Chanson de Jerusalem* survive but these works were intended primarily for public performance: it takes little effort to imagine a group of knights gathered in a torchlit hall to listen to the valiant feats of Godfrey and Bohemond in the Holy Land. Other epics such as the famous *Song of Roland* (set in the eighth century and featuring the wars of Charlemagne, the greatest Christian emperor of all), were composed almost immediately after the First Crusade and also reflected a theme of holy war. Yet it was not just in writing and performance that the First Crusade was remembered. Churches and monasteries were decorated with images that suggested the struggle between Christianity and its enemies, while numerous round churches, meant to represent the Holy Sepulchre itself, were constructed across the Latin West; for example, in Cambridge, Northampton, San Stefano in Bologna and Asti in Piedmont. In other words, the memory of the First Crusade percolated deep into the physical, political and spiritual culture of western Europe.

Pope Eugenius repeatedly cast his own actions as following in the footsteps of 'Pope Urban, our blessed predecessor'. Again and again he urged knights not to let slip the legacy of their fathers: 'It will be seen as a great token of nobility and uprightness if those things acquired by the efforts of your fathers are vigorously defended by you, their good sons. But if, God forbid, it comes to pass differently, then the bravery of the fathers will have proved diminished in the sons.'[7] Naturally, the pope also set out the spiritual rewards for the participants: the remission of all confessed sins and an assurance that those who died en route would be treated as martyrs.

King Louis tried to launch the crusade at his Christmas court at Bourges, and while his nobles were moved by the plight of Edessa they postponed a formal commitment until an assembly at Vézelay, in northern Burgundy, in March 1146. In part, their reticence was coloured by the wait for *Quantum praedecessores* to arrive from the papal court: the need for formal authorisation to begin the crusade was essential. Louis' desire to take part in person was also a cause for concern. We must remember that no monarch was on the First Crusade and although King Sigurd of Norway (the 'Sigurd Jorsalfar' of Edvard Grieg's eponymous suite of 1892) went to the Holy Land in 1109–10 and various Spanish rulers had fought in the reconquest, Louis was the first major crowned head to aspire to such a commit-ment in the Levant. The fact that, to date, he had been a mediocre monarch did not help either. The king had managed to antagonise his most powerful noble, the count of Champagne, and had also alienated many churchmen; the burning of a church at Vitry with 1,300 people inside being a particularly ghastly episode. By 1145, peace was restored and this, in conjunction with the king's need to make good his sins, could help to explain why he was so keen to travel to the Holy Land. Another worry for the French court was the succession. In 1137 Louis had married Eleanor, the beautiful and strong-willed heiress to the duchy of Aquitaine, but by the time of the crusade they had only one child – an infant daughter. An ongoing civil war in England was a stark reminder of the perils of a disputed succession; a son was vital. One way around the problem was for the queen herself to go on the crusade. She came from a family of crusaders – her father, William IX (a famous troubadour) had taken part in the 1101 crusade and her uncle, Raymond of Poitiers, was the prince of Antioch. Some writers suggest that Abbot Bernard told Eleanor that if she went to Jerusalem, she would be rewarded with a son. As we shall see, however, while the crusade made a significant impact on the royal marriage it was not in the positive way origin-ally envisaged.

'The mellifluous doctor': The Preaching and Miracles of Bernard of Clairvaux

On Easter Sunday 1146 the cream of the French nobility assembled at Vézelay to hear a sermon by Abbot Bernard. Arguably, this was his most mesmeric performance ever and such was the power of his oratory that crowds, inflamed by the wish to help the Holy Land, surged forwards and begged to take the cross. So immense was the demand, one source reported, that the abbot was forced to tear crosses from his own clothing because all the pre-prepared insignia were used up.[8] A contemporary list of the senior nobles at Vézelay shows that almost all of them had First Crusade ancestors – a fact that vividly illustrates the resonance of Eugenius' call for sons to continue the work of their fathers.[9]

In the months after Vézelay, Bernard continued to recruit in France. In his own, surely ironic, words, he told Eugenius: 'As for the rest, you have ordered and I have obeyed and your authority has made my obedience fruitful. "I have declared and I have spoken, and they are multiplied above number": towns and castles are emptied, one may scarcely find one man amongst seven women, so many women are there widowed while their husbands are still alive.'[10] The point was made, however: many thousands had taken the cross.

The abbot also sent letters across Europe and dispatched preachers to spread the word: this was the most organised attempt to secure support for a crusade to date. The churches and market squares of the West echoed to the stirring words of Eugenius' *Quantum praedecessores* and, to complement it, Bernard's own distinctive appeal for action. Centuries later, the power of his words is still evident in his letters – simply reading them out loud shows this even more:

> Now is the acceptable time, now is the day of abundant salvation. The earth is shaken because the Lord of Heaven is losing His land, the land in which He appeared to men . . . For our sins, the enemy of the Cross has begun to lift his sacrilegious head there, to devastate with the sword that blessed land, that land of promise . . . What are you doing, you mighty men of valour? What are you doing, you servants of the Cross?

I call blessed the generation that can seize an opportunity of such rich indulgence as this, blessed to be alive in this year of jubilee, this year of God's choice. The blessing is spread throughout the whole world, and all the world is flocking to receive this badge of immortality . . . But now, O mighty soldiers, O men of war, you have a cause for which you can fight without danger to your souls: a cause in which to conquer is glorious and for which to die is gain."

Bernard was sharp enough to appreciate he could exploit the emerging economic strength of towns and tradesmen, and he appealed to them in terms they would understand: 'But those of you who are merchants, men quick to seek a bargain, let me point out the advantages of this great opportunity. Do not miss them. Take the sign of the Cross and you will find indulgence for all the sins which you humbly confess. The cost is small, the reward is great.'[12]

In the autumn he set out on a gruelling seven-month tour to preach in the Low Countries and Germany. His tasks were threefold: to recruit more crusaders, to deal with a threat to the Jews and to enlist the king of Germany himself. In all three cases, he emerged triumphant – a conclusion that only served to reinforce his conviction that God favoured the crusade. Again and again, Bernard's unparalleled oratorical skills invoked profound religious feelings in his audience. As he progressed through Flanders and into the Rhineland huge crowds flocked to hear him and reports of miracles were widespread. It has been calculated that 235 cripples were healed, 172 blind people recovered their sight, as well as cures for the deaf and dumb, demoniacs and others; there was even one raising of a person from the dead.[13] At times the atmosphere became so fevered that the crowds threatened to crush him; on several occasions, like a modern movie star, he was trapped in his overnight accommodation and had to flee through a back exit. Notwithstanding this delirium the abbot convinced thousands more people to take the cross.

As with the First Crusade, however, the call to fight God's enemies was regarded by some as an excuse to turn upon the Jews. A renegade Cistercian preacher named Radulf (close to the Hebrew word *radof*, meaning 'to persecute') inflamed audiences in the Rhineland with his anti-Semitic language and incited outbreaks of violence against communities in Cologne, Worms, Mainz and Speyer. Bernard was

furious because Radulf had broken biblical injunctions against killing
the Jews. The abbot had worked hard to control the preaching precisely
to ensure that everyone stayed, in modern parlance, 'on-message'. He
wrote to Radulf and commanded him to stop, but when this failed
Bernard went to see him in person and ordered him back to his
monastery in disgrace. Compared to the killing spree of the First
Crusade, the events of 1146–7 were reined in far more quickly and were
on a much lesser scale – a small consolation to the Jews themselves.[14]

The recruitment of King Conrad III of Germany was of prime
importance to the scale and scope of the Second Crusade. The German
contribution to the First Crusade had been constrained by the conflict
between empire and papacy but with that resolved it was logical that
the most powerful secular monarch in Europe should act in partnership with the Church and head Christ's army. Conrad himself had been
to the Holy Land to serve the Christian cause in 1124–5 and he was a
highly experienced warrior. At first, however, he seemed reluctant to
take part in the crusade: his lands – which stretched from the Danish
border to Poland, across Bavaria and into Italy, as far south as the Papal
States – were in turmoil. At least five major conflicts were aflame and
it would have been reckless of him to leave home. He enlisted Bernard's
help to quell the troubles and with the spellbinding presence of the
abbot in play, 'the serenity of peace suddenly shone forth again'.[15]
Around Christmas 1146 news arrived at the royal court that Duke Welf
of Bavaria, the king's main rival, had taken the cross. This ensured that
he would not be remaining in the West to foment trouble in Conrad's
absence – now the king could act. Bernard's hagiographer described
a dramatic scene in Speyer Cathedral when the abbot was seized with
the Holy Spirit during Mass. He turned to Conrad, reminded the king
of the Last Judgement, and asked how he would respond to the question of Christ: 'O man, what have I not done for you that I ought to
have?' Bernard described Conrad's exalted standing, his physical strength
and his vigorous soul; in other words, he made the case that he had a
Christian duty to act in the Lord's cause. The king burst into tears and
cried out: 'Now I recognise clearly that this is a gift of divine grace,
nor now shall I be found to be ungrateful . . . I am ready to serve Him!'
A swell of noise filled the cathedral as the audience sounded their
acclaim. Bernard turned to the altar and picked up a cloth cross,
approached the king and pinned it on him; the most powerful secular

ruler in Europe had become a crusader – another advance in the history of medieval holy war.[16] As a piece of hagiography this account may have overemphasised the abbot's role because Conrad knew full well that Bernard would ask him to take the cross, and to turn him down in front of such a huge congregation would have been unthinkable. In reality, he had already decided to join the crusade. Thus, Conrad and Louis were both committed to following in the footsteps of the First Crusaders: optimism ran high across Christian Europe.

The Ambition of the Second Crusade: Holy War on Three Fronts

Around this time we can discern a bold change in the aims of the crusade. This was not part of some preconceived master plan, but was a blend of the opportunism of secular and religious rulers within the broader climate of holy war. It transformed the Second Crusade from a bid to recapture Edessa into a hugely ambitious attempt to expand Christendom on three fronts: the Holy Land, Iberia and the Baltic. The first manifestation of this was in the late autumn of 1146 when Eugenius wrote to the Italian trading port of Genoa to urge its citizens to take part in the campaign. Their response would not take them to the Levant, however, but to Spain, and it produced one of the few real successes of the crusade.

Back in 1095–6, as the excitement of the First Crusade gripped Europe, many Spanish knights aspired to take the cross for the Holy Land to secure remission of all their sins.[17] Their own region had a complex history of holy war that dated back to the conquest of the peninsula by Islamic forces during the eighth century; by the late eleventh century a series of small Christian kingdoms had recovered the northernmost regions. They lived in reasonable harmony with their Muslim neighbours, on some occasions working with one local Muslim lord against another and, at other times, demanding what amounted to protection money to keep the peace. Under the influence of the Reform Papacy, spiritual rewards began to be offered to those who died fighting to reconquer Christian lands. In 1085 King Alfonso VI of Castile and León captured Toledo to mark an important step forward, but men such as Rodrigo Díaz (immortalised as El

Cid by Charlton Heston in the 1961 movie) carved out careers as hired hands, fighting for whoever paid them. It was only in his last major commission, the defeat of the Almoravids of Valencia, that El Cid (meaning 'the leader') acquired the heroic status inflated by Christian writers early in the following century and then embraced by modern politicians such as General Franco. Urban II's launch of the First Crusade gave an added sharpness to Christian–Muslim relations in the peninsula. Yet the pope had to work hard to prevent a haemorrhage of warriors away from the area and he wrote: 'it is no virtue to rescue Christians from Saracens in one place, only to expose them to the tyranny and oppression of the Saracens in another.'[18] The symbols and ideology of crusading to the Holy Land soon seeped into Spain and men from Iberia fought at home and in the East. Gradually, the two theatres of war were brought into parity and it is certain that by 1123 the remission of all sins was offered to crusaders in both the Levant and Spain. As recruitment for the Second Crusade gathered momentum the Genoese struck agreements with Count Ramon Berenguer of Barcelona and King Alfonso VII of Castile and León to attack the southern Spanish city of Almería in 1147 and the more northerly settlement of Tortosa in 1148.[19] These parties had all fought the Spanish Muslims for decades, advancing their territorial holdings and securing commercial privileges, but this time they chose to bring their campaign under the formal umbrella of papal approval and to secure the full array of spiritual rewards on offer.

It was not just Iberia that saw increased interest in the crusading cause around this time; for example, as Bernard drew towards the end of his travels he addressed an assembly of German nobles at Frankfurt in March 1147.[20] While many expressed enthusiasm for the expedition, a number ventured a new and radical idea – a concept that would mark a further extension to the range of crusading warfare. To the east of Germany lay lands occupied by pagan tribes known generically as the Wends, peoples who worshipped a panoply of gods and held meetings at sacred groves and springs. In line with the basic idea of attacking the enemies of the faithful, the north German nobles refused to set out for the Holy Land 'because they had as neighbours certain tribes given over to the filthiness of idolatry' and wanted to fight their pagan neighbours instead.[21]

Conflict between Christians and pagans had simmered for centuries.

The Christians had made slow progress through a combination of conquest and conversion but there was constant tension between these two means of advance because sometimes the nobles' support for the churchmen was overridden by their desire for land, an approach that could provoke savage reprisals on the defenceless clerics. Bernard of Clairvaux, however, possibly swept along by the tide of confidence created by his preaching, agreed that the Wends were suitable targets for the crusade. In his most controversial statement of all he said: 'At the council at . . . Frankfurt, the might of the Christians was armed against them [the pagans] and that for the complete wiping out or, at any rate, the conversion of these peoples, they [the Germans] have put on the Cross, the sign of our salvation; and we, by virtue of our authority, promised them the same spiritual privileges as those enjoy who set out for Jerusalem.'[22] Theologians and historians alike have been troubled and perplexed by this apparently obvious breach of the biblical injunction against forced conversion: no clear explanation is apparent. One possibility is that some of the pagans were apostates – they had reneged on their conversion, therefore, as heretics they could be killed. Alternatively, the abbot could have learned that many previous campaigns in the north had ended when the pagans paid off the attackers and underwent some token form of conversion, a process that did little to advance the Christian cause.[23] It is possible this edict was an attempt to ensure a more permanent solution was reached. Eugenius gave his agreement to the idea (not that he had much choice by that time) and issued the papal bull *Divina dispensatione* in April 1147 in which he referred to the wars in Iberia, the Holy Land and the Baltic as part of a single enterprise. Thus, the grand scale of the Second Crusade was made clear and, as several contemporaries noted, Christendom sought to extend its frontiers.[24]

The Conquest of Lisbon

As the main German and French armies prepared to march across southern Europe and Asia Minor, one particular group set out for the Holy Land by sea.[25] Southern England, Normandy, Flanders and the Lower Rhineland (around Cologne) had long-standing ties from trade and regional politics; when the crusade appeal spread into these areas it was logical to sail, rather than to travel to the East by land.[26] In fact, a few northern European contingents had sailed to the Levant at the time of the First Crusade, so such a practice was not unheard of. In the autumn of 1146 a criss-cross of communications must have passed over the English Channel and along the northern European coastline making the arrangements to co-ordinate the expedition. In the end a fleet of around 180 ships assembled in the port of Dartmouth ready to make the journey to Jerusalem. No especially famous figure led this force: a nephew of Godfrey of Bouillon, Count Arnold of Aerschot, was the most prominent of the Rhinelanders; Christian of Gistel, a castellan, led the Flemings, and Hervey of Glanvill the Anglo-Normans. Tensions between the various armies of the First Crusade had shown how destructive bickering between contingents could be, and to try to ensure reasonably good terms between the troops they made a sworn association:

Amongst those people of so many different tongues the firmest guarantees of peace and friendship were taken; and, furthermore, they sanctioned very strict laws, as for example, a life for a life and a tooth for a tooth. They forbade all display of costly garments. Also they ordained that women should not go out in public; that the peace must be kept by all, unless they should suffer injuries recognised by the proclamation; that weekly chapters be held by the laity and the clergy separately, unless perchance some great emergency should require their meeting together; that each ship have its own priest and keep the same observances as are prescribed for parishes; that no one retain the seaman of another in his employ; that everyone make weekly confession and communicate on Sunday; and so on through the rest of the obligatory articles with separate sanctions for each. Furthermore, they constituted for every thousand of the forces two elected members who were to be called judges or *coniurati*, through whom the cases of the constables were to be settled in accordance with the proclamation and by whom the distribution of moneys was to be carried out.[27]

The holy city was not, however, their first target – instead it was Lisbon, at the time in Muslim hands. King Afonso Henriques of Portugal (1128–85) knew of the planned crusade and he probably made some informal contacts with the north Europeans. A reference in the contemporary eyewitness account known as *The Conquest of Lisbon (De expugnatione Lyxbonensi)* spoke of Afonso 'knowing of our coming'. It seems too much of a coincidence that the fleet decided to set out so far in advance of the main land armies; they would have arrived in the Levant a whole season ahead of Louis and Conrad and then used up vital resources just waiting around. Their departure in the spring of 1147 allowed them to engage in another arena of holy war and to secure valuable booty as well. While there is no surviving papal bull for this campaign the participants were already signed with the cross and a case for the spiritual value of their actions could be constructed with ease.[28]

From Afonso's perspective, this was not an opportunity to miss: he had only just started to use the title *'rex'* and to capture Lisbon would both enhance his credentials as a holy warrior and extend his lands. The bishop of Oporto greeted the crusader fleet when it arrived in northern Spain and he tried to convince them of the worth of what they were doing. He outlined the destruction wrought by the Muslims and to convey his point he used the extraordinarily brutal image of a butchered woman:

To you the Mother Church, as it were with her arms cut off and her face disfigured, appeals for help; she seeks vengeance at your hands for the blood of her sons. She calls to you, truly, she cries out loud. 'Execute vengeance upon the heathen, and punishments upon the people [Ps. 149:7].' Therefore, be not seduced by the desire to press on with the journey that you have begun; for the praiseworthy thing is not to have been to Jerusalem, but to have lived a good life along the way; for you cannot arrive there except through the performance of His works . . . Therefore, reclothe her soiled and disfigured form with the garments of joy and gladness.[29]

The offer of the freedom to sack the city for three days after it was captured proved a further incentive and the crusaders duly agreed to stay and help Afonso. Thus a blend of secular and spiritual motives were firmly in play. Lisbon lies on the banks of the River Tagus a few miles in from the Atlantic: its castle still stands on top of one of the city's many hills and in the mid-twelfth century the fortress walls extended down to the shoreline to embrace the heart of the settlement. From the besiegers' viewpoint this proved to be a model campaign.

Unlike, for example, the terrible hardships endured at Antioch by the First Crusaders, the land around Lisbon was extraordinarily rich in fish and fruit.[30] The discovery of the city's main storehouses, which lay outside the walls, was an even greater bonus because it deprived the defenders of supplies. The Christians were also advantaged by the political situation in Islamic Iberia and North Africa.[31] The peninsula was ruled by the Almoravid dynasty, but by the mid-twelfth century their popularity had waned and the ultra-pious, hard-line Almohads began to sweep aside their co-religionists whom they viewed as weak and corrupt. In other words, just as the First Crusaders profited from dissent in the Muslim Near East, so the Lisbon crusaders benefited from a power struggle at the western edge of the Islamic world. In consequence there was no hope of a relief force for the defenders of Lisbon, another considerable help to the crusaders.

The siege was not, however, an entirely straightforward affair. The natural strength of the city's defences and the determined resistance of its inhabitants proved desperately hard to wear down. For much of the summer, the Christians made limited headway; they tried to construct huge siege towers – one was over thirty metres high, but the enemy set fire to it. The Anglo-Norman contingent made catapults and arranged a series of shifts to keep up a relentless barrage of stones and missiles, but again little progress was apparent. Eventually, however, the lack of food and outside help began to wear the Muslims down. Peace negotiations were opened although they quickly descended into Muslim diatribes against the divinity of Christ and allegations of the crusaders' greed.[32] Once more the assault was renewed: to the east of the city the Flemish-Rhineland contingent dug an elaborate series of multi-galleried tunnels but even though this brought down a section of the wall, the defenders managed to barricade it quickly enough to prevent entry. The Anglo-Normans dragged up another siege tower and Raol, the eyewitness author of *The Conquest of Lisbon*, brandished a piece of the most talismanic relic of all, the True Cross, as he gave an impassioned final oration designed to inspire the crusaders to victory. He reminded the men of the sacrifices that they had made and promised them success. Raol made it clear that he would be in the thick of the battle himself, trusting in divine blessing to protect him from danger. The crusaders wept with emotion and fell to their knees to venerate the relic. With these spiritual preparations completed, the onslaught began.[33] Slowly they heaved the tower towards the enemy. The Muslims tried everything possible to break, crush or ignite the structure but it was too well protected by skins and padding. Inexorably it closed in on the walls – with the drawbridge just over a metre away from the battlements the defenders' nerve broke. Starving and desperate, they could see there was no point in further resistance and so they sued for peace: a negotiated surrender was infinitely preferable to the likely horrors of an uncontrolled sack.

With the fall of Lisbon King Afonso had taken possession of a prized target in the reconquest, although the city of Coimbra remained the capital of Portugal for several more centuries. Most of Lisbon's inhabitants were treated well enough to stay *in situ* because, as we saw in the Latin East, if they were killed or exiled then the resultant ghost town was of little use to the conquerors. The crusaders received their promised booty and settled down to wait for the winter to pass. Once it was safe to venture to sea again – probably in late February – they set sail for the Levant to fulfil their vows and to pray at the Holy Sepulchre.

Final Preparations for the Crusade: Sermons and Ceremonies

Back in France and Germany the crusaders readied themselves to depart. They needed to mortgage and sell land to finance their journeys and such was the demand for precious metals that some churches were forced to melt down relics and religious vessels to supply the crusaders. Groups of warriors began to assemble and we can often see more than one family representative ready to go: it is striking how many sets of brothers took part in the Second Crusade, as well as a few fathers and sons too – once again, the old cliché of crusaders being landless younger sons is proved groundless.[34]

In the weeks before the crusade set out, the anticipation and excitement were fuelled by several major public events. Eugenius had journeyed to Paris and his presence added a special gloss to the spiritual preparations. He presided over a series of ceremonies that probably included a sermon by Abbot Peter the Venerable of Cluny on the importance of the Holy Sepulchre, and the dedication of a series of fourteen windows in the abbey of Saint-Denis to commemorate the achievements of the First Crusaders. Two of these roundels survive in a museum in the United States; the other twelve were destroyed during the French Revolution but fortunately engravings of them remain. Some depict the great pre-crusading heroes of Christian history, Charlemagne and Constantine, others show a trio of kings being given the martyr's crown: the majority tell of the battles, sieges and triumphs of the First Crusade. In sum they formed a series of inspirational scenes designed to imbue the crusaders of 1147–8 with the values of their magnificent predecessors.[35]

Saint-Denis was also the location for an emotional farewell to King Louis himself on 11 June 1147.[36] The crowds present witnessed a brilliantly choreographed event designed to display Louis' piety to maximum effect and to secure divine favour. As Louis journeyed to the abbey he stopped at a leprosarium and, with only two companions, entered. The patronage of lepers, who were kept separate from society by reason of their terrifying disease, was a deliberate echo of Christ's care for those similarly afflicted. At Saint-Denis itself, the sense of expectation was tremendous. Excited crowds waited for a glimpse of their crusading king, although the extreme heat caused his mother to faint. Louis paused in front of everyone and asked to be given the *oriflamme*, the vermilion banner mounted on a golden lance that was equated with Charlemagne's standard. Then he entered the abbey: the congregation within the cool, shadowy church fell silent. At the altar stood Abbot Suger, Abbot Bernard and Pope Eugenius himself – a gathering of Europe's elite churchmen – and in front of them lay a golden-plated casket that contained the remains of St Denis, the patron saint of the Capetian dynasty and the protector of France. Louis fell to the ground and prostrated himself in front of the altar. Eugenius and Suger carefully opened a small door on the casket and tenderly pulled out the silver reliquary holding the relics to allow the king to venerate the saint more closely and to be inspired in his holy task. After this Suger presented Louis with the *oriflamme* and Eugenius gave him a wallet, the traditional symbol of a pilgrim, and a reminder that a penitential journey remained a central part of crusading ideology. The pope blessed the king before Louis and his companions went to dine in the monks' refectory to emphasise their change in status from earthly knights to holy warriors.

Tensions at Constantinople and Defeat in Asia Minor

Conrad of Germany set out ahead of Louis and marched swiftly through Hungary towards the northern edge of the Byzantine Empire. In theory, his reception there should have been good because his sister-in-law had recently married Emperor Manuel Comnenus, but the woeful discipline of his army (perhaps some 35,000 in number) caused serious friction with the locals and provoked a series of skirmishes. In contrast to the First Crusade, the Greeks had not invited the westerners into their lands and they feared crusader aggression.[37] It was a natural disaster that brought most trouble for the Germans, though. By early September they had reached Choerobacchi, just to the west of Constantinople, where they camped on a wide floodplain. Heavy overnight rainfall overnight caused a flash flood to cascade down from the mountains and a torrent of water ripped through the Germans' camp, carrying away huge amounts of equipment and drowning men and horses alike – a disturbing signal of divine disapproval.[38]

The Germans then arrived outside Constantinople. The Greeks wished to move their visitors along as fast as possible in order to prevent a link-up with the French crusaders and, through the usual carrot-and-stick routine – an offer of transportation over the Bosphorus and the provision of markets – they managed to induce the Germans to cross into Asia Minor. The Bosphorus may be only 550 metres wide at one point but, given the Greeks' control of shipping, it was a genuinely formidable barrier and after Conrad had moved, 'the queen of cities', as the Greeks described their capital, was safe from one western army at least.

Once in Asia Minor Conrad was supposed to wait for Louis but, as he admitted later, he became impatient to attack the Turks and chose to advance ahead. The Germans split their forces into two: a group of pilgrims were to take a slower, and nominally safer, route around the coast of Asia Minor while the king and the bulk of the knights and foot soldiers planned to forge directly towards northern Syria. Accounts differ but it seems that the cumulative effects of a hopelessly over-optimistic rate of march, which in turn led to a short-fall of supplies, coupled with possible treachery from their Greek guides and fierce harassment by the Seljuk Turks, culminated in a crushing defeat. Footmen were slaughtered in their thousands and although Conrad himself was wounded, most of the better-armoured knights survived and began to retreat.[39]

Within a few days they encountered the first of the French crusaders. Their colleagues were astounded: the Greeks had claimed that the Germans were surging victoriously towards northern Syria and when the truth emerged it was taken as clear evidence of Byzantine duplicity. Louis' and Manuel's relationship had been troubled from the start.[40] Manuel's recent wars with the principality of Antioch, presently ruled by Queen Eleanor's uncle, Raymond, plus his recent decision to sign a twelve-year truce with the Seljuk sultan of Iconium, were perceived as indications of hostility to his fellow Christians. Prior to the crusade's departure the emperor had written to Louis and asked him to swear fealty and return lands formerly held by the Byzantine Empire; in other words, to repeat the oaths of the First Crusaders. The French king declined, but as he drew nearer to Constantinople, Manuel's demands for fealty, from the French nobles at least, grew more insistent. This was driven by the actions of a third party – the Sicilians: the Byzantines' old enemy and, by coincidence, fraternal allies of the king of France. At this most delicate of moments King Roger II of Sicily sent a powerful fleet to invade the Peloponnese peninsula, to ravage the city of Corinth and then to smash Athens. Manuel was terrified that the French would join forces with the Sicilians and threaten Constantinople itself. To counter this Louis was subjected to the full splendour of Byzantine diplomacy: he enjoyed escorted visits to countless glittering churches, he was entertained with sumptuous banquets and given audiences with the emperor himself. John Kinnamos, a Byzantine writer, noted that when the two rulers met in front of a grand assembly, Manuel was placed on a throne and Louis on a much lower stool: an unmistakable hierarchy. Still the French resisted Manuel's calls for fealty – in fact, a vociferous minority in the crusader army even wanted to attack Constantinople and it was only the Greeks' familiar combination of incentives and bullying – poor supplies outside the city and the promise of ample markets across the Bosphorus – that induced the French to move.[41]

In the aftermath of the German retreat Conrad and Louis met and the two armies joined together to begin a more circuitous march around the coast, a frustratingly slow process because of the innumerable inlets and rivers that had to be crossed. Conrad soon decided that his injuries were such that he had to rest and, thanks to the efforts of his sister-in-law, Empress Eirene, he was invited to winter in Constantinople. Of course, with most of the German troops gone and with no prospect of Conrad upstaging him, Manuel could afford to be magnanimous and he personally attended to the king and nursed him back to full health.

In the meantime, Louis and his troops had turned inland along the Maeander valley where, in mid-December, they routed a Turkish force that tried to block their fording of the river. By early in the New Year they were in mountainous territory and it was here that disaster struck.[42] On 6 January 1148 Geoffrey of Rancon commanded the vanguard as it moved over Mount Cadmus. He led the troops along at a brisk pace and by the end of the day had crossed the summit and started down the far side – well out of sight of the slow-moving baggage train and foot soldiers in the middle of the army; still further behind, the rearguard had not yet broken camp. The Turks constantly shadowed the crusaders and soon glimpsed their opportunity. As the ponderous wagons and the lightly armed footmen laboured over the mountain, the Seljuks pounced. They loosed volley after volley of arrows and bombarded the panic-stricken Christians from above and below: men and animals plummeted to their deaths and the Turks seized huge amounts of booty. Meanwhile, far ahead, the vanguard camped for the night, oblivious to their tragic error. Word of the attack eventually got back to Louis in the rearguard and the king and his household charged out to try to save the day, but by now the Turks were in total control of the situation and many of the royal entourage died. At first glance this seems an amazingly amateurish mistake – the loss of contact between contingents sounds so basic, but on closer examination, a few mitigating factors emerge. The French army probably numbered at least 20,000 and to move over such awkward terrain was a seriously difficult task. Roads were rudimentary and the baggage train and troops probably extended for six miles. In unfamiliar territory it is perhaps understandable how such a situation could have developed because the mountains constantly broke up any sight lines and it became impossible to hold a proper formation.

The vanguard waited in trepidation for their friends to appear. Throughout the night men emerged from the gloom in ones and twos

to tell of their escape and to report the death of friends and comrades:
a grim list of the missing, presumed dead, was compiled. Louis survived
and soon took drastic action to try to ensure that such a catastrophic
breakdown in order was never repeated. In an unprecedented move
(and one not replicated by any later crusader king) he turned over the
running of the entire army to the Knights Templar. This, only a
couple of decades after their foundation, was a telling indication of the
respect with which the warrior-monks were viewed, as well as a sign of
the damage to Louis' own morale. The crusaders swore to establish
fraternity with the Templars and to obey their commands in full. With
discipline established the army marched onwards and duly reached the
southern Turkish coast without further setbacks.

Eleanor of Aquitaine and the Scandal at Antioch

In February 1148 Louis and Eleanor finally arrived at Antioch where
Prince Raymond, her uncle, eagerly awaited their presence. The
prospect that the Second Crusade would fight in northern Syria was
of real excitement to Raymond because it meant he could tackle the
neighbouring Muslims of Aleppo; it also opened out the possibility
that he could gain sufficient power to shrug off Byzantine overlordship, a situation he loathed. As the crusaders prepared to leave France
the prince had sent them gifts to win their favour and now he welcomed
his guests with processions and fine entertainments. Raymond was
certain that his close ties to the Capetian royal family would aid his
cause and there is even a suggestion that he commissioned the epic
Old French poem *Chanson des Chétifs* in honour of their visit.[43] Yet
within weeks the situation had turned very sour indeed. When a
formal assembly of Antiochenes and crusaders met to discuss a
campaign in the north, the idea was, to Raymond's complete horror
and fury, rejected. The sources suggest that Louis' wish to make his
pilgrimage to the holy sites drew him towards Jerusalem, yet while
there may be some truth in this, it does not seem convincing when
set against the wider context of the crusade. More pertinently, the
deteriorating condition of Edessa, the original target of the expedition, could have contributed towards the decision to leave Antioch. In
October 1146 the local Armenians had tried to break free from Muslim

rule only to be crushed with the utmost ferocity. The walls of the citadel were shattered and many thousands of Christians were killed or sent into slavery. A northern Syrian writer of the late twelfth century offered an almost apocalyptic description of the city: 'Edessa was deserted of life: an appalling vision, enveloped in a black cloud, drunk with blood, infected by the cadavers of its sons and daughters! Vampires and other savage beasts were running and coming into the city at night to feed themselves on the flesh of the massacred people.'[44] In other words, the city was no longer worth recovering.

The crossing of Asia Minor must have exhausted Louis and his men and the losses of horses and equipment were further serious problems. The presence of Conrad in the kingdom of Jerusalem (he had sailed there after his convalescence, well supplied with money and horses by Manuel) was another pull towards the south. Finally, an unwillingness to help Raymond, whose status as a vassal of the Greeks was known, is also relevant because the French blamed much of their misfortunes in Asia Minor on Byzantine guides and the Greeks' dealings with the Seljuks. With his strategy in ruins, a furious Prince Raymond became hostile to King Louis and it is from this point onwards that the infamous cause célèbre of the Second Crusade emerged – the alleged relationship between Queen Eleanor and her uncle.

Our sources for these events are problematic: William of Tyre wrote in the 1170s (although he claimed to have researched the matter closely) and, while the Englishman John of Salisbury met the king and queen on their journey home in mid-1149, he did not compose his *History of the Popes* until 1164. William suggested that Raymond resolved to steal Eleanor from the king in revenge for Louis' unwillingness to fight in Syria. William stated categorically that 'she disregarded her marriage vows and was unfaithful to her husband.'[45] John was less certain, but indicated that 'the attentions paid by the prince to the queen and his constant, indeed almost continuous, conversation with her aroused the king's suspicions.'[46] This latter issue might be explained by the fact that, unlike Louis, the prince and his niece were both Occitan speakers, the language of their native southern France; to an outsider, a 'secret' language could have aroused suspicion. A later comment ascribed to Eleanor that the king was 'more monk than man' gives a sexual twist to the situation.[47]

It is frustratingly difficult to reach a definitive conclusion on the matter: the need to preserve a royal bloodline meant that an affair would have been hugely dangerous, but not, of course, impossible. On the other hand, John of Salisbury and William of Tyre were serious, sober writers, not given to sensationalism for its own sake. The most contemporaneous piece of evidence has been widely ignored by historians and is from a letter sent to the king by Suger, the regent of France in 1149. The abbot wrote: 'Concerning the queen, your wife, we venture to congratulate you, if we may, upon the extent to which you suppress your anger, if there be anger, until with God's will you return to your own kingdom and see to these matters.' While this is not a categorical statement of an affair it is a strong indication that rumours concerning Eleanor's behaviour were in circulation at the time of the crusade and that even back in France, Suger was aware of them, whether true or not. In short, it was widely believed that the queen had deserted her marriage bed.

The Siege of Damascus and the Humiliation of the Second Crusade

On 24 June 1148 a general assembly gathered at the town of Palmarea, near Acre. This was the most splendid congregation of rulers and lords in the history of the crusader kingdom. Two reigning European monarchs, along with members of their families, senior churchmen and nobles, met with Baldwin III and Melisende and the leading figures in the kingdom of Jerusalem to decide where to attack. Given the tensions between Raymond and Louis a campaign in the north was unlikely. Notwithstanding recent periods of friendship between the Franks and the Damascenes – largely brought on by a mutual fear of Zengi of Aleppo and Mosul, but now ended by the Syrian city's rapprochement with Zengi's son and successor Nur ad-Din – the choice of Damascus was almost a foregone conclusion, although the port of Ascalon remained in Muslim hands too. Damascus, however, was one of the great cities of the Islamic world and the chance to take a place of such spiritual and strategic importance had to be grasped.[48]

The crusader armies marched from Tiberias to Banyas and then over Mount Lebanon to begin the gentle descent towards Damascus. The city lies on a flat plain overlooked by Mount Kasouin to its north and with the small, but vital, River Barada running through it. The most dominant feature of the region (and indeed still surviving outside the modern urban sprawl), were the immense orchards that surrounded most of the city and extended for up to five miles towards the west. The close, densely packed trees were a difficult obstacle for a large army to breach, but in spite of this the Franks decided to go ahead because the fruit and irrigation canals offered immediate supplies of food and drink, and they believed that if they broke through these defences then morale in the city would collapse.

King Baldwin led his men into the orchards where they were subjected to a strange form of guerrilla warfare quite beyond their military experience.[49] Barricades blocked the paths, the mud walls that delineated each plot were pierced by lances thrust out of special peep-holes, and arrows peppered the crusaders from the watchtowers that stood over each smallholding. Slowly, the Christians worked their way through the trees and emerged on the plain in front of the city. Once there the German knights used their favoured tactics, dismounting from their horses to fight with swords and shields so as to push the Damascenes back to the walls. Conrad was at the front of his troops and so great was his ferocity that he reputedly severed the head, neck and shoulder of one opponent with a single mighty blow. At this point the crusaders looked as if they were on the verge of a spectacular success, poised to add their own great chapter to the annals of holy warfare. Then, curiously, they moved away from their hard-won position to the west and marched over to the other side of the city where there were no orchards, water supply or moat, only, allegedly, a low wall. Later, the crusaders would complain vehemently that they made this move on the advice of the local Franks, but once established in this location, they quickly ran out of food and could not then return to the orchards because of new barricades. Thus, with antagonism between the crusaders and the local lords growing fast, the armies reluctantly began to break camp. The finest collection of warriors in Christendom had been compelled to turn tail after only four days – an unimagined ignominy. They had not even been defeated in battle; it was far more humiliating for them to abandon the attack than to lose some epic military engagement. It seems that accusations that the Franks took

bribes from the Damascenes to lift the siege – a common enough practice in Levantine warfare – offered the crusaders their most acceptable
explanation for this turn of events. While it had the merit of exculpating
the westerners from responsibility for the fiasco, it created a legacy of
distrust between Europeans and the Franks that simmered for decades.
What the Muslim sources tell us, however, is something slightly different.

In the same way that parts of al-Sulami's jihad sermon of 1105
resembled crusade preaching, reports of the Damascenes' spiritual
preparations during the siege echo crusader practices prior to military conflicts. As the citizens assembled in the hall and courtyard of
the Great Umayyad Mosque, the revered Koran of Caliph Uthman
(579–656) was shown to the crowd and the people sprinkled their heads
with ashes and prayed for divine aid.[50] This veneration of the Koran
and the acts of humility recall the scene at Saint-Denis just over a year
earlier with Louis and the relics of his own patron saint. Preachers
urged the Damascenes to defend their holy city, and infused with jihad
fervour, the Muslims were ready for battle. A subsequent engagement
on the eastern side of Damascus proved inconclusive, but it showed
the crusaders that resistance was hardening; more importantly, it gave
time for relief forces to approach. Some reinforcements arrived from
the Beqaa valley and Nur ad-Din himself paused at Homs, ready to
march south to Damascus. On this basis, the Christians' attempt to
move the focus of their attack and achieve a quick victory becomes
understandable. When the defences there proved stronger than anticipated it was clear that a retreat was the prudent course of action.
At this point it is possible the Damascenes made payments to the
Franks (rather than the crusaders) to ensure their departure and therein
lay the basis for allegations of duplicity on the part of the local barons.

A furious Conrad soon left for home: in contrast, Louis and Eleanor
remained in the Levant for almost a year to visit the holy sites. Given
the enormous sense of expectation prior to the campaign, it was
inevitable that people sought to apportion blame. We have seen that
some opprobrium fell upon the Frankish nobility, but the crusaders
were held responsible too. Some of this was general in nature: the
contemporary 'Chronicle of Morigny' decried the expedition as having
achieved 'nothing useful or worth repeating'; the poet Marcabru called
the leaders 'broken failures'; John of Salisbury claimed it had irreparably
damaged the Christian faith.[51] For the first time, therefore, people

seriously questioned the value of crusading and the events of 1147–8 probably deterred many from taking the cross in future. Bernard of Clairvaux came in for severe criticism and he was forced to give sermons and write a treatise to explain what had happened. His answer was to point to the sins of man in general and to remind people of the mysterious ways of the Lord. Eugenius too felt a backlash from people because the number of letters issued by his chancery saw a huge decline – an indication that people were less inclined to turn to the papacy for confirmation or recognition of their rights; in other words, the standing of the *curia* had dropped because the crusade had failed.[52]

To the Muslims of the Near East, the collapse of the expedition was a source of huge delight. Previously they had feared the western armies but now, as William of Tyre wrote: 'they mocked at the shattered strength and broken glory of those who represented the substantial foundations of the Christians.'[53] Nur ad-Din led an invasion of Antioch and in June 1149, at the Battle of Inab, he killed Prince Raymond of Antioch, the Franks' most formidable warrior. The panic-stricken Franks appealed to Europe to help 'the oppressed Mother Church of the East', but a combination of exhaustion on the part of those recently returned crusaders, the need to raise more funds and a general lack of morale meant that even though Eugenius promised the usual spiritual rewards, there was no worthwhile response.[54]

The Second Crusade in the Baltic

The Second Crusade's two other theatres of war produced very mixed results. The campaign against the pagans of northern Europe proved a grave disappointment but the expeditions to Almería and Tortosa in eastern Spain were successful. Within three months of Eugenius' endorsement the Wendish crusaders (as the northern campaigners have become known) set out. Their motives seem a confused combination of the clerical wish to convert the pagans and the nobles' desire for land and vengeance for recent enemy incursions. A joint Danish–Saxon force attacked the town of Dobin, just inland from the Bay of Wismar.[55] This was the stronghold of Niclot, leader of the Abodrites, and it was defended by a combination of earthworks, waterways and the surrounding marshlands. Niclot proved a dangerous opponent who struck hard at the Danish ships while they prepared to engage. Mutual distrust amongst the attacking forces surfaced: the Saxons suggested that the Danes were pugnacious fighters at home but unwarlike abroad, while the Danes disdainfully stated that 'only self-indulgence and sausages' came from Germany. More seriously, there was a disjunction between Bernard's 'death or conversion' theme and the aspirations of the crusaders themselves. The latter questioned whether it was sensible to kill the locals because if this happened there would be no one to tax or make a livelihood from. The fighting was desultory and after a while the Slavs agreed to convert to Christianity and to release their Danish prisoners. As one local writer observed, however, theirs was a false baptism and they kept the able-bodied prisoners anyway.[56]

A second crusading army containing many north German bishops and nobles, as well as a notable Polish contingent, laid siege to Stettin to the north-east. This quickly descended into the realms of farce when the defenders displayed crosses above their citadel – they had been converted to Christianity a couple of decades previously! The attack was therefore either a product of complete ignorance on the part of the crusaders or else the wish to conquer a strategically important site, regardless of its religious allegiance. The clergy managed to prevent an assault from taking place; as a local churchman pondered: 'if they had come to confirm the Pomeranians in the Christian faith, then they ought to have done this through the preaching of bishops, not by arms.' Another writer noted, 'thus that grand expedition broke up with slight gain.' While the northern Europeans were attracted to the offer of spiritual rewards, the rigorous aspirations of Bernard and Eugenius were far out of line with the existing practices of conversion combined with political submission.[57]

Success in Spain: The Capture of Almería and Tortosa

In eastern Spain, by contrast, the interests of the papacy, the Genoese and the local rulers coalesced much more comfortably and this gave the Iberian crusaders a very strong focus. As we saw above, the Genoese and King Alfonso VII of Castile and León had made a formal contract to attack the city of Almería, deep in the south of Muslim Spain. Around the same time, Eugenius had issued a crusade bull to the people of Italy and also encouraged the Genoese to fight at Almería.[58] It is possible that the pope had learned of this expedition, or else he was approached by the Genoese themselves, and he decided to endorse the move as part of a wider campaign of Christian expansion. Other sources report that negotiators sent to secure the involvement of Count Ramon Berenguer IV of Barcelona included a bishop who urged him to join the other parties 'for the redemption of their souls'. The participants stood to gain the spiritual privileges of a crusader, as well as carefully demarcated financial, commercial and/or property rewards: the Genoese would get one-third of the town, the king two-thirds. Ramon also made his own agreement with the Italians to besiege Tortosa the following year on much the same terms. The Spanish bishops exhorted their people to join the crusade and to 'go bravely and surely to battle', to have their sins pardoned and 'with victory [to] assure them once more that they will have all the gold that the Moors possess.'[59] An explicit promise of financial gain would have been abhorrent to Bernard of Clairvaux, but in this context represents some recognition of what motivated the Iberian crusaders.

In the late summer of 1147 a fleet of sixty-three galleys and 163 other ships left Genoa and in October began to attack the port from the sea. After a successful landing, the siege began in earnest with the construction of towers and catapults. The arrival of Alfonso VII provided further momentum and they soon broke down a section of the wall. On 17 October the crusaders poured into the city and 'with the help and favour of God' put the place to the sword. In a dramatic contrast to the peaceful surrender of Lisbon (only a week later) thousands of Muslims were killed or enslaved. The citadel resisted for four days but capitulated on the payment of a huge sum of money. Alfonso now had an outpost in the south of Iberia and the Genoese possessed another vital trading station. Their fleet sailed north to lie up over the winter before heading on to its next target, Tortosa.[60] Many southern French nobles, including a contingent from Narbonne led by Viscountess Ermengarde, contingents from the Templars and the Hospitallers and, amazingly, a group of Anglo-Norman veterans who had fought at Lisbon, joined in. The city had substantial walls and a formidable citadel but skilful use of siege towers by the Genoese brought them to the edge of victory. The defenders parleyed – if, after forty days, they were not rescued by the Muslims of Valencia, they would surrender: the crusaders agreed. The Christians successfully blockaded Tortosa to the south and on 30 December 1148 with no prospect of relief, the city opened its gates to a peaceful conquest.

A contemporary Genoese charter reveals the city's comfortable assimilation of crusading ideology and the blossoming sense of civic pride that would be a hallmark of medieval Italy: 'they have captured the city for the honour of God and all of Christianity and they have determined to remain in control of the city out of the greatest necessity of Christians, and most of all because they know that it is honourable and useful to the city of Genoa.'[61] There was no contradiction here between the prospect of secular and spiritual rewards. As we have seen before it is too simplistic to frame holy war and the pursuit of profit as a dichotomy. Pisa, Genoa and Venice were as full of churches as every other contemporary city: in other words, they too had strong religious motives to defeat the Muslims. The fact that Eugenius must have known about the commercial contracts between Genoa, Alfonso VII and Ramon Berenguer, yet still issued bulls in favour of the crusade suggest that he too recognised the practicalities of the situation. The Genoese believed their success was evidence that God approved of their motives. At the heart of medieval Genoa, a few streets up from the docks, lies the cathedral of St Lawrence. This striking building – the spiritual centrepiece of the city – is cloaked in the black and white horizontally striped stonework so typical of Italian Romanesque architecture. Inside, on the south wall of the nave, the surviving fragments of a fresco depict the capture of Almería and Tortosa.[62] This image encapsulates the essence of crusading for the Genoese: to them there was no clash between the overlapping aims of holy war, conquest and commerce: everyone had acted in concert and all of the Christian community benefited. Aside from the massacre at Almería, deep in Muslim Spain, a policy of conquest and assimilation operated in Iberia, broadly similar to that in place in northern Europe; again born out of a need to rule lands effectively in the future. Ultimately, in spite of its grandiose ambitions, in Spain alone did the Second Crusade manage to extend the frontiers of Christendom.

5

Saladin, the Leper King and the Fall of Jerusalem in 1187

The Rise of Nur ad-Din and the Revival of Jihad

In spite of the defeat of the Second Crusade outside the walls of Damascus, it would be a serious mistake to regard the period down to Saladin's capture of Jerusalem in 1187 as one of inevitable decline for the Franks – on the contrary, there were times when the Christians seemed poised to take the ascendancy. Saladin's ultimate success came about through a complicated cocktail of the political and the personal, a spectrum that encompassed good fortune and sheer opportunism, clever strategy and the ability to arouse religious passion.

Within weeks of Louis VII's departure for home in June 1149 the leading nobles and churchmen of Jerusalem gathered to celebrate the reconsecration of the Church of the Holy Sepulchre. With the completion of Fulk's and Melisende's plans the building at the spiritual heart of Christendom assumed much of the form that we see today. Pilgrims could process around such holy sites such as the tomb of Christ, Calvary (the place of Christ's crucifixion), the Chapel of St Helena (where the True Cross was found), the Grotto of the Cross (where it was kept), the prison of Christ and other, lesser shrines, all under one roof. The creation of a single, splendidly decorated building, rather than the slightly dilapidated structures found by the First Crusaders, constituted far more appropriate surroundings for the glorification of God. The rededication ceremony took place on 15 July 1149, a date chosen with particular care because it was the fiftieth anniversary of the crusaders' capture of Jerusalem in 1099. Thus the new church recalled why that great expedition had taken place and boldly perpetuated the link with continued Christian custody of the Holy Land.[1]

Soon, however, such convivial feelings evaporated as Baldwin III,

encouraged by certain of his advisers – perhaps themselves jealous of
the queen's favourites – sought to end the regency of Queen Melisende
and take full control of the kingdom. Baldwin was now over twenty
years old and his age certainly permitted such a move, yet Queen
Melisende was reluctant to step aside. She had proven a successful
and widely admired ruler and since standing up to Fulk in 1134 she
had exercised power in a variety of forms for almost seventeen years.
Throughout history, the voluntary surrender of authority has proven
immensely difficult and it was beyond Melisende. The kingdom's
nobility polarised and two separate courts came into being; each issued
its own documents and judgements. The situation escalated and armed
confrontations took place before mediators established peace. By 1152
Melisende agreed to allow her son full power and Baldwin started to
rule in his own right. It seems, however, that the relationship between
the two survived and the queen continued to fulfil important roles
within the royal family.[2]

The most dramatic events in this period took place in northern
Syria. Buoyed by the failure of the Second Crusade, Nur ad-Din began
to take the jihad to the Franks with a ferocity and zeal as yet unseen.
In token of his victory at Inab in June 1149 he dispatched the head
and right arm of Raymond of Antioch to the caliph of Baghdad.[3]
Unlike Zengi, who had used Turkish titles (such as *atabeg*, or ruler)
to emphasise his ties to the Seljuks, Nur ad-Din took Arabic titles
that reveal his focus on jihad, the promotion of Sunni orthodoxy, and
the establishment of justice. His own name meant 'light of the religion' and he was repeatedly described as *al-mujahid* (fighter in the
holy war) and *al-adil* (the just). It was through Nur ad-Din that
the Muslim counter-crusade took its most significant steps forward.
He is overshadowed by his successor, Saladin, a man whose
contemporary biographers have done much to keep his reputation
buoyant to the present day. Aside from his role in modern-day politics, Saladin will (literally) loom large for any visitor to Damascus
because his modern equestrian statue stands just outside the medieval
citadel, while his well-preserved tomb is just adjacent to the Great
Umayyad Mosque. To find Nur ad-Din's burial place requires a fair
amount of detective work in amongst the mesmerising warren of
streets and alleys in Old Damascus. At one of his madrasas (teaching
schools) we can peer through a small, barred window to see a drab

cenotaph of unknown (but not medieval) age in a dirty, unlit chamber – hardly the memorial of a hero of the holy war. Of course, it was Saladin who actually removed the Christians from Jerusalem, yet this triumph would have been almost impossible without the immense spiritual, social and military commitment of Nur ad-Din who managed the hitherto unprecedented feat of drawing together the religious and noble classes of Muslim Syria.

One manifestation of Nur ad-Din's style can be seen in the foundation of a new madrasa in Aleppo around 1150. Madrasas were central to his policies because they offered a way to spread his religious and political agenda and also served as a place to train officials. They were closely associated with Islamic traditionalism – and, by definition, they challenged the Shi'a, a group whom he unrelentingly targeted as a destabilising, heretical force in the Muslim world. Nur ad-Din wanted to unify the Islamic Near East and to eradicate heterodoxy; only then would he be able to deal with the Franks. He also chose to locate the Aleppan madrasa in a former church, thus symbolising his recent victories over the Christians.[4]

Nur ad-Din's next major success was to take power in Damascus. As we saw above, at the time of the Second Crusade there was a rapprochement between the two parties and Nur ad-Din's marriage to the daughter of Unur, former ruler of the city, sealed this pact. To extend his authority further the emir used a combination of military threats and a strong moral message to remind the citizenry of their obligation to the jihad and to suggest that their own rulers were dangerously sympathetic towards the Christians. Nur ad-Din blockaded the city and convinced the inhabitants to open the gates to him. This was a substantial step forward in his struggle against the Franks: for the first time in the history of the Latin East, the two most important cities of Muslim Syria were under the rule of the same man. As William of Tyre observed: 'a formidable adversary arose . . . This change was decidedly disastrous to the interests of the kingdom.'[5]

Yet Nur ad-Din's rise was not without setbacks. A defeat by the Franks near Krak des Chevaliers in 1163 seems to have prompted a personal reappraisal and the emir decided to abandon all luxuries and to dedicate himself to the holy war. In this drive for personal devotion and austerity the emir pursued his own inner jihad as a way to seek God's favour for the wider holy war. The ideas generated in Nur ad-Din's circles emphasised martyrdom and the reward of Paradise for those who lost their lives fighting the infidel. They also supported the writing of *al-Quds* literature, work that stressed the holiness of Jerusalem and its importance as a place of pilgrimage – thus was made clear the need for Muslims to recover the city.[6] In connection with this, around 1169, he ordered the construction of an elaborate *minbar* (pulpit) destined for the al-Aqsa Mosque in Jerusalem; a clear statement of his intent to conquer the city for Islam. Ibn Jubayr saw it in 1182 and rhapsodised about its beauty: 'The art of ornamental carving had exhausted itself in its endeavours on the pulpit, for never in any city have I seen a pulpit like it or of such wondrous workmanship.'[7] More pertinent to Nur ad-Din's endeavours were the *minbar*'s multiple inscriptions that proclaimed the victory of Islam over the infidel. A letter from Nur ad-Din to the caliph of Baghdad expressed his aim clearly: 'to banish the worshippers of the cross from the Aqsa Mosque . . . to conquer Jerusalem . . . to hold sway over the Syrian coast.'[8]

King Baldwin III of Jerusalem and the Battle for Egypt

Faced by such a formidable opponent the Franks needed a strong leader of their own and, in the form of King Baldwin III, they found an energetic and effective monarch. In 1153 he took the port of Ascalon to give the Franks control over the entire eastern Mediterranean coastline; this, in turn, meant that the Egyptian navy could no longer use Ascalon to harass the merchant and pilgrim fleets that were so vital to the survival of the Frankish states. While this triumph was partially neutralised by Nur ad-Din's seizure of Damascus it showed that the Franks remained a powerful force. In the remainder of the 1150s Baldwin fought a series of campaigns against Nur ad-Din with honours shared fairly evenly.

In light of the disastrous Second Crusade and the rising threat of Nur ad-Din, the king set aside previous tensions with Byzantium and elected to establish a closer relationship with the Greeks: they were, after all, the leading Christian power in the eastern Mediterranean. He proposed a marriage with a Byzantine princess and, after an embassy to Constantinople bore Baldwin's handwritten assurance that he would abide by the envoys' negotiations, the thirteen-year-old Princess

Theodora was dispatched to Jerusalem with a dowry and a bridal suite of huge value. This consisted of gold and gems, garments and pearls, tapestries, silks and precious vessels – a real demonstration of Byzantine wealth. They were married in September 1158 and, by way of reciprocation, when Emperor Manuel Comnenus became a widower, he married Princess Maria of Antioch on 25 December 1161.[9]

While Baldwin proved a competent ruler of Jerusalem, the calibre of Prince Raymond of Antioch's successor was far inferior. His widow, Princess Constance (daughter of Melisende's sister Alice), was unwilling to accept any of the candidates on offer.[10] She was only nineteen years old and had already produced four children: in part she may – understandably – have been reluctant to marry again. She had been betrothed to Raymond at the age of eight and presumably, on this second occasion, she wanted more of a say in the matter. Thus she turned down a trio of eminent nobles, two of whom were powerful figures from the West. Yet in political and military terms the need for her to take a husband was urgent. Baldwin III did not want the principality to follow Edessa into Muslim hands and he could not keep travelling up to Syria to protect Antioch and thereby leave Jerusalem vulnerable. He consulted his mother and Melisende was dispatched north to sort out her recalcitrant niece. At a family crisis meeting the queen was joined by another of her sisters, Hodierna of Tripoli, and together they tried to impress upon Constance the gravity of the situation. Still the princess resisted and she did not marry until, a year later, she felt a personal attraction to Reynald of Châtillon, a young French knight who may have come out with the Second Crusade.[11] Her decision brought to prominence one of the most notorious and influential figures of the entire crusading movement. After the Battle of Hattin in 1187 Reynald was executed by Saladin himself, yet to merit such a distinction was merely the climax of a career that displayed quite special brutality. While Reynald's violence towards Muslims is well documented, his behaviour towards his own co-religionists was, at times, equally appalling. A few years after his wedding the prince fell out with Aimery, the aged patriarch of Antioch, a man whom Reynald suspected of trying to undermine his marriage plans and who continued to make plain his dislike of the prince. Aimery began to voice his opinions too loudly for Reynald's taste and he was seized. The prince personally conducted him to a tower on the citadel of

Antioch and there, on a hot summer's day, high above the city, he had the old man tied to a chair and his bare head smeared with honey. Flies, bees and mosquitoes swarmed around Aimery for hours and yet no one dared to help him or protect him from the blazing sun or the tormenting insects until Reynald signalled an end to the grotesque torture.[12]

In November 1161, as the prince and his troops rode home after a successful raid into Muslim lands, they were cornered and seized, and Reynald was sent in chains to Aleppo. He spent the next sixteen years as a prisoner; during this time he is said to have learned Arabic but, as his actions later showed, he nursed a deep and festering hatred of his captors. By the time he was freed, however, Baldwin III would no longer rule Jerusalem. He died of consumption in February 1163, only thirty-three years old, and because he had no children the succession passed to his brother, Amalric.

William of Tyre, our main source for events in the Latin East, was personally acquainted with Amalric and acted as his chancellor and as tutor for his son; as he also stated, the *Historia* – an account of the Frankish East from the First Crusade to the author's own day – was written, in part, at the king's suggestion.[13] All of this means that he was supremely well placed to give a character portrait of his patron. William described him as quite tall and good-looking with receding blond hair and a full beard, although he noted that the king was troubled by his weight and had breasts 'like those of a woman hanging down to his waist'.[14] Amalric's personality was described in some detail: he was confident and assertive with a fine knowledge of customary law; he enjoyed reading and talking to people from distant lands, he was also pious and trusting of others. He was, however, said to be taciturn (in contrast to his affable brother, Baldwin III), relentless in his demands on Church revenues and a womaniser.

His reign (1163–74) was dominated by the struggle for Egypt. Both Amalric and Nur ad-Din recognised the vulnerability of the Fatimid regime and each sought to join with, or to remove, this ailing dynasty and thereby secure the unparalleled riches of the Nile for themselves. William of Tyre described the incredible wealth and fertility of Egypt. He wrote of 'the marvellous abundance of all good things there and of each individual commodity; the inestimable treasures belonging to the prince himself; the imposts and taxes from the cities both on the coast and farther inland; and the vast amounts of annual revenue. . . . the people, devoted to luxurious living and ignorant of the science of war, had become enervated through a period of long-continued peace.'[15]

In the case of Nur ad-Din there was a further dimension to the conflict because he would take on his principal Muslim enemies, the Shi'a, and their Cairo-based caliphate. On five occasions between 1163 and 1169, Amalric invaded Egypt. These campaigns were characterised by a bewildering series of alliances and counter-alliances, first between the Egyptians and the Franks against the Syrian Muslims, and then between the Egyptians and the Syrians in opposition to the Franks. Amalric achieved some notable successes: in 1167 his troops entered Alexandria and for two or three days flags bearing the Christian cross fluttered above this mighty Muslim city, a situation that seems so incongruous it is hard to bring to mind. The threat of an Egyptian-Syrian relief force caused the king to withdraw, however. Amalric knew the conquest of Egypt would be a huge challenge and he sought help from western Europe and Byzantium. Along with several other leading figures in the Frankish hierarchy he sent a series of appeals to the pope and King Louis VII of France. These emotive and keenly pitched messages transmitted hope and the expectation that Louis, as ruler of the homeland of crusading, would act; one letter stated: 'Great sadness! How disgraceful it will be to all the peoples and to you if this land, land in which your relatives spilt so much blood, so finely situated and having acquired so much fame, may be violated by evil people and allowed to be destroyed.'[16] The pope preached a couple of new crusades and while several important nobles visited the East, and the Pisans – keen to get a priority standing in the prime market of Alexandria – sent fleets in 1167 and 1168, there was not the large-scale expedition the king so desperately needed. An invasion of Egypt in late 1168 proved a disaster. Amalric's retreat in January 1169 left the stage free for Nur ad-Din's lieutenant, Shirkuh, to murder the ruler of Egypt and to seize power in the country for himself.

Saladin's Rise to Power in Egypt

When Shirkuh began to govern Egypt he took on the same titles and offices as used by the Fatimid regime; an absurd pretence given that the latter were Shi'ite and the invaders Sunni. From a pragmatic perspective, however, this was an undeniably wise policy given the relatively small size of his forces and the danger of overturning such a fundamental aspect of Egyptian life so quickly. When Shirkuh died in March 1169 – of a heart attack brought on by his immense girth – he was succeeded by his nephew, Salah al-Din Yusuf ibn Ayyub, known to the Franks and to posterity as Saladin.

He was of Kurdish stock, born in Takrit in 1138.[17] His father, Ayyub (hence the name of Saladin's dynasty, the Ayyubids) and his uncle, Shirkuh, were successful warriors, and at the age of fourteen the latter secured him a place in the service of Nur ad-Din in Aleppo. He received a good education and within a few years he had become the *shihna* (a sort of police chief) of Damascus, a role that provided him with an appreciation of politics and administration that would serve him well. He became close to Nur ad-Din, in part through a shared love of polo, a game both were said to excel at. Imad ad-Din wrote that Nur ad-Din 'was passionately fond of polo and would often go out in the dark and, as the day began to break, play by the light of candles, and Saladin would ride out to play with him every morning.'[18] Like his father and uncle, Saladin was a short man, whose most noted features were piercing dark eyes and a neat beard. Notwithstanding his military background and evident equestrian skills, Saladin was said to have been reluctant to join the Egyptian campaigns, although by 1167 he was fully involved in events at the siege of Alexandria.

After Shirkuh's death Saladin assumed the position of vizier, the de facto ruler of the land, and it is at this point he is said to have experienced a profound change in character and attitude. While some of this could be explained as idealised rhetoric, it seems true that a new-found focus and drive emerged. Ibn Abi Tayy, a near contemporary, wrote: 'He repented of wine-drinking and turned away from idle pleasures, he was vigilant in government and dismissed all negligence, donned the garment of religion and observed the rule of the Holy Law, the clear guide. He girt up his loins for serious endeavour and dedication. He poured out on people from his generosity and the abundance of his liberality floods of his goodness, far removed from human experience. To him came envoys and visitors and he was sought out with jewels of orations and gems of poetry.'[19] Thus the foundations for a good Muslim ruler were present – strict religious observance, justice, charity and, of course, the need for a cultured and sophisticated court.

He began to use this position to destabilise the standing of al-Adid, the Fatimid imam or spiritual leader.[20] Saladin provoked a fight with the imam's black infantry regiment, the force that underpinned his authority, and he duly defeated them and executed the survivors. He fought off a combined Frankish-Byzantine invasion at the coastal city of Damietta in the autumn of 1169 and then secured the pacification of Upper Egypt to assure his authority in the south. In accordance with a familiar practice in the Muslim world he then buttressed his position by the appointment of family members to senior posts in the government. His father became the treasurer of Cairo and his brother Saphadin was made ruler of the Yemen. He founded Sunni law colleges, dismissed Shi'a judges and, after he had secured the allegiance of the administrative classes (many of whom were Sunni anyway), he felt strong enough to omit the name of al-Adid from Friday prayers, thereby removing one of the great symbols of power in the Islamic world (the other being the minting of coins) from the imam. Within days al-Adid was dead – possibly killed by one of Saladin's brothers – and Sunni Islam had swept aside its bitter rival. Such progress aside, looming over this burgeoning family enclave was the spectre of Saladin's relationship with Nur ad-Din.

The extension of Sunni Islam was, of course, a source of delight to Nur ad-Din; yet his ability to control Saladin had become a cause of deep concern. As the man responsible for the young man's advancement he understandably felt that his protégé owed him some degree of loyalty; the Ayyubid family's growing entrenchment in a land of such immense riches and the clan's acquisition of so many key political positions were a threat to his authority. In September 1171 Nur ad-Din summoned Saladin to join him at the siege of the Frankish castle of Kerak in Transjordan.[21] Saladin did not appear, blaming tensions in Cairo for his absence; his commander was not remotely impressed and made his displeasure clear – he even threatened military action. The Ayyubid clan debated how to react if Nur ad-Din were to invade Egypt. Saladin's father spoke out, saying that they should obey Nur ad-Din, but later, in private, told his son that this had been a façade and that he should simply avoid open dissent with the Syrian.[22] The Ayyubids were clearly playing a long game here and realised that as yet, they could not afford open war with their former patron. Saladin's behaviour during this period poses a major challenge to his image as a selfless holy warrior. Some contemporaries were explicit about the fact that he knowingly defied his overlord and that his wish to rule over the Yemen, for example, was motivated by the need for a safe refuge should Nur ad-Din defeat him. It seems that Saladin had exploited the collapse of the Fatimid dynasty to establish his family's position in the wealthiest land of the Near East. He had acted quickly and decisively to make the most of the situation but in doing so he acquired a taste for independence. For Nur ad-Din's part, the ongoing danger of Frankish invasions and his own plans to attack Antioch and Jerusalem were obvious reasons why he was reluctant to provoke a civil war. Yet there seems little doubt that he had lost control over Saladin whose approach looked increasingly out of step with the jihad against the Christians.

Notwithstanding these disturbing tremors across the Islamic Near East, the Syrian Muslims' acquisition of Egypt caused consternation in the Frankish lands. William of Tyre wrote that 'the wise men of the kingdom began to realise that the subjugation of Egypt by the Turks had been a serious injury to us and our situation had become materially worse.'[23] Amalric dispatched Archbishop Frederick of Tyre, the most senior figure yet to be used as a diplomat, in an attempt to convince his co-religionists in the West of the need to act. The king wrote that the Christian territories were being ground away and broken up by the forces of Islam. He argued that the possibility of being block-aded by land and sea would prevent the safe passage of pilgrims – an effort to show how the spiritual well-being of all the faithful would be affected. Personal meetings with the pope, King Louis VII of France and King Henry II of England raised Frederick's hopes, but he had arrived at an inopportune time. The two monarchs blamed each other for the threat of invasion, and gathering tension over the Thomas Becket affair added a further complication. By the autumn of 1170, however, Frederick may have convinced Henry – who was also the nephew of King Amalric – to set out on a crusade the following spring. Unfortunately for the Holy Land, and for a certain archbishop, the murder in Canterbury Cathedral put paid to such plans. In the end, Frederick of Tyre was unable to secure anything more than tearful expressions of regret and promises of money – but not the crusade Amalric required.[24]

Probably Amalric's most ambitious diplomatic efforts involved the Byzantine Empire. William of Tyre related that in early 1171 the king and his courtiers discussed how best to secure help: most recommended another appeal to the West – hardly an innovative line of thought. The king agreed to this, but then gathered his inner circle about him and made a further suggestion. Against a flurry of protest he decided to journey to Constantinople and to pay homage to Emperor Manuel Comnenus in person. In doing so he hoped to convince the Greeks to help defend the Holy Land. For the crowned ruler of Christ's city to make such a voyage and to submit to the authority of another monarch was a clear indication of the danger from the Muslim world. Amalric's actions suggested deep scepticism that the West would ever respond to his embassies and a perception that his marriage ties with the Greeks, plus their shared task of custodians of the holy places against the advance of Islam, would be reasons enough to prompt a reaction. In March the king reached Constantinople where he was welcomed in the magnificent style that was the trademark of the Byzantine court. William of Tyre described games, races at the hippodrome, banquets and celebrations, but he chose not to state explicitly what Amalric and Manuel discussed. Instead he used the rather elliptical statement that the king and the emperor made a treaty agreeable to them both, perhaps wary of how his western European readers would respond to Amalric's submission.[25] John Kinnamos, a contemporary Byzantine official, had no need of such circumspection and he wrote: '[Amalric] came to Byzantium to petition the emperor . . . obtaining what he sought he agreed to many things including his subjection to the emperor on those terms.'[26] By way of demonstrating his concern for the Holy Land Manuel also sponsored a series of construction projects to enhance important religious sites, most notably the fine Byzantine mosaics (complete with Greek inscriptions) that still adorn the nave of the Church of the Holy Nativity in Bethlehem.[27]

In late July 1174 a Sicilian fleet of almost 200 vessels, with 1,000 knights and 500 Turcopoles (lightly armed cavalry), landed on the beaches of Alexandria and started to invest the city. The Sicilian forces were extremely well equipped and constructed siege towers, battering rams and catapults that hurled specially shipped black volcanic rocks from Mount Etna. The attack seemed particularly well timed because on 15 May Nur ad-Din had died. Religious differences apart, even William of Tyre paid tribute to him as 'a just prince, valiant and wise and, according to the traditions of his race, a religious man.'[28] He was an inspirational leader and had provided real impetus to the cause of the jihad. Imad ad-Din wrote his funeral eulogy that included this statement:

Religion is in darkness because of the absence of his light [a pun on Nur
   ad-Din's name which meant the 'Light of Religion']
The age is in grief because of the loss of its commander.
Let Islam mourn the defender of its people
And Syria mourn the protector of its kingdom and its borders.[29]

Although Nur ad-Din and Saladin were at loggerheads, the demise of the senior ruler of the Muslim Near East must have provoked considerable uncertainty. In Alexandria, fierce resistance curtailed the Sicilians' initial momentum but, confusingly for the crusaders, there was no sign of support from the kingdom of Jerusalem. In fact, by this time the Christians too had lost their leader. On 11 July Amalric succumbed to an attack of dysentery: Greek, Syrian and Frankish doctors had laboured in vain for several days to save him, but at thirty-eight years old he was laid to rest alongside his brother in the Church of the Holy Sepulchre.

The Reign of the Leper King, Baldwin IV of Jerusalem

The near-simultaneous loss of Nur ad-Din and Amalric obviously had a profound impact upon both Christian and Muslim lands. Saladin provided the Islamic world with an ambitious and experienced figure poised to extend his power and take the holy war to his enemy. On the Frankish side, however, Amalric was succeeded by his thirteen-year-old son, Baldwin IV, and, to exacerbate the inevitable uncertainties of a minority king, the youth was rumoured to have leprosy, the most feared medical condition of the medieval age.[30]

Baldwin would rule for almost eleven years, although at the time of his coronation it is unlikely that the outward symptoms of the illness were visible. William of Tyre described how, when still a boy,

Baldwin was playing with his friends and while the other boys cried out in pain during their fights the prince 'endured it all patiently, as if he felt nothing . . . At first I supposed it proceeded from his endurance, but I discovered that he did not feel pinching or even biting in the least. I began to feel uneasy . . . Repeated fomentations, oil rubs and even poisonous remedies were employed without result . . . For, as we recognised in the process of time, these were the premonitory symptoms of a most serious and incurable disease which became plainly apparent.'[31] Once the king reached puberty the leprosy took a firmer hold and plunged him deeper and deeper into disability, often associated with fevers; the illness would then plateau and he could reassume some level of authority.

As the nobility gathered to elect Amalric's successor, Baldwin's health was already a cause for worry, but the diagnosis was by no means certain – if he proved healthy this would be a terrible slight to the youth. The best compromise was to choose Baldwin and then find his sister Sibylla a husband who could be a suitable regent or king if necessary. Baldwin was duly crowned on 15 July 1174 – the seventy-fifth anniversary of the capture of Jerusalem by the First Crusaders: in theory, an auspicious day. Health aside, the new king was described as a skilled rider, as having a quick mind and a love of stories.

The first man to act as regent during Baldwin's minority was the arrogant and autocratic Miles of Plancy; such traits were entirely inappropriate to the unsettled atmosphere of the time and he was murdered on the streets of Acre.[32] His replacement, Count Raymond III of Tripoli, emerged as one of the most influential and ambitious men of the land, as well as a potential candidate for the throne of Jerusalem on account of his status as the king's cousin. Because our main source, William of Tyre, was a partisan of the count we have a closely observed impression of the man: 'He was a thin man . . . not very tall with dark skin, straight medium-coloured hair and piercing eyes . . . He had an orderly mind, was cautious, but acted with vigour. He was more than averagely abstemious in his eating and drinking habits and although he was liberal to strangers he was not so affable to his own men.'[33] The contemporary Muslim writer Ibn Jubayr saw him as a man of 'authority and position . . . he is qualified to be king . . . he is described as being shrewd and crafty.'[34] Raymond came to head one of the two rival factions who vied for control over the kingdom.[35] The other was led by Baldwin's mother, Agnes. She was a more controversial figure, in part because her gender opened her to some harsh, if stereotypical, criticism. William of Tyre hated her for denying him the premier ecclesiastical job in the land, that of patriarch of Jerusalem. To him, therefore, she was 'relentless in her acquisitiveness and truly hateful to God'.[36] Other writers cast aspersions on her morality. In reality, as Baldwin's mother, Agnes was in a position of considerable influence and her guiding hand was vital in his maintenance of power and resisting the ambitions of Count Raymond.

It is likely that within a year or so of his coronation the king's leprosy became certain and thus it became imperative to find a husband for Sibylla. William Longsword, marquis of Montferrat (in northern Italy, near Turin) appeared an ideal candidate. He was related to the ruling houses of France and Germany and could be expected to represent the interests of Jerusalem at the highest levels. He came to the Levant in November 1176; within weeks Sibylla was pregnant, but in May 1177 William fell ill and died two months later to reopen the issue of regency.[37]

In the meantime Saladin had started his bid to rule the Muslim Near East. He marched to Damascus where he took control of the city and married his former commander's widow – a reasonably common course of action in the Islamic world and a move designed to associate a newcomer with the former regime. Twice Saladin's opponents employed the Assassins to try to murder the sultan although both attempts failed. With Saladin portraying himself as the champion of Sunni orthodoxy, the Assassins were a prime target for suppression. The Shi'ite sect soon found a way to resist: if the Sunni rulers of Aleppo were prepared to tolerate the Assassins' presence around their nearby base at Masyaf, then it was worth trying to kill their common enemy. In the first attack, Assassins infiltrated the sultan's camp only to be recognised as outsiders. In the ensuing scuffle one of Saladin's emirs and several of his soldiers were killed, but the sultan remained unharmed. In May 1176, Assassins again used disguise to penetrate his camp and this time they managed to stab him, but armour under his clothes prevented serious injury. Thereafter Saladin was forced to take highly elaborate precautions against future attempts on his life, including sleeping in a tent on stilts.[38]

Not everything worked in Saladin's favour, however. In the summer of 1177 the arrival of a large crusading expedition under Count Philip of Flanders (following in the footsteps of the four expeditions made by his father, Count Thierry), resulted in a campaign in northern Syria. When Saladin saw the bulk of the Christian army heading away from Jerusalem he moved his own forces up from Cairo to the southern borders of the kingdom near Gaza. Baldwin IV had, unsurprisingly, been left behind, but it now fell to him 'already half dead' as one writer commented, to draw upon his courage and to ride against the Muslims.[39] Saladin was far too confident in his numerical superiority and failed to anticipate any active resistance from the Christians. He neglected to post sentries and when his men forded a stream near Montgisard the Frankish knights charged and destroyed the central section of the Muslim army. One of Saladin's family was killed and the sultan himself only narrowly avoided being slain.[40] While the Franks incurred losses themselves – perhaps as many as 1,000 men died, and 750 were said to have been treated at the Hospital of St John in Jerusalem – in terms of morale this provided a massive boost.[41] News of the triumph reached the West and was widely circulated. Paradoxically, of course, this meant that it became even harder to convince Europeans to help the Holy Land – how could the settlers be *so* desperate for support if they had just won such a great victory?

As her brother performed heroics on the battlefield, Princess Sibylla's period of mourning had come to an end. She had given birth to a baby boy, named Baldwin, but now it was necessary to find her a new husband and potential regent. The settlers turned to their ancestral homeland of France. In a letter to King Louis VII, the leper admitted his terrible infirmities and asked that a powerful French noble be sent to the Levant in order to take charge of the holy kingdom because 'to be deprived of one's limbs is of little help in carrying out the work of government . . . no one can heal me. It is not fitting that a hand so weak as mine should hold power when fear of Arab aggression daily presses upon the holy city and my sickness increases the enemy's daring.'[42] Baldwin tried to lead as best he could and his level of determination was astonishing: by now he could not climb onto a horse unaided and his limbs showed severe deformities.

Romance at the royal household soon brought forward another candidate to marry Sibylla. Guy of Lusignan, a young French knight, caught Sibylla's eye and she set her heart on marrying him. Guy and Sibylla became lovers, yet the princess needed the approval of her brother, who insisted that it was his prerogative to choose the husband of the royal heiress. When the king discovered the affair he was furious and wanted to have Guy stoned to death, but the master of the Knights Templar and other nobles calmed him. In any case, the blossoming relationship could serve a political purpose as well. By coincidence, Raymond of Tripoli was marching towards the kingdom of Jerusalem, a move that seemed to presage a possible coup. His ally, Baldwin of Ibelin, had long admired the princess and was keen to marry her. When the king learned of Raymond's approach he moved quickly to retain control over the situation and authorised the marriage between Guy and Sibylla. The wedding took place in Holy Week 1180, a breach of strict canon law and a sign that there was no wish to delay.[43] Any threat to topple the king required Sibylla to be free to marry and now this possibility had been frustrated. A clear division in the Latin East was apparent with the powerful Ibelin clan lined up with Count Raymond in opposition to Baldwin, Agnes, Guy and Patriarch Heraclius of Jerusalem.

The patriarch was a controversial character and much maligned by William of Tyre, largely because he envied Heraclius for securing the premier ecclesiastical position in the land. The latter seems to have been a rather worldly character, blessed with good looks and some considerable charm with women.[44] He was known to have a mistress, Pasque, the wife of a draper whom he rewarded so richly that the man consented to the affair. After the cuckold died, Heraclius set up Pasque in a fine house and provided her with beautiful clothes and precious jewellery. As she passed by, people would exclaim 'There goes the patriarchess!' On one particularly excruciating occasion a messenger burst into a meeting of the High Court shouting, 'Sir, patriarch, I bring you good news!' Heraclius assumed that this was something for the benefit of the kingdom and asked him to announce it: 'The Lady Pasque has given birth to a daughter!' Not, perhaps, the forum in which a patriarch of Christ's city would have wished such tidings to be broadcast.

The king's leprosy was now acute and the possibility of abdication must have been raised. The High Court urged him to become reconciled to Count Raymond and the two men duly met. Some sense of Frankish unity – however temporary or shallow it turned

out to be – was welcome, especially because one of their most important supporters, the Byzantine Empire, had become hostile. Manuel
Comnenus, whose military might had done much to deter Muslim
aggression, died in September 1180; William of Tyre described him
as 'a great-souled man of incomparable energy'.[45] Within a couple
of years, a backlash against Manuel's pro-western policies produced
a fiercely anti-Frankish stance in Constantinople.[46]

Tensions Rise: Reynald of Châtillon's Red Sea Raid of 1182 and Saladin's Invasions of 1183 and 1184

By mid-1182 the truce had expired and Saladin stepped up the jihad
with an incursion towards Beirut. Stern resistance from the defenders
and the prospect of a Frankish relief fleet prompted the sultan to
withdraw, thus marking a second setback in succession; evidently the
Christians were still highly formidable opponents. In fact, the Franks
soon took to the offensive themselves. Prince Reynald of Antioch,
now a member of the nobility of Jerusalem through his marriage to
the widowed heiress of Transjordan, planned a raid of breathtaking
audacity. Reynald ordered the construction, in kit form, of five galleys
which were transported by camel from Kerak down to the Gulf of
Aqaba, reassembled and then launched. Saladin suspected that the
vessels would be used against the castle of Eilat and the routes across
the Sinai peninsula which linked his Egyptian and Syrian lands. While
he was correct in the former belief, the latter was wrong – Reynald's
plan was far more daring: he directed his men down the Red Sea
where no Christian ship had been seen for centuries and where, in
consequence, there was no Muslim navy or coastal defences.[47] The
Christian fleet was free to prey upon commercial and pilgrim traffic
between Egypt and the Arabian peninsula and could menace the
holiest cities of Islam, Mecca and Medina, the birthplace and the burial
place of the Prophet himself. As Ibn Jubayr, a contemporary Muslim,
wrote, 'it shocks the ears for its impiousness and profanity.'[48] Such a
move sharply compromised Saladin's position as the defender of Islam.
The fact that he was occupied fighting his fellow Muslims in northern
Syria rather than protecting the haj pilgrimage route added to his
embarrassment.

The Christians raided a town on the Egyptian coast, then crossed over the Red Sea and landed north of Jedda where they continued to cause havoc. Some locals feared this signified the approach of the Day of Judgement. Reynald was described as 'the Elephant', a reference to the name of an Abyssinian king who had led a Christian invasion of Mecca in 570.[49] It was believed that he wanted to remove the Prophet's body from his tomb in Medina and the locals sent urgent messages to Cairo. After a few weeks, al-Adil, Saladin's brother (popularly known as Saphadin) managed to get ships of his own transported overland and they chased the Franks down to the Red Sea port of al-Hawa. The Christians were eventually cornered, forced to abandon ship and to flee inland; unbowed, they headed towards Medina. Only a day from the holy city they were trapped in a waterless ravine and either killed or surrendered. The 170 captives were sent throughout Saladin's lands to be publicly executed – a clear contravention of Islamic law that directs the sparing of those who surrender voluntarily. So great was Saladin's fury and embarrassment that he showed no mercy at all. Two of the men were dispatched to Mina, the place where animals are sacrificed in the course of the haj, and there they had their throats cut like sacrificial beasts.[50] Prince Reynald, as the instigator of the plan, was the object of Saladin's greatest anger, however, and the sultan vowed to kill the author of such an affront to Islam.

By 1183 Baldwin's health had started to decline further: he was blind, his hands and feet were severely damaged and he had to be moved around in a litter. When the king was afflicted by a particularly bad fever he formally designated Guy as regent and asked all the nobles to swear homage to him, although he made his brother-in-law promise not to try to take the crown during his own lifetime. The Franks also faced financial problems: the pressure exerted by Saladin had taken a toll on the kingdom's finances and in 1183 a variety of taxes were levied on all its inhabitants, regardless of race, tongue, creed or sex while the gold coinage issued by the crown was also much debased.[51] The resources raised by such measures could be used to hire mercenaries, a contingency that became essential in the summer of 1183 when Saladin – emboldened by finally securing control over Aleppo – invaded. In the face of this crisis Guy summoned the entire military strength of the kingdom as well as enlisting any Italian merchants and western pilgrims who happened to be in the Levant. They marched to the Springs of Sapphoria in central Galilee and then proceeded to shadow the Muslim armies for two weeks before Saladin withdrew. Was this a success, in that the Christians lost no territory and hardly any men? Or was it a humiliation that the largest Frankish army yet assembled barely struck a blow in anger? William of Tyre commented that some nobles had been unwilling to offer Guy good advice because they feared that if he scored a great victory it would be impossible to unseat him. Guy was a victim of his own inexperience and the vicious political rivalry of the time. The ethos of such a militaristic society also counted against passivity, regardless of how effective a strategy it can be judged with hindsight. Criticism of Guy's leadership reached a crescendo, and when Baldwin recovered his health he summoned the High Court of Jerusalem and dismissed his brother-in-law from the regency. By way of sealing his disapproval of Guy's performance the king asked Raymond of Tripoli to lead the army and conduct public business when he was unfit to do so. To help define the succession he also had his five-year-old nephew crowned as his co-ruler, Baldwin V.[52]

In 1183 and 1184 Saladin returned to the offensive with two attempts on the huge castle of Kerak in Transjordan. The first of these sieges took place just after the marriage of Sibylla's younger sister, Princess Isabella (aged twelve) and Humphrey of Toron. In one of the strange instances of chivalric courtesy that – confusingly – lie alongside the rhetoric of holy war, the wedding party sent food down to the besiegers. In return, the couple were accorded the privilege of having the bridal suite exempted from bombardment for one night. More significantly, on both campaigns, the castle resisted Saladin's attacks.[53]

The Final Descent into War

Baldwin continued his effort to prevent Guy taking power, although he worried that as Baldwin V's stepfather he would exercise the regency again. A contemporary source explained that Guy had 'neither the knowledge or ability to govern the kingdom'.[54] King Baldwin turned to Raymond to fulfil this role, although the High Court insisted that the royal castles should be held by the Military Orders, a sign that some feared the count had his own designs on the crown. Raymond in turn insisted that someone other than he should be appointed the personal guardian of Baldwin V in case the child's unexpected death could be blamed on him. Finally, and most intriguingly, it was agreed that if Baldwin V died, the succession – which would rest between Sibylla and Isabella – was to be determined by the joint decision of the pope and the rulers of France, England and Germany. This, in theory at least, marked a startling surrender of authority by the nobles of Jerusalem and was a mark of how divided and seemingly bereft of self-regulation they perceived themselves to be. It reinforced their overt reliance on powerful western rulers for support as well as gesturing towards Christendom's shared responsibility for the defence of the Holy Land.

This emotive issue had been raised by successive embassies to the West during the 1170s and early 1180s. Discouragingly, in 1181, Pope Alexander III had issued a crusade appeal that said: 'the king [Baldwin IV] is not such a man as can rule that land, since he . . . is so severely afflicted by the just judgement of God, as we believe you are aware, that he is scarcely able to bear the continual torments of his body' – a crushing verdict on the settlers' position.[55] In 1184–5 the Franks dispatched the most senior ambassadors they had ever sent to Europe. Clearly the king could not make the journey himself but Patriarch Heraclius of Jerusalem and the masters of the Templars and Hospitallers formed a genuinely prestigious trio.[56] The envoys struggled over the Alps and moved northwards to Paris where they offered King Philip II the keys of the walled city of Jerusalem and the Tower of David. This was an attempt to induce him to emulate the Emperor Charlemagne, the role model for all medieval monarchs, who accepted these symbols in the year 800 and took the city under his protection. In the perilous circumstances of 1185 Philip was well aware of the huge responsibilities this would entail and, given the fragility of his own power in France, he politely declined.

The envoys then crossed the English Channel to seek out King Henry II who, as a man who had made previous promises to crusade and, as the closest living relative of Baldwin IV on the male side of his family, was the most logical target for the embassy. In late January 1185 they met him at Reading Abbey where Heraclius gave an impassioned sermon about the terrible danger in which Christ's land found itself. He also offered Henry the keys to Jerusalem and the Tower of

David, and while the king was said to have shown the objects great devotion he too avoided accepting them. Instead he called an assembly of the churchmen and nobles of England, as well as King William of Scotland, to the Hospitaller headquarters at Clerkenwell in March. Again Heraclius implored his audience to act but it seems that the nobles were unwilling to allow their monarch to leave his kingdom. While the patriarch could make a strong moral case for Henry to journey to the Levant, in reality the situation there was so complex and troubled that it was hardly an attractive proposition. The usual expressions of regret and promises of financial support followed and Heraclius convinced a few English nobles to commit themselves to a crusade, but the large-scale expedition he so desperately desired did not materialise. As an aside, in the weeks between the Reading and Clerkenwell assemblies, the patriarch also consecrated the Temple Church in London, familiar to a wider audience from its place in *The Da Vinci Code*. This circular chapel, designed as a copy of the Holy Sepulchre itself, was a clear signal of the Templars' vocation and their wealth in being able to finance such a fine building.[57]

By the time Heraclius returned to the Levant, however, Baldwin IV had finally – mercifully – passed away: he was buried alongside his ancestors at the foot of Mount Calvary in the Church of the Holy Sepulchre. While one might judge that he held on to power for too long, and that the combination of his unpredictable health and his desire to exercise authority caused serious inconsistencies in the government of the land, it is undeniable that his bravery in confronting a horrific illness induced respect even amongst his enemies. Imad ad-Din wrote that 'in spite of his infirmities they [the Franks] were loyal to him, they gave him every encouragement . . . being satisfied to have him as their ruler . . . they were concerned to keep him in office but paid no attention to his leprosy . . . he was obeyed by them . . . and saw that there was peace amongst them.'[58]

Both Saladin and Raymond of Tripoli wanted a truce and in the spring of 1185 settled upon a two-year arrangement. The sultan used this period to his advantage and in March 1186 he finally persuaded the ruler of Mosul to acknowledge him as overlord and to give him military help if required. His empire now consisted of Egypt, Syria and the Jazira (northern Iraq today, including Mosul) – a vast series of lands, tenaciously assembled and maintained in a loose confederation by Saladin's military strength, his persuasive diplomacy and his repeated calls to jihad and reminders of the duty of good Muslims to evict the Christians from Jerusalem.

In the summer of 1186 Baldwin V died: he had been a sickly child for much of his life and his passing was hardly unexpected. Predictably there were rumours that Raymond now planned to take the throne for himself and he seemed to confirm such suspicions when he tried to gather together the majority of nobles at Nablus. It seems, however, that he had underestimated the level of support for Sibylla, and when a significant number of senior figures, including Prince Reynald and Patriarch Heraclius, assembled for Baldwin's funeral it was this latter group that seized the initiative by backing Sibylla (rather than her younger sister, Isabella, or Count Raymond) as the next monarch. The main stumbling block was Guy, already cast aside by the leper king for his perceived lack of leadership ability. It seems that Sibylla was required to divorce Guy before she could become queen. With the connivance of Heraclius, she agreed to this, on the condition that she alone could select her new husband. Sibylla announced her divorce from Guy and then turned to the assembled nobles and said:

> I, Sibylla, choose as king and husband, my husband: Guy of Lusignan who was my husband. I know him to be a man of prowess and honour, well able, with God's aid, to rule his people. I know too that while he is alive I can have no other husband for, as the Scripture says, 'Those whom God has joined together, let no man put asunder.'[59]

Her dumbstruck audience could only watch in silence as the queen placed the royal crown on Guy's head. Her actions were within the letter of the agreement and this brilliant and breathtakingly audacious move carried the day. Queen Melisende would have delighted in her granddaughter's political acumen and brazen determination to preserve power. This was also a very open show of her love and loyalty towards Guy. Roger of Wendover, an early thirteenth-century English writer, was impressed: 'A most praiseworthy woman, to be commended both for her modesty and for her courage. She so arranged matters that the kingdom obtained a ruler while she retained a husband.'[60] But tensions between Guy's men and the locals continued to emphasise his status as an outsider, and compromised his ability to draw the disparate factions together. After the coronation his Poitevin associates infuriated the people of Jerusalem by singing: 'Despite the *pulains*, we shall have a Poitevin king': *pulain* was a term to describe the second and third generation Frankish settlers in the Levant.[61]

Raymond and the Ibelins were furious at being outfoxed and the count's ambition drove him towards the Muslim camp. He struck a deal that allowed Saladin's army to move through his Galilean lands if, in the future, the sultan would make him king. It almost beggars belief to register that one of the most powerful Frankish nobles was an ally of the leader of the jihad just under a year before the fall of Jerusalem. Quite how Raymond expected this arrangement to tally with Saladin's principles of holy war was unclear. As Ibn al-Athir noted: 'Thus their [the Franks'] unity was disrupted and their cohesion broken. This was one of the most important factors that brought about the conquest of their territories and the liberation of Jerusalem.'[62]

In the winter of 1186 Prince Reynald attacked a caravan crossing his territory in Transjordan, an act contrary to the ongoing truce.[63] When he refused to compensate the Muslims, Saladin had an excuse to fight – not, by this stage, that he was going to do anything else. The pressure he had generated through the creation of his fragile coalition meant that nothing other than all-out holy war would satisfy his allies: if he failed to attack, then his confederation would undoubtedly disintegrate. His forces gathered at Damascus and once the truce had formally expired on 5 April 1187, the sultan began to launch a series of exploratory raids. Thanks to the foolhardy sense of honour of Gerard of Ridefort, Master of the Templars, the Franks soon suffered a major defeat. With a force of only 140 knights and against the advice of his colleagues whom he accused of cowardice, he rashly decided to engage a Muslim army of 7,000. Only three Templars – including, ironically, Gerard – escaped, while other casualties included the master of the Hospitallers, Roger of Moulins. The Battle of Cresson is often overlooked because of the events at Hattin two months later, but the loss of over 100 of the Christians' finest troops, as well as one of their senior commanders, was a significant blow to morale and resources.[64] Saladin's aggression finally pushed Raymond of Tripoli into some form of homage – however superficial – to King Guy, and he duly expelled the Muslims from his lands. Ibn al-Athir noted that after the Battle of

Cresson the count's vassals had threatened to withdraw their allegiance to him if he failed to act.[65]

The Battle of Hattin, July 1187

By the summer of 1187 both sides had gathered their men for battle.[66] The Franks drew together almost the entire military strength of the kingdom of Jerusalem: the Military Orders put forward about 600 knights while only skeleton garrisons remained in the towns and castles. The total Christian force probably numbered around 16,000; Saladin held a worthwhile advantage with at least 20,000 troops, of which perhaps 12,000 were mounted. Once across the River Jordan the sultan presented the Franks with the same dilemma as four years previously – should they fight, taking an even greater risk given the lack of almost any other troops beyond the army in the field? Or should they repeat the strategy of 1183, shadow the Muslims and wait for their forces to break up? Count Raymond appeared to have more to lose than most because on 2 July Saladin's army besieged his wife in the citadel of Tiberias. This carefully calculated test of chivalric resolve was designed to trigger Guy's responsibilities to rescue the wife of his vassal, although at first the ruse seemed unlikely to succeed. The Franks, assembled at their customary muster-point at the Springs of Sapphoria, held firm because to reach Tiberias required a twenty-mile march across an arid plateau in the height of the summer. Ibn al-Athir believed Raymond – ignoring the captivity of his wife – advocated inactivity; he claimed the count argued 'If [Saladin] takes Tiberias he will not be able to stay there and when he has left it and gone away we will retake it; for if he chooses to stay there he will be unable to keep his army together, for they will not put up for long with being kept away from their homes and families.'[67] A council of war on 2 July confirmed this strategy and the camp went to sleep believing that they were to remain at Sapphoria. Late at night, however, Gerard of Ridefort sought a private audience with the king.

In the flickering candlelight of the royal tent, the master of the Templars, who had shown his rampant antipathy towards Islam at the Battle of Cresson three months previously, repeatedly urged the king to fight. He reminded Guy of what had happened the previous time he took a passive approach and that Raymond of Tripoli, the very man who now advocated caution, had been the beneficiary. While the king had been accused of cowardice in 1183 he could now rebut such claims in the most emphatic fashion possible. This discussion was not simply about strategy, however; underlying Gerard's persuasive sugges- tions was a deep personal animosity towards Raymond. Back in the 1170s, when Gerard was a lay knight, the count had promised him a good marriage to the heiress of the castle of Botrun. Yet Raymond reneged on the agreement and gave her to a Pisan merchant in return for her weight in gold. Gerard was hugely insulted to be displaced by an Italian trader and stormed off to Jerusalem where he joined the Templars. Now, a decade later, at this time of crisis, he had a chance to face down his hated rival: 'Sire [Guy], do not trust the advice of the count for he is a traitor, and you well know that he has no love for you and wants you to be put to shame and to lose the kingdom . . . let us move off immediately and go and defeat Saladin.' [68]

Guy vacillated: should he hold to the advice of his council and risk his reputation again, or should he change his mind and act boldly at the risk of losing the Holy Land? In the end it seems the psycholog- ical scars of his earlier humiliation were too deep to ignore and, in a dramatic volte-face, on the morning of July 3 the king commanded the heralds to sound the order to march. The nobles were both horri- fied and amazed; they asked on whose advice such a decision had been taken. Guy sharply rebuffed them and simply told them to obey him and get ready to move.

Under normal circumstances, the twenty miles from Sapphoria to Tiberias was a day's hard march; the problem was that by breaking camp the Franks abandoned their only sure supply of water and then offered themselves up as a very slow-moving target to the Muslim forces – in other words they surrendered the strategic initiative. The vanguard was Count Raymond, in the centre was King Guy and in the rear, the Knights Templar. The Christians advanced eastwards and reached the springs of Turan about seven miles away. This seemed a good place to pause, but they pressed onwards, a move that Saladin himself believed was fatal. In a letter written immediately after the battle he suggested that 'the Devil seduced [Guy] into doing the oppo- site of what he had in mind and made to seem good to him what was not his real wish and intention. So he left the water and set out towards Tiberias . . . through pride and arrogance.'[69] In fact, the springs at Turan were simply insufficient to sustain the Christian army and they had no choice but to keep going. In contrast, to the south, Saladin was comfortably provisioned at the village of Kafr Sabt and now he utilised his superior numbers to divide his troops and sent some to seize Turan and prevent a Frankish retreat. At this point he had effectively surrounded the Christians: 'they were as closely beset as in a noose, while still marching on as though being driven to a death that they could see before them, convinced of their doom and aware the following day they would be visiting their graves', Beha ad-Din grimly observed.[70] The sultan dispatched some of his cavalry to crash into the Templars, a tactic that slowed up the entire march. Time and again Muslim mounted archers poured arrow-fire into the Christian lines, yet the Franks dared not break ranks and charge for fear of losing any sense of order at all. It was no longer possible to reach Tiberias that day and Guy decided to camp overnight on the plateau. A few nearby cisterns offered a little water but the evening brought no real respite after the exertions of the march and the harrowing Muslim arrow-fire. Imad ad-Din offered this excited description of the situation, first recapping the events of the day: 'The day was hot, the [Frankish] people were on fire [with the heat], the midday sun shone with an incessant strength. The troops had drunk the contents of their water bottles and had nothing more. Night separated the two sides and cavalry barred both the roads. Islam passed the night face to face with unbelief, monotheism at war with Trinitarianism, the way of righteousness looking down on error, faith opposing polytheism. Meanwhile several circles of hell prepared themselves and several ranks of heaven congratulated themselves; Malik [the guardian of hell] waited and Ridwan [the guardian of heaven] rejoiced.'[71]

Saladin's troops continued to enjoy plentiful supplies as camels carried barrels of water up from Lake Tiberias. They were boosted further by the delivery of 400 loads of extra arrows intended to kill the remaining Frankish horses and to prevent the Christians from using their famed charge. Morale in Saladin's camp soared – 'they could smell victory in the air and . . . they became more aggressive and daring . . .' Dawn broke at around 4.30 on the morning of 4 July and, as the first fingers of light crept over the hills of eastern Galilee, the exhausted Christian soldiers stirred themselves for another day of torment.[72] Guy's doomed army soon set out yet the Muslims did little to bother them, preferring to wait for the full heat of the day to sap their opponents' strength even further. With the wind blowing towards the Christians Saladin commanded his men to set fire to the dry brush that lay close to the Frankish forces, thus parching their throats even more. Yet another level of distress was generated by the constant drumming and sounding of horns and bugles, a fearsome noise designed to add a sense of hopelessness and disorientation amongst their opponents.

Slowly the Franks trudged forwards but now the Muslim horsemen grew ever closer. Saladin himself rode up and down his lines, encouraging and restraining his men as appropriate. His archers 'sent up clouds of arrows like a swarm of locusts' and killed many of the Frankish horses, while the lightly armoured Christian foot soldiers suffered heavy losses as they dragged their tired and dehydrated bodies eastwards.[73] Controversially, Count Raymond led his own men (around 200 knights) in a charge towards the enemy lines only for the Muslims to open ranks and let him pass through to gallop down the hill away from the main plateau. Some felt this was further evidence of his friendship with Saladin; a more practical interpretation suggests that it made little sense to resist a group of men trying to flee – furthermore, given the lie of the land, they would hardly turn around and try to fight uphill back through the Muslim army. For those Christians that remained, Raymond's escape was a further blow.

The Frankish advance had almost ground to a halt. The foot soldiers' morale was all but broken and they decided to stop and make camp on a hill now known as the Horns of Hattin. This is the crater of an ancient volcano and it still stands proud and isolated on the bare and largely uninhabited plateau. Today, the discordant clank of distant sheep's bells is the only sound to break the silence on this tough, barren landscape. With nothing else to disturb the scene one can pause and imagine the desperate struggle played out below. To the east lie the glittering waters of Lake Tiberias – a tantalising sight for the desperate Christian soldiers; the 'Horns' are formed by the northern and southern sides of the crater, while the western edge of the rim is broken to leave a natural ramp down to the plateau. Back in 1187, the surviving foot soldiers struggled up to the crater where they must have found some shelter from the relentless Muslim bombardment – yet they probably realised as well that there was no chance of escape. Guy knew the knights needed to stay with the archers to have any protection for themselves and, with the king's red tent at their centre, the Christians prepared to play their last cards.

Given their desperate position the Franks had few options open to them – perhaps their best hope was to strike a single decisive blow. The remaining knights gathered together and twice hurled themselves down the slope towards the compact group of Muslim horsemen who guarded Saladin. The plan was to kill the sultan in the belief that if he died then the remainder of his forces would simply crumble away. It was a bold idea that came perilously close to success: certainly the troops around Saladin suffered heavy losses; the sultan himself was said to have been pale with worry and anxiously tugging at his beard. On both occasions, however, the Muslims rallied and forced the Christians back up the hill. After the second of these counter-attacks most of the knights were reduced to fighting on foot while their exertions had only increased their thirst. Down the hill, Saladin's son watched his men surge into the crater. He turned to his father and shouted 'We have beaten them!' Ibn al-Athir reported Saladin's curt response: '"Be quiet! We have not beaten them until that tent falls."' As he spoke Guy's tent crumpled. The sultan dismounted, prostrated himself in thanks to God Almighty and wept for joy.'[74] The Christian cause was broken; Guy himself was taken soon after, as was the True Cross, a huge gold and jewelled object that contained the wood upon which it was believed that Christ was crucified. The spiritual importance of this as the talisman of the Christian army was something clearly understood by the Muslims: 'In their [the Franks'] eyes, its capture was more important than the loss of the king; it was the worst thing that happened to them on the field of battle because that cross was irreplaceable . . . its veneration was their prescribed duty . . . they fainted at its appearance . . . they gave their blood for it. So when the Great Cross was taken, great was the calamity that befell them and their vigour disappeared.'[75]

In the aftermath of the battle Saladin could at last extract vengeance on Prince Reynald.[76] The sultan ordered King Guy and the prince to be brought before him. Exhausted and thirsty the two dishevelled warriors knelt at his feet. Saladin gave Guy a cup of cool, refreshing iced julep water – this was a sign of safe conduct and the king gratefully took it and drank. When the king moved to pass the cup to Reynald, Saladin rebuked him and said that he had not offered a drink to the prince. He then gave Reynald the choice of converting to Islam or facing death: apostasy was never an option and the prince declined the proposal, thereby sealing his own fate. The sultan had not forgotten the insult of Reynald's attack on Medina, nor his raid on the pilgrim caravan, and he struck out with a terrible blow from his scimitar. Some claimed that Reynald died from this, other sources suggest that it severed an arm and Saladin's bodyguards rushed forwards to hack the mortally wounded man to death. In any event, this marked the end of one of the foremost Frankish nobles, a man of mercurial temperament, great military skill, but also unremitting brutality. To some in the West he was viewed as a true martyr and a text titled the *Passio Reginaldi* (*The Passion of Reynald*) was written to lament his death and to urge revenge for his loss.[77]

The captured Templars and Hospitallers fared little better. As the bitterest enemies of Islam and as a religious order who would never convert or pay ransoms, they were doomed. Herded together for a mass execution, their death was especially grisly because Saladin summoned his Sufi holy men to perform the task. These individuals were unaccustomed to wielding blades and so the wretched event became even more prolonged than necessary. Piles of bones were said to have remained visible for years afterwards. The other prisoners – nobles, knights and foot soldiers alike – were shackled together, thirty to a single rope. For the wealthy there was the prospect of ransom, for the others it was the slave auctions of the Middle East, although with such a glut on the market the sellers complained bitterly about low prices. Saladin, meanwhile, sent out messages to proclaim his success and he memorialised his achievement by ordering the construction of a Dome of Victory on the site of the battle.[78]

Saladin Recovers Jerusalem for Islam

The kingdom of Jerusalem now paid heavily for committing so many of its resources to the field at Hattin: the land lay almost defenceless. Saladin's armies swept through the Christian territories and within weeks the majority of settlements had fallen to his men. Only Tyre, Kerak,

Tripoli, Antioch and a few northern castles held out. Jerusalem itself, the ultimate prize, awaited the sultan. 'Islam wooed Jerusalem . . . making heard above the cry of grief from the [Dome of the] Rock . . . the reply . . . to bring the exiled faith back to her own country and dwelling place and to drive away from the al-Aqsa those whom God drove away with his curse. Saladin marched forward to take up the reins of Jerusalem that now hung loose, to silence the Christian clappers and allow the muezzin to be heard again . . . to purify Jerusalem of the pollution of those races, of the filth of the dregs of humanity.'[79]

The few remaining Frankish knights gathered for the final defence of the holy city. Given the enormous disparities between the two armies the Christians knew full well that the situation was hopeless, but out of duty and desperation they had to make a stand. Patriarch Heraclius, Balian of Ibelin and Queen Sibylla led the resistance in a city crowded with refugees from across the Latin East. The leadership ordered the walls to be strengthened and catapults were constructed to help in the fight.

The siege began in late September and for five days the Muslims circled the city looking for a weak spot. They fixed on the northernmost section – ironically at exactly the same point the First Crusaders had broken in eighty-eight years earlier. Fierce exchanges of arrow and artillery fire followed and both sides suffered heavy losses as the Franks made a series of sallies. So extreme was the situation inside Jerusalem that Heraclius actually preached a crusade and formally offered the remission of all sins to those who helped to resist the attack. Strictly speaking, only the pope or his authorised agents could launch a crusade, but in these circumstances the patriarch felt little need to follow protocol.[80] Frankish women cut off their children's hair and priests and nuns processed barefoot around the shrines of Jerusalem to try to convince God to save them, but to no avail.

Soon the Muslims seized the outer defences and a special shield-wall enabled archers to set up a continuous rain of arrow-fire; meanwhile, a group of sappers began to mine the walls. At this point the defenders realised that all was lost and they started to parley. A delegation was sent to ask Saladin for terms, but interestingly – and in complete contrast to the sultan's general reputation for mercy – he reacted angrily and shouted: 'I will treat you only as you treated the inhabitants when you conquered it in [1099], by killing, enslaving and

requiting evil with evil.'[81] Balian requested a personal audience with
Saladin but he met with the same uncompromising response. Perhaps
expecting this, he set out an alternative proposal to the sultan: if the
Christians were not granted their lives then he swore that they would
kill their wives and children, destroy all their property, slaughter the
5,000 Muslim prisoners in their hands and then dismantle the Dome
of the Rock and the al-Aqsa Mosque stone by stone. They would then
sally out and fight with nothing at all to lose to kill as many Muslims
as possible. In other words, Saladin would have to pay such a high
price to avenge the atrocities of the First Crusade that his own achievement would be irrevocably stained, and the holy places of Islam
destroyed.

The leading emirs advised the sultan to offer terms – everyone to
be ransomed within forty days or to be treated as a slave. Men would
be freed for ten dinars, women for five and children for two. Balian
offered 30,000 dinars on behalf of all the poor and this was accepted.
A treaty was sealed and the keys to the city were carried out – at last,
Saladin had achieved his great ambition.[82] On 2 October 1187 the emir
made his formal entry into Jerusalem – by a wonderful coincidence
this was also the anniversary of the Prophet's Night Journey from
Jerusalem into heaven – a cause for even greater celebration. As the
city surrendered to his army and the banners of Islam flew proudly
over the battlements, Saladin could reflect on the thirteen hard years
that he had spent entreating his fellow Muslims to follow the jihad
and reclaim Jerusalem for their faith. Once his troops entered the city
a small group quickly headed for the Dome of the Rock, on top of
which stood a large golden cross. They scrambled to the top of the
dome and toppled the cross to the ground shouting: 'God is great!'
Truly this moment symbolised the triumph of Islam.[83] To emphasise
his victory Saladin had the cross, which was made of copper coated
with gold, sent to the caliph of Baghdad who, in turn, demonstrated
his contempt for Christianity by burying it beneath the threshold of
the Bab al-Nuri Mosque in Baghdad in order that his people could
tread upon it as a sign of disrespect.[84]

The sultan's holy men purified the Dome of the Rock and the al-
Aqsa Mosque (the former headquarters of the Templars) with rose
water and a week after the conquest they held Friday prayers. A
Damascene preacher, Ibn al-Zaki, won a competition (each competitor

had sent in a manuscript of their sermon) to have the honour of giving the first sermon in the al-Aqsa Mosque. He had foreseen the reconquest of Jerusalem ten years before and, dressed in a fine black robe given to him by the sultan, he delivered a powerful piece of oratory. Ibn al-Zaki reminded his audience of the centrality of Jerusalem to Islam as the dwelling place of Abraham, the location for the Prophet's ascent to heaven, the first direction of prayer for Muslims and as the place where mankind will assemble on the Day of Judgement. He compared Saladin's victory to that of the Prophet himself at the Battle of Badr (624) and mentioned the presence of angels, seen in 1187 and reported in 624 as well. He reminded his listeners that the victory was God's doing, not their own, and he encouraged them to stay firm in their jihad. Saladin himself – described as 'the champion and protector of God's holy land' – thoroughly approved of the call for Muslims to stay united for the sake of Jerusalem.[85]

The sultan commanded that Nur ad-Din's great pulpit be brought from Aleppo and installed in its proper place. The workmanship of this object was praised by everyone who saw it, and it stood *in situ* until 1969 when an arsonist destroyed it.[86] Patriarch Heraclius was allowed to leave Jerusalem as a free man; moreover, he was permitted to take many of the riches of his church with him. Some of Saladin's advisers suggested that the sultan should have kept these treasures but he took only the statutory ten dinars. Queen Sibylla was treated courteously and permitted to travel with her retinue to see King Guy in prison at Nablus. Ibn al-Athir recorded that 60,000 men were present in Jerusalem and that most gave the ransom or were covered under Balian's payment. In the end, the 16,000 Frankish men, women and children who could not offer anything were made captive. The local Christians were, however, allowed to stay and keep their houses as long as they paid the customary tribute levied on non-Muslims.

Notwithstanding his earlier determination to kill the defenders of Jerusalem, once he had taken the city Saladin exhibited the courtesy for which he is famed. This particular anecdote is from a Christian source, so there is no danger it was fabricated by one of the sultan's own literary admirers.[87] A group of women and daughters of men killed or captured at Hattin came to the sultan and begged him to tell them which of their menfolk were still alive and in captivity. Saladin ordered an enquiry and, once he had discovered who had survived, he ordered the husbands or fathers of the womenfolk in his presence to be released. To those who were not so fortunate he gave gifts and riches according to their station and 'they praised God and man for the kindness and honour Saladin had shown them.'[88]

As a backdrop to the sultan's victory lay one certainty: the Christian world would respond with a new crusade. A chance event gave that campaign a vital starting point: only one port of real consequence had escaped Saladin's conquests – Tyre. In August 1187 Conrad of Montferrat, a younger brother of William Longsword, Queen Sibylla's first husband, landed there with a few companions. Conrad was completely ignorant of the fall of Jerusalem and Saladin's rapid conquests, yet his arrival gave the knights in Tyre a glimmer of hope and they prevented the Muslims from taking the last remaining maritime outlet in the kingdom. Some have criticised Saladin for his decision to seize Jerusalem before he had secured the strategically crucial coastline. In reality, however, the presence of the marquis at Tyre was purely coincidental and even then, he might well have been defeated. In the event, thanks to Conrad, the Christians preserved the most tenuous handhold imaginable and – crucially – a bridgehead for the next crusade.

6

'Nowhere in the world would ever two such princes be found': Richard the Lionheart, Saladin and the Third Crusade

Richard the Lionheart and Saladin are, above all others, the two figures from crusading history who have captured the popular imagination. Through deed and legend the confrontation between these two colossi of the medieval world has shaped the public perception of the crusading age over the centuries. In the West, a blend of romance and pride in the actions of the mighty warrior Richard are coupled with a whiff of disapproval for his supposed neglect of England during exotic escapades in the Orient; Saladin, meanwhile, is seen as a man of integrity, sophistication and good grace. In the Islamic world, Richard has been pilloried as the man responsible for the cold-blooded slaughter of thousands of Muslims at the siege of Acre – a personification of Christian hatred of Islam; Saladin has emerged as the hero who recovered Jerusalem and then fought off the formidable Third Crusade (1189–92).

It is beyond dispute that eyewitnesses on both sides recognised that the two main players in the Third Crusade were exceptionally charismatic men. They never met face to face because Saladin thought it improper 'to fight after meeting and eating together. If he [Richard] wants to talk, an agreement must be settled before it can happen.'[1] In the course of peace negotiations at the end of the crusade the bishop of Salisbury had a personal audience with the sultan. While previous (and future) accounts of crusades often caricatured and demonised Muslims, the image of Saladin was usually the opposite, a legacy of his behaviour after the siege of Jerusalem and during the Third Crusade. The bishop told Saladin that 'if one were to take your qualities and his [Richard's] together then nowhere in the world would ever two such princes be found, so valiant and so experienced', a neat testimony to both men.[2] Events in the course of the expedition formed Richard's reputation for bravery in battle, a matter of paramount importance to contemporaries: 'He bore himself with indescribable vigour and superhuman courage into the mass of Turks not turning tail for anyone, scattering and crushing all he met; he mows the enemy with a sword as if he were harvesting them with a sickle. It could justly be said of his memorable blows that whoever encountered one of them had no need of a second.'[3] He was compared to the pantheon of ancient, biblical and legendary heroes, Judas Maccabaeus, Achilles, Alexander and Roland. Saladin himself was said to have regarded Richard as too reckless, although perhaps the most interesting assessment of the king was by the sultan's close associate, Beha ad-Din, who noted that he possessed judgement, experience, audacity and astuteness. He wrote: 'Just look at this guile in eliciting what one wants by soft words at this moment and by harsh ones the next! We pray to God to keep the Muslims safe from his evil, for they had never been tried by anyone more devious or more bold.'[4] The recognition of his bravery, combined with political and tactical acuity, offers a pertinent starting point to relate the events of the crusade.

Christendom Responds to the Fall of Jerusalem: King Richard takes the Cross

Saladin's victory at the Battle of Hattin and his subsequent capture of Jerusalem were heavy blows to the people of Europe. Given the dire warnings of previous years, the Franks' defeat was hardly a total surprise but the loss of the True Cross and the holy city itself were hugely traumatic for Latin Christendom: the aged Pope Urban III was reported to have died of shock. As details of events in the Levant filtered back through merchants and refugees, his successor began to formulate a response. Pope Gregory VIII issued the bull *Audita tremendi*, a dramatic and emotional appeal to Christians to help recover Christ's patrimony:

> On hearing with what severe and terrible judgement the land of Jerusalem has been smitten by the divine hand . . . the psalmist laments, 'Oh God, the heathens are come into thy inheritance.' . . . Anyone who does not weep at such a cause for weeping, if not in body, at least in

his heart, would seem to have forgotten not only his Christian faith
. . . but even his very humanity. From the very magnitude of the peril
with those savage barbarians thirsting after Christian blood and using
all their force to profane the holy places and banish the worship of
God from the land . . . What a cause for mourning this ought to be
for us and for the whole Christian people![5]

In contrast to the studied indifference shown to earlier appeals for
assistance, now, at this time of unprecedented crisis, a sense of honour
and Christian duty impelled all the major royal houses of Europe to
act. The first to take the cross (in the late autumn of 1187) was Richard,
count of Poitou and duke of Aquitaine, the eldest son of King Henry
II of England. Contemporaries were impressed: a Limousin troubadour wrote: 'He who is count and duke and will be king has stepped
forward and by that his worth has doubled.'[6] In January 1188 King
Philip II of France and Henry II met to discuss the ongoing differences between them, but when the archbishop of Tyre arrived to
report on the disastrous situation in the East, his impassioned sermon
prompted the two kings to take the cross as well. In March 1188, the
most powerful ruler in Europe, Emperor Frederick Barbarossa of
Germany, took the cross at a huge assembly of nobles and churchmen
at Mainz. Meanwhile, notwithstanding their promise to crusade, Henry
and Philip continued their perennial squabbling until the former's death
in July 1189, and this brought Richard to the throne.

He was crowned at Westminster Abbey on 13 September, aged thirty-
two, a man of mercurial character and a far more complex individual
than the compulsive warmonger he is so often perceived to be.[7] Few
details are known of his appearance: some writers say he was tall,
long-limbed and with red-golden hair – a suitably heroic combination.
Around the time of his death, however, he was described by an eyewitness as overweight and pale. Richard was certainly highly literate and
he was fluent in Latin, as well as the Occitan tongue of his upbringing.
He also enjoyed music and wrote highly competent troubadour songs
– his mother was, after all, Eleanor of Aquitaine, patroness of the
greatest writers of the day who included Chrétien de Troyes, the
author of *The Knight of the Cart* (*Lancelot*) and *The Story of the Grail*
(*Perceval*), the latter being the basis of the entire Holy Grail myth.[8] In
terms of personality, Richard could have the most volcanic temper.

In Sicily, for example, he could not defeat an old rival in a tournament and completely lost his cool, commanding the man never to show his face in his presence again. On the other hand, he was very generous to his followers and to favoured religious foundations. He was said to be conventionally pious, attending Mass daily and, unsurprisingly, enjoyed church music. By the time of the crusade he was also a hugely experienced military man who had fought and trained for many years. Two particular forms of warfare dominated his life: most typical was the raid, or *chevauchée*, a rapid incursion into enemy lands designed to destroy crops, seize booty and break morale. Richard had also besieged numerous towns and castles during his struggles with both his father and Philip in south-western France. The most obvious gap in his military curriculum vitae was battles; in fact he had fought in only one prior to the Third Crusade, in southern France in 1176. The reason for this was, as a writer earlier in the century had noted: 'the rewards of victory could be won by other means which did not involve the penalties of defeat.'[9] Without wishing to state the obvious, the hand of fate could deliver a calamitous blow. The fate of King Harold of England in 1066 showed that the loss of a ruler might mean immediate disaster for his people and it is striking how rare pitched battles were in western Europe during the twelfth century. Copies of the late fourth-century military manual of Vegetius, *De re militari*, were in existence at the time and this advised that a battle should only be fought with a four-to-one manpower advantage. On this basis, caution was the guiding principle behind much of Richard's strategy during the crusade – although such an approach did not extend to situations where the king acted in response to the initiatives of others, as we will see at Jaffa, for example. Contemporary ideas of chivalry and honour were other aspects of the king's upbringing that are visible in Richard's actions in the Holy Land. A highly developed – perhaps oversensitive – appreciation of prestige and standing were further, very prominent, features of the king's personality.

Once his coronation was over Richard began to organise the affairs of his realm and to plan his crusade. Under Henry II, England had evolved the most sophisticated royal administration of the day and this meant the crown could collect substantial revenues, much of which could be spent on the new campaign. Records survive to show some of the preparations Richard made.[10] He clearly appreciated the need for proper reserves of money, food and weaponry – all matters that the monarchs on the Second Crusade had conspicuously failed to address. Thus, he gathered 14,000 cured pig carcasses from Essex and Lincolnshire, 50,000 horseshoes from the Forest of Dean, as well as immense stores of cheese, beans and wine.

The Second Crusade had struggled to cross Asia Minor and with the Byzantines now hostile to the West and, as we shall see, the army of Frederick Barbarossa likely to consume most of the available supplies en route, the English and French kings resolved to sail to the Levant. This decision enabled Richard to eliminate the poor and unarmed pilgrims who had so hampered the previous crusade because places on ships were limited and had to be paid for. In total a force of around 17,000 set out from England and Wales. At Vézelay in June 1190 Richard and Philip agreed to share the profits of conquest evenly, although even this apparently simple arrangement proved a fertile source of controversy.

King Guy of Jerusalem and the Survival of the Holy Land

While these preparations got underway, several smaller expeditions had already reached the eastern Mediterranean hoping to bring relief to the beleaguered defenders of the Holy Land. Their initial target was the port of Tyre, held by Conrad of Montferrat. With King Guy still in captivity, the marquis had assumed de facto control of the remaining settlement in the kingdom of Jerusalem. He issued charters to the Genoese (long-standing allies of his) and granted them commercial rights in the city in perpetuity.[11] In late 1187 Saladin made a second attempt to take the port when he sent in forces by land and sea. The sultan tried to exert emotional pressure on Conrad by offering to exchange Conrad's father, William the Elder, taken captive at Hattin, in return for the city. The Muslims paraded William in front of the walls only for Conrad to shoot at him with a crossbow. When Saladin threatened to kill the prisoner the marquis is said to have retorted that this would be a good thing because a wicked man would have a good end and he would have a martyr as a father. A few days later the Christians broke the naval blockade and the Frankish knights drove the land-based Muslims from the walls; on 1 January 1188 Saladin retreated.

King William II of Sicily dispatched a fleet of fifty galleys and 500 knights and these forces helped to keep Tripoli and Antioch in Christian hands, as well as reinforcing Tyre. In May 1188 Saladin decided to release King Guy. He was liberated near Tortosa, in northern Syria on condition that he swore to give up his kingdom and go overseas. Guy chose to interpret the latter clause in a rather confrontational fashion and sailed the few hundred metres to the island of Ruad, just offshore from Tortosa claiming this fulfilled the letter of the agreement. He then waited for his beloved Queen Sibylla. They had been allowed to meet once, at Nablus, when the king was a prisoner. Within a few days the queen arrived and 'they exchanged kisses, they intertwined embraces, their joy elicited tears, and they rejoiced that they had escaped the disasters which had befallen them.'[12] Guy, however, remained a king without a kingdom. Conrad refused to let him enter Tyre and continued to exercise full power himself. Guy's supporters gathered at Tripoli and after failing to gain entry to Tyre, marched on southwards to Acre, the best port on the coast.

To lay siege to Acre was an audacious ploy: at first the Muslim defenders could not even understand why the Christians had appeared, and when they realised the king's plan they started to jeer him. Guy's forces numbered about 9,000, of whom 700 were knights; he was also joined by a Pisan fleet that swiftly blockaded the city by sea. The Christian land army pitched camp on nearby Mount Turon and started to dig in. Saladin had not expected that Guy, the man most believed responsible for the defeat at Hattin, would take the battle to the Muslims in such an outrageous fashion. Within three days the sultan's army arrived and he quickly established his own forces, therefore 'those who had come to besiege were themselves besieged'.[13] Thus began the siege of Acre, a visceral, gruelling struggle that would last for over two years.

The Christians were soon reinforced by a substantial fleet from northern Europe, as well as more Sicilians and Italians. The Templars and the Hospitallers sent in contingents, and even Conrad joined the battle – he could hardly let his rival take all the glory for himself. By early 1190 the two men were, in theory at least, reconciled when the marquis recognised Guy's title, although he kept Tyre for himself.

In spite of repeated Muslim attacks the Christians were now, literally, entrenched. They constructed palisades, fortifications and all the necessary support networks to live and fight. The Germans set up a horse-driven milling machine; people planted herbs and crops and markets began to operate. Similarly, the Muslim camps acquired the attributes of a permanent settlement such as marketplaces, cookhouses and, so it was reported, 1,000 baths, created by digging holes in the ground, lining them with clay and filling them with hot water.[14]

With the stream of newcomers helping to cushion any Frankish losses, conditions for the Muslims inside Acre began to deteriorate substantially. All the time the siege dragged on, Saladin had to maintain a credible army in the field. Naturally, he still retained a considerable residue of prestige from his achievements at Hattin and Jerusalem, but he continued to face an immense challenge in trying to control a diverse group of forces, some of whom were less than devoted to his leadership. Ibn Jubayr wrote of the sectarian tensions he witnessed within the Muslim Middle East in the mid-1180s as Saladin struggled to hold together his fragile coalition.[15] The majority were not professional soldiers and needed to return home at harvest time and to be paid. The victories of 1187 had provided large sums of money, but now Saladin was on the defensive, his sources of income in decline. Most worrying of all was the response of the West. The smaller waves of crusaders were troublesome enough: still to come were the forces of the three greatest Catholic monarchs of the day. The sultan knew the western armies were gathering strength and, eventually – inevitably – a potentially devastating response would descend upon him.

The Expedition of Frederick Barbarossa

The first, and potentially the most powerful, of these campaigns was the crusade of Emperor Frederick. Frederick had thirty-six years' experience as the ruler of the largest and wealthiest lands in Christendom. Known as Barbarossa on account of his close-cropped red beard, he was a veteran of the Second Crusade's troubled march over Asia Minor and the failed siege of Damascus. Strangely, however, he chose to repeat a landward march. He could have commissioned a fleet from the Venetians (with whom he was on good terms) but decided to lead his forces of perhaps 30,000 through Byzantium and across the Seljuk Empire. One source claimed Frederick feared a prophecy that he would die in water – something that would prove uncannily accurate, regardless of the route he selected.[16] The march through Hungary went according to plan but the Byzantine emperor, Isaac Angelos, had an alliance with Saladin and tried to hinder the German advance. Frederick knew that he was militarily stronger than the Greeks and bullied the Byzantines into submission; thus he entered Seljuk lands in good order. By the late spring of 1190, however, he was finding the crossing of Asia Minor far harder. Arrangements for food supplies collapsed and the Turks constantly harassed the German crusaders. The Anatolian plateau was almost waterless and many of the knights' horses died in this barren landscape; troop losses started to mount dramatically too. In mid-May the army reached the Seljuk capital of Iconium where, in spite of their weakened condition, the Germans took the city. The emperor negotiated proper supplies and then continued southwards towards Christian Armenia. By this point, Saladin was feeling enormous trepidation.[17] The siege of Acre continued to soak up large numbers of his men yet he needed to send troops northwards to confront the imminent arrival of the Germans. The sultan tried hard to reinvigorate his people with the spirit of jihad and he looked to the caliph of Baghdad for further backing; on this occasion he was successful and the nobles of northern Syria and Iraq dispatched contingents to help resist the infidel.

Good fortune soon gave the sultan a vital boost: on 10 June 1190 Frederick tried to cross the River Saleph in southern Cilicia. He slipped and drowned; thus he died in water, as foretold. More seriously, this was a calamitous blow to the Christian cause. His death extinguished morale in the German crusade and many knights returned home. Some carried on to Acre but they had been grievously weakened by their ordeal in Asia Minor. The arrival of a figure possessing Frederick's authority had the potential to end the siege of Acre and his unparalleled status would probably have prevented the political tensions that hampered relations between the French and English crusaders. As the sultan's administrator, al-Fadil, perspicaciously observed: 'if [Frederick] is broken, as it is said, then after him the unbelievers will be building on a shattered foundation.'[18] Saladin himself was hugely relieved to avoid a confrontation with the mighty Barbarossa.

The Siege of Acre: Attrition, Disease and Stalemate

For a short while at least, the sultan could breathe a little easier – it would be another year before the next wave of crusaders arrived. In the meantime the siege of Acre dragged on; conditions over the winter of 1189–90 became so bad that the armies could not fight. Such close engagements inevitably saw long periods of inactivity and rather like the famous football match across the trenches between German and English troops in World War I, the adversaries in this holy war began to interact. Beha ad-Din wrote: 'They got to know one another, in that both sides would converse and leave off fighting. At times people would sing and others dance, so familiar had they become over time, and then after a while they would revert to fighting.'[19]

Starvation and disease were inevitable bedfellows of such grim conditions. People began to hoard food and the cost of the most basic provisions rocketed. The poor ate grass and herbs, horses were worth more dead than alive and no part of the dead animal was left to waste; people who fell in battle were reckoned more fortunate than those who perished slowly by famine and illness. The only thing available in any reasonable quantity was wine, but those who overindulged were weakened even further. The wealthy organised collections for the less fortunate but it was the arrival of a grain ship that saved the day for the crusaders. In the winter of 1190 excessive rains prompted an epidemic of some tortured form: the soldiers' limbs swelled up, people's teeth fell out and then they succumbed to an agonising death. Large numbers of crusaders perished and amongst the most significant fatalities were Queen Sibylla and her young daughters. This tragedy reignited the succession issue because Guy was king only by right of marriage and the bloodline of the royal house now passed to Sibylla's younger sister, Isabella. Conrad's ambition to become king was ever more manifest – aside that is, from the inconvenient matters of his own earlier marriages to an Italian woman and Theodora Angelos of Byzantium, as well as the existence of Isabella's husband, Humphrey lord of Toron. Humphrey had turned down a chance to become king in 1185 and his opponents taunted him for a stammer and his alleged effeminacy:

As nature doubts whether to make a man or girl,
You are born, O lovely, a boy who's almost a girl.[20]

Conrad exploited the fact that Isabella and Humphrey had been betrothed when she was only eight and married at eleven; this was under the age of consent which meant the union was therefore void. Conrad is said to have abducted Isabella – described as a beautiful young woman with a pale face and black hair, devoted to her husband – and then bribed various churchmen to annul the marriage to Humphrey and to preside over the new union. Many of the ecclesiastical hierarchy were outraged – aside from the alleged abduction, Conrad was an adulterer, a bigamist; furthermore the marriage was technically incestuous in canan law because Isabella's sister had been wedded to Conrad's brother, William Longsword. Guy, of course, continued to claim that he was the crowned king of Jerusalem: all of this meant that when Richard and Philip arrived in the Holy Land they would need to decide who was the rightful monarch.

Saladin, meanwhile, tried ever harder to dislodge the Christian army, aware that Acre was by far the best bridgehead for the crusaders. He repeatedly appealed for the support of his co-religionists and he urged the caliph of Baghdad to encourage people to help him: 'In the presence of a clear danger, Muslims remain indifferent in giving aid to their comrades, yet those around us [the crusaders] are inflamed by zeal. The times are hard and demand tough, merciless men: this war is unlike other wars, it needs seasoned and brave troops . . . where are the Muslims? God forbid that they are abandoning Islam.'[21] The sultan certainly led by example, sharing in the privations of his troops and doing much to create his reputation for justice and generosity. While we must beware of the tendency of Saladin's biographers to exaggerate their subject's qualities, the basic principles of his behaviour can be clearly recognised in the reports of Christian contemporaries too. In early April 1191 his men captured a group of Franks, including an extremely old man without a tooth left in his head. Saladin asked, through his interpreter, why he had come to the Levant at such an age: 'to go on pilgrimage to the Sepulchre' came the reply. The sultan was so impressed with the man's devotion that he gave him gifts, a horse, and freed him.[22] Two months later – with the siege of Acre about to reach its denouement – a Christian woman was brought before him by the Muslim guards. Raiders had taken her three-month-old infant from the Frankish camp to sell at a slave market. The mother was understandably grief-stricken but the crusader princes mentioned Saladin's mercy and advised her to ask for help. She explained the situation to the sultan who ordered that the infant be found. He learned that it had been sold and so instructed the buyer to be refunded the purchase price and then handed the baby over to its mother. Beha ad-Din watched as mother and baby were reunited – the whole of the sultan's retinue wept for joy; mother and baby were then escorted back to the Christian camp.[23]

King Richard and King Philip: Crusading Rivals

Back in the West, the main crusader armies were almost ready to set out. Philip had made a contract with the Genoese to transport his force of 650 knights to the Levant and he reached Sicily in September 1190. Part of Richard's forces sailed directly to the Levant but the king and most of his troops went to Messina in Sicily where he would stay from September 1190 until April 1191. Appeals from the Holy Land begged Richard to get going but, in spite of the desperate situation at Acre, his thorough and cautious approach meant that he resolved other issues before continuing eastwards. The time spent in Sicily allowed the king to gather even more money and resources and to organise his own marriage – although not in a way many had anticipated.

The contrast in the arrival of the two kings reveals much about their respective characters and the amount of money each had. Philip sailed in with no fanfare at all, but Richard arrived 'with great ships and galleys, in such magnificence and to such a noise of trumpets and clarions that a tremor ran through all who were in the city. The king of France and his men and all the chief men, clergy and people of Messina stood on the shore, wondering at what they had seen and heard about the king of England and his power.'[24] In theory, Philip was Richard's overlord but reality seemed to demonstrate that the junior partner had a much greater profile and far more money – something that Muslim writers would also notice as the crusade wore on.[25] It was, however, the issue of the English king's marriage that created the greatest tension. Richard had been betrothed to Philip's sister Alice since they were children. Now, however, Richard wished to secure the southern borders of Aquitaine and through the work of his mother, Eleanor, arranged to marry Berengaria of Navarre. Eleanor, by now in her late sixties, had a particularly close relationship with Richard. Aside from her son's strategic aims, she also wished him to spurn Alice because she was the daughter, by a later marriage, of her first husband, Louis VII. Eleanor duly travelled to Navarre to collect the bride and then escorted her to southern Italy to present her to the king. Once this was done, Eleanor returned to England to share the regency of the land with a senior churchman. Not content with rejecting Alice, Richard chose – rather crassly – to compound the insult to the French princess' honour by claiming, almost certainly unfairly, that she had slept with his father, Henry II. So offensive was this rumour that, from this time onwards, it practically crippled the Anglo-French relationship. In fact, it was deemed necessary to wait until Philip had departed from Sicily before it was safe to bring Berengaria over to Messina.

Richard had another specific aim during his stay in Sicily. Tancred of Lecce, who ruled the island, owed him a considerable sum of money from the dowry of Richard's sister, Joan, wife of Tancred's predecessor, William II (d.1189). The Sicilian was unwilling to repay this and in response Richard stormed the capital city of Messina and flew his banners above the walls until Tancred complied. The two men then exchanged gifts to seal their goodwill. In the course of this diplomacy the king mentioned that he had with him Excalibur, the sword of King Arthur, the hero of medieval romances and celebrated king of Britain. It had been 'found' by monks of Glastonbury Abbey and presumably Richard had brought it with him as a symbol of his own standing and self-image. Tancred admired the sword and asked if he could have it – Richard agreed and in return accepted four large transport ships and fifteen galleys.[26] Such an unsentimental exchange of this talismanic item shows the Lionheart's calculating, organisational streak and his determination to achieve victory.

Practical matters notwithstanding, in the course of his stay at Messina the king was moved by the spiritual purpose of his campaign as well. For all Richard's macho politicking he remained a pious Christian and Roger of Howden recorded a moment when the king was overcome by his own sinfulness. He called all the clergy with him to assemble and then, naked, he threw himself to the floor and, holding three scourges, confessed his sins to them.[27] In this context, we can see the power and attraction of the papal indulgence that offered a crusader the remission of all his sins.

Winter weather meant it was impossible to leave Sicily until the spring of 1191. Philip of France was the first to depart, setting sail on 30 March and reaching Acre four weeks later. This provided the major injection of men, food and equipment the Christians so desperately needed. Philip's status meant that he was accorded a magnificent reception and the presence of figures such as Count Philip of Flanders (who had been to the Holy Land in 1177–8) and Duke Hugh of Burgundy added to the sense of anticipation amongst the Franks of the Levant.

The French constructed screens covered in polished iron to protect their crossbowmen and they launched a fierce bombardment towards the walls of Acre. Philip ordered specialist miners to dig under a section of the battlements. They shored up the passage, set it on fire and brought the wall down; a contingent of knights scrambled through the breach but were forced back. It became clear to the defenders that they were near breaking point and they communicated this to Saladin in the main camp. Some writers indicate that Philip could have taken the city without Richard's presence but the French king decided to wait in order for them to share in the conquest, as agreed at Vézelay. The meaning of this arrangement became sorely tested in the aftermath of Richard's journey from Sicily to Acre. As the fleet passed Cyprus a storm blew up and drove ashore the ships of Joan and Berengaria where they were seized by Isaac Comnenus, the ruler of the island. Isaac was a renegade member of the Byzantine imperial family and another ally of Saladin; foolishly he started to threaten his prisoners. 'Not unnaturally we were spurred to revenge', wrote Richard, who landed his own forces and quickly took Limassol.[28] Isaac fled but Richard soon captured his opponent, bound him in silver chains in recognition of his status, and packed him off to the Hospitaller castle of Marqab in the principality of Antioch.[29] By chance, therefore, the king had acquired a rich, fertile land that was a perfect springboard for future crusades. Cyprus later became a place of refuge for those driven from the mainland and acted as a prominent and long-standing part of the Catholic presence in the eastern Mediterranean. It may seem contradictory that Richard had taken the lands of a fellow

Christian, but Isaac was in alliance with the Muslims and had reputedly maltreated his prestigious female prisoners because of their allegedly heretical, that is non-Orthodox, beliefs. In the short term, Richard saw Cyprus as a source of money and he imposed a punitive levy of fifty per cent on all possessions. When his own administration ran into trouble, the king promptly sold the island to the Templars for 100,000 bezants, thus raising the prospect of an independent territory owned by the warrior-monks. What this sale also meant was that Richard had refused to share the profits of his conquest with Philip. This seemed contrary to their agreement at Vézelay but Richard claimed that it only applied to gains made in the Holy Land and not en route, a provocative reading of the terms that only served to increase Philip's animosity towards his rival.

Richard married Berengaria at Limassol on 12 May 1191. Soon after the festivities he was visited by King Guy, himself a Poitevin. Guy's opponent, Conrad, had already secured the support of his relative, King Philip, and now the nominal ruler of Jerusalem pledged homage to the English monarch. Thus the two rivals in the Holy Land had each linked up with one of the antagonistic crusading kings to add a further dimension to the intrigues of this campaign.

Richard in the Holy Land: Triumph at Acre

On 8 June 1191 Richard received a rapturous reception as he landed at Acre. 'The most valiant of kings has arrived, the best warrior in all of Christendom . . . Their trust was in King Richard', as one writer commented.[30] With barely a hint of irony, Richard of Devizes suggested that 'the king was greeted with as much joy as if he had been Christ himself returning to earth to restore the kingdom of Israel.'[31] The Christians had bragged about his strength and when he appeared amidst great pomp and ceremony with twenty-five galleys full of men, stores and weapons, 'his coming', reported Beha ad-Din, 'had a dread and frightening effect on the hearts of the Muslims.'[32] King Philip paid his men three gold bezants a month: Richard immediately showed his wealth and his competitive nature by offering four to anyone who would join his troops.[33] Further supply ships followed, this time containing his siege equipment. The Christians were greatly encouraged and launched a fierce assault on the walls of Acre but Muslim resistance remained strong. Catapults named 'Bad Neighbour' and 'The Catapult of God' launched a relentless barrage of stones (some brought especially from Messina) into the city. Within Acre, a catapult known to the crusaders as 'Evil Cousin' inflicted much damage to the Frankish machines and other weapons discharged Greek fire. Sometimes, they caught the Christians off guard and managed to destroy a ram or catapult. The crusaders faced not simply the defenders of Acre, but Saladin's troops as well. When those in the city were under attack they would sound a drum to signal their co-religionists behind the Christians to launch an assault of their own. As the three armies pounded away at each other, the defenders of Acre grew ever more desperate; the Christians continued to exert maximum pressure on the walls, but still had to defend themselves from fierce attacks by Saladin's men. The sultan sent in a huge supply ship with 650 fighting men to try to break into the harbour at Acre and to bolster the defenders. It was met by an English fleet and in spite of destroying some of these vessels it was forced to scuttle itself rather than have its cargo fall into Christian hands.

Briefly, in late June, the Christians lost momentum. Both Richard and Philip fell ill with 'arnaldia', possibly scurvy, and had to take to their beds. Richard was determined not to let this deflect him and he ordered himself carried to the walls in a great silken quilt and there, protected by a screen, fired his crossbow at the city. Needless to say, such resolution was inspirational to his troops. A fortification in the north-east of the city known as the 'Accursed Tower' became the focus of Richard's efforts and he offered two, then three, and then four gold bezants to anyone who could remove a block of stone from it. Meanwhile his engineers dug a mine underneath, only to find a Muslim counter-mine blocking their path. The defenders burst through into the Christian tunnel: in such a cramped, dark space, with the tunnel held up by temporary pit props, it must have been a confusing and especially terrifying fighting environment; the two forces agreed a mutual truce and the crusaders had to withdraw.

Finally the 'Accursed Tower' was brought down, but still the Muslims resisted: 'had they not been infidels no better people could have been seen', marvelled the eyewitness Ambroise.[34] By now, however, the walls of Acre had been pounded, pierced and shattered so many times that the situation had become truly untenable. The defenders sent another envoy to Saladin to ask that he make peace with the Christians to save them from even greater distress. The sultan's own forces were losing heart and his secretary reported that it was getting ever harder for him to persuade them to fight. Negotiations began but Saladin could not agree to the crusaders' demands. Matters were to be taken out of his hands, however. The garrison became so desperate that they unilaterally struck a deal with Conrad of Montferrat to surrender. The terms included: their own freedom in return for the city, the handover of all its siege engines, equipment and ships, 200,000 dinars, 100 specified prisoners and 1,500 unnamed captives from Saladin's jails, and, most prized of all, the return of the True Cross. Certain hostages would also be given by the Muslims and the obligations were to be fulfilled within a month.[35] A swimmer escaped from Acre to bring this unwelcome news to the sultan on the morning of 12 July 1191. He was devastated by this turn of events – his authority had been ignored and he was to be bound by a treaty that he had not consented to. He was about to send a message telling those in Acre to wait, but at that very moment 'the banners of Unbelief, its crosses, emblem and beacon were raised over the walls of the city.'[36]

At last the crusaders had achieved their goal: the defenders marched out, although their resolute bearing surprised and impressed the Christians because in spite of their terrible ordeal they made no outward sign of sorrow or humiliation. The crusaders then entered the devastated port, crying out with joy and giving thanks to God for their success. Richard's and Philip's banners were raised over the walls and towers and the city's contents and property divided equally. The only note of discord was an incident that concerned Duke Leopold V of Austria – a veteran of Frederick Barbarossa's crusade – who, by this point, had been fighting at Acre for almost two years. As a noble of considerable standing he felt entitled to fly his banner from the walls as well – King Richard disagreed because he did not want a mere duke to share any part of the triumph and the Austrian standard was 'cast into the dirt and trampled upon as an insult.'[37]

As we saw earlier, the simmering rivalry between King Guy and Conrad of Montferrat over the throne of Jerusalem was paralleled in the tension between Richard and Philip. As a partisan of Conrad's, the French ruler proposed to hand over all his acquisitions to the marquis – Richard felt this was wrong and that Guy, as the king, was the appropriate beneficiary.

The need to settle the crown became even more pressing with the news that Philip intended to return home forthwith. Rigord, one of the few near-contemporary French sources to comment on the crusade, explained this by reference to the king's continued ill health and irritation at the arrogance of Richard; however, some writers note that he wished to assert his rights to Flanders, a land without a ruler since the death of Count Philip at Acre on 1 June.[38] None of these ideas are mutually exclusive and in the absence of an eyewitness account taking Philip's part it seems reasonable to assume a combination of all three reasons. This was a propaganda gift to the English chroniclers and they scorned the move: 'What an extraordinary way of discharging a vow, when he had hardly entered the country and had such brief triumphs against the Turks!'[39] While Philip spent a considerable amount of money on the siege of Acre and his efforts there proved highly important in the capture of the city, some commentators argued that as the most prestigious monarch present he had a particular responsibility to lead the recovery of the Holy Land. In spite of many efforts to make him change his mind, Philip resolved to leave on 1 August. Four days prior to then, a compromise was arranged over the succession to Jerusalem. It was agreed that Guy should hold the throne for his lifetime but because Conrad had married Isabella, the legitimate heiress to the kingdom, on Guy's death the crown would go to his rival. This arrangement preserved Guy's status as the crowned and anointed monarch but recognised the legitimacy of Conrad and Isabella's wedding, endorsed the royal bloodline and, de facto, noted Conrad's popularity and military strength.

Just before he embarked for home Philip swore that he would not attack Richard's lands or people while he was away – as a crusader, in theory, the king of England's territory was under the protection of the Church. As time would show this was not a promise that Philip kept, and the threat of his interference in Angevin lands proved a constant distraction for Richard over the next couple of years. The bulk of the French crusaders remained in the East, now under the command of Duke Hugh of Burgundy.

As Richard oversaw the reconstruction of Acre's defences the Muslims dragged out fulfilling the terms of surrender. Saladin seemed in no hurry to gather the Frankish prisoners together or to locate and hand over the True Cross. Several weeks passed by and after repeated requests for information, Richard believed that Saladin was simply

playing for time. The longer Richard remained at Acre, the better the
sultan could prepare his defences elsewhere and gather more men to
attack the crusaders on their march south. Around 19 August Richard
called a council to debate the matter and the meeting resolved to kill
all the Muslim prisoners, excepting the most important who could be
ransomed. The following day 2,700 men were marched out in front of
Saladin's camp and beheaded in cold blood. The stark, straightforward
brutality of this act is one of the most controversial incidents of the
entire crusading period. One hundred years later, in June 1291, the
slaughter of Christians at Acre was justified by the Muslims as revenge
for Richard's actions; modern commentators also cite it as a landmark
of western savagery.[40] Why, then, did the king and his council order
such an act? Some writers state that it was done to avenge the thousands of Christians who died at the siege of Acre between 1189 and
1191, although this seems rather a long delay between the capture of
the city and the executions for such an emotional response. Practical
strategic reasons were probably more prominent – even Beha ad-Din
mentioned both Saladin's hesitation and the fact that the Christians
would not want to guard and feed so many prisoners with the main
army absent to the south.[41] With every passing day the king could see
the impetus from his victory ebbing away. The chance to capitalise on
this hammer blow to Saladin's prestige was fading and the Muslims
were obviously steeling themselves to make his next task even harder.
Seen in these terms, Saladin's delaying tactics gave the crusaders little
choice. While one could indicate that the sultan had butchered knights
of the Military Orders after the Battle of Hattin, his eventual decision
to show mercy to the inhabitants of Jerusalem was some form of counter-
balance. Some westerners condemned the episode; for example,
Ansbert, the author of an account of Frederick Barbarossa's crusade,
and Sicard of Cremona argued that they should have been made slaves.[42]

To the watching Muslims the slaughter of their friends and co-
religionists was an appalling and horrific experience. While the
struggle at Acre had been extraordinarily hard there is no doubt that
the massacre of so many prisoners in such a terrible fashion ratch-
eted up the religious intensity of the conflict considerably. Over the
next few months, any crusaders – men or women – unfortunate
enough to fall into Muslim hands were summarily executed – this
need for vengeance demanded an outlet.[43]

Within Acre itself, boredom had taken hold of the crusaders. Churchmen complained that the men became consumed by lust: prostitutes were readily available and this, combined with heavy drinking, had brought on a collapse in morality. The authorities acted and when the orders to march south were given the only women permitted to travel were elderly laundresses and flea-pickers.[44]

The March to Jaffa and the Battle of Arsuf

On 22 August the host set out along the coast in immaculate formation. King Richard was in the vanguard, King Guy and the Military Orders were in the centre with the French contingent at the rear. A baggage train marched between the fighting men and the sea and those who carried the equipment often swapped duties with colleagues in the main force to share the burden. Alongside the army a fleet provided essential supplies; this in itself was a feat worthy of praise because the prevailing wind in the eastern Mediterranean runs from south to north, requiring the ships to tack into the breeze.

The conditions on the march were terrible – the heat was oppressive and there was constant harassment from the Muslims. Ambroise vividly described the Muslim way of fighting, praising their horses: 'there are no better anywhere in the world; they seem to fly like swallows', and cursing their tactics: 'When the Turk is followed he cannot be reached. Then he is like a venomous fly; when chased he flees; turn back and he follows.'[45] Beha ad-Din admired the Christians' stoicism as they endured a relentless series of forays and suffered constant bombardment with arrows and missiles, a scene played out to a constant throbbing drumbeat and the braying of bugles. Losses of horses were particularly grim and the crusaders themselves began to resemble pincushions with as many as ten arrows or crossbow bolts protruding from their chain mail. Ambroise claimed that 'never did rain or snow or hail falling in the heart of winter fall so densely as did the bolts which flew and killed our horses – many would know if I was lying; there you could have gathered the bolts in armfuls like the gleaners gathering the corn in cut fields.'[46] The need to remain fully armed caused sunstroke to become commonplace and more and more men were evacuated to the ships. Yet the crusaders trudged onwards and as the army moved past Haifa, Mount Carmel and Caesarea, Saladin realised that he needed to halt its progress sooner rather than later.

Just through the forest north of Arsuf lies a plain and there Saladin massed his forces, gathered from Egypt (the crusaders marvelled at the black-skinned Nubians), the Jazira and all across Syria. With the drums, cymbals and trumpets at full volume, thousands of Muslims hammered through the dust towards the crusader army. Again and again they charged up, poured their arrows into the Christian host and wheeled away. Saladin's holy men roused the jihad spirit in his troops and for a while the sultan believed that he had his enemy cornered.[47] This was certainly the most intense bombardment faced by the crusaders and the discipline required not to react tested the knights' patience to its absolute limits. Their sense of honour screamed at them to cast aside strict military protocol. The Hospitaller master shouted: 'St George, will you let us be defeated like this?' He rode up to Richard and complained about the shame of the situation, as well as marking the huge losses of horses. 'Put up with it, Master,' was the curt response. Richard recalled the need for caution instilled into him as a youth, and he did not want to respond to the Muslims because a shapeless pursuit would break his ranks and present Saladin with an opportunity to obliterate the crusader forces. The king wanted to charge on his terms and had prepared a prearranged signal – yet he did not get to use it: a Hospitaller and an English knight charged of their own accord. So tense were the nearby units that they followed suit and hurled themselves after the enemy. Richard reacted immediately: even though his plan was in ruins he was sharp enough to realise that a charge from only one section of the Christian army would likely be defeated and he too thundered into the Muslims 'faster than the bolt from a crossbow', as Ambroise eulogised.[48] The massive impetus of the crusader charge, so potent in theory, but so rarely unleashed in the Levant, smashed into Saladin's troops and its impact was devastating. Richard himself 'did such deeds at that time that all around him, behind and beside were the bodies of Saracens who fell dead.'[49] The centre of the Muslim army was punched back and the survivors took to wholesale flight leaving a trail of slain soldiers and horses. Some rallied, however, most notably Saladin's own elite Mamluk units, marked out by their yellow banners, and these men offered fierce resistance and killed a number of knights. Another push by the crusaders inflicted further losses on the Muslims and by then the Christians had the field of battle to themselves. While the Muslim casualties were nowhere near enough to break Saladin's strength, once again the sultan's aura of success had been breached and his despondency and frustration were manifest to all in his entourage.

The crusaders reached Jaffa (just south of modern Tel Aviv) where they had to make an important strategic decision – should they carry on south and take the mighty fortress of Ascalon, thus threatening Saladin's communications with Egypt, or should they go directly to Jerusalem? Richard, ever the strategist, opted for the former, but the French forces and the majority of the army wanted to aim for the holy city itself. Jaffa was refortified – although in the course of this work boatloads of prostitutes arrived from Acre to bring 'an increase in the army of sin and filth, ugly deeds and lust... what bad shields and defences with which to reconquer the land and heritage of God', complained Ambroise.[50]

The First Attempt on Jerusalem: The Lionheart Thwarted

Over the next few weeks, Richard's caution was again manifest. To ensure the advance on Jerusalem could be properly sustained he carefully rebuilt several fortresses along the route. As he inched towards the holy city an intense diplomatic exchange began to take place; in tandem with the bloodshed of holy war a dialogue proposed a peaceful settlement. Admittedly, the agendas of the various parties were wildly different. Beha ad-Din reported that Saladin really favoured the continuation of the jihad because he feared that if he died the Franks would ignore any deal and carry on fighting. The Christians were deeply divided: Conrad of Montferrat negotiated with Saladin to try to enhance his power and he even raised the prospect of attacking the crusaders left in Acre. For his part, Richard was probably most concerned to discover any weaknesses in the Muslim camp. At times his proposals for the division of Jerusalem – such as shared custody of the city and a corridor of land to the coast – have a surprisingly modern ring to them. He was certainly in close contact with Saladin's brother, Saphadin. The two men met on several occasions, exchanging gifts and learning of their mutual love of music. They were described as parting 'in amity and in good spirits as firm friends', and at one event Richard knighted some of Saphadin's Mamluks, bestowing the ultimate honour for a western knight on his opponent's finest troops.[51]

Probably Richard's most outlandish scheme involved the marriage of his sister, Joan, to Saphadin. The couple would rule the coast, the castles of the land and Jerusalem, but the Military Orders were to hold all the villages and Richard was to return home. Saladin himself was sceptical as to the seriousness of the idea but agreed to it anyway; the one person not consulted was Joan and she, predictably, was furious. She demanded that Saphadin convert to Christianity before they were wed – how else could she allow him to have carnal knowledge of her? The plan never progressed far but the principle of shared ownership of the land and Richard's insistence on a Christian presence in Jerusalem while the Muslims kept the Dome of the Rock would be endlessly revisited over the next few months. Both sides were feeling the pressure of this sustained conflict; physically, financially and politically (in terms of keeping their forces together) this was a struggle of epic proportions.

Between 30 October and 22 December 1191 the crusaders advanced only about forty miles. Torrential rains and cold brought great misery to both sides with more losses of animals and supplies. Just before Christmas they reached Beit Nuba, a day's ride from Jerusalem. There was a burst of optimism: 'God, we thank you! Now we will see your Sepulchre!'[52] But the local Franks and the knights of the Military Orders began to express ever deeper reservations about the wisdom of laying siege to the city. The Christians were scared that Saladin would surround them as he had done at Acre; they also feared that their supply lines to the coast would be cut. Furthermore, they suggested that if they gained control of the holy city it would be very hard to hold on to; by definition, crusading was a temporary condition – after fulfilling his vow the crusader returned home, leaving insufficient men to reinforce Jerusalem. One alternative was to refortify Ascalon, thereby damaging Saladin's contact with Egypt and confirming Frankish control of the seaboard.

On 13 January 1192 the retreat was announced – a calamity to the rank and file. They had struggled so hard to get (literally) within sight of their goal, and to reject what appeared a real chance to regain Christ's sepulchre for the faithful caused profound melancholy and mutters of discontent. Most of the French left immediately and went to Acre. Richard moved down to Ascalon where his fractious army tried to rebuild the city. The Pisans and the Genoese, allies of Richard and Philip respectively, also came to blows, demonstrating further the frustrations and tensions that permeated throughout the Christian forces.

The spring sailing season brought bad news. Messengers from England announced that Prince John was trying to take control of the land and had removed all the king's counsellors and ransacked the treasuries. Richard's departure would have brought the campaign in the Holy Land to a grinding halt; without his powerful personality and leadership qualities the will to fight on would disappear. The need to consider a peaceful settlement became even more pressing, therefore. On top of this, the situation amongst the nobles of Jerusalem had also deteriorated. In spite of the agreement that Guy could remain king for life it was apparent that he enjoyed little confidence from the local nobility. Conrad, for all his double-dealing, was a man who they believed understood war. They pleaded with Richard to change the earlier agreement and to become reconciled with the marquis, who it must also be remembered was a clear partisan of the French. Ever the pragmatist, Richard reluctantly acknowledged the desires of the Frankish nobility and dispatched messengers to tell Conrad of his change of heart. The news was greeted with considerable enthusiasm in the Frankish cities and gave the Christians a renewed sense of purpose for the forthcoming campaigning season – perhaps with greater unity they might achieve some success. Guy was not left entirely empty-handed because Richard managed to sell him Cyprus. The Templars had proven heavy-handed rulers and the locals attempted to massacre the garrison of Nicosia. The master realised his men could not control the island and he turned it over to Richard, who promptly made a deal with Guy, who retained his royal status and began a period of Lusignan rule on the island that would last until the 1470s.[33]

Conrad himself was understandably delighted but, on the evening of 28 April, as he took a stroll along the streets of Tyre following dinner with the bishop of Beauvais, two men set upon him. The marquis was caught entirely unawares and his assailants slashed and stabbed at him. People rushed to help and one of the attackers was killed, but it was too late and Conrad died of his wounds. The other assailant claimed that he worked for the Old Man of the Mountains, the master of the Assassins, who held a long-standing grudge against the marquis for seizing one of their ships at the port of Tyre. Other sources suspected Richard's involvement, but simply murdering the marquis would have been an extremely foolish way to nullify the recent arrangements. Given the inevitable backlash it was unlikely that the king really was responsible; nonetheless, his well-known animosity towards Conrad and the hatred of Leopold of Austria and Philip of France ensured that 'news' of his complicity in the murder soon became commonplace around Europe.

One further consequence of Conrad's murder was that Isabella – as the surviving member of the ruling house of Jerusalem – was obliged to face a third marriage. Count Henry of Champagne was a prominent crusader and he was a nephew of both King Richard and King Philip. This, combined with his experience and popularity, meant that he was an ideal candidate to rule Jerusalem. Richard consented to the plan, although he was not convinced that Henry should marry Isabella because of the immorality of her marriage to Conrad; presumably the king was worried about the legitimacy of any offspring. The Franks of the Holy Land had no such concerns and they urged Henry to wed the heiress. Isabella was famed for her beauty: 'as fair as a gemstone', avowed Ambroise, and the count stated his desire to marry her. 'I would have done the same,' volunteered Ambroise, making his own feelings towards the princess perfectly clear.[54] A French bishop performed the marriage and the citizens of Acre gave Henry a rapturous reception. The streets were hung with drapes, censers full of incense dangled from the windows and the city's clergy escorted him to the main church, presented him with relics, including a piece of the True Cross, and then led him to his palace.

Throughout the early summer of 1192 messengers continued to arrive from Europe bearing the tidings that John, encouraged by Philip of France, persistently stirred trouble in England and Normandy. Richard was downcast by these stories and feared that if he did not depart soon he would lose his kingdom. The other crusader nobles decided to march on Jerusalem regardless of Richard's mood, and when they broke this news publicly the Christian forces were suffused with enthusiasm. The king continued in his depression: the prospect that he would leave, for whatever good reason, was highly unpopular and he was the subject of much criticism. Yet a monarch's primary duty was to his kingdom, and this pressure – when combined with the strategic concerns of the Holy Land – undoubtedly, and understandably, trapped him. Eventually a Poitevin priest talked to Richard, reminded him of his previous achievements and stressed his duty to those he could help most easily: 'now everyone . . . says that you are the father and brother of Christianity and if you leave her without help now, then she is dead and betrayed.'[55] Such talk pulled the king out of his lethargy and he called for his crier, who announced his lord would remain in the Holy Land and that all should prepare to march.

A Second March on Jerusalem: Saladin Fights Back

On 7 June 1192 the Christians prepared for another assault on Jerusalem. This time progress was rapid and within four days they had reached Beit Nuba. As he led a reconnaissance mission the king caught sight of Jerusalem on the horizon – but this proved the closest he would get to his goal. So near were the Christian forces that Saladin decided to poison all the wells around the city. The sultan was highly anxious and his men feared that after the defeat at Acre, Jerusalem would fall too. The strain of holding an alliance of the Muslim Near East was immense: ever more of the sultan's time was spent trying to convince his co-religionists to come and help, and their inadequate responses tested his remarkable powers of persuasion to the limit. As Beha ad-Din noted, there were times when he needed 'to mend feelings and to enhance his authority'. Yet he could still inspire his troops, as this rousing speech shows: 'Know today that you are the army of Islam and its bulwark, as you are aware that the blood of Muslims, their property and their offspring depend on your protection. There are no Muslims who can face the enemy but you. If you turn your reins away, they will roll up these lands as one rolls up a scroll. This is your responsibility.'[56]

The crusader army had to pause for a month to wait for King Henry to join them and during this time there was another debate as to strategy. In reality, the arguments of the spring had not changed: the French and the main army still wanted to besiege the holy city, but Richard and the local knights did not. The king also expressed another, perhaps more selfish motive, albeit a sentiment that showed his sense of honour and an awareness of a wider political and historical spectrum. When asked why he would not march on Jerusalem he answered: 'You will never see me lead a people [in an undertaking] for which I can be criticised and I do not care if I am disliked for it.' He then explained that the defences of the holy city were said to be formidable and that Saladin could cut his supply lines to the coast: 'If I were to lead an army and besiege Jerusalem and such a thing were to happen to their loss, then I would be forever blamed, shamed and less loved.' Richard argued that 'we must work through those who live in this land and [also] through the advice of the Templars and the Hospitallers.'[57] The fact that it was now the height of summer and water was scarce sealed the decision to turn around. Again the rank and file were utterly despondent as they headed back to Acre.

Buoyed by this news, Saladin seized the initiative for the first time in months, and launched a lightning attack on Jaffa. His sappers quickly undermined the walls and the town fell, which left a small garrison of Franks trapped in the citadel. The sultan's forces blocked help coming from overland, which meant that relief could only arrive by sea. Richard rushed south as fast as he could and once at Jaffa the Christian ships paused, unsure as to whether the entire town was already in Muslim hands. One defender escaped and swam out to the crusader fleet where he reported that if the Christians landed immediately there was still a chance for the castle to hold on. Richard urged the boats towards the shore and even before it beached he leapt into the surf, firing his crossbow as he waded to land. Beha ad-Din was present ('all this went on before my eyes') and he described the king, red-haired, in a red tunic accompanied by a red banner rushing into the fray.[58] The Itinerarium peregrinorum conveys the ferocity of his onslaught: 'With no armour on his legs he threw himself into the sea first . . . and forced his way powerfully on to dry land. The Turks obstinately opposed them on the shore . . . The outstanding king shot them indiscriminately with a crossbow he was carrying in his hand and his elite companions pursued the Turks as they fled across the beach, cutting them down. At the sight of the king they had no more spirit in them; they dare not approach him.'[59] The Muslims were terrified and fled, Richard reached the citadel and had his banner unfurled on top of the wall.

Saladin's men were ashamed by their rout and swore revenge.

At dawn on 5 August 1192 they mounted a surprise attack on the crusader camp outside the city. Richard's force was small, but despite being outnumbered the Christians vigorously resisted enemy charges before a signal from the Lion banner triggered the crusader counter-charge. Once again, Richard led from the front; his superb fighting ability caused western writers to rhapsodise about his strength and prowess: 'His right hand brandished his sword with rapid strokes, slicing through the charging enemy, cutting them in two as he encountered them.'[60] Amidst this desperate conflict the importance of chivalric etiquette remained apparent. Saphadin so admired the king's bravery that he sent two fine Arab horses for Richard to use in the battle. Set against the background of a holy war such a gesture seems wholly paradoxical, yet it showed the shared values of the warrior elites and the close bond between these two individuals.

For a while it appeared the Christians would be driven back into Jaffa but again, Richard's daring – some might say reckless – charges pushed the Muslims back. At one point he was almost swallowed up by their ranks but he slashed his way free, and when he killed an important emir, the other soldiers lost heart and a space appeared around him. For the second time in five days the Lionheart had humiliated Saladin's troops and shown himself worthy of a place in the pantheon of great warriors.

The Crusade Ends: Diplomacy and Peace

At this stage the king and the sultan were like two heavyweight boxers, who after fifteen rounds of brutal pounding, are so weary they lack the strength to deal the knockout blow. Both suffered from ill health and each had domestic political troubles. News of Philip's and John's meddling continued to arrive from the West while, in the face of multiple setbacks, Saladin's authority was in decline. Beha ad-Din wrote that the army was 'weary and showing signs of disaffection', and mentioned tensions in the east of the sultan's domains and disputes with the caliph of Baghdad.[61]

Further negotiations took place through August, gilded by the usual diplomatic courtesies. Richard's illness left him with, apparently, a yearning for pears and plums. The fruit – properly iced – was duly sent to him; its delivery also provided another opportunity to gather information about Christian morale and resources. For a while the possession of Ascalon was a sticking point but in the end Richard conceded. On 2 September 1192 a three-year truce was agreed whereby the Christians would keep the coastline from Jaffa to Tyre. Pilgrims could enter Jerusalem freely, although the king himself refused to visit the holy city in such circumstances.

Many of the crusaders did, however, make the pilgrimage where they were treated with considerable courtesy by the senior Muslims. In hugely emotional scenes they were able to venerate the Holy Sepulchre, Mount Calvary and other important sites, weeping and kissing the places where Christ had lived and died; Saladin even showed some of them the True Cross. The bishop of Salisbury had a personal meeting with the sultan. Saladin offered to grant the bishop a wish and after due reflection he answered that he would like two Latin priests and two Latin deacons to worship at the Holy Sepulchre, the Church of the Nativity in Bethlehem and in Nazareth, where they would live off gifts made to them by visitors: Saladin graciously agreed.[62]

On 9 October 1192 Richard set sail for home from Acre, although it is clear that he intended to return. 'Ah Syria! I commend you to God. May the Lord God, by his command grant me the time, if it is his will that I may come to your help! For I still expect to save you.'[63] Events would prove otherwise: in the course of the crusade Richard had generated a comprehensive network of enemies across Europe, a situation that required him to travel home in disguise.[64] By December 1192 he reached Vienna when he was discovered. The king spent the next fifteen months as a prisoner, first in the dungeons of Duke Leopold and then those of Emperor Henry VI of Germany. Finally, on 4 February 1194, after the payment of the colossal sum of 100,000 marks, Eleanor of Aquitaine was able to welcome her son home. It was the payment of this punitive sum, so soon after the expense of the crusade, rather than the cost of the expedition itself, that has done much to create the impression that the expedition almost bankrupted the country. After a ceremonial re-coronation at Winchester Cathedral in April 1194 Richard set about restoring order in his lands. With great generosity – or misjudgement – he pardoned John for his serial misdemeanours and then set about recovering the lands in Normandy taken by King Philip. This process would embroil him for years and it was in the course of one of these

campaigns that he was wounded by a crossbow bolt at Chalus-Chabrol
in the Limousin. The injury became infected and gangrene claimed the
most famous warrior-king in English history on 6 April 1199.

His performance during the Third Crusade had gained him an international reputation – across both the Christian and the Muslim worlds
– as a leader and as a warrior. Perhaps the testimony from the latter
group is most telling; after all, they dismissed the majority of westerners as greedy, unclean barbarians. Ibn al-Athir characterised him
thus: 'The king was an outstanding man of his time for bravery,
cunning, steadfastness and endurance. In him the Muslims were tried
by an unprecedented disaster.'[65] Richard was not simply a violent lout.
Wars were not just won on the battlefield, but by planning and administrative competence as well. Without doubt his military daring inspired
his men, but alongside this, his meticulous attention to detail and
strategic caution created the circumstances in which his bravery could
shine through. He was also a keen diplomat; at times, such as in his
dealings with King Philip, he showed no subtlety at all, but his carefully nurtured relationship with Saphadin constituted a vital subplot
to the progress of the Third Crusade.

In terms of outcome, the expedition failed to achieve its ultimate
aim of the recovery of Jerusalem. It did, however, provide the Franks
with a tolerably firm hold on the coastline and an economically viable
territory. With Cyprus, Acre and Tyre in Christian hands there existed
a series of genuine bridgeheads for future crusades. Compared to the
situation in late 1187 when Tyre survived thanks only to the chance
arrival of Conrad of Montferrat, the position had been transformed.
With regard to the development of crusading, apart from the raw
power of the preaching bull *Audita tremendi*, the Third Crusade was
notable for the dominant role played by the secular monarchs and the
low-key involvement of the papacy.

The Death of Saladin

Richard's departure from the Holy Land was a cause of much fear
in the Frankish East, but the existence of a truce and the king's
promise to return offered a breathing space.[66] Ironically, had the king
remained in the Levant over the winter of 1193 – as he intended at

one stage – circumstances would have presented him with a tremendous opportunity to reverse the gains made by Saladin. On 4 March 1193, worn out by six years of almost continuous campaigning, the sultan died in Damascus where his simple wooden tomb can still be seen today. He was the hero of the Islamic world.

The capture of Jerusalem was the apogee of his lengthy career and this gave him the credibility to survive the setbacks at Acre, Arsuf and Jaffa. He could argue that he had seen off the challenge of the three greatest monarchs of the West and that Islam's third most important city remained in Muslim hands. Had Saladin lived, once the three-year truce expired, he would have been free to renew the jihad against the settlers. Arguably his greatest achievement was to gather and then to hold together – just about – a broad coalition of the Muslim Near East in the face of increasingly poor military results. Saladin was not a great battlefield general; his triumph at Hattin was down more to Frankish foolishness than his own skill. His gifts were more as a man of huge personal charisma and consummate political ability. While he was undoubtedly a pious individual determined to accomplish the obligations of the jihad, he did not shrink from conflict with his fellow Muslims – and not just the heretical Shi'a, but also his political opponents in the Sunni world. His flagrant disregard of Nur ad-Din's instructions during the early 1170s was redolent of spectacular self-interest, and this aspect of his career must always be borne in mind in the course of any wider discussion. Any final assessment might see him as primarily motivated by religion, yet not blind to political advantage, a man who used all the weapons at his disposal to draw his fellow Muslims together and to achieve Islam's greatest success against the crusaders to date. Abd al-Latif visited him in late 1192 and wrote these words soon after his death: 'I found a great king who inspired both respect and affection, far and near, easy-going and willing to grant requests. His companions took him as a model . . . [When he died] men grieved for him as they grieve for prophets. I have seen no other ruler for whose death the people mourned, for he was loved by good and bad, Muslim and unbeliever alike.'[67]

7

'An example of affliction and the works of hell': The Fourth Crusade and the Sack of Constantinople, 1204

On 8 January 1198 Lotario de Conti di Segni was elected Pope Innocent III. At thirty-seven years old he was one of the youngest men ever to hold the title; during his dynamic pontificate (1198–1216) crusading reached new levels of intensity and diversity, both in theory and in practice: the enemies of the Church – inside and outside Christendom – were identified, challenged and, in some cases, defeated. Innocent was convinced that the faithful could overcome the loss of Jerusalem and the failure of the Third Crusade. He believed passionately that God had called the crusades and that it was the duty of all Christians, not just the warrior classes, to support the true cause. Yet for the crusades to succeed, people had to win divine favour and to do this required a society purified from sin. This ambitious agenda often brought him into conflict with secular powers and, at times, Innocent's desire far overreached his means but he, of all popes, had a clear aim in mind: 'to eliminate from the Holy Land the filth of the pagans.'[1]

Innocent's pontificate saw crusading unleashed in new directions: against heretics in southern France (the Albigensian Crusade), against political opponents of the papacy in southern Italy and, more by accident than design, against the Christian Byzantine Empire, an event that culminated in the horrific sack of Constantinople in the Fourth Crusade. He also encouraged crusading in north-eastern Europe and Spain, as well as the Holy Land. So great was contemporary enthusiasm for holy war that one of the most legendary episodes of the medieval age, the Children's Crusade – a mass migration of the young intent upon reclaiming Jerusalem – also took place during his pontificate.

The Procession in Rome, May 1212

Events in Rome during May 1212 reveal Innocent's way of thinking and provide a truly startling demonstration of his understanding of a Christian society working through God to defeat His enemies – on this occasion in Spain.[2] The struggle against the Iberian Muslims was at a critical point and the pope knew that King Alfonso VIII of Castile planned to fight a major battle in southern Spain the week after Pentecost on 20 May. By way of securing divine favour for the Christians, Innocent decided to stage an enormous procession in Rome.

Records show that Innocent ordered the *entire* population of Rome – probably about 50,000 people – to gather on 16 May: men, women and the male clergy were instructed to assemble at three churches. Mass was sung and the processions set out. Each party marched behind a particular cross; nuns led the secular women, the men were led by Hospitaller brothers, and the clergy headed by monks. No one was permitted to wear gold, jewellery or silk; everyone was to walk barefoot, to pray and to repent of their own sins and the sins of man, and to ask for salvation. As thousands of voices rose and fell in prayer and lamentation it must have created an amazing ebb and flow of sound. The three processions snaked their way through the streets of Rome and channelled their spiritual energy towards the heavens; eventually they reached the open space in front of the Lateran Church where all fell silent. Meanwhile the pope, the bishops and the cardinals emerged from the chapel of the Sancta Sanctorum bearing a relic of the True Cross and then joined the waiting crowd in the Lateran square. Innocent preached a sermon that almost certainly emphasised Christ's sacrifice on the cross and explained how a crusader would follow Christ and serve and repay Him through his efforts on earth. The assembly then divided. The women went to the Church of Santa Croce where they heard Mass and a prayer for God's intercession on behalf of his warriors in Spain, after which they dispersed. The men entered the Lateran Church, still in their subgroups of clergy and laymen, where Innocent presided over Mass; next they went to Santa Croce where the intercessory prayer was said to end the proceedings. Once home, unless sick, everyone was to fast on bread and water. While we can presume that children, the aged and the infirm did not participate, and that some individuals must have chosen not to join in, the likelihood was that the majority of Rome's inhabitants were involved. For Innocent even to conceive of the idea of directing an entire city to pray for a conflict taking place hundreds of miles away (and one with no direct Roman interest in it) shows the spectacular breadth of his vision of Christian brotherhood. Praying for crusaders overseas was not an innovation, but this rigidly prescribed focus by one city was indeed a novelty. No realistic parallel can be drawn in the western world today; maybe a major state funeral will interest large parts of a capital's population or perhaps protests against a particular event, such as kidnappings in South America, have a similar effect, but the idea of trying to compel an entire city to gather for a higher cause is outside of our experience.

The Battle of Las Navas de Tolosa did not take place until July 1212, but – crucially for Innocent's way of thinking – the Christians prevailed. The triumphant pope read Alfonso's letter to the people of Rome and the victory, self-evidently, was proof that the procession had influenced the result. Thus, if people's spirituality was directed correctly – and that meant the prayers of the entire community – then God would favour them.

The Crusade Against Markward of Anweiler

At the start of Innocent's pontificate, the chances of a successful campaign appeared less propitious. A crusade to the Holy Land directed by Henry VI of Germany had promised much but after his advance forces recaptured Beirut and Sidon, the emperor's death in 1197 (before he set out in person) brought the enterprise to a close.[3] The Holy Land remained in Muslim hands, therefore. In Iberia, Christian forces had been smashed at the Battle of Alarcos (1195) and the six rival rulers of the kingdoms of Spain continued their long-running feuds. Around the same time, a smaller, but no less significant, struggle took place in southern Italy and its proximity to the papal lands spurred Innocent into a rapid – and, in the long term, highly significant – extension of the concept of crusading.[4]

On the death of Henry VI, a dispute arose over possession of his southern Italian and Sicilian lands. Henry's marshal, Markward of

Anweiler, wished to be regent for the child heir, Frederick (later Emperor Frederick II), and possibly planned to rule in his own right. Markward allied with Philip of Swabia, another claimant to the German throne, and together they threatened to squeeze the papal lands in central Italy into oblivion. Markward's brutal military campaigns made strong progress and the pope became so desperate that he contemplated unleashing the ultimate weapon in his spiritual armoury: the crusade. In March 1199 Innocent claimed, rather tendentiously, that Markward impeded the planning of the new campaign to the Holy Land and he threatened holy war against the German.

By the autumn of 1199 Markward – perhaps foolishly – had made an alliance with Muslim groups in Sicily and in November the pope responded to this by offering people who fought his German enemy the same indulgence as those who went to the Holy Land. He wrote: 'He [Markward] has called on their [Saracens] help against the Christians . . . and so as to stimulate their spirits more keenly . . . he has spattered their jaws with Christian blood and exposed Christian women to the violence of their desire . . . Who would not rise up against him who rises against all and joins the enemies of the Cross so that he might empty the faith of the Cross and, having become a worse infidel than the Infidels, struggles to conquer the faithful?'[5]

Markward's treaty with the Muslims gave Innocent an obvious reason to initiate a crusade; primarily, however, it was the danger posed to papal lands that pushed him to act. In doing so, Innocent gave life to the idea that political opponents of the Church were appropriate targets for a holy war, a concept that – ironically – in future would find its greatest expression in the conflict with Innocent's young ward, Frederick. There is little evidence that the localised crusade against Markward ever really blossomed. The pope used the French nobleman Walter of Brienne, from a proud crusading dynasty in the county of Champagne, to try to protect his interests. Walter duly raised an army and between 1201 and 1203 he managed to hold off the German until the latter's death as a result of surgery for kidney stones. The contemporary *Gesta Innocenti* reported that at one battle Walter 'received the blessing and indulgence from the papal legate . . . [and that] a shining golden cross was seen carried miraculously before the count'.[6] The indulgence hints at a crusading ethos while the reference to a golden cross certainly indicates a belief in divine favour. Walter himself succumbed to wounds suffered in a battle in 1205 but his family's service would not go unnoticed. Four years later, the French crown and the nobility of Jerusalem, with Innocent's blessing, chose his younger brother, John of Brienne, to marry their heiress to Jerusalem and to take the crown of the holy city.

The Origins of the Fourth Crusade, 1198–1201

While these events were of considerable concern to Pope Innocent, they were of secondary importance compared to his efforts to regain the Holy Land. The limited progress of the Third Crusade and the German Crusade of 1196–7 meant it would require another major expedition to take back Jerusalem.[7] Within months of his accession as pope, Innocent issued a new crusade appeal, *Post miserabile*. Its compelling language exhorted the faithful to act and it railed against the destructive infighting that so crippled the response of the rulers of England, France and Germany:

> Following the pitiable collapse of the territory of Jerusalem, following the lamentable massacre of the Christian people, following the deplorable invasion of that land on which the feet of Christ stood and where God, our king, had deigned before the beginning of time, to work out salvation in the midst of the earth, following the ignominious alienation from our possession of the vivifying Cross . . . the Apostolic See, alarmed over the ill fortune of such calamity, grieved. It cried out and wailed to such a degree that due to incessant crying out, its throat was made hoarse, and from incessant weeping its eyes almost failed . . . Still the Apostolic See cries out, and like a trumpet it raises its voice, eager to arouse the Christian peoples to fight Christ's battle and to avenge the injury done to the Crucified One . . .[8]

To shame his audience into action Innocent even pretended to quote a Muslim who mocked the Christians' failures. The pope also criticised the arrogance of earlier crusaders (presumably a reference to the dissent between Richard and Philip during the Third Crusade) and urged new recruits to set out in the correct frame of mind, unclouded by vanity and greed.

Innocent dispatched preachers to France, England, Hungary and Sicily, although he ignored Spain, where the reconquest continued, and Germany because it was torn apart by civil war. The death of Richard the Lionheart in April 1199 and tensions over Philip's marital status prevented two obvious candidates from taking the cross, but in November 1199 the elite knighthood of northern France assembled for a tournament at Écry-sur-Aisne, just north of the city of Rheims, in the county of Champagne. There is a paradox here because during the twelfth century the Church consistently censured tournaments as events that promoted the sins of pride, envy and murder. In contrast, the contemporary nobility were – with no exaggeration – utterly addicted to the thrill and opportunity of such occasions. They were the perfect platform on which to gain status and, more pertinently, to train for war. The massed charges by teams of up to 200 knights, in an arena that ranged across several miles, was the closest possible replica of real warfare. The idea of a tournament was to capture and ransom opponents, rather than to kill them, but deaths were not uncommon. After such competitions the nobles gathered to feast, dance and listen to stories and songs – particularly epics that told of the heroes of the First Crusade such as the *Chanson d'Antioche*. This was, Church disapproval aside, the ideal environment in which to nurture crusading enthusiasm and it is no coincidence that the two comital houses with the greatest crusading traditions, the counts of Flanders and Champagne, were ardent tournament-goers.[9]

Count Thibaut of Champagne and Count Louis of Blois both had splendid crusading lineages. Thibaut's father had ruled Jerusalem from 1192 until 1197 when his dwarfish entertainer toppled from a balcony and pulled him to his death. At twenty-eight years old Louis was already a veteran of the Third Crusade, a campaign that had seen his father's death at the siege of Acre. Once these men took the cross several other important nobles followed suit, including Geoffrey of Villehardouin, a senior figure on the expedition and the author of a memoir of his experiences.[10] (Rather than the Latin texts composed by clerical writers that so dominated accounts of crusading during the twelfth century, the growth of vernacular literacy amongst laymen meant that accounts of the sort Villehardouin wrote became more common.) Simon de Montfort, a noble from the Île-de-France, was another to join the crusade at Écry and within a couple of months

Count Baldwin of Flanders also committed himself to the expedition. Thus it was the nobility of northern France who came to form the nucleus of the Fourth Crusade.[11]

In the spring of 1200 they gathered at Soissons and started to plan their campaign. Here they made a decision that, unforeseen by them, was to have the most profound consequences for the direction of their expedition and, ultimately, for the history of Christendom itself. The crusaders resolved to sail to the Levant and, given that Pisa and Genoa were at war, they approached the other maritime experts of the day, the Venetians. Pope Innocent had already sent a legate to the city to petition their involvement so this link-up dovetailed with papal thinking anyway.

In March 1201 a specially deputed group of crusaders arrived in Venice to arrange the terms of passage. There they encountered one of the most amazing figures in medieval history: Doge Enrico Dandolo, a man already over ninety years of age and who, for at least the previous two decades, had been blind.[12] In spite of his handicap Dandolo was an individual of enormous energy and drive whose behaviour on the campaign would attract strong praise and sharp criticism alike. Bishop Gunther of Pairis (a Cistercian monastery in Alsace) described him thus: 'He was, to be sure, sightless of eye, but most perceptive of mind and compensated for physical blindness with a lively intellect and, best of all, foresight. In the case of matters that were unclear, the others always took every care to seek his advice and they usually followed his lead in public affairs.'[13] To Pope Innocent, however, he behaved in an outrageous fashion that did nothing but cause the crusaders to fight Christians rather than Muslims. Dandolo had governed Venice since 1192 and was clearly a hugely experienced and able politician. After a few days' consideration the Venetians made their response to the crusaders' request:

> We will build horse transports to carry 4,500 horses and 9,000 squires with 4,500 knights and 20,000 foot sergeants travelling in ships. And we will agree to provide food for all these horses and people for nine months. This is the minimum we will provide in return for a payment of four marks per horse and two marks per man. All the terms we are offering you would be valid for one year from the day of our departure from the port of Venice, to do service to God and Christendom,

wherever that might take us. The total cost of what has just been outlined would amount to 85,000 marks.[14] And what's more, we will provide, for the love of God, fifty armed galleys, on condition that for as long as our association lasts we will have one half of everything we capture on land or at sea, and you will have the other. Now you should consider whether you have the will and the means to go ahead.[15]

The envoys duly agreed to these terms, but the doge still needed the approval of the people of Venice. Such was the scale of this undertaking that it would require the city to suspend its entire commercial operations for a year to fulfil the treaty – a breathtaking and unprecedented commitment. At a meeting held in the mosaic-covered splendour of St Mark's Cathedral, Villehardouin himself addressed the congregation.[16] He implored the Venetians, as the greatest seafaring power of the time, to act to help recover Christ's land. He sought to harness their civic pride and their commercial aspirations to the intrinsic religiosity of the age. Of all the Italian communities, the Venetians are frequently imagined as money-grabbing mercenaries, devoid of the spirituality of many of the other crusaders.[17] In large part, the outcome of the Fourth Crusade is to blame for this, but as we will see, their behaviour does not entirely merit such opprobrium. They had already taken part in the First Crusade and the 1124 crusade that captured Tyre; on both occasions they eagerly sought relics, just as the other crusaders had. The numerous churches in Venice bear obvious testimony to their conventional, and deep-seated, spiritual values. As Villehardouin reached the climax of his speech, he fell to his knees and cried out to the congregation for help. The doge and crowd responded with cries of 'We agree! We agree!' and with 'this great outpouring of piety', as Villehardouin described it, the pact was sealed and the Venetians had joined the crusade.[18]

The execution of these terms came to exert an unyielding and pervasive influence on the outcome of the Fourth Crusade, far beyond anything that could have been calculated or forecast. The costs per individual were broadly in line with what the Genoese had charged King Philip during the Third Crusade, but it was the sheer scale of the project that proved the devastating structural flaw that drew the expedition to its terrible conclusion. The numbers promised were massive, particularly given the absence of a major monarch to pull troops along with him. By way of comparison, Frederick Barbarossa had led 12,000–15,000 men on the Third Crusade, while the money required to pay the Venetians amounted to twice the annual income of the English or French crowns.[19] Yet Villehardouin and his colleagues were highly experienced nobles, many of whom had taken part in the Third Crusade; how could they have been so mistaken? Either they must have been confident in promises from people in northern France who planned to take part in the crusade, or else they were breathtakingly – and criminally – optimistic.

One further dimension to the campaign was a secret agreement between the leadership and the doge to begin the crusade with an assault on Egypt, rather than the Holy Land; the intention was to use the former as a staging post en route to Jerusalem.[20] Sound strategy and considerable financial advantages lay behind such a plan. As we saw earlier, King Amalric of Jerusalem had made several attempts to conquer Egypt, the Sicilians attacked Alexandria in 1174 and Richard the Lionheart had favoured an invasion of the Nile as a prelude to an approach on Jerusalem in 1191. The immense resources of Egypt offered unparalleled opportunities to the Christian military while control of the coastline would all but guarantee Frankish security at sea. If Egypt came under Frankish power then the Muslim world – which, since Saladin's death in 1193, was in a highly fragmented condition anyway – would certainly struggle to recover. The existence of an ongoing truce between the kingdom of Jerusalem and Muslim Syria was a further reason to begin the campaign on the Nile because this arrangement excluded Egypt.

For the Venetians, the chance to become the pre-eminent trading city in Alexandria was impossible to resist. The city was by far the greatest commercial centre in the Mediterranean, yet by the year 1200 Dandolo's people conducted only 10 per cent of their trade there: by contrast, the Pisans and the Genoese held a much stronger position. The pope frowned upon dealings with the Muslims, especially in materials of war such as iron and timber, but in the run-up to the crusade Innocent was flexible enough not to alienate the Venetians and he condoned trade in non-military goods. Dandolo himself had visited Egypt in the 1170s so he was well aware of this tremendous opportunity. If the crusade succeeded, then it would bring the most phenomenal wealth to Venice and, of course, be the crowning achievement of Dandolo's time as doge.

The fact that it might then lead to the recovery of Jerusalem itself would only add further lustre to his triumph.

It must be said that this was a hugely ambitious scheme – previous campaigns had seen pretty limited Christian progress in Egypt, although the plan to deliver a large force by sea marked an advance on previous strategy. The decision to take 4,500 horses required the construction of dozens of special galleys, each equipped with slings to carry the beasts, as well as low-level doors that, on landing, could be opened to allow mounted knights to pour straight out of the ship and into battle. In other words, these vessels were a form of medieval landing craft and disgorged, in the form of a charging crusader, the equivalent of an armoured car. The Venetians had fifty of their own battle galleys, headed by the vermilion-painted ship of the doge, along with around sixty to seventy large sailing boats that each carried up to 600 passengers and a hundred crew. In total it would need about 30,000 Venetians to man the whole fleet – possibly half the adult population and another indication of the scale of the city's commitment.

The envoys made a down payment of 5,000 silver marks so the work could start immediately and then headed back to France, eager to announce the agreement. By the time they arrived home, however, the crusade had been dealt a heavy blow because the charismatic young Thibaut of Champagne had fallen ill and died on 24 May 1201. The death of this immensely popular figure provoked genuine distress in the region: 'no man of his era was loved more by his vassals and by others', as Villehardouin wrote.[21] He could have been an inspirational and unifying figure to the crusaders and his presence might well have drawn many more to take the cross. The epitaph on his richly decorated tomb in Troyes (sadly, no longer extant) revealed his loss as a potential crusader, as well as showing a belief that he would attain the heavenly Jerusalem:

Intent upon making amends for the injuries of the Cross and the land of
    the Crucified
He arranged the way with expenses, an army, a navy.
Seeking the terrestrial city, he finds the celestial one;
While he is obtaining his goal far distant, he finds it at home.[22]

Thibaut's passing meant that the crusade needed a new leader, a man of comparable authority and connections. The nobles decided to contact someone from outside France – perhaps a move designed to broaden the crusade's appeal – and approached Boniface, marquis of Montferrat. We have already met his brothers, namely, William Longsword, briefly the husband of Sibylla of Jerusalem and father of Baldwin V; and Conrad, the man chosen to rule Jerusalem but murdered (probably) by the Assassins in 1192. Boniface could boast, therefore, a formidable crusading ancestry. The Montferrat clan also had a history of involvement with Byzantium because another brother, Renier, had married into the imperial family in 1179, although three years later he was poisoned by the usurping Angeloi dynasty. Conrad himself had served as the commander of the imperial army later in the decade before political intrigue forced him to flee for his life in the summer of 1187. Given this history, plus family ties to the ruling houses of France and Germany, coupled with his long experience of war and diplomacy (he was in his mid-forties), Boniface was a genuinely astute choice. The marquis travelled up to Soissons and there, in late August, he formally took the cross.[23]

For the remainder of 1201 and into early 1202 preaching and preparations for the crusade gathered pace. The most intriguing – and potentially sinister – development took place at Christmas 1201 at the court of Philip of Swabia, king of Germany, in Hagenau. Boniface was visiting his relative when the king's brother-in-law, Prince Alexius of Byzantium, arrived to seek help. This meeting has aroused considerable suspicion over the years: some have seen it as the foundation stone of an alleged agreement with Boniface that eventually led to the sack of Constantinople. A few years earlier, the prince's father, Isaac Angelos, had been the victim of a coup led by his brother who now ruled Byzantium as Alexius III. Isaac was blinded and, along with his son, Prince Alexius, cast into prison. The young prince managed to escape and now he haunted the courts of Europe trying to persuade relatives to restore him and his father to their rightful position. While his pleas had some emotional leverage, the fact that the Angeloi family themselves had brutally removed the previous dynasty and that Isaac had allied with Saladin counted against his cause. In any case, the way events on the crusade developed were so unexpected and, in several cases, so far outside of the prince's control that the idea of a plot hatched at Hagenau is not sustainable. Prince Alexius also visited Innocent, but the pope showed little interest in the case.[24]

The Crusaders Gather in Venice, 1202

During the late spring of 1202 the northern French crusaders set out on their great campaign. As they headed southwards many travelled via the mighty waterways of the Seine and Saône, before they crossed the Alps and moved into northern Italy to assemble at Venice. Here, during the long hot summer, the catastrophic miscalculation of the previous year's treaty became apparent. Contingents of crusaders arrived in small groups: every so often the appearance of a senior noble would boost morale, but in essence only a fraction of the huge numbers of men promised actually gathered. Those waiting were stuck out on the Lido, an island seven miles from the main city, prudently housed there by the Venetians to ensure they could not cause any trouble. By August, only about 12,000 of the stipulated 33,500 men had turned up. Dandolo began to fear the whole plan would collapse and all the sacrifices that he had induced the Venetians to make would be in vain. He appealed to the crusaders: 'Lords, you have used us ill, for as soon as your messengers made the bargain with me I commanded through all my land that no trader should go trading, but that all should help prepare this navy. So they have waited ever since and have not made any money for a year and a half past. Instead, they have lost a great deal, and therefore . . . you should pay us the money you owe us. And if you do not do so, then know that you shall not depart from this island before we are paid, nor shall you find anyone to bring you anything to eat or to drink.'[25]

In desperation the leadership pooled their resources but still fell 34,000 marks short of the 85,000 owed to their hosts. Both parties here faced a deeply uncomfortable dilemma: the crusaders were aware they had made a contractual obligation and that any failure to fulfil it would entail a substantial loss of face. They might have to return home, ridiculed as the men who had reneged on their vows – in such a status-conscious society this was practically unthinkable. On Dandolo's part, he had persuaded his people to make this huge effort and now it seemed as if it had been a terrible mistake. Not only would this ruin his own standing as doge but it would catastrophically compromise Venice's finances. It would be an error, however, to view Dandolo as nothing other than a ruthless commercial operator. While the well-being of Venice was – rightly, given his role as doge – central to his actions, he had also chosen to become a crusader. His own father, grandfather and uncle had taken part in the crusade of 1122–4: in the same way that the French were proud of their crusading ancestry, so was the Venetian.[26] His age and blindness were, of course, immense barriers to his participation; at a ceremony in St Mark's he cried out: 'I am an old man, weak and in need of rest, and my health is failing', yet he pleaded to be allowed to take the cross and 'protect and guide' his people; the congregation bellowed their support: 'We beg you in God's name to take the cross', and thus Dandolo bound himself even closer to the cause of the crusade.[27]

Religious sentiment aside, he needed to find a way forwards for all concerned, and here we can see his ability to accommodate the seemingly contradictory demands of holy war and his place as ruler of Venice. By now it was September, and as the autumn weather drew in the chances of a safe journey to Egypt receded. Given the need to make good some of the Venetians' losses, and the presence of a large, morally and financially indebted military force, he proposed an assault on the Croatian city of Zara, 165 miles to the south-east. The Zarans had been former subjects of Venice but had broken free from its overlordship – this represented an ideal opportunity for Dandolo to regain control. There were, however, two serious catches to this scheme: the Zarans were Christians and their present overlord, King Bela III of Hungary, was a crusader. In theory, therefore, his lands were under the protection of the Church and should not be attacked – let alone by another crusading force. Aware of the acutely controversial nature of such a plan the expedition's leadership chose not to make an official announcement to the troops and simply gave the order to depart.

The Siege of Zara and the Envoys of Prince Alexius

In October 1202 the Fourth Crusade set sail from Venice. After months of procrastination and disappointment the relief of finally starting their journey invigorated everyone. The fleet of almost 200 vessels made a magnificent sight, at the head of the flotilla the winged-lion banner of St Mark fluttered and snapped above the vermilion galley of Doge Dandolo. The French crusaders hung their own brightly coloured shields from the sides of their boats and everyone sang hymns to invoke divine blessing for their campaign. The eyewitness Robert of Clari was moved to describe the spectacle as 'the finest thing to see that has ever been since the beginning of the world.'[28]

By this time, however, Pope Innocent had learned of the crusaders' plan to go to Zara and he told his legate, Peter of Capuano, to forbid the assault and to threaten them with excommunication if they disobeyed. This was a major weapon in the Church's spiritual armoury – complete withdrawal from the community of Christians, including all church services and the sacraments; in other words, certain damnation. Yet Peter, who was with the army and could fully appreciate the crusaders' terrible dilemma, chose not to prevent the fleet sailing to Zara and thereby gave a tacit endorsement of the plan: for him, of paramount importance was the need for the crusade to get going.

Within the ranks of the crusaders themselves, however, there was a huge split. One group of nobles, led by Simon de Montfort, opposed the diversion to Zara and strove to frustrate Dandolo's scheme. He told the Zarans that none of the French crusaders would attack them and encouraged the defenders to turn down Venetian attempts to negotiate a surrender. The doge was disgusted by the actions of his French colleagues: 'You made an agreement with me to help me capture it and now I call on you to do so.'[29] From Simon's perspective the decision to turn the crusade against his co-religionists – whatever the justification – was utterly unacceptable: 'I have not come here to destroy Christians', was his crisp assessment.[30] Abbot Guy of les Vaux-de-Cernay, a churchman from Simon's contingent, obtained a copy of the pope's letter and read it out to the assembled nobles. At news of Innocent's disapproval, a physical struggle ensued and Simon had to intervene to stop the doge's men murdering the abbot. After such an open confrontation it was inevitable that the count would withdraw from the attack. On 13 November 1202 the siege of Zara began in earnest. The Venetian and French crusaders began to set up towers, catapults and, most threateningly of all, mines. As the siege machinery bombarded the defences the tunnelling advanced well; the creation of such a lethal attacking device usually meant the end of any resistance and once the Zarans learned of its construction they agreed terms of surrender.

By the end of 1202 the crusade was at least underway. Some progress had been made towards paying off the Venetians, although to Innocent, the price of this was, in moral terms, far too high. He wrote to the crusaders at Zara in excoriating terms: 'Behold, your gold has turned into base metal and your silver has almost completely rusted since, departing from the purity of your plan and turning aside from the path onto the impassable road . . . you should have hastened to the land flowing with milk and honey, you turned away, going astray in the direction of the desert.' He could not see how God would favour men who had behaved in such a fashion. To Innocent it was the Venetians who were to blame and he accused the crusaders of paying the Devil the first fruits of their pilgrimage and falling in amongst thieves (that is, the Venetians). He pronounced a sentence of excommunication against the crusaders as a punishment for their actions.[31] Given the spiritually catastrophic consequences of such a decree many crusaders were deeply worried and a group of fearful churchmen made their way to the pope to beg for absolution. Innocent listened to their pleas and promised to consider the matter.[32] The episode at Zara was a harsh lesson in just how limited papal control over crusading actually was. Firstly, Innocent's own legate had ignored his orders, and then the bulk of the main army went completely against a clear directive. While the pope's power to call a crusade and to care for souls was unchallenged, the practicalities of an ongoing military expedition relied on consent to ecclesiastical authority for any of the further levers to have an impact. The French crusaders' contractual failure, coupled with the Venetians' threat to withdraw their shipping, meant that it was pragmatism – wrapped up in an argument about being able to carry on the crusade in the first instance – that won the day. For a man such as Pope Innocent, whose belief in the power and sanctity of his office was absolute, this was an infuriating and horrifying development.

The crusaders spent the winter of 1202 encamped outside Zara. Just before the end of the year envoys arrived representing Prince Alexius. They made a carefully pitched proposal, artfully designed to appeal to the needs and interests of all involved in the crusade:

Since you have left home in the cause of God, right and justice, you should, if you are able, restore their inheritance to those who have been wrongly dispossessed . . . If God permits you to restore Alexius to his inheritance, he will place the entire empire of Byzantium in obedience to Rome, from which it has formerly been cut off. Secondly, he understands that you have spent your own money and are now poor. Therefore, he will give you 200,000 marks of silver and provisions for the whole army, both the great men and the lesser. He will also go with you in person to the land of Egypt, accompanied by 10,000 men (or he will send them at his expense if you think that would be better). He will provide you with such service for one year. And throughout his life he will maintain 500 knights in the land overseas, supported with his own money.[33]

This brilliant piece of diplomacy seemed to offer advantages to everyone. For Innocent there was a prospect of the submission of the Greek Orthodox Church, something that popes had desired for centuries. The deal also enabled the crusade to continue – an obvious attraction to the pope and also, of course, to the expedition's leaders. The problem of the debt to the Venetians would disappear and the Christians' military resources would be dramatically enhanced. The shortfall of men at Venice would be cancelled out and the prospect of a garrison force in the Levant answered another long-running need of the Latin East. The catch was, that in return for this, Prince Alexius wanted to be restored to the throne of Constantinople, something that might require the crusaders to fight their way into the city and install him by force.

Once again, the prospect of attacking a Christian city provoked huge controversy amongst the crusaders. The fact that Prince Alexius' father had been illicitly dispossessed of his throne was, as the Byzantine envoys observed, an important point because the notion of regaining land wrongfully taken was a central element in the concept of crusading. Yet many in the rank and file experienced deep disquiet. Some felt that Dandolo's enthusiasm for the plan was driven by financial motives and a desire to avenge the arrest and ill-treatment of Venetians in Constantinople in 1171. By the early thirteenth century, however, relations between the two powers were mended and due recompense had been made; this was not really, therefore, a relevant issue.[34] The northern French crusaders, such as Baldwin of Flanders and Villehardouin, were determined to push through the plan and they tried hard to persuade their colleagues to consent. Given his earlier opposition to the siege of Zara it was inevitable that Simon de Montfort should dissent and he chose this moment to leave the main expedition and take his knights directly to the Holy Land. This did not deter the other nobles and they summoned the prince's envoys to the doge's quarters in Zara where they swore to the agreement.[35] From this moment onwards the crusade was heading for Constantinople.

Pope Innocent had released the French crusaders from the vow of excommunication on condition they perform penance for their sins, but the Venetians showed no contrition and therefore remained outside the Church. Innocent required an oath from the crusaders that they would behave correctly in future, although the phrasing of his pronouncement created an ambiguity. The men would: 'neither invade nor violate the lands of Christians in any manner, unless, perchance, they wickedly impede your journey or another just or necessary cause should, perhaps, arise, on account of which you would be empowered to act otherwise.'[36] Intentionally or not, the clause 'just or necessary cause' gave the crusaders a loophole to justify their future actions and for some – probably incorrectly – to infer papal support for their decisions.

The First Siege of Constantinople, 1203

The expedition left Zara in late April and sailed down the Adriatic to Corfu where it was joined by Prince Alexius. After a few weeks the crusaders gathered themselves together and set sail for Constantinople on 24 May 1203. While many thousands of crusaders and merchants had seen Constantinople over the years, little could prepare newcomers for its size and splendour. With a population of around 350,000 it was far in excess of anything in the West – Paris, Rome and the Italian trading cities reached perhaps the 50,000–60,000 mark. The three and a half miles of land defences, fully double-walled and with a moat, were the greatest urban fortifications in Christendom; the rest of the city was guarded by the smaller sea walls while a chain protected the entrance to the inlet of the Golden Horn. Close to the waterfront lay the magnificent Bucoleon Palace, while behind it lay the massive bulk of the Hagia Sophia, arguably the greatest church in the world. Villehardouin noted some of the crusaders' reactions:

> Now you can be assured that those who had never seen Constantinople before gazed at it for a long time, barely believing that there was such a great city in all the world. They saw its high walls and mighty towers, with which the city was completely encircled, as well as the fine palaces and impressive churches, of which there were so many that none could believe it if he did not see it with his own eyes, and they could be seen the length and breadth of the city which is the sovereign of all others. Know that there was no man there so bold that his flesh did not tremble, which should come as no surprise for never was such a great project undertaken by as many men since the creation of the world.[37]

Only now did they realise the immensity of the challenge that lay ahead of them if Prince Alexius was not accepted back by his people. The crusaders made camp in the area of Scutari on what we now call the Asian side of the city. In early July a group of boats set out to parade Prince Alexius before the sea walls. The prince and his allies anticipated a tumultuous acclaim and the start of a peaceful and easy entry to the city: 'Behold your natural lord,' they called out.[38] Yet as the crusaders' boats bobbed offshore, most of Constantinople remained utterly indifferent except a few who hurled abuse and taunts at the young man. Such a reception shattered the prince's assurances that he would be welcomed by a grateful crowd, relieved to have respite from the cruel tyrant Alexius III. The emperor exploited over a century of tension between the Byzantines and the crusaders to encourage the idea that the prince and his western allies intended to deprive the Greeks of their liberty and to subjugate them to the pope. The fact that Prince Alexius had never governed Constantinople, plus his youth and his recent lengthy absence from the city were further reasons why he lacked a natural groundswell of support. The crusaders ushered their chastened ally away and despondently turned back for camp.

Their first point of attack was to be the suburb of Galata on the northern bank of the Golden Horn. The army divided into seven divisions according to regional identity, a move intended to preserve the co-ordination and discipline so vital in winning battles. On the night of 3 July 1203 the crusaders prayed for victory as they prepared to make the largest amphibious landing yet attempted in the medieval West. The fleet moved across the Bosphorus and as the boats drew close to the shore, archers and crossbowmen sent a hail of fire towards the Greeks. Once the ships touched the shallows the horse transports opened their doors and disgorged the mounted knights who surged ashore. Troops had gathered to resist the landing, but rather than confront the crusaders at this most vulnerable time they simply retreated.[39]

The following day brought more success for the westerners with the capture of the Galata Tower, the main defensive structure of the area and, more importantly, the breaking of the chain across the Golden Horn which gave the Venetian fleet clear access to the Greek navy, a decrepit force that had been neglected for decades by successive emperors; it was duly routed.[40] Control over the Golden Horn also provided safe harbour for the Venetian vessels, and the presence of their ships bobbing just opposite the city walls brought home to the Greeks the menace posed by the crusaders.

The attackers debated their next move. The Venetians chose to launch an assault from scaling ladders on the ships; the French preferred to fight on land. They repaired a bridge over the Golden Horn (again with a curious lack of opposition from Alexius III), and set up a fortified camp on the northern edge of the city. Given the size of Constantinople a blockade was unrealistic, and when Alexius III finally began to order sallies and raids the crusaders started to run low on food. By mid-July they had only three weeks' supplies left and their momentum looked fatally stalled. In desperation, on 17 July, they launched a twin-pronged assault. The Venetians sent a hail of arrows and stones towards the walls while a small group pounded at the fortifications with a battering ram. In one memorable incident the aged Doge Dandolo showed unparalleled courage and leadership qualities.[41] Angered by the failure of his people to engage closely with the Greeks he commanded the crew of his galley to pull ahead of the others. With the banner of St Mark fluttering close by, the blind old man stood proudly at the prow of his ship. When the boat grounded he ordered himself carried ashore and, as he had hoped, once his men saw that their commander's banner had landed, they hastened forwards, fearful of being shamed by his example. The intensity of this thrust terrified the defenders and a crucial first bridgehead was gained. Alexius III dispatched a contingent of the feared Varangian guard to stem the Venetians' advance and while these Russian and Scandinavian mercenaries managed to halt the attack, the Italians responded by starting a fire. Fanned by a strong westerly wind the flames soon consumed about 120 acres of the eastern side of the city – another serious blow to the inhabitants.

The trauma of seeing dense clouds of black smoke billowing over Constantinople belatedly prompted Alexius III to act and he led out the bulk of his army to confront the crusaders in front of the great Theodosian walls on the north-eastern edge of the city. The westerners were terrified by the immensity of the Byzantine forces. While precise figures for the Greek army are unknown – it must have been many thousands – the crusaders (excluding the Venetians) by now numbered around 500 knights, 500 other mounted men and around 2,000 foot soldiers. Back at their camp the cooks and stable lads donned pots and horse blankets for protection, so great was their fear of being overwhelmed. As the Byzantines drew up the crusaders advanced towards them in tight formation. Some of their leaders wanted to stop or retreat to camp, but others counselled them to hold their nerve and, in the face of seemingly hopeless odds, the westerners continued to move resolutely forwards. A small waterway, the River Lycus, barred their way, yet Alexius III, far from choosing this moment to unleash a tidal wave of his own troops, decided to withdraw behind the city walls. The reasoning behind such a baffling move is almost impossible to fathom. Certainly the Greeks feared the impact of a crusader cavalry charge, but the Byzantines' numerical advantage surely meant they could sustain a degree of loss. The crusaders were adamant that it was their martial vigour that had won the day. Hugh of Saint-Pol proudly reported: 'When they saw that we were brave and steadfast and that we moved forward . . . in formation and that we could not be overrun or broken they rightly became terrified and confused. Retreating before us they dared not fight by day.'[42] Villehardouin experienced an overwhelming sense of relief: 'Know that God has never delivered any people from such great danger as He did the army that day. Know moreover that there was no man present so brave that he did not feel very glad about this.'[43] The long-held stereotype of the effeminate and unwarlike Greek had been confirmed.

The blow to Byzantine morale was catastrophic. There was fury inside Constantinople and the eyewitness Niketas Choniates wrote that Alexius III 'returned in utter disgrace, having only made the enemy more haughty and insolent.' Given their fast-expiring supplies of food, the emperor need only have contained the crusaders for a matter of days before they would have been obliged to leave or to sue for peace. Choniates was scathing about Alexius III's behaviour: 'it was as though he had laboured hard to make a miserable corpse of the city, to bring her to utter ruin in defiance of her destiny, and he hastened her along her destruction.'[44]

On the night of 17 July the emperor gathered as much money as he could find and fled Constantinople. The following morning senior Byzantine officials went to his predecessor, the sightless Isaac Angelos and, in contravention of the customary practice of refusing to crown a blind man, offered him the imperial robes and insignia. They hoped the returnee ruler would influence his son, Prince Alexius, to call off his allies and they sent messengers to the crusaders' camp seeking peace. As news of events overnight broke, a huge cheer erupted from the westerners; from the verge of defeat, God had granted them victory – and with relatively few casualties. Then, in due fulfilment of the agreement between Prince Alexius and the Crusaders, the youth was enthroned as co-emperor with his father.

Villehardouin led an embassy into the city for talks to confirm that Isaac would uphold his son's promises. The envoys passed in front of the gathered Byzantine courtiers, attired in their customary splendour. Isaac was appalled when he learned the details of Alexius' pact with the crusaders, but given the latter's obvious ascendancy he could not resist. Villehardouin reported his reaction: 'In truth, this agreement is a most burdensome one, and I do not see quite how it can be fulfilled. However, you have done both my son and myself such a service that if you had been granted the whole empire you would have well deserved it.'[45] While Villehardouin may have massaged the moral worth of Isaac's words, as well as hinting at some of what was to come, this assessment of the onerous nature of the deal was true enough.

The crusaders withdrew over the Golden Horn and camped in the

Galata district of the city. They were well provided with food and most took the opportunity to visit the churches of Constantinople and to see the many magnificent collections of relics. This was also an ideal time for the crusaders to appreciate the Greeks' true wealth and to learn exactly where their treasures were stored.

The westerners sent home a series of triumphant letters that carefully portrayed the merits of their actions and pointed out the advantages of their decision to go to Constantinople.[46] Innocent remained highly antagonistic towards the doge, although several crusade leaders made a point of stressing his virtues and described a man 'who is prudent, discreet and skilled in hard decision-making'.[47] They also reminded Innocent of the immense advance in spiritual authority that had accrued to the papacy: 'We carried on the business of Jesus Christ with His help, to the point that the Eastern Church (whose head is Constantinople), along with the emperor and his entire empire, reunited with its head, the Roman pontiff . . . acknowledges itself to be the daughter of the Roman Church.'[48]

A Troubled Peace and the Descent into War

In his coronation speech, Alexius IV clearly envisaged problems in fulfilling this promise: 'we will prudently and with all our might, influence the Eastern Church towards the same end'; in other words, he was unable to guarantee the Orthodox clerics would follow his lead – a sign of his own weakness as much as anything else.[49] Alexius IV also began to hand over the vast sums of money he owed the crusaders, although he was soon compelled to melt down precious icons and relics to pay his allies, a move that provoked deep hostility from his own people. Choniates wrote of the subversion of the Byzantine state and 'of revered vessels seized from churches with utter indifference and given over to the enemy troops as common silver and gold.'[50]

By the late summer of 1203 it was too late to invade Egypt, although that certainly remained the crusaders' intention. Instead they decided to help Alexius IV and set out on a tour of the region designed to consolidate his authority and to raise money. As the young emperor acknowledged, 'You should know then that the Greeks hate me on account of you. If you leave I will lose this land and they will put me to death.'[51] Alexius also promised to supply the westerners with all necessary supplies and to help the Venetians prepare their fleet ready to embark in the spring of 1204.[52]

While Alexius IV and the leading French crusaders were away, tensions between the Greeks and the remaining westerners took a serious turn for the worse. A group of crusaders attacked a small mosque – probably built for Muslim traders during Isaac's alliance with Saladin – near the shoreline of the Golden Horn. The occupants begged the locals for help and, only too pleased to turn against the hated invaders, many citizens rushed to join the fray. In response, as they had done during the first siege of Constantinople back in June, the crusaders started a fire, although this time the consequences were incomparably worse. The blaze lasted for three days and ripped through areas of wooden housing, turning more than 400 acres of the city into a smouldering, charred wasteland. Understandably the Greeks were outraged at this vandalism of their precious city, and any westerners living in Constantinople – including several thousand traders based there – had to flee and take shelter in the crusaders' camp at Galata.[53]

Isaac remained obliged to keep melting down precious objects to pay the westerners. In a play on his family name of Angelos, Choniates condemned him as 'the incendiary angel of evil', but by mid-November he stopped handing over any money and tensions grew. The return of Alexius IV and the northern French nobles brought even further trouble. The lack of cash infuriated the crusader leadership, but Alexius knew they could not set sail for Egypt at that time of year and that they relied on him for food. Violence and skirmishing grew ever more frequent and eventually both sides called for a formal summit.

The crusader delegation brought along the sealed documents that testified to the agreement between Alexius and themselves. They reminded him of his moral and financial duties but now added a threat: if he failed to comply, 'you should know that from this time forward they [the crusaders] will not regard you as their lord or friend. Instead they will recover what is owed to them by whatever means necessary . . . they have never acted deceitfully and it would be against the custom of their country to do so.'[54] This warning, combined with the slight on the Greek character, provoked outrage and the envoys barely escaped the palace alive. Alexius IV, of course, could neither deny the oath, nor, in a hall of his own people, favour the westerners.

Dandolo made one last attempt to recover the situation. He approached Alexius in person and urged him to remember what the crusaders had done for him, but the young man was so paralysed by his own political weaknesses that he dismissed the doge with insults. Dandolo exploded with rage: 'Wretched boy! We dragged you out of the filth and into the filth we will cast you again. And I defy you, and I give you warning that I will do you all the harm in my power from this moment forwards.'⁵⁵ 'And so the war began', as Villehardouin succinctly observed.⁵⁶

On the night of 1 January 1204 the Byzantines made their most confrontational move yet. They filled seventeen vessels with combustible materials and, with the wind behind them, dispatched this deadly, floating pyre towards the Venetian ships. If the Greek boats became enmeshed with those of the Italians then the crusaders would be at the mercy of the Byzantine Empire. A watchman sounded the alarm and the doge ordered galleys to row out to the burning boats, throw grappling irons onto them and pull them out into the channel. Against a backdrop of jeering locals the Venetians accomplished this task quite brilliantly and saved their ships.

Such an aggressive action only increased the likelihood of full-scale confrontation. A Byzantine noble known as Murtzuphlus (a nickname meaning 'mono-eyebrow') emerged to focus the opposition to the westerners. Anger towards Alexius IV and his increasingly feeble father Isaac reached a peak. 'Like a boiling kettle to blow off a steam of abuse', a mob barged into the Hagia Sophia and demanded that the senate and leading churchmen elect a new ruler.⁵⁷ Candidate after candidate declined such a dangerous role until a young noble named Nicholas Kannavos was seized and, against his will, anointed emperor on 27 January. Later that day a desperate Alexius IV turned to the crusaders for help but his invitation for them to enter the city proved the final act of provocation to his enemies. That night, Murtzuphlus arrested him and cast him into prison. Within hours the usurper was crowned emperor (with the formal title of Alexius V). Now there were four holders of the imperial title in Constantinople – a ridiculous situation for one of the greatest institutions in Christendom, and a sign of just how moribund the Byzantine Empire had become.

Within days Murtzuphlus killed Kannavos and Isaac: he also started to refortify the defences of Constantinople and his energetic style inspired the imperial forces. Three Venetians were captured and Murtzuphlus commanded them to be suspended from hooks in front of the city walls before he personally set them alight in a gruesome demonstration of his personal hatred of westerners. Predictably, he withdrew food markets from the crusaders which forced them to forage over considerable distances. Murtzuphlus planned to ambush one such raiding party but, disastrously for him, he lost not only the battle but also the great talisman of the Byzantine army, an icon of the Virgin, described as 'a fellow general' by Choniates. To the crusader Robert of Clari this was inevitable because, as a usurper, the Greek 'had no right to carry it and so was defeated'.[58] Murtzuphlus foolishly tried to deny the loss to his people, and when the crusaders learned of this deception they cheerfully paraded the icon in front of the walls to humiliate their rival.

Last-ditch attempts at diplomacy failed and, as Choniates pithily noted, 'Their inordinate hatred for us and our excessive disagreement with them allowed for no humane feeling between us.'[59] Murtzuphlus still feared that the crusaders might join with Alexius IV, and so on 8 February he strangled the young man; a grim end to the life of an individual whose efforts to assume his personal inheritance had provoked consequences of such terrible magnitude. To the crusaders, the murder of Alexius IV provided a powerful justification for the removal of his killer. Now, camped outside an implacably hostile city, hundreds of miles from home, denied food, and in no condition to continue to the Holy Land, their options were extremely limited. If they gave up it would be a cause of intolerable shame and criticism, and their justification for going to Constantinople in the first instance had become redundant. In these circumstances, they decided to assault the city and to remove the treacherous Murtzuphlus.[60]

The Sack of Constantinople, 1204

Both sides prepared for war. The Venetian ships were equipped with, as Robert of Clari wrote, 'marvellous engines'. They lashed together yardarms to form bridges about 110 feet long, suspended high on the mastheads and covered with hides to protect the attackers from missiles. These huge tubes would be brought up to the city walls to disgorge the crusader knights onto the battlements. Similar devices had been deployed the previous summer and, in an effort to counter them, Murtzuphlus ordered huge wooden towers to be constructed on top of the walls along the Golden Horn. These unwieldy creations, projecting perilously outwards from the fortifications, and in some cases six or seven storeys high, were covered in vinegar-soaked hides to protect them from missiles and flames. The end result must have looked like some freakish shanty town, but they were to play a crucial role in resistance to the attack.[61]

As the crusaders organised their resources they also planned the division of their conquest. The senior leadership drew up what is known as the 'March Pact' in which they agreed that all booty was to be centrally pooled with the first call being to pay off remaining debts to the Venetians. The identities of the Latin emperor and the patriarch were to be decided by a committee of six Frenchmen and six Venetians, a reflection of the parity of effort that the two groups had put into the enterprise. A further committee would allocate the lands of the Byzantine Empire to the conquerors while, naturally, the Venetians were guaranteed a position of economic dominance. The need to bring stability to the new empire was recognised in a decision to put off sailing to the Holy Land until 1205; finally, oaths were taken to try to prevent assaults on women and churchmen in the aftermath of the capture.[62]

On 8 April 1204 the crusaders loaded their ships, then sought absolution for their sins from the priesthood and prayed for divine aid. The next day the fleet – almost a mile long according to Villehardouin – began the short journey over the Golden Horn. Arranged in their familiar divisions, they moved across the inlet. In some areas a narrow strip of land lay between the fortifications and the water and it was here the French set to work. Scaling ladders were put to the walls and siege engines began to bombard the city; in turn, the defenders fired back their own missiles and poured boiling oil down onto the besiegers. Murtzuphlus proved an able commander and his sharp direction brought proper spirit to the Greeks' resistance. The weather conditions helped him too – a contrary wind prevented the Venetian ships from drawing as near to the walls as they had hoped. Being unable to engage closely, the crusaders withdrew, to a huge cheer from the Greeks. Morale in the crusader camp was, unsurprisingly, fragile.

The leadership acted quickly to prevent a complete collapse of hope and tried to encourage the troops; the clergy argued that the day's events were simply a divine test of the crusaders' resolve. They preached powerful sermons that claimed the Greeks were 'worse than the Jews' and that their disobedience to the papacy merited punishment. In consequence, the crusaders were justified in their actions and deserved divine blessing and remission of their sins.[63]

Four days later a second assault began. Again there was a period of fierce bombardment from both sides: 'cries from the battle were so great that it seemed that the whole world was quaking', wrote Villehardouin.[64] At first it looked as though the Byzantines were holding firm but a fortuitous change in the breeze finally brought the crusaders' ships up to the walls. Robert of Clari described what happened next: 'by a miracle of God, the ship of the bishop of Soissons struck against one of the towers, as the sea, which is never still there, carried it forward.'[65] Some of the Venetian vessels were lashed together in pairs and, appropriately enough, the *Paradise* and the *Lady Pilgrim* were the ships whose ladders locked one of the towers in a lethal embrace. Fortified by a potent combination of prayers and the offer of 100 silver marks to the first man onto the walls, crusaders gathered at the exits of their fortified bridges, swaying high above the deck and conscious that a mistimed jump would cause them to plummet to their death. Once over the dizzying chasm there remained the small matter of the defenders . . . A Venetian leapt across only to be killed, but two French knights succeeded in creating the space for others to join them and soon the first crusader banner fluttered above the battlements of Constantinople. To make real progress, however, required an entrance at ground level.

On the shoreline a group of men from Amiens hacked and battered away at a small, bricked-up door.[66] As stones and debris thudded down onto their protective mats and shelters they managed to breach the makeshift barrier. Aleaumes of Clari, a belligerent priest, volunteered to be the first to enter. He had to struggle through a hole about the size of a small fireplace, beat off the waiting Greeks and then resist long enough to allow his colleagues to follow. As he crawled through the gap, blows rained down on top of him but, incredibly, he survived and then, much to the defenders' horror, he stood up, stepped forwards and began to fight. Such was their fear of this seemingly indestructible man that the Greeks fled, leaving Aleaumes to call back for his friends to join him. Once into the streets this small group of crusaders soon found a gate and forced this open to allow mounted knights to pour into Constantinople and seal the city's fate. By nightfall the districts close to the Golden Horn had fallen and the crusaders paused to rest. Overnight Murtzuphlus decided to emulate Alexius III by fleeing; once news of this spread, the senior figures who remained decided to surrender. The Greeks hoped that their submission would prevent any further violence, but to the crusaders the removal of any active opposition meant they could begin the sack of Constantinople in earnest.

As the mob fanned out across the city, the senior nobility hurried to secure the imperial palaces. Boniface of Montferrat took the Bucoleon, where he found 'such a store of precious things that it is impossible to describe the treasures that were in that palace, for there were so many they were endless and innumerable.'[67] While the takeover of the palaces was relatively orderly, the rank and file completely ignored their earlier vows to behave with restraint. Infuriated at their dismal treatment by the Byzantines, fortified by a belief in divine favour and inspired by pure and simple greed, they despoiled churches and houses and killed and savaged without distinction. 'So those who denied us small things have relinquished everything to us by divine judgement', was the sanctimonious obser-vation of Baldwin of Flanders.[68] The crusaders ransacked the Hagia Sophia, the spiritual heart of Byzantium. Drunken westerners cavorted beneath its magnificent mosaic ceiling, a prostitute danced on the altar and then straddled the patriarch's chair; meanwhile pack animals were brought in to carry away the spoils of war. Elsewhere, even Latin churchmen joined this orgy of acquisitiveness. Abbot Martin of Pairis found the treasury at the imperial foundation of the Church of the Christ Pantocrator. He grabbed the feeble old Orthodox monk who guarded the precious objects stored there and bellowed at him: 'Come, faithless old man, show me the more powerful of the relics you guard. Otherwise understand that you will be punished immediately with death.'[69] The quivering monk handed over what he had and the abbot departed, his robes bulging with booty like an incompetent shoplifter. Such an image, regardless of explanations of divine favour, is hard for us – and indeed for some contemporaries as well – to see in anything other than an overwhelmingly cynical light. Immense numbers of relics made their way back to the churches of western Europe. While the four horses and the objects in the treasury of St Mark's in Venice are the most famous of these, many other crusaders gave precious objects to their local churches when they returned home.[70]

It was not just the fabric of Constantinople that was shattered, its people were brutalised too – even nuns were violated. Nicholas Mesarites, a contemporary Byzantine author, wrote of 'westerners tearing children from mothers and mothers from children, treating the virgin with wanton shame in holy chapels, viewing with fear neither the wrath of God nor the vengeance of men.'[71] To the Greeks, such behaviour was inexcusable. Choniates argued passionately that the crusaders were exposed as greedy fraudsters, sinners against Christ. He compared Saladin's humane treatment of his captives at Jerusalem in 1187 with the brutality of the westerners against their fellow Christians; the implication was clear: even a Muslim was superior to the barbaric crusaders.[72]

Even though many of the crusaders had taken loot for themselves the conquerors gathered mountains of spoils to share out. The Venetians were finally paid off and individuals given specific amounts according to their rank. The next major decision was to elect an emperor.[73] On 9 May the committee assembled and after a long debate it voted for Count Baldwin of Flanders. To Boniface of Montferrat, the nominal leader of the crusade, this was something of a blow, but he conceded with some grace; in any case, Baldwin was recognised as a good choice. A week later, dressed in the magnificent imperial robes, the Fleming was anointed and crowned the emperor of Constantinople, one of the greatest titles in the known world. The fate of Doge Dandolo is worth mentioning too. Given his extreme age he wrote to the pope and asked to be released from his pilgrimage vow to go to Jerusalem. Innocent remained furious with the doge for his behaviour at Zara and his lack of any subsequent remorse. Thus, one imagines, the pope took grim pleasure in rejecting the request. Innocent assured Dandolo that because the doge was so important to the leadership of the crusade it would be dangerous to agree to his petition because it might endanger the expedition. Politely checkmated, the doge could argue no further, although the issue soon became irrelevant when he died in June 1205.[74]

In the aftermath of the conquest of Constantinople the Latins fought hard to extend their power. Boniface of Montferrat took control of Thessalonica, the Venetians seized Crete and Corfu to form essential parts of their trading empire and the Villehardouin clan established themselves in the Peloponnese.[75] There was, of course, opposition. Murtzuphlus was soon captured and executed, but other Greek nobles became a focus for anti-Latin feelings and the hostility of the Christian king of Bulgaria was a further distraction. It was fighting the latter's armies at Adrianople in April 1205 that Louis of Blois was killed and Emperor Baldwin seized and never seen again. This disastrous defeat led to the first of a series of appeals for help from western Europe. In the same way that many men had returned home after the First Crusade, so the Latin Empire of Constantinople (as it is known) suffered from a lack of manpower too. In part this was a consequence of its unforeseen creation. While it possessed ties with certain regions, such as Flanders, Montferrat and Venice, the thirteenth century saw a multiplicity of different draws on crusading enthusiasm. Some proved much closer to home than the Latin Empire and because it could never possess the allure of the holy city of Jerusalem, it was doomed to be something of a poor relation to the Holy Land.

One of the most intriguing reactions to the Fourth Crusade was that of Innocent III.[76] He had, as we saw, tried to prevent the expedition from attacking Christian lands, although the caveats within these directives proved easy to circumvent or to ignore. The pope's early reaction to the news of the capture was very positive. He wrote in November 1204 that God had transformed the Byzantine Empire from 'the proud to the humble, from the disobedient to the obedient, from schismatic to Catholic.'[77] He was prepared to award full crusading privileges for the defence of the Latin Empire and continued to speak of 'the miracle that has come to pass in these days' into 1205.[78] By midsummer of that year, however, his tone had changed. First, the legate on the crusade released the men from their vows to go to the Levant – a realistic move given the vulnerability of the empire, but one that ended Innocent's hopes of the crusade ever reaching the Holy Land. More seriously, visitors to Rome began to detail the full atrocities of the sack – matters passed over by the crusaders' reports of the event – and the pope learned of the terrible violation of women and the destruction of churches. He was appalled at the sordid, grasping behaviour of the crusaders and noted that the Orthodox Church would have no wish to acknowledge papal primacy if it saw in the Latins 'nothing except an example of affliction and the works of hell, so that now it rightly detests them more than dogs.'[79] To Boniface of Montferrat he railed, 'you turned away from the purity of your vow when you took up arms not against Saracens but Christians . . . preferring earthly wealth to celestial treasures.'[80] Most dramatically of all, we sense a spiritual crisis in the head of the Catholic Church, baffled by the ways of the Lord and wondering how his God could let such a thing happen. 'Who can know the mind of the Lord?' was his troubled and unsettled conclusion.[81]

The Fourth Crusade remains one of the most controversial of all crusading expeditions. While conspiracy theories have accused the pope, the Venetians and various of the crusade leaders of plotting the diversion to Constantinople, none of these can be sustained. Originally, the campaign planned to attack Egypt but it was the disastrous terms of the Treaty of Venice that drew the crusaders to Zara and then laid them open to the offer of Prince Alexius. Ironically, therefore, it was a Greek who steered the campaign towards Constantinople; otherwise, there is no hint that this was a realistic desire on the part of anyone. The chronic instability of the Byzantine Empire during the early thirteenth century, combined with the desperation and the determination of the crusaders – men whose military expertise had become so honed and reinforced in the course of their experiences – gave them the opportunity to pull off an improbable and tragic victory, and an event still remembered in the Orthodox world today.

8

From 'little foxes in the vines' and the Children's Crusade to the Greatest Church Council of the Age

The closing decades of the twelfth century saw the emergence of several powerful new forms of spirituality across western Europe.[1] A thriving economy brought widespread urban expansion and considerable personal gain, but this financial boom clashed with a growing interest in a pure and simple existence, modelled on a life of apostolic poverty. In tandem with this, increasing numbers of lay people openly questioned both the wealth of the Church and the moral qualities of some of its clerics. Men such as Waldes of Lyons gave up a comfortable lifestyle to follow a more spiritual approach and his calls for austerity attracted numerous followers. Notwithstanding his overt criticism of the Church, Waldes was, at heart, still fairly close to orthodox Catholicism, although his demands to be allowed to preach in public were rejected by the papacy, jealous to preserve proprietorship of what it regarded as the true interpretation of the gospels.[2] Around the middle of the century, however, another strand of religious belief began to surface: Catharism (from the Greek *kathare* meaning 'pure'), a radical set of ideas that posed a profound challenge to the power of the Catholic Church. To fight this threat Pope Innocent launched the Albigensian Crusade, a conflict that brought the horrors of holy war to the heart of Christendom and engendered levels of atrocity unseen in Europe since the barbarian invasions. As one contemporary lamented, the launch of the crusade was 'the decision that led to so much sorrow, that left so many men dead with their guts spilled out and so many great ladies and pretty girls naked and cold, stripped of gown and cloak. From beyond Montpellier as far as Bordeaux, any that rebelled were to be utterly destroyed.'[3]

The Rise of Catharism

Two of the prime reasons why Catharism posed such a danger to the Church lay in the broad appeal of its beliefs and the fact that it did not rely on a single charismatic leader but had a well-established hierarchy. At the heart of the faith was dualism, the belief that a Good God had created all spiritual matter, including men's souls, and an Evil God (Satan) had created all material and corporeal things.[4] Christ had come to earth, but only took on a human appearance to avoid entering a physical body. He told the Cathars how to achieve salvation through the baptism of the spirit, an act known as the *consolamentum*, a process that could be administered only by a spiritual elite, the *perfecti*. These men and – crucially – women, renounced all property, vowed never to kill any human or warm-blooded beast, to consume no products of sexual intercourse such as meat, cheese, eggs or milk, to tell no lies and abstain completely from sex which was the means of physical procreation and intrinsically evil. Most Cathars found these rules an impractical way to exist and followed as modest a life as possible. They rejected the Old Testament, the Eucharist, baptism and only took the *consolamentum* – thus obtaining salvation – as they neared death. The concept of a female priest was unheard of in the Catholic Church, but given the restricted outlets for women's spirituality anyway it represented another powerful attraction of this new faith. The simple tenets of Catharism were easy to understand; the *perfecti* seemed to lead genuinely pure lives – especially compared to the venality of the existing hierarchy. Local lords did little to shift the newcomers and some welcomed the spiritual rigour they seemed to bring.

Catharism originated in south-eastern Europe and it first appeared in the West, probably carried by traders and returning crusaders, during the 1140s in Cologne and southern France. Another group surfaced in Oxford in 1166, but King Henry II swiftly ordered the detention of the thirty individuals involved. Punishment was swift and harsh: their brows were branded, they were stripped to the waist, flogged and driven out of the city to perish in the bitter winter cold: the sect was never again seen on English shores. Other Cathar communities, however, thrived and the papacy felt compelled to pass formal legislation to outlaw the heretics at the Third Lateran Council in 1179: 'since the loathsome heresy of those who some call the Cathars ... has grown so strong that they no longer practise their wickedness in secret, as others do, but proclaim their error publicly and draw the simple and the weak to join them, we declare that they and their defenders and those who receive them are under anathema ... [therefore, they will not receive Mass] or burial amongst Christians. We also grant that to faithful Christians who take up arms against them ... a remission of two years' penance.'[5]

Catharism flourished most strongly in southern France. Culturally and linguistically, the Languedoc was entirely distinct from northern France (the *langue d'oc* – *oc* means 'yes'). It was the home of the troubadour poets, of remote rural villages; a rugged land of castles clinging to rocky spurs, of fertile valleys and the broad floodplain of the River Rhône easing out into the Mediterranean. Based far to the north, the Capetian kings had no worthwhile influence in the Languedoc and while the counts of Toulouse were figures of considerable standing, most local power structures were highly fragmented. The Catholic Church was poorly developed in comparison to the well-established hierarchies of northern France; many urban clerics were perceived as greedy and indolent, while the rural clergy were often ill-educated men who lived openly with their mistresses and children. Such conditions were ripe for Catharism to enter communities and, with the support of the local nobility, it put down the most tenacious roots. The Church sent special delegations of Cistercian monks to try and bring the heretics and their supporters back into the fold. Cathar *perfecti* and Catholic clergy held numerous debates, but unsurprisingly neither conceded their beliefs were wrong. When Innocent III became pope, these efforts intensified; given his determination to guard the Christian faith, he saw that Catharism needed to be utterly eradicated.

Even before Innocent's pontificate, churchmen had described the region around Toulouse as 'a great cesspit of evil, with all the scum of heresy flowing into it', and 'the mother of heresy and the fountainhead of error ... When heretics spoke, everyone applauded.' The city itself was 'so diseased that, from the soles of its feet to the top of its head, there was not a healthy piece in it'; the solution offered was simple – to stun, sever, and raise up the head on a sword.[6] This highly emotive language of pollution and contamination formed the basic register in the fight against the Cathars; the body of the Mother Church itself was said to be threatened from within, as if by a cancer, and only a sword could cut it out. In 1204 Innocent tried to persuade King Philip of France to eradicate the wild beasts who planned to destroy the Church. The pope offered him the same remission of all sins as a crusader to the Holy Land if he would go to Toulouse and crush the man seen as the Cathars' principal protector, Count Raymond VI of Toulouse. Philip declined the invitation, as he would repeatedly do in the future.[7] It was another four years before the confrontation with the Cathars escalated into outright conflict. The situation became tinder-dry with the repeated failure of preachers to convince the heretics to recant; indeed, according to the near contemporary William of Tudela, their attempts met with derision: 'People in this region think more of a rotten apple than sermons.'[8] The conflagration itself was largely precipitated by the murder of a papal legate, Peter of Castelnau, in January 1208. Peter had spent months trying to bring the heretics to heel and in the course of his travels, as he waited for a ferry to cross the River Rhône, he was fatally stabbed in the back by one of Count Raymond's vassals. When the news reached Rome, Pope Innocent was furious; he lit a candle and, in the name of St Peter, he dashed it to the floor and cursed the murder.[9]

The Launch of the Albigensian Crusade

Without hesitation Innocent called for a crusade: 'In the name of Christ and in my name . . . drive the heretics out from the virtuous.'[10] Thus the weapon that had been used so frequently against God's enemies overseas and at the edges of Christendom was deployed in the heartlands of western Europe against a people that were, of a sort, Christians (they approved of the New Testament) and who certainly lived amongst, and were supported by, Catholics. This marked another extension in crusading theory, although the familiar justification of a defensive war was fulfilled by the threat Catharism posed to the Church: 'Attack the followers of heresy more fearlessly even than the Saracens – since they are more evil – with a strong hand and an outstretched arm. Forward then soldiers of Christ! Forward brave recruits to the Christian army! Let the universal cry of grief of the

Godfrey of Bouillon and Adhémar of Le Puy head the armies of the First Crusade. Taken from a thirteenth-century manuscript of the Old French *Histoire d'Outremer* of William of Tyre.

Patriarch Aimery of Antioch tied to the citadel of Antioch where Prince Reynald smeared his head with honey and released a hive of bees on him, an act of revenge for the ageing churchman's opposition to his marriage to Princess Constance. Taken from a thirteenth-century manuscript of the Old French *Histoire d'Outremer* of William of Tyre.

Marriage of Guy of Lusignan and Queen Sibylla of Jerusalem. Taken from a thirteenth-century manuscript of the Old French *Histoire d'Outremer* of William of Tyre.

Carved ivory cover, ornamented with turquoises, rubies and emeralds and showing a king carrying out the six acts of mercy specified in the Book of Matthew. Taken from the Psalter of Queen Melisende probably presented to her by her husband King Fulk of Jerusalem. The bird is a falcon, a pun on Fulk's name.

Saladin's mausoleum in Damascus. Next to the original medieval tomb (left) stands a marble structure presented by Kaiser Wilhelm II after his visit of 1898.

Seal of Richard the Lionheart.

Seal of Emperor Frederick II, ruler of Germany, Sicily and Jerusalem.

Aerial view of Hospitaller castle of Krak des Chevaliers, southern Syria.
This 1920s photograph shows locals' houses still within the fortifications,
prior to their removal by the French.

Burning at the stake of the Grand Master of the Templars, James of Molay, and Geoffrey of Charney on 18 March 1314 on a small island in the River Seine.

Portrait of Sultan Mehmet II, conqueror of Constantinople 1453.

State visit to Jerusalem of Kaiser Wilhelm II of Germany in October 1898.

Contemporary cartoon from *Punch*, drawing a parallel between Richard the Lionheart's failure to take Jerusalem during the Third Crusade and General Allenby's entry into the city in 1917.

THE LAST CRUSADE.

Cœur-de-Lion (*looking down on the Holy City*), "MY DREAM COMES TRUE!"

'Pershing's Crusaders', poster of the first official film report of the US Army in Europe, 1918.

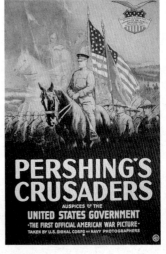

The Jarrow Crusade, 1936.

U.S. Army Sergeant, identified as Kelly, 38, from Chipley, Florida, steps on a carpet depicting Saddam Hussein and Saladin, at the Office of Reconstruction and Humanitarian Assistance (ORHA) base in Baghdad, 11 May 2003.

Holy Church arouse you, let pious zeal inspire you to avenge this monstrous crime against your God!'[11] The Cathars were rebels against God, dangerous adversaries sent by the Devil to ensnare the faithful and lead them to hell: the contagion of heresy had to be torn out from society and proper order restored.

Peter of Castelnau was hailed as a martyr and when, several weeks after his death, the legate's body was transferred to its proper tomb it was 'found to be as whole and unimpaired as if it had been buried that very day. A marvellous perfume arose from his body and clothing.'[12] In contrast to this story of Catholic purity, the Church portrayed the heretics as vile, depraved creatures who engaged in endless orgies and barely clung to the vestiges of humanity. One writer described how a Cathar 'fell into such depths of madness that he emptied his bowels beside the altar in a church and by way of showing contempt for God wiped himself with the altar cloth.'[13]

In the autumn of 1208 Cistercian preachers toured northern and eastern France to whip up support for the crusade. Recruits wore the sign of the cross and received all the privileges, protection and spiritual rewards of a crusader to the Holy Land. King Philip was too worried about a possible invasion by King John of England to take part, but many senior nobles took the cross. The duke of Burgundy, the count of Nevers, the count of Saint-Pol and the count of Montfort all committed themselves to God's cause. These families had proud traditions of crusading that stretched back to the capture of Jerusalem in 1099. The count of Saint-Pol's predecessor, Hugh, had been one of the leading knights on the Fourth Crusade until his death from gout in January 1205. Count Simon de Montfort was another veteran of that expedition although as we saw, he could not stomach the idea of attacking the Christian city of Zara and so left the campaign in the autumn of 1203 to sail directly to the Holy Land. With the guiding hand of Pope Innocent at his back, Simon would emerge as the champion of the Church and over the next decade his struggle with Count Raymond came to inflict horrific suffering across the towns and castles of south-western France.

The first target of papal rage was the count of Toulouse, a man who had been excommunicated in 1207 for his apparent tolerance of the heretics. 'You cherish heretics, you yourself are strongly suspected of heresy . . . you stand convicted as an adversary of the Gospel . . . we cannot allow such an injury to the Church to go unpunished . . . [your]

territory will be taken from you . . . The wrath of the Lord will not be turned from you . . .', thundered Innocent.[14] In reality, Count Raymond was probably not an active Cathar, but he was undoubtedly sympathetic to their cause and resented what he came to see as a blatant attempt by the northern French crusaders to steal his lands. Raymond's career attracted starkly opposing assessments. Peter of les Vaux-de-Cernay, a partisan of the Montforts, stated that 'the count was a vicious and lecherous man . . . from early youth he lost no opportunity to seek out his father's concubines and felt no compunction about bedding them – indeed none of them could please him unless he knew that his father had previously slept with her . . . Always he acted as a limb of the Devil, an enemy of the Cross . . . a veritable treasury of all sins.'[15] To his supporters, however, he was 'valiant, joyful and strong', and when, later in the crusade, he entered Toulouse to eject the French he was greeted as 'the morning star, risen and shining upon us! Our lord who was lost!'[16]

With the crusade poised to attack his lands Count Raymond tried to deflect the Church's ire and made a humiliating public submission to the papal legate in Saint-Gilles, the town of his family's patron saint. Today Saint-Gilles is a sleepy village a few miles distant from the Mediterranean, yet it still possesses one of the most famous Romanesque churches in Europe and its magnificent tympanum features imagery connected with the rich crusading history of the counts of Toulouse.[17] In the course of his supposed reconciliation Raymond was led naked to the church doors where, in the presence of the papal legate and other leading clerics, he swore to obey the papacy. He was then robed and scourged by the legate to absolve him of his sins and taken into the church. So great was the crowd that Raymond had to leave through the crypt and pass – by neat irony – the tomb of the murdered legate, Peter of Castelnau. The count then took the cross himself, although this was soon declared the act of a false and faithless man by the hostile Peter of les Vaux-de-Cernay.[18]

The Siege and Sack of Béziers

The main crusade continued to head relentlessly southwards and soon it entered the lands of another man accused of harbouring heretics:

Raymond-Roger Trenceval, the viscount of Béziers. His hometown stands on a commanding hilltop location overlooking the broad flood-plain of the River Orb. On 21 July 1209 the citizens who lined its walls caught their first glimpse of a distant dust cloud: slowly it grew bigger and bigger; movement rippled underneath the billowing mass and gradually came into focus. Sunlight reflected off armour, banners bearing bright red crosses cracked in the early evening breeze, warhorses snorted and whinnied beneath their masters while carthorses strained to haul heavy wagons. This was a force with lethal intent: an army of 20,000 crusaders set upon the destruction of the Cathar heretics, some of whom sheltered defiantly behind the town walls.[19]

Bishop Reynald of Béziers stood in his cathedral and tried to convince the inhabitants to surrender. His voice breaking with fear, he urged the people to reconsider their resistance. He brandished a list of the names of the 220 individuals suspected of heresy and warned of the dire consequences if they were not handed over. The citizens' response was crisp – they told the bishop 'they would rather be drowned in the salt sea than take his advice'. They cared little for the distant authority of Rome and had faith in their own beliefs and the strength of their town walls; as one contemporary drily observed, however, 'an evil gift the men of Béziers received when they were told to stand firm and give battle.'[20]

Reynald carried the news out to the crusader army. Grim-faced, Abbot Arnold Amalric of Citeaux, the papal legate and leader of the expedition, ordered the siege to begin on 22 July. At first the defenders were confident – one crusader was seized, mutilated and thrown off a bridge. The senior crusading nobles gathered to discuss strategy; Béziers appeared very well fortified. Yet as they talked, cries of 'To arms! To arms!' rang out from their lines. The most unpredictable element of the crusader army, known as the *ribauds* – basically the servants and hangers-on – had become fed up with the citizens' mockery and charged towards the walls. Armed with little more than clubs and picks they began to batter and smash away at the defences and their ferocious onslaught provoked panic.

Astonished by the *ribauds'* progress the crusading knights rushed to put on their armour and to join the fray. At the sight of the heavy knights gathering in formation, courage deserted the men defending the city and they abandoned the walls and the gates. The crusaders swarmed into Béziers, inflamed with religious zeal and determined to reap material rewards for their success in the holy war; the *ribauds* scented riches beyond their wildest dreams and began to seize and hoard everything they could. With a frenzied energy the crusaders started to ransack the houses, shops and palaces; meanwhile the inhabitants sought refuge in the cathedral. Soon it was packed full with desperate people; the priests sensed their impending fate and donned vestments for a Mass for the dead and the bells tolled a funeral lament. As the town fell, the crusaders faced a dilemma because they could not decide who was guilty of heresy and who was not. They were painfully aware that Catholics – even those tainted by association with the unbelievers – were mingled amongst the heretics. 'What shall we do, Lord?' they asked Abbot Arnold Amalric. Might some of the Cathars pretend to be Catholics to avoid death and then continue to spread the contagion of heresy once the crusaders had gone? The abbot was stony-faced; an example had to be made to all the enemies of the Church. Calmly he uttered one of the most chilling phrases in the history of medieval Europe, words that sealed the fate of thousands of innocent men, women and children: 'Kill them all. God will know his own.'[21]

At this uncompromising edict the massacre began. The *ribauds* and the knights went to work with, to a modern reader, a stomach-churning enthusiasm and soon the piercing shrieks of the dying assailed the ears of those inside the cathedral. The smell of smoke began to permeate into the building as nearby houses and shops were torched in the anarchic, frenzied atmosphere of the sack. Soon the flames spread to the cathedral itself and, barricaded inside their supposed place of sanctuary, thousands were incinerated in the house of God. So intense was the heat that the cathedral split into two and central Béziers became one enormous funeral pyre. Warfare in western Europe had reached a new level of horror, and all in the name of God. The message was plain: heresy would be extinguished at all costs.

Carcassonne was next in line to the crusaders and it surrendered relatively quickly; the viscount of Béziers (who had fled there for safety) was taken prisoner and he soon died in custody. By the autumn of 1209, however, the crusaders began to melt away because their terms of service were set at only forty days' fighting and they wanted to return home. Only a few remained in the south and the rebels started to regain much of their lost land.

Simon de Montfort, Hero of the Church

While Raymond of Toulouse had lain low during these events, his patent lack of enthusiasm for the crusade soon brought him into open opposition to the Church once more. As noted above, his principal opponent was Simon de Montfort, a man who perfectly fused the secular and spiritual motives of a crusader. Simon was driven by a deep conviction that he was doing God's work and a sense of moral certainty that he was entitled to take over the lands of the heretics. Physically, he was a powerful man, which caused the pope to pun that the lord of Montfort was 'the Strong Mountain' (*mons* and *fortis*) sent by Christ to defend the Church. A contemporary admirer described him as 'eloquent of speech, eminently approachable, a most congenial comrade-in-arms, of impeccable chastity, outstanding in humility, wise, firm of purpose, prudent in counsel, fair in giving judgement . . . and totally dedicated to the service of God.'[22] To an opponent, he was a man who 'destroys and devastates, a man devoid of pity'.[23] As time moved on, however, his desire to conquer and hold lands in his own right even began to provoke disquiet in the Church and aroused ever more fierce opposition in the south.

In 1213, the prospect of a new crusade to the Holy Land brought a brief cessation to hostilities, but so embedded were the respective hatreds that this calm lasted only a matter of months. Between 1209 and 1218 Simon fought no fewer than thirty-nine sieges; some lasted only hours, others took months. He was capable of terrible atrocities: at the castle of Bram all the defenders except one were blinded and had their noses cut off. The remaining prisoner was blinded in only one eye and told to lead this pitiful procession of brutalised troops back to the rebel lands.[24] On another occasion he ordered the buildings of Toulouse to be so ravaged that a man could pass straight into the city without pause. Roofs, workshops, chambers and doorways were ripped out: 'such was the noise, dust and damage,' wrote William of Tudela, 'that it felt like an earthquake . . . in every street, men were in tears, their hearts and spirits overcome by darkness.'[25] Yet Raymond's resistance – in large part an attempt to hold on to his own ancestral lands – enabled Catharism to survive, especially in the more remote areas of the Languedoc where its adherents continued to practise their beliefs and spread their gospel. The *perfecti* moved from village to village, preaching to the people and setting up formal Cathar communities of men and (separately) women, rather like monasteries. The fight swayed back and forth as every year, waves of crusaders arrived, the heretics retreated to the countryside and then came back to the towns and castles once the danger had passed. It was like a simmering pot that all too often came to the boil, but Simon was iron-willed in his determination to bring the Languedoc to orthodoxy and to take the lands and titles of those whom he defeated. He had spent eight months besieging Toulouse when, on 25 June 1218, he was struck on the head by a catapult stone. The anonymous continuator of William of Tudela reported that the machine was worked by noble-women, girls and wives – perhaps a sign that everyone was involved in the defence of their city. Such a comment was also intended as a slight on Simon with the suggestion that 'mere' women had fired the fatal shot. In any case, 'a stone struck Count Simon on his steel helmet, shattering his eyes, brains, back teeth, forehead and jaw' and he died immediately.[26] He had certainly brought the power of the Catholic Church and the northern French nobility to the Languedoc, and at times, he had borne down hard upon the heretics. Unsurprisingly, he was loathed by the southern French as this scathing assessment of the epitaph on his tomb shows: '[It says] that he is a saint and a martyr who shall breathe again and be seated in the kingdom [of heaven] . . . If, by killing men and shedding blood, by damning souls and causing deaths . . . by kindling evil and quenching good, by killing women and slaughtering children, a man can in this world win Jesus Christ, certainly Count Simon wears a crown and shines in heaven above.'[27] Four years later Count Raymond died, marking the end of the first phase of the war.

The Church continued to fulminate against the heretics, but for a time the military situation became a little calmer. Amaury de Montfort and Raymond VII of Toulouse, the sons of the two great warriors, moved towards a compromise. In the mid-1220s, however, a new player appeared. King Louis VIII of France (1223–6) hitched his territorial ambitions in southern France to the papacy's ongoing holy war against the Cathars to trigger a new crusade.[28] Louis was, of course, following in the crusading footsteps of his father, Philip, his grandfather, Louis VII and his great-uncle, Hugh of Vermandois, although they had all been to the Holy Land. In 1226 the king led a large army southwards and received the submission of Avignon and Albi. At the Treaty of Paris in 1229 the lords of southern France were compelled to accept royal authority and a concerted attempt was made to deprive the heretics of their places of refuge.[29] Yet the Cathar belief system still persisted and with less military action during the 1220s it recovered much of its vigour. While there had been periods when the crusade made great progress, ultimately, it must be judged to have failed to uproot Catharism.

The Inquisition

The final phase of the conflict saw the papacy make its most calculating effort to destroy the heretics.[30] Churchmen realised that warfare and preaching could be avoided by those who wished to escape detection and so they developed a new mechanism to flush out the heretics and to create fear and suspicion in the very heart of their communities. The result was the fearsome Inquisition, headed by the crack troops of the medieval Church, the Dominican friars. They were university-trained experts in theology, yet their personal poverty and mendicant vocation meant they lacked the worldly trappings of the Church hierarchy and so could not be accused of the greed or moral failings of many of their predecessors.

The Inquisitors' powers were unfettered: homes could be searched, anywhere a heretic was known to have stayed was to be destroyed, repentant Cathars were resettled in places where no heresy had been discovered.[31] No one other than churchmen was permitted to possess copies of the Old and New Testament, and those whose confession of heresy was obtained under torture were to be imprisoned as a penance. The new measures made it far harder for the Cathars to move around and to live peacefully. An Inquisitorial Manual from 1245–6 gives a stark insight into the sophisticated disputation procedures available to extract confessions. If a village was suspected of heresy, all males over fourteen and females over twelve were required to come forward and make a statement of orthodoxy. If under suspicion – and anyone could, in complete anonymity, point the finger at a fellow villager – they had to confess, to recant from all heresy and swear to pursue and seize other heretics. Everyone known to have given *perfecti* food and hospitality, or listened to sermons, had their names recorded; many came to the friars of their own volition, trying to pre-empt arrest. Those who confessed had to perform pilgrimages and other acts of penance and to wear a yellow cross for the rest of their lives. People who refused to abjure the heresy were handed over to the secular authorities and burned to death. One measure that aroused special ire was the practice of condemning deceased heretics and then exhuming their bones to be burned 'in detestation of so heinous an offence'.[32] All of this generated – as it was intended to do – a climate of fear and suspicion that would fragment communities for decades. From the point of view of the Church, it began to yield results and many *perfecti* were forced to live as outlaws, or were identified and handed over to the authorities.

Inevitably, people reacted violently to this intrusive and arbitrary justice. At Albi in 1234, the inquisitor, Arnold Catalan, went to dig up the bones of a woman but he was confronted by a crowd led by a local knight. They began to hit Arnold on the chest, to slap his face and drag him away by his clothing and he only narrowly escaped being pushed into the River Tarn. Arnold retreated to the safety of the cathedral where a frenzied mob demanded his head be cut off, put in a sack and thrown into the water. The inquisitor excommunicated the entire town, a measure which led to peace negotiations and the withdrawal of the censure. Many of his colleagues were not so lucky and a number of clergymen were assassinated as they tried to implement the inquiry.

On 28 May 1242, William Arnold, the leader of the Inquisition, was ambushed and slaughtered in a remote town, twenty-five miles southeast of Toulouse, by men from the castle of Montségur, the focal point of Cathar resistance. Such an atrocity inevitably provoked a response and troops sent by Louis IX (1226–70) invested the Cathar stronghold the following summer. Penned into the fortress were 361 people, including children, of whom 211 of the total were *perfecti*.[33] Montségur stands almost 4,000 feet above sea level on a rocky outcrop around fifty miles south of Toulouse: it remains resonant of its role in history, shrouded in mist, a melancholy and ravaged structure that stands over a place of death and destruction. It was not until March 1244 that a group of servants were able to scramble up the precipitous north-eastern edge of the crag. They took the guards by surprise and captured the tower. The larger part of the fortress remained secure, but the besiegers' foothold allowed them to bring up more men and to inten-sify their assault. The defenders realised their resistance was futile – or as William of Puylaurens, a near-contemporary author, commented: 'the faithless could not withstand the onset of the faithful'. They accepted a promise that their lives be spared while the Cathar believers were handed over. William related that 'the heretics were invited to accept conversion, but refused. They were confined to an enclosure made of pales and stakes. This was set on fire, they were burned and passed on to the fire of Tartarus.'[34]

The fall of Montségur in March 1244 marked a watershed. With the death of so many *perfecti* the Cathars lost a major part of their spiritual elite. This last intervention by the French crown, combined with the rigour of the Dominican inquisitors, had finally cracked the heretics' resistance and while their beliefs persisted for a few more decades, fundamentally they had been broken. While Innocent's crusade had failed, its successor, the Inquisition, proved a far sharper and more subtle weapon in the fight against heresy.

The Children's Crusade of 1212

In spite of Pope Innocent's unsuccessful efforts to regain the Holy Land, one startling manifestation of popular support for crusading took place in 1212 – the near-legendary Children's Crusade.[35] Over the centuries this strange event has metamorphosed into a tale of lost innocence, greed, debauchery and sheer fantasy. As early as the mid-thirteenth century, writers started to gild the story. One claimed that the whole episode was initiated by two clerics who had been imprisoned by the leader of the Syrian Assassins, the Old Man of the Mountains. The men were freed on the promise that they would bring him back a group of young boys; therein lay the 'explanation' for the crusade. For some commentators, the naivety of the young was fit to be mocked, for others, it was an excuse to blame unscrupulous Italian merchants who allegedly sold their hapless passengers into slavery; a few were dispatched to Baghdad where they were said to have been martyred or set to hard labour.[36] In reality, the Children's Crusade was far less exciting than these exotic vignettes, although for us, its importance lies in its ability to illuminate the age of crusading under Innocent III.

In essence, the Children's Crusade was an unauthorised, popular movement. It has become known as a crusade because of its aims – to recover Jerusalem and the True Cross; in fact, within a year of its demise a preacher calmly commented on the 'innocent children who became crusaders the other year'.[37] The idea that a group of children and young people could reach, let alone recover, the Holy Land from the Muslims was, of course, utterly ridiculous. What it reflected, however, was a sense of frustration with the efforts of the powerful and the wealthy, that is, the failure of the Third Crusade and the diversion of the Fourth. In line with contemporary admiration for apostolic poverty and a belief in the virtue of the poor and the pure, the sense that divine providence would bring victory to this most worthy enterprise took these adventurers far from their homes and created an extraordinary legacy.

The 'crusade' began in the late spring of 1212 near the town of Chartres, about sixty miles south-west of Paris. This was a region with a rich history of crusading – some relics from the Fourth Crusade had been given to the cathedral, although in the form of Simon de Montfort, at least one notable local figure had shown his disapproval for the events of 1203–4. At the feast of Pentecost (13 May), groups of peasants, shepherds and servants gathered at the cathedral for the ceremonial display of an important relic, the tunic worn by the Virgin Mary as she gave birth to Christ. A week later prayers were said for the fight against the Muslims in Spain, and this combination of religious ceremony and preaching stirred a fervent, if unexpected, response. The 'Chronicle of Mortemer' noted: 'In the realm of France, boys and girls, with some more mature males and old men, carrying banners, wax candles, crosses, censers, made processions, and went through the cities, villages and castles, singing aloud in French, "Lord God, raise up Christendom! Lord God, return to us the True Cross!" . . . this thing, unheard of in past ages, was a wonder to many . . .'[38] The tender years of many of these devotees has aroused much comment and it seems likely that, at this stage at least, a large proportion of young children aged between seven and fourteen took part in these processions. The lack of clergymen involved is conspicuous, again an indication of the popular nature of this movement, while the desire to recover the True Cross shows the undimmed significance of this relic to the people of the West, even twenty years after its loss to Saladin.

To stimulate the enthusiasm of these people further would need a charismatic leader, and the sources name a young shepherd, Stephen of Cloyes, as the figure who emerged. Stephen had a vision from God in which Christ appeared to him as a pilgrim. The shepherd treated him kindly and so the pilgrim revealed his identity and gave him letters to deliver to the king of France at Saint-Denis, just north of Paris. Stephen and the *pueri* headed towards Saint-Denis, gathering even more adherents en route, and by the time they reached the town the group numbered several thousand. Saint-Denis was a place rich in crusading history, as we saw at the time of the Second Crusade. Stephen handed over his letters to royal counsellors and they duly held discussions with the king. Taken to its logical conclusion this was an attempt to pressure the king to lead a new crusade, but Philip was resolutely not interested. Given Stephen's many followers there must have been some concern about public order and the king was advised to order the pilgrims to disperse. The 'Chronicle of Laon' said: 'And so this boyish revival was terminated as easily as it had begun. But it seemed to many that by means of such innocents gathered of their own accord, the Lord would do something great and new upon the earth, which turned out to be far from the case.'[39] This seems a regret- tably tame ending to such an effusion of religious fervour, but over the next few weeks some of the *pueri*, undeterred, stayed on the road and headed eastwards towards Cologne and the Rhineland, set to follow the old route taken by Peter the Hermit on the First Crusade.

Their arrival prompted a new outbreak of enthusiasm amongst the poor and the young, and thousands are said to have taken the cross deter- mined to make the pilgrimage to the Holy Land, to recover the True Cross and to seek a better life. Cologne Cathedral holds a magnificent reliquary that houses the relics of the Magi (the three kings) and was, therefore, an appropriate place to begin a pilgrimage. The crowds drawn to the adventure believed that they had been chosen by God, and at this stage, they were warmly received by locals as they headed south through Germany in July and August. People gave them gifts and food and others joined the expedition. By now the crusade was headed by another charis- matic young man, Nicholas of Cologne, who carried a T-shaped cross (known as a tau), a symbol of the exodus of the Children of Israel from Egypt; they, of course, had followed their leader and crossed the sea dry-footed – perhaps some of Nicholas' followers believed the same would happen when they arrived at the Mediterranean.

Unfortunately for the pilgrims their march coincided with one of the hottest summers on record and the effort needed to cross the Alps sapped the strength and the conviction of many in Nicholas' band; every day more of his troupe fell by the wayside or returned home in shame. By late August the few thousand survivors had reached the port of Genoa in north-western Italy. Unsurprisingly, the pragmatic sea captains refused to offer free passage to such a rabble and quickly extinguished the dreams of many of these hopeful, yet utterly naive, travellers. Some settled in Genoa, others went west to Marseilles where they were also rejected by the seafaring community. The remainder wandered home, no longer welcomed so kindly, but ridiculed for their stupidity. Nicholas probably went to Rome, and although he did not meet Innocent in person the pope undoubtedly heard about the young pilgrims' activities. The Children's Crusade was an unofficial, popular movement, but it had demonstrated the desire of non-knightly classes to contribute to the crusades and Pope Innocent was sharp enough to try to harness this in his next formal crusade appeal for the Holy Land.

Quia maior, issued in April 1213, marked a significant change in the direction and form of papal appeals.[40] As we shall see below, it urged everyone to become involved in the campaign, not just knights and nobles but also townsmen, the poor and the infirm. It is no coincidence that Innocent took this step in the few months after the Children's Crusade reached Italy and this, rather than the legends of later writers, represents its true legacy. Nicholas himself managed to hang around Rome and southern Italy and he left Brindisi with the armies of the Fifth Crusade in 1217. Thus he became a 'legitimate' crusader after all, and took part in and survived an expedition to the East.

The Diversity of Crusading: Spain and the Baltic

After the successes of the Second Crusade (1145–9) the pace of reconquest in Iberia slowed and the character of the crusading movement in the peninsula changed. In contrast to crusading in the Holy Land there was little involvement of external forces and most progress was a consequence of local and regional initiatives.[41] The concept of the Military Order proved immensely popular in Iberia and the foundation of several organisations, such as the Order of Santiago (1170) and the Order of Calatrava (1158), institutionalised the struggle with Islam. While the Christian kingdoms of northern Spain began to grow in strength, the Muslims of Iberia experienced a period of upheaval with, by 1172, the removal of the ruling Almoravid dynasty at the hands of the austere Berber tribesmen of Morocco, a group known as the Almohads.[42] In 1195 Almohad armies exploited rivalries between the Christian kingdoms to crush them at the Battle of Alarcos, near Toledo.[43] So soon after the loss of Jerusalem to Saladin this latest disaster raised fears that Islam was poised to sweep aside Christianity in the peninsula as well. Such had been the antipathy between the warring factions of León and Castile that prior to this battle the ruler of the former had preferred to ally with the Muslims rather than join with his co-religionists. The shock of Alarcos was sufficiently profound to prompt a degree of Christian co-operation and with the accession of Innocent III the papacy began to offer increasing encouragement to the Iberian crusade. As we saw earlier, the most spectacular manifestation of this was the 1212 penitential procession in Rome. When King Peter II of Aragon called for outside help, Innocent appealed to the French and, with a positive response, the Christians assembled their most formidable force for years. At the same time, the Almohads were struggling with rebellions in North Africa and, to exacerbate their situation, Calpih al-Nasir was a weak, paranoid figure who executed many of his most able lieutenants.[44]

By July 1212 the Christians had made steady progress southwards and they brought their opponents to battle in mountainous terrain near Las Navas de Tolosa, roughly midway between Christian Toledo and Muslim Granada. The kings of Castile, Aragon and Navarre all took to the field, although most of the French were absent after a dispute over the distribution of booty. The crusaders confessed their sins and called for divine help in their struggle; their prayers were soon answered when the Christian cavalry burst through the enemy lines and put them to flight. Al-Nasir fled, leaving many splendid treasures, including the beautiful tapestry that covered the entrance to his tent, an object that still hangs in the monastery of Las Huelgas near

Burgos.[45] His silken tent, golden lance and standard were all sent to the papal court and an exultant Innocent translated and read out Alfonso VIII's victory letter to a public assembly – irrefutable evidence that the procession and prayers in Rome had induced divine favour.[46] Alfonso's message resounded with crusading imagery: 'Our Lord slew a great number of them with the sword of the cross', and although his estimates of the enemy dead – 100,000 – and the Christian losses – only twenty to thirty – may have been somewhat exaggerated, the point was made: the Muslims had suffered a savage defeat and the Christians could establish firm control over much of southern Iberia. While Innocent saw the victory at Las Navas de Tolosa as an inspiration to the Christian cause, he adduced it as a reason to suspend the crusade in the peninsula and to concentrate on the Holy Land. Progress halted for a couple of decades until the capture of the Balearic Islands (1235), Cordova (1236), Valencia (1246) and Seville (1248). Protected by the Sierra Nevada mountains, however, the kingdom of Granada remained in Muslim hands for more than 200 years, meaning that the reconquest was far from complete. The battle at Las Navas de Tolosa has become a seminal moment in Spanish history because it was the point at which the divided kingdoms began to work together; indeed, within a few decades the absent rulers of León and Portugal found their way into the story of the battle as well, accounts of which almost entirely exclude the role of the papacy because in terms of generating a national identity it was the Spanish alone – 'Soli Hispani' – who had fought for God, the Catholic faith and Spain.[47]

Crusading in North-Eastern Europe

In the course of the Second Crusade Pope Eugenius III had brought the war against the pagans of northern Europe into parity with the campaigns in the Holy Land and Spain. This situation did not, however, continue and there was no ongoing papal initiative in the region.[48] Local princes and churchmen organised further campaigns of conquest and conversion to Livonia, southern Estonia and Prussia. During the late twelfth and early thirteenth centuries, efforts at missionary work gathered momentum as the Church sought to provide proper instruction for the people now under Christian authority. Innocent quickly appreciated the need to defend these new acquisitions; he also tried to counter the trend of forcible conversion, something contrary to canon law. In papal thinking, however, the need to preserve these Christian outposts justified the use of violence, 'to root out the error of paganism and spread the bounds of the Christian faith'.[49] The pope granted partial indulgences to various expeditions in the Baltic: in other words they did not receive the full forgiveness of sins and the protection of property granted to crusaders in the Holy Land, Spain or against the Cathars of southern France. While the Baltic campaigns shared the idea of service to God they were not, at this point, regarded as equals. Innocent had created a hierarchy of crusading with the Baltic placed behind these other holy wars; presumably a judgement on their perceived spiritual merits and the threat posed to the Christian faith therein.

In the decades after Innocent's pontificate this approach changed when Honorius III (1216–27) brought the Baltic crusades back on a par with the campaigns to the Holy Land, probably a reflection of his interest in the emergent mendicant orders of the Franciscans and the Dominicans.[50] Missionary work needed support, and crusades could help to defend both the newly converted and the missionaries themselves. In the 1230s the Teutonic Knights arrived in Prussia. Originally founded during the Third Crusade, this new group of warrior-monks soon established itself as an important institution in the Levant.[51] Given its national origins it also became a natural outlet for crusading ideas in the Baltic and Prussia and the papacy provided it with considerable support and freedom of action.[52] By 1245 Innocent IV had awarded the Teutonic Knights the right to recruit crusaders at any time, thereby removing the need for him to grant permission for a specific campaign. The war against the pagans became, therefore, a perpetual crusade, a ceaseless struggle against the enemies of the faith. As the experience of the Holy Land showed, taking territory was one thing, but holding it was often a much harder matter. Yet the Teutonic Knights soon became such a powerful and wealthy institution they were capable of doing just this, and the Order secured promises from the papacy and the German Empire that it could keep the conquered lands for itself. As we shall see, this was hugely significant because in later centuries it meant the Teutonics became a sovereign power in their own right in north-eastern Europe.

The Fourth Lateran Council (1215) and the Call for the Fifth Crusade

With his crusades against Markward of Anweiler, the Cathars of southern France, the Muslims of Spain, as well as the ill-fated Fourth Crusade, we can see Innocent III's near obsession with fighting the enemies of the faithful. To this list one might add calls for a crusade against heretics in Milan in 1212–13 and hints that he considered a campaign against King John of England for his persistent disobedience to papal instructions.[53] The popular enthusiasm for the Children's Crusade was a manifestation of continued public support for holy war and in April 1213 Innocent issued *Quia maior*, one of the most powerful and forceful crusade appeals of all time.[54] Innocent's sense of passion blazed forth and he demanded action to recover the holy places, 'because at this time there is a more compelling urgency than there has ever been before to help the Holy Land in her need.' He argued that God could have saved Jerusalem if he had wished, but because of man's sins he had created a test of their faith and now offered the people who fought for him a chance of salvation. To the individuals who rejected this opportunity Innocent had a threat: 'those who refuse to pay him the servant's service that they owe him in a crisis of such great urgency will justly deserve to suffer a sentence of damnation on the Last Day of severe Judgement.' The pope castigated ungrateful Christians for rejecting Christ's 'ancient device' that would deliver salvation to them. He sought to arouse their feelings by describing the slavery and suffering of captive Christians and he delivered a scathing denunciation of 'the false prophet Muhammad, who has seduced many men from the truth by worldly enticements and the pleasures of the flesh', a typical attack on the alleged immorality of the Muslims. Innocent even cast the situation in an apocalyptical framework when he reminded his audience that, according to the Revelation of St John, the end of the beast, that is, Muhammad, would happen in 666 years, of which almost 600 had passed.

Innocent sought to capitalise on the hunger for crusading apparent in the Children's Crusade by taking the radical step of broadening his appeal beyond the usual warrior classes. He indicated that those who were unsuitable, or unable to go in person, but who paid for a soldier to go in their place would also receive full remission of their sins. He also offered partial remission of sins to those who provided money for other crusaders. Innocent's vision of Christianity pulling together was restated in his commands that communities should organise processions, prayers and alms-givings to show their support for the crusade and to gain God's favour – in other words, events similar to the display in Rome in 1212. Innocent offered some practical ideas too. He urged abbots, bishops and all the clergy, as well as cities, villages and castles to contribute to the crusade. He also asked the Italian mercantile cities to provide vessels for the campaign, which showed the importance of shipping as the method of transportation to the eastern Mediterranean. As noted above, he temporarily suspended the crusades in Spain and southern France on the basis that they were making good progress and the needs of the Holy Land were more urgent.

To bring the spiritual attention of the Catholic Church into proper focus, Innocent then organised the Fourth Lateran Council, an event advertised years in advance, to give himself a platform to address the largest gathering of churchmen and lay leaders in the medieval period.[55] This most dazzling of public ceremonies took place over several days in November 1215 when more than 400 bishops, archbishops, patriarchs and cardinals, numerous representatives of cathedral chapters and monasteries, as well as envoys from the rulers of France, Germany, Hungary, Jerusalem, Cyprus and Aragon, plus Count Raymond VI of Toulouse (keen to defend himself against accusations of heresy), gathered to hear Innocent set out his vision for the faithful. This was an astounding display of papal power and undoubtedly the apogee of Innocent's – and probably any medieval pope's – pontificate. The new crusade loomed large on the agenda and Innocent added a boost to *Quia maior* by legislating that the clergy should give one-twentieth of their annual income to the crusade – a very unpopular move amongst the clerics, but a way to show lay people that the Church (with its obvious wealth) truly supported the expedition. The pope promised that he and the cardinals would make an even bigger donation to the campaign – one-tenth of their income; he also commanded the secular authorities to prevent Jews from charging interest on loans to crusaders.[56]

At the forefront of his message was a total obligation on mankind to obey the divine mandate of the crusade. Once again he castigated those who were unwilling to take the cross: the sense of threat in

Innocent's crusade appeals was something barely apparent in earlier papal bulls and showed his unwavering belief in the necessity and moral right of the cause. His final strictures demanded a four-year peace throughout the Christian world, an attempt to head off another common reason why crusades had struggled; those who broke this order were threatened with excommunication.

Innocent intended the crusaders to gather at Brindisi in southern Italy in June 1217 and he hoped to send God's army on its way in person. In the event he did not live to see his grand plan fulfilled. In April 1216 the pope addressed an enthusiastic crowd of potential crusaders at Orvieto and, in pouring rain, as the throng clamoured to take the cross he insisted on fixing the insignia to everyone who had taken their vows. Soon after it was apparent that he had caught a chill, but the pope travelled on to Todi and then to Perugia, where his condition began to weaken considerably and he died on 16 July 1216. By some astonishing error, no one was left to guard his body in the cathedral and the following morning the corpse of the most powerful man in Christendom lay almost naked, stripped of its precious clothes and starting to putrefy: 'How brief and how vain is the treacherous glory of the world' as one contemporary observed.[57]

His pontificate had been a period of astounding energy, confidence and challenges for the Church. Innocent truly believed that as the Vicar of Christ he was responsible for the souls of everyone, that all Christians should be subject to his authority and that the crusade was a means by which he could maintain and extend this guardianship. As we have seen, he made some progress in Iberia and (at the time of his death) against the Cathars, but the Fourth Crusade was a disaster and the Fifth Crusade would struggle to gather momentum against a background of turmoil in the German Empire and the continued warfare between England and France. As the pope himself wrote in one of his treatises: 'I have done as well as I could, but not as well as I wished.'[58]

9

'Stupor mundi' – *The Wonder of the World: Frederick II, the Fifth Crusade and the Recovery of Jerusalem*

'The emperor, as the custodians [of the Dome of the Rock] recall, had a red skin, and was bald and short-sighted. Had he been a slave he would not have been worth 200 *dirham*. It was clear from what he said that his Christianity was simply a game to him.'[1] This dismissive and derogatory description by a contemporary Damascene writer hardly brings to mind a crusading hero in the mould of Richard the Lionheart – yet it was Frederick II of Germany who recovered Jerusalem, rather than the great warrior-king. The fact that Frederick achieved this while an excommunicate and without striking a single blow signals what an intriguing and controversial personality he was. To his enemies in Christendom he was a heretic, a false crusader, a friend of Muslims and Mongols, a man hostile to the Church; for some, he even represented an apocalyptic figure; the fourth beast in the vision of the prophet Daniel. To his admirers, however, he became known as '*stupor mundi*' (the wonder of the world); a linguist, a patron of science, a philosopher, a mathematician, an astrologer, the author of the definitive treatise on falconry: an archetype for the renaissance man. He was also a victorious crusader and the most powerful ruler in medieval Christendom.[2]

Frederick spent the majority of his childhood and adolescence in the cultural and ethnic melting pot of southern Italy where Byzantine, Norman Sicilian and Islamic influences overlapped and blended to glorious and, usually, harmonious effect. The royal palaces were modelled on the cool chambers and highly decorated buildings of North Africa; Muslim and Christian officials worked alongside one another and some of the imperial bodyguard were followers of the Prophet too.[3] Frederick himself was fluent in Arabic – surely the greatest advantage of all in his dealings with the Muslim world simply because the barrier of language is such a potent cause of fear and mistrust. The emperor was a highly educated, literate man who also spoke the Sicilian dialect, as well as Latin, Greek, French and German. He engaged in debates and correspondence about issues such as the location of Paradise, Purgatory and Hell. He also enjoyed entertainments, particularly dancing, although his reported enthusiasm for the performances of female Muslim artistes atop large glass balls formed just one of several charges of immorality laid against him by the papacy. There seems little doubt that the women at his court lived in some form of harem, kept in seclusion and cared for by eunuchs. One must be careful not to paint too rosy a picture of Frederick's involvement with Arab peoples because in 1224 he savagely attacked a group of Sicilian Muslims who had resisted royal rule. It would, however, be fair to say that he was entirely familiar with the culture of the Muslim Near East and he had a manifest appreciation of what was important to its people.

The Fifth Crusade: Preparations and Personnel

Frederick's crusading career began with the disastrous Fifth Crusade of 1217–21. As we saw in the previous chapter, Pope Innocent III had prioritised the recovery of the Holy Land above all else. Preparations for a new campaign to the East were well underway at the time of his death in July 1216; a year earlier, however, as preaching for the expedition reached its highest pitch, it gathered a surprise recruit. During Frederick of Hohenstaufen's coronation ceremony the young man astounded onlookers in the magnificent octagonal marbled church at Aachen when he took the cross, a commitment of enormous magnitude for the young monarch. Since the death of his parents in 1197 and 1198, Frederick had, in effect, been a ward of the papacy. Innocent III had carefully preserved his rights to the German throne and, in return, anticipated a close and fruitful relationship between the leading secular and ecclesiastical powers of Christendom. In the short term the papacy paid little heed to Frederick's actions at Aachen because it wanted to steer the crusade for itself; the harsh lessons of the Fourth Crusade's diversion to Constantinople were still painfully apparent. Innocent's successor, the aged Honorius III, chose only to involve the king after the expedition had actually set out – yet once Frederick became actively engaged in the crusade, the fate of the Holy Land came to overshadow his life for well over a decade and his career in the Levant did much to accelerate the secular powers' removal of crusading from papal hands.

The Fifth Crusade was an odd campaign; it lacked a dominant leader and was marked by a bitter rivalry between the papal legate, Pelagius of Albano, and King John of Jerusalem; it was also unique for the enormous influence of visions and prophecy; finally, as a distant backdrop to events in the Levant, Europe began to sense the first destructive tremors of the Mongol invasions of the Near East.[4] In the autumn of 1217 armies led by Duke Leopold VI of Austria and King Andrew II of Hungary reached Acre. Their forces fought the Muslims near Mount Tabor and then settled down to construct the enormous castle of Athlit for the Knights Templar. With walls over thirty metres high and eight metres thick it dwarfed any previous fortification in the Levant; by way of comparison, most castles of the early twelfth century had walls around two to three metres thick.[5] This reliance on huge defensive sites, in part a consequence of the small Frankish field army, coupled with advances in building technology, typified the settlers' strategy during the thirteenth century and leaves us with some of the most impressive visual reminders of their presence.

In May 1218 the nobles of Jerusalem and the knights of the Military Orders were joined by the Austrians, as well as new arrivals from Frisia, the Rhineland and the Italian trading cities; a truculent Andrew of Hungary had already departed for home. The crusaders prepared to attack Egypt – the strategy favoured, although never implemented, by both Richard the Lionheart and the Fourth Crusade. Their first target was the port of Damietta on the northern Egyptian coast at the end of a branch of the Nile. A formidable obstacle immediately blocked the crusaders' bid to move up the river – a huge chain suspended between the city and, on the opposite bank, an immense tower. For weeks and months the crusaders pressed around Damietta and its stubborn satellite. A concerted assault finally caused the tower to surrender in August 1218. Yet the crusaders could not exploit this propitious moment because by now the Nile was in full flood and, in any case, some of the German and Frisian crusaders had chosen to return west by the autumn sailing. In their place, contingents of

English, French and Italian crusaders arrived, including the papal legate, Pelagius of Albano.[6]

Within days Saphadin, the aged and infirm Sultan al-Adil, died on 31 August 1218, and Egypt, Syria and Iraq fragmented into a series of regional powers; Sultan al-Kamil took power in Cairo and it was he who led the defence of Damietta. To block the Nile he ordered the sinking of a series of boats across the river. To overcome this barrier the crusaders fixed upon a particularly ingenious solution, namely, to enlarge a nearby canal that connected the Nile to the Mediterranean. The presence of men from the Low Countries, a region familiar with complex hydrography through the reclamation of large areas of land from the North Sea, provided the necessary engineering skills to deepen the old canal and bypass the barrier. Local labourers and prisoners of war were pressed to help and a two-mile stretch of water was sufficiently modified to permit ships to pass. The completion of this scheme allowed the siege to tighten further although Damietta's defenders remained resolute.

An atmosphere of gloom pervaded the winter of 1218–19; a flood devastated the crusader camp and an outbreak of scurvy took a heavy toll as well. One crusader described the position thus: 'What are we doing here, dearest companions? It is better for us to die in battle than to live like captives in a foreign land.'[7] In the summer of 1219 Duke Leopold of Austria left for home and morale in the camp fell further. Men were bored, their minds paralysed by the unendingly dull vista of sea and sand; food was often in short supply and the Christians remained pinned between Damietta and a large Muslim army. The hot Egyptian summer sapped the energy of both sides and stalemate ensued. James of Vitry, the bishop of Acre, wrote that 'we were in the grip of despair'.[8]

Prophecy and Visions on the Nile Delta

In the course of the crusaders' stay outside Damietta one arrival was of particular interest: Francis of Assisi, the man who founded one of the greatest orders of friars in Christendom. The Franciscan vocation was to spread the faith to all and, for that reason, the fearless cleric decided to try to convert Sultan al-Kamil. The saint's biographers praised his boldness in visiting the sultan.[9] Al-Kamil treated him with proper respect but, unsurprisingly, was not swayed from Islam. The emergence of conversion as a theme in Europe's dealings with the wider world is one of the most striking developments of religious and cultural life of the thirteenth century and the close, if paradoxical, relationship between crusading warfare and the Church's efforts to convince others of the need to become a Christian, formed a central part of that.

The concept of reaching out beyond the bounds of Latin Christendom also applied to contact with the Eastern Christian Churches. It is estimated that almost 20 per cent of the Egyptian population were Copts – a Monophysite Christian group who believed in the divinity, but not the humanity, of Christ and were thus theologically divided from the western Church. Some in the papal court hoped for a grand Christian alliance against the forces of Islam: James of Vitry wrote from Acre in 1217 that 'The Christians of the Orient, as far away as Prester John, have many kings, who, when they hear that the crusade has arrived, will come to its aid and wage war on the Saracens.'[10] Prester John was a quasi-mythical figure who had existed on the fringes of Europe's imagination for decades. He was thought to rule a Christian empire to the east, a notion based upon the memory of preaching in India by the apostle Thomas.[11]

Once the invasion of Egypt was underway the crusaders made contact with the Copts and in mid-1219 a prophecy, written in Arabic, was given to Pelagius.[12] The legate was told its meaning and he became intrigued; it updated a ninth-century Nestorian tract to include Saladin's capture of Jerusalem. This was followed by the prediction that an army from the West, led by a tall man with a lean face, would take Damietta and Egypt. Furthermore, a king would come from over the mountains and conquer Damascus while the king of the Abissi would destroy Mecca. The Abissi meant the Abyssinians, in other words, the powerful Christian kingdom of Ethiopia. Pelagius – in what, to a modern reader, seems a moment of alarming hubris – believed that he was the tall man with the thin face. He had the document translated into Latin and sent it back to western Europe where it was widely circulated.

In the meantime, the position inside Damietta had become desperate and in the autumn of 1219 Sultan al-Kamil suggested terms that included the return of the True Cross, the city of Jerusalem and other former Christian lands, and all prisoners. In return he wanted to keep Damietta and the strategically valuable castles of Kerak and Shaubak in Transjordan. On the surface this seemed immensely advantageous to the Christians, yet it provoked a furious debate in the crusader camp – Pelagius, the clergy, the Templars, the Hospitallers and the Italian merchant communities were against it because they felt victory was imminent; with Damietta taken, the remainder of Egypt would fall and lead to a permanent reconquest of the Holy Land. On the other hand, King John of Jerusalem, most of the northern European crusaders and the Teutonic Knights preferred the certainty of having possession of Jerusalem. Pelagius won the argument and al-Kamil's proposal was rejected.

Within a few days, on 5 November 1219, Damietta capitulated. Al-Kamil had tried time and again to bring relief to his co-religionists but to no avail; it seemed as if the legate was right to turn down the sultan's offer. Inside Damietta the crusaders found a city filled with the dead and the dying, but also containing immense riches. King John was entrusted with control of Damietta and it became part of the kingdom of Jerusalem. John minted coins bearing the legend 'Iohannes rex' and 'Damietta' to demonstrate the permanent nature of the conquest and his place as its ruler.[13] Yet the need for reinforcements remained acute and the leadership issued a desperate appeal to the pope for more money and manpower; most particularly they wanted Frederick to fulfil his vow. Pelagius' control over the income sent by the papacy (the result of levies in the West) meant his influence increased considerably. While other leaders simply ran out of money and went home, and John of Brienne could not fund large numbers of troops himself, Pelagius' treasure chest allowed him to dictate the direction of the crusade.

Over the next few months the expedition stalled as contingents from the West came and went – a revolving-door effect that meant there was little continuity. John and Pelagius quarrelled over strategy while the king also had to return to his territories in the Levant to face attacks from Damascus. The crusader army stayed encamped outside Damietta; any sense of advantage from its capture soon evaporated. In the summer of 1220 an imperial fleet reached Damietta bearing the news that Frederick planned to join the campaign later in the year. In the event he had to postpone his plans because of troubles in Sicily. The arrival of the emperor himself, presumably accompanied by a massive army, would, in theory, do much to secure victory. In the meantime, the crusaders remained pinned on the coast and, as with any military force that lies idle, discipline in the army degenerated and prostitution and gambling became rife. From the Muslim perspective this was a vital period of calm. The fall of Damietta had been a considerable blow; Ibn al-Athir, a contemporary Aleppan writer, claimed 'thus all the lands in Egypt and Syria were on the point of being overcome and all the people were fearful of them [the Franks] and had come to expect disaster any morning or evening. The population of Egypt wanted to evacuate their land for fear of the enemy, but it was not a time to escape, for the enemy had encompassed them on every side.'[14] While al-Kamil issued desperate pleas for help to his brothers in Syria he also began to consolidate his own resources and to harass the Christian camp.

As the tedious, torpid months of 1220 and 1221 wore on, the clergy began to pay even greater attention to a number of new prophecies. More than almost anything else from the medieval period, the idea of trusting a prophecy seems peculiarly alien to the present day – a real whiff of superstition before the age of reason took over – yet the senior churchmen of the time were ideologically predisposed to recognise the biblical provenance of such ideas and to have faith in them. In any case, several of the predictions appeared to have come true: for example, Hannan's prophecy had indeed foretold the Christian capture of Damietta in 1219.

In the spring of 1221 a text known as the *Relatio de Davide* reached James of Vitry. He considered this work so important that he dispatched numerous copies to the West where the recipients included the pope and the chancellor of Paris University.[15] The letter described how David, the great-grandson of Prester John, had attacked Persia and taken cities such as Bukhara, Samarkand and Khurasan. The story was 'confirmed' by the amazing adventures of a group of Frankish prisoners who had been captured in Egypt and dispatched by al-Kamil to the caliph of Baghdad to try to convince him to help. The caliph sent them on to 'David' (in reality a Mongol warlord), who, realising that these men were fighting the same Muslims as he was, ordered them back to Frankish Antioch and thence they returned to Damietta! Given the Christians' almost complete ignorance of the Mongols' existence, plus the men's obvious linguistic limitations, it is not surprising they had failed to appreciate the true identity of their captors. On the other hand, because the latter seemed hostile to Islam and ruled the areas said to be governed by Prester John, it appeared reasonable to suppose that this was indeed King David bringing the fight to Islam from the east. The reality, for both Christianity and Islam, was incalculably more sinister because this was an early report of the most westward foray to date of Chinggis Khan, emperor of the Mongols and arguably the most terrifying warlord in history; by *c.*1240 the Mongol military machine would conquer lands from the China Sea to Hungary – the greatest land empire of all time.[16] The fact that the *Relatio de Davide* mentioned the Mongol destruction of the Christian kingdom of Georgia was one inconsistency the clerics failed to take due note of, but in essence James and Pelagius were so receptive to the prophecies that they accepted the bulk of these works as fact.

The Copts soon gave Pelagius a third treatise, allegedly written by St Clement, which recorded the prophecies of St Peter himself. The *Book of Clement* predicted the capture of Damietta, and presaged that the decline of Islam and its defeat would be signalled by the meeting in Jerusalem of two kings, one from the east and one from the west, in a year when Easter fell on 3 April. The next two occasions such dates would align were 1222 and 1233. Once again Pelagius believed he recognised what was happening. The king from the west was evidently Frederick and his counterpart was King David, about whom the *Relatio de Davide* had just reported such positive progress. For Jerusalem to be in Christian hands by the appointed time the crusade had to get a move on, starting with the capture of Cairo. Coupled with clerical anger at the continued moral decay in the Christian camp, this prophecy, along with the arrival of a group of imperial crusaders led by Duke Louis of Bavaria, jolted the leadership into action.

The March Southwards and the Collapse of the Fifth Crusade

Pelagius made an impassioned speech in which he called upon the crusaders to march south. The need to depart immediately was compounded by the timing of the annual Nile flood – roughly early or mid-August to mid-November – which gave the Christians an extremely narrow window to operate in; the army set out on 17 July 1221.[17] The Muslim world, meanwhile, had responded to al-Kamil's pleas for support and started to pull together. The rulers of Damascus and Iraq came to help al-Kamil and his call to resist the infidel: 'I have set out on a jihad and it is essential to fulfil this intention' began to take effect.[18]

Hundreds of boats began to move up the Nile. They contained 1,200 knights, 400 archers and many non-combatants; a similar-sized force remained in Damietta. Ibn al-Athir commented on the crusaders' apparent self-belief – or their naivety: 'The Franks, because of their overconfidence, had not brought with them sufficient food for a number of days, only imagining that the Muslim armies would not stand against them and the settlements and the hinterland would all be left in their hands, so that they could take from them all the provisions they wanted.'[19] The Christians placed a heavy reliance on supplies from their fleet, and at first all appeared well; the army and accompanying vessels moved south in tight formation, reminiscent of the textbook advance by Richard the Lionheart's forces from Acre to Arsuf during the Third Crusade. By 24 July, however, ferocious Muslim attacks had slowed their pace; King John advocated a withdrawal but he was shouted down by his colleagues. The further the army moved from Damietta the greater became its dependence on ships coming up the Nile. The Egyptians quickly realised this and exploited their local knowledge to the full. Al-Kamil seized his chance and dispatched boats to a back canal and slipped behind the Christians. The plan worked to perfection; the crusader shipping was blocked and the army's supplies quickly dwindled. By late August the crusaders accepted they could make no more headway and decided to retreat to Damietta. In contrast to the ordered march towards Cairo, the return journey was an utter fiasco; almost a parody of a military operation. The crusaders set out under the cover of darkness but soon lost any advantage because, having drunk all their remaining wine, they set fire to the camp making their intentions entirely plain. Noisy, inebriated, hampered by many sick and wounded men, plus the fact that by now the Nile was in full flood, they were easy prey for al-Kamil's troops. The Egyptians opened sluice gates to restrict the Christians' path even further and by 28 August there was no choice but to surrender. The crusaders had to hand over Damietta – a humiliating contrast to the offer that Pelagius had so haughtily rejected.

Many blamed Pelagius for the defeat. The Frenchman William the Clerk wrote: 'Because of the legate who governed and led the Christians, everyone says that we lost that city through folly and sin . . . For when the clergy take the function of leading knights certainly this is against the law. But the clerk should recite aloud from his Scripture and his psalms and let the knight go to his great battlefields. Let him remain before the altars and pray for the warriors and shrive the sinners. Greatly should Rome be humiliated for the loss of Damietta.'[20]

The troubadour Peirol, who had been at Damietta, targeted Frederick:

> Emperor, Damietta awaits you
> And night and day the White Tower weeps
> For your eagle which a vulture has cast down therefrom:
> Cowardly is the eagle that is captured by a vulture!
> Shame is thereby yours, and honour accrues to the sultan.[21]

Still others put the responsibility at the pope's door, but Honorius regarded Frederick to be at fault and on 19 November 1221 he gave vent to his feelings. A letter phrased in the most disparaging terms claimed the whole Christian world had waited for the emperor's departure but his failure to crusade had demeaned the sacred offices of both pope and emperor. Ominously, Honorius suggested that he had been too easy on the emperor and from now onwards he would be far less tolerant. There is no doubt that Frederick's repeated promises to appear in person had influenced the crusade considerably, but the constant coming and going of the other contingents, the dubious reliance on prophecies, squabbles between Pelagius and King John, and the increased cohesion of the Muslims were more important in denying the expedition any chance of success.

Frederick, King of Jerusalem and Excommunicate Crusader

Frederick restated his determination to fulfil his vow and, over the next few years, he made further preparations. He showed a willingness to learn from the troubles of the Fifth Crusade by commissioning shallow-draughted ships for use in the Nile.[22] In spite of his personal enthusiasm, the German nobility was indifferent and this caused another postponement; the papacy dispatched more preachers to try to rouse greater levels of support. Although the *curia* recognised there were good reasons for these delays, its patience was about to expire and a parallel dispute with Frederick over Church rights in Sicily gave an extra edge to Pope Honorius' demands. At the Treaty of San Germano in June 1225 – ten years after he had first taken the cross – the emperor submitted to an outrageous and demanding series of conditions that bound him to go on crusade or face the severest penalties. He agreed to depart on 15 August 1227 and promised to fight in the East for two years; during this time he was to pay for the maintenance of 1,000 knights. He would provide fifty fully equipped galleys and one hundred transport ships capable of carrying a total of 2,000 armed men with three horses each, plus ancillary personnel. He also consented to give 100,000 ounces of gold in five instalments into the custody of the patriarch of Jerusalem, King John and the master of the Teutonic Knights, Hermann of Salza. The gold would be returned to him at Acre, but if he did not reach the Levant it could be spent in defence of the Latin East. Lastly, Frederick accepted that if he failed to crusade then he would be placed under a ban of excommunication, the harshest penalty the Church could impose on a person, casting them out from the community of the faithful and placing their soul in danger of perpetual torment.

Frederick's involvement in the Holy Land had increased in April 1223 when it was decided that he should marry Isabella, the heiress to the kingdom of Jerusalem. In August 1225 the emperor sent a fleet of galleys to bring back his fiancée to Sicily, although a curious ceremony took place at Acre where Isabella received her wedding ring and a bishop performed the marriage with Frederick *in absentia*. The queen reached Brindisi in November where she met her husband and the marriage was celebrated properly.

In theory, Frederick was supposed to wait until he arrived in the Levant to assume the title of king of Jerusalem from Isabella's father, John of Brienne, whose own claim to the crown had rested upon his marriage to Isabella's dead mother, Marie. Frederick was far more ambitious, however; he disregarded assurances from his own envoys that John could hold the kingdom for life and seized the title for himself. John was outraged and sought support from Honorius; the pope duly condemned the emperor's actions as 'no less prejudicial to your own reputation than to the interests of the Holy Land', but could do little else.[23] At this stage of his career Frederick had assembled a stupendous array of honours and the addition of the kingship of Jerusalem to his imperial title and the crown of Sicily meant his power far exceeded anyone else's in Christendom. While becoming the ruler of Jerusalem certainly pulled Frederick towards a campaign in the East, it also meant that the Holy Land became just one element amongst his portfolio of dominions and his actions in the Levant would always be to some extent influenced, or potentially complicated, by affairs elsewhere in the empire. Frederick's new title also sparked an increased German presence in the kingdom, most particularly through the Teutonic Knights, who had gained considerable prestige during the recent campaign in Egypt. Like the Templars and the Hospitallers they combined martial activity with the care of pilgrims and, as the recipients of generous gifts of lands, became highly important in the affairs of the Latin East.[24]

Back in Europe recruitment for the crusade gathered momentum and a good number of northern Germans took the cross, as well as a strong contingent from England. In the summer of 1227, as required by the pope, they moved over the Alps and began to gather at Brindisi. Ironically, given the earlier lack of manpower, the problem now became one of overcrowding and a lack of food. In the intense heat of an Apulian summer disease broke out. Fearful of breaching his promise to the pope, Frederick ordered a first group of ships to set sail ahead of him. Several members of the imperial court fell ill, then the emperor himself was laid low. He moved along to Otranto but it became impossible to continue and he went to the thermal town of Pozzuoli to recover. Common sense dictated that the new pope, Gregory IX (1227–41), should waive the strict application of the Treaty of San Germano; an illness was hardly something Frederick could control. Yet Gregory would not even receive the imperial ambassador; he had to act now, 'or seem like a dog unable to bark', as one contemporary wrote. Frederick's ban of excommunication was invoked – no one in the Christian community was to have any contact with him.[25] Gregory's letter to the emperor pulsed with anger and disgust. He recounted how Innocent III had protected the young man: 'see if there is any grief like that of the apostolic see, your mother, who has been so often and so cruelly deceived in the son, whom she suckled, in whom she placed confidence that he would carry out this matter, and on whom she has heaped such abundant benefits.' He emphasised that Frederick had now broken four oaths to help the Holy Land and was henceforth subject to the excommunication he had voluntarily submitted to. Gregory censured the emperor directly for the failure of the Fifth Crusade and claimed that it was his prevarication that had caused the loss of Damietta. He also blamed him for the death of many crusaders in the summer of 1227 because his delays had trapped them in the unhealthy ports of southern Italy. Another of Gregory's letters concentrated on the emperor's alleged misde-meanours: his abuse of Church rights in Sicily, his use of Muslim soldiers in his army and hostility to the Templars and Hospitallers. The first of these points in particular suggested that Gregory saw the excommunication as an opportunity to advance long-standing papal claims against imperial power in Sicily, rather than dealing solely with the matter of the crusade. He also argued that Frederick took 'more account of the servants of Muhammad than those of Christ', an early sign that the emperor's contact with Muslims was a target for papal ire.[26] The belief that Frederick's actions had impeded the crusade had some broader currency as well. Roger of Wendover, a contemporary English writer, noted a widely reported vision in which Christ appeared in the sky, suspended on the cross, pierced with nails and sprinkled with blood, 'as if laying a complaint before each and every Christian of the injury inflicted upon him by the emperor'.[27]

Meanwhile the Germans who had sailed ahead to the Latin East helped to establish the castle of Montfort as the headquarters of the Teutonic Knights; they also took control of Sidon and fortified Jaffa and Caesarea. Once recovered, Frederick still wanted to fulfil his vows – in part to try to clear his name, but also to enforce his title to Jerusalem and to assist the Christian cause. At this moment fortune finally presented him with an opportunity to accomplish all three of those aims.

The rulers of Egypt, Sultan al-Kamil, and Damascus, Sultan al-Mu'azzam, were fierce rivals and in 1226 the former sent his vizier, Fakhr al-Din, on a mission to Sicily. The envoy offered to return

Jerusalem to the Christians if the emperor would join him in an attack on Damascus. Almost forty years earlier, Richard the Lionheart had enjoyed a good relationship with Saphadin during the Third Crusade but Frederick, above all other western rulers during the age of the crusades, was particularly open to the idea of diplomatic engagement with the Muslims, in part on account of his own multicultural upbringing. The emperor sent an embassy to al-Kamil that bore splendid gifts, including a favourite horse with a jewel-encrusted saddle of gold. Just to cover all possible options, however, the imperial envoys also visited Damascus to sound out al-Mu'azzam. The response was exceptionally direct: 'I have nothing for your master but my sword.' Nevertheless, Frederick's approach to the Damascenes worried al-Kamil sufficiently for him to send Fakhr al-Din to Sicily again where it is likely that he was knighted by the emperor – a clever twist in the developing concept of chivalry as a broad-minded westerner bestowed the prime manifestation of his own warrior code on a Muslim.

In November 1227, al-Mu'azzam died, and in consequence al-Kamil's need to make peace with the emperor became far less compelling. For Frederick, however, the momentum behind his crusade steadily gathered pace; it seems that public sympathy lay with his account of the conflict with the papacy – for example, a riot against Gregory IX forced him to flee from Rome. The death of Isabella of Jerusalem soon after the birth of a son, Conrad, was a serious setback, however. Frederick was now simply king by right of his dead wife (much as John of Brienne had been) but he insisted on maintaining his title rather than acting as regent on behalf of the infant. Rumours spread that Frederick was responsible for Isabella's death – a ridiculous idea, but one that provided the emperor with another incentive to clear his name through a successful crusade.

Frederick in the Holy Land: A Triumph of Diplomacy

Frederick set sail from Brindisi on 28 June 1228; thirteen years after he had taken the cross, his crusade was underway. The imperial fleet reached Cyprus in late July; 500 knights had already sailed east in April, and several imperial vessels remained at Acre from the previous year's sailings. Technically, Frederick was the imperial overlord of Cyprus and he demanded custody of the boy-king Henry, as was his right. He symbolically asserted his power at a banquet on the island. John of Ibelin, who had acted as regent for Henry, was made to serve wine and cut meat for the emperor – an imperial custom, but one that humiliated the locals. This unpleasant situation escalated further when a group of imperial soldiers entered the hall to intimidate the native barons. Frederick required ten years' income from the period of John's regency as well as the custody of the Ibelin fief of Beirut. John argued that the latter issue was a matter for the High Court of Jerusalem; as far as the money was concerned, he claimed that it had been spent on the defence of Cyprus. While Frederick's actions had a basis in strict legal terms, his abrasive and confrontational attitude did little to secure support from the local baronage.

It was early September 1228 when Frederick landed at Tyre. The Templars, Hospitallers and clergy greeted him with huge enthusiasm, prostrated themselves at his feet and kissed his knees; on account of the ban of excommunication they could not give him the customary kiss of peace on his face. The emperor's status placed the Military Orders and clergy in a peculiarly difficult position – they were, as a religious institution, subject to papal authority and should, in theory, have shunned him. At the same time, however, he was the most powerful ruler of the West, the king of their lands, a source of immense potential patronage and, most important of all, actually present in the Levant; 'in hope that by his [Frederick's] means there would be salvation in Israel.'[28] The emperor sent envoys to Gregory trying to persuade him to lift the ban but to no avail and the pope urged people to shun Frederick. As his army left Acre the German invented a neat ruse to get around this problem: those groups uneasy about an association with him marched a day behind and followed orders issued in the name of God and Christendom, rather than the emperor.

Diplomatic contacts opened with al-Kamil, although by now the sultan was unenthusiastic about a deal. Nonetheless, a combination of careful negotiation and a fear of Frederick's military strength brought him to terms. As Ibn Wasil, a contemporary Muslim observer who later visited the court of Frederick's son Manfred, wrote: 'when the emperor reached Acre al-Kamil found him an embarrassment, for al-Mu'azzam . . . had died . . . [but] it was not possible to turn [Frederick] away because of the terms of the earlier agreement and because it would have led him to lose "the goals on which his heart was set" at the time. He therefore made a treaty with Frederick and treated him with great friendship.'[29] The phrase about losing 'the goals on which his heart was set' indicates that al-Kamil saw the crusaders as a serious threat to his own power. By this time imperial forces in the Levant formed a potent task force: up to ninety galleys, a transport fleet of one hundred oared galleys capable of carrying horsemen (possibly 1,500 in number) and with the requisite shallow draught and manoeuvrability to penetrate deep into the Nile Delta.[30]

The emperor's old acquaintance Fakhr al-Din was the chief Muslim negotiator and in Frederick he found someone capable of playing the diplomatic game to the full. The crusader pointed out that he had come to Jerusalem at al-Kamil's invitation, moreover, he needed to achieve something to preserve his own reputation – in any case, surely the sultan could relinquish a defenceless city. Frederick impressed the Muslims with a series of conversations and questions about philosophy (including Aristotle's *Logic* which he was reading at the time), geometry and mathematics. The combination of charm, backed up with substantial military force, paid off: on 24 February 1229 a truce was sworn for ten years, five months and forty days, and it was agreed that Jerusalem should be handed over to the emperor, albeit with several provisos: the walls were to remain demolished; no land around it was to be held by the Franks, although pilgrims could use a narrow corridor linking the city to the coast; the al-Aqsa Mosque and the Dome of the Rock were to stay in Muslim hands, although the Franks might still visit them; the Christians also recovered Bethlehem and Nazareth to secure the three holiest sites for their faith. In many respects, therefore, these terms echo those rejected by Pelagius during the Fifth Crusade.

Controversy was almost inevitable with such extraordinarily sensitive issues at stake. The agreement sparked nearly as much dissent in the Islamic world as it came to provoke in the West. Many Muslims regarded it as deeply shameful that Saladin's recovery of Jerusalem from the infidel had been cast aside. Sibt Ibn al-Jawzi, a contemporary Damascene writer, described the episode as a 'disaster . . . so great a tragedy that public ceremonies of mourning were instituted . . . [I] presided over a meeting in the Great Mosque of Damascus to speak of what had occurred.'[31] Al-Kamil justified his actions by claiming the city was without walls and that once the truce expired he could drive the unbelievers out; in any case, he observed, the Muslims still administered their own sacred sites.

Frederick approached the holy city in mid-March 1229, accompanied by his host, the *qadi* of Nablus. One wonders what the emperor's emotions were as he laid eyes upon Jerusalem: in spiritual terms, it was the centre of his faith and its recovery was desired by all of Christendom, yet as the capital of his kingdom, it had been stripped of its defences and probably looked pretty dilapidated. Muslim reports of Frederick's visit to the Dome of the Rock may have been tinged with an element of propaganda as they tried to play down the fact that he had taken control of Jerusalem. They show him as rather casual in his Christianity, but by contrast interested in, and respectful of, Islam. He admired the *mihrab* in the Dome of the Rock yet when he saw a Christian priest about to enter the al-Aqsa Mosque carrying a bible he scolded the man in the harshest of terms and threatened to kill him if he behaved so tactlessly again. The emperor read out an Arabic inscription on the Dome of the Rock that said 'Saladin purified this city of the polytheists' and teasingly enquired, 'Who would these polytheists be?' After he had stayed overnight in the city, the emperor asked why the muezzin had not called the morning prayer, and was told by his host that it had been silenced out of respect for the emperor. Frederick responded: 'my chief aim in passing the night in Jerusalem was to hear the call to prayer given by the muezzins and their cries of praise to God during the night.'[32] He asked the *qadi* if he would have expected the bells to be silenced in a reciprocal visit to Sicily; the emperor also gave generous donations to the custodians and holy men of the sanctuary. Sibt Ibn al-Jawzi concluded that 'it was clear from what he said that he was a materialist and that Christianity was simply a game to him.'[33] While the Muslims were impressed with Frederick's learning they seemed baffled by his apparent indifference to his faith; this may have reflected his understandable dislike of the contemporary papacy, rather than a deeper lack of religious feeling. Most crusaders were intolerant of Islam and overtly devoted to their own faith – Frederick, it seems, was not so easy to categorise.

To his opponents in the West the emperor's willingness to engage with the Muslims and his long discussions with them – in the incomprehensible Arabic tongue – were further signs of his moral decay. Undeniably, however, he had achieved a tremendous success. On 17 March 1229, Frederick, accompanied by pilgrims and crusaders, entered the Holy Sepulchre to pray. Throughout the entire history of the crusades this surely stands as the moment of supreme irony: an excommunicate crusader took possession of Christ's tomb wearing full imperial regalia and implementing his own claim to the throne of Jerusalem. To Frederick it was the ultimate justification of his actions – God had unambiguously endorsed his behaviour and permitted the German crusaders to recover the holy city. The following day, in a frequently misunderstood ceremony, he placed the imperial crown on his own head, not, as often stated, the crown of Jerusalem. He was, in his own mind, already king of Jerusalem and this act of crown-wearing was a conventional aspect of ceremonial behaviour for rulers across medieval Europe.[34]

Hermann of Salza read a speech on Frederick's behalf. He cast back to the emperor's assumption of the cross at Aachen in 1215; he related the problems in fulfilling the vow and decried the malicious stories that others had fed the pope, a device to remove Gregory from direct blame for the troubles. Here, then, was a call for peace with the papacy, a chance to move on from the bitterness of the previous decade. The emperor seized the moment to spread news of his triumph and a letter to King Henry III of England gives the emperor's side of the story with, in today's terms, an impressive, and probably justified, level of spin: 'By a miracle rather than by strength that business [the recovery of Jerusalem] has been brought to a conclusion, which for a length of time past many chiefs and rulers of the world . . . have never been able to accomplish by force, however great . . . [but] Jesus Christ, the Son of God, beholding from on high our devoted endurance and patient devotion to His cause . . . brought it about that the sultan of Babylon restored to us the holy city, the place where the feet of Christ trod.' Thus Frederick made it clear to all that he had received God's favour; by implication, therefore, the status of excommunicate had been unwarranted. He continued: 'We, being a Catholic emperor, wore the crown which Almighty God provided for us from the throne of His majesty, when of especial grace, He exalted us on high amongst the princes of the world . . . it is more and more evident that the hand of the Lord has done all of this . . . and has raised up the horn of salvation for us in the house of His servant David.'[35] The sheen of imperial authority now gleamed even brighter with Frederick's succession to the throne of King David, a Christ-king, divinely ordained. Where the emperor stretched the truth a little further was in a claim that he was allowed to rebuild the city walls of Jerusalem (this was not so) and in his outline of the Christian position on the coast.

In response to the coronation, Patriarch Gerold of Jerusalem declared an interdict against Frederick and banned church services in Jerusalem, although his ruling arrived after the ceremonies outlined above. The Templars and the Hospitallers came into open opposition against the emperor, in part frustrated by his generosity towards the Teutonic Knights; the local clergy and some of the nobility feared his interference in their affairs as well. Patriarch Gerold wrote an incendiary and innuendo-laden letter to people in the West, and suggested that 'the conduct of the emperor . . . from beginning to end, has been to the great detriment of the cause of Jesus Christ and to the great injury to the Christian faith; from the sole of his foot to the top of his head, no common sense could be found in him . . . After long and mysterious conferences, and without having consulted anyone who lived in the country he suddenly announced one day that he had made peace with the sultan.'[36]

The day after his crown-wearing, Frederick departed from Jerusalem and headed towards Acre. The news that a papal army led by John of Brienne, the former king of Jerusalem, had invaded his lands in Sicily demanded urgent attention. These events exposed the difficulties in governing lands far distant from one another – Frederick had to cut short his stay in the Levant to preserve authority elsewhere in his dominions; the fact that it was the head of the Catholic Church who compromised his efforts in the Holy Land merely added another twist to the tale. In Acre itself tensions between the emperor and the Templars escalated. Rumours grew that Frederick planned to abduct the master of the Order and take him back to Apulia; imperial troops blockaded the Templars' quarters as well as those of the patriarch. By late April Frederick's ship was poised to sail; he appointed representatives to govern on his behalf, although they would face a tough struggle against the legally minded nobles of Jerusalem whose insistence on preserving their rights meant that the imperial faction could never assert itself.

Frederick was ready to leave early in the morning of 1 May; such was the ill feeling towards him that this was no grand send-off, but a private, hurried affair. As he waited on the quayside by the butchers' quarter some hostile locals spotted him and began, first, to jeer and then to pelt him with offal. John of Ibelin arrived on the scene and, in spite of his disagreements with Frederick, reminded the unruly butchers who their king was and that he deserved their respect. This amazing little cameo brought to an end one of the most controversial crusades ever – not contentious because of some atrocity, but on account of a diplomatic agreement between Christianity and Islam. The image of a shower of stinking pigs' innards raining down upon the most powerful ruler of the medieval age is an extreme indication of the passions the emperor's expedition aroused. In spite of the immensity of his achievement Frederick's uncompromising determination to impose his authority as king of Jerusalem had alienated the nobility of the Levant, a group whose support could have added real lustre to his triumph. In the West, what should have been the crowning achievement of his life was clouded in contention and propaganda.

Frederick arrived back at Brindisi on 10 June 1229. Gregory tried hard to displace him from southern Italy and Sicily to prevent the empire continuing to surround the papal states. The pope raised troops to invade, although he stopped short of calling a crusade against the excommunicate, and his soldiers wore the symbol of the keys of St Peter rather than the cross. Imperial forces had resisted strongly and a groundswell of support enabled the emperor to sweep aside his enemies. He also confiscated lands owned by the Templars and Hospitallers in southern Italy as a punishment for their opposition to him in the Holy Land. After months of threats and insults – Gregory, for example, described the emperor as 'the disciple of Muhammad' – agreements in the summer of 1230 brought peace. Frederick managed to preserve his hold on northern Italy, Germany and Sicily (as he always wished) although he promised the Sicilian Church elections free of interference and to return the properties of the Military Orders. On August 28 the ban of excommunication was lifted and thus Frederick had eventually emerged the victor, although he was careful not to humiliate the pope. At a private dinner at Anagni, Gregory, Frederick and Hermann of Salza gathered together to plan the way forward for the Christian cause.[37] In the short term, peace between

Frederick and al-Kamil ensured a period of calm but by the mid-1230s Gregory started to make sure that a new crusade would be ready to set out once the agreement expired.

The Barons' Crusade: Military Disaster, Diplomatic Success

In 1234 the pope dispatched preachers across Europe. While the response from imperial lands was muted, France and England reacted with vigour to begin what is known as the Barons' Crusade.[38] A swathe of the French nobility, headed by Thibaud IV, the count of Champagne and king of Navarre, took the cross. From England, Richard earl of Cornwall, brother of Henry III and brother-in-law of Frederick II, led a large contingent. Neither King Louis IX of France nor Henry III joined the expedition, in part out of mutual suspicion. In Louis' case his youth may also have counted against him (he was only twenty years old) although his later career would show an unmatched devotion to the crusading cause. Henry expressed some interest in the defence of the Holy Land and the settlers continued to target him for support. In the summer of 1247 he was sent a relic of the Holy Blood by the patriarch of Jerusalem and the masters of the Templars and Hospitallers. On 13 October the king personally carried the crystal vase that contained Christ's blood from St Paul's Cathedral to Westminster Abbey, and after Mass and a sermon it was presented to the clergy. Henry also had rooms at Westminster's royal palace decorated with stories of the First Crusade, and while he assumed the cross in 1250 he never actually went to the Levant.[39]

The year after Thibaud took the cross, the papacy received a desperate appeal for help from Baldwin II, the Latin emperor of Constantinople. So alarmist was the tone of this message that Gregory decided to direct Thibaud to Constantinople instead of the Holy Land. Thus the tragedy of the Fourth Crusade continued to play itself out; the morally questionable circumstances in which the Latin Empire was created, coupled with the fact that Constantinople lacked the spiritual pull and unparalleled status of Jerusalem, caused the count to decline this proposal.[40] Gregory tried to withhold papal funding for his campaign but Thibaud was rich enough to crusade from his own resources (although he did mistreat the Jewish communities in his lands to raise cash). If one considers the deviation of the Fourth Crusade to Constantinople, the success of the excommunicate Frederick II in recovering Jerusalem and now Thibaud's resistance to attempts to steer him towards the Latin Empire, papal control over crusades can be seen to be in tatters – yet impressive levels of recruitment for the Barons' Crusade showed that the basic *idea* of fighting for God in the Holy Land remained strong.

The French crusaders sailed from Marseilles on the autumn passage of 1239. Once in the Levant they had to decide whether to attack Egypt or Damascus. In the meantime they raided enemy territory in Palestine. In one such episode the count of Brittany gathered rich booty but his success was to have a fatal coda. The sense of competitiveness so indelibly ingrained in the chivalric mentality of western European knights dictated that if one noble achieved great feats in battle, his colleagues should emulate, or exceed, him. A large group of nobles led by the count of Bar and the duke of Burgundy crossed into Egyptian territory near Gaza. They rode through the night and then paused to rest, planning to wait until dawn when the locals brought out their livestock. Foolishly the crusaders had camped in a narrow, sandy valley, factors that would ruin their horses' ability to manoeuvre. They settled down to what seems like a picnic: 'rich men had cloths spread and sat down to eat, for they had brought plenty of bread, poultry and capons, cooked meat, cheese and fruit, as well as wine in casks and barrels.' This showed fatal disrespect for their enemies. A Christian writer noted in a rather ominous tone: 'Then they learned that Our Lord will not be served in this way.'[41] Muslim scouts had observed their presence and the Egyptian commander used watchfires to assemble his troops. By first light on 13 November he had placed a large force of crossbowmen, archers and slingers on the hills around the valley while he stationed cavalry at the exit. A huge crash of drums and a blast of horns announced his intention to attack. The crusaders tried to resist but soon exhausted their supplies of arrows and crossbow bolts; the enemy closed in and in spite of fierce resistance the Christians succumbed to fatigue and their opponents' sheer weight of numbers. Many of the knights were taken captive and sent to the major cities of Egypt where they were paraded through the streets and pelted with animal excrement. A victory mosque at

Beit-Hanun still marks this Ayyubid triumph. A few months later the garrison of the Tower of David in Jerusalem was ejected too.[42]

In the spring of 1240, fearful of the strength of his co-religionists in Egypt, the ruler of Damascus sought an alliance with the Franks. Thibaud decided to turn to diplomacy and made a treaty whereby he recovered control of the castles of Beaufort and Sidon and secured recognition of Christian rights to the lands west of the River Jordan, although in reality this territory was still in the hands of the Muslim ruler of Transjordan. Many crusaders were angered by this policy – they could not understand why such a powerful group of knights did not fight. Papal legate Friar William of Cordelle concluded a sermon with the words: 'For God's sake, good people, pray to our Lord, beg him to give the commanders of this host their hearts back, for you can be sure they have lost them through their sins! Such a huge force of Christians ought to be able to attack the unbelievers in any place at all if they had God on their side.'[43] Some fighting took place when Thibaud's men seized Jerusalem to enable the count to make a pilgrimage to the holy city. Another positive development was the recognition of Christian claims to Transjordan by its governor. The count's moves towards the Damascene axis had, potentially, one flaw: the fate of the prisoners from the Battle of Gaza who remained in Egyptian hands. Thibaud tried to secure their release through a truce with Sultan Ayyub of Egypt, but this was angrily opposed by the Military Orders who disliked dealing with him. Other western crusaders wanted revenge on the Muslims, regardless of the danger to their captive colleagues. Thibaud realised that he had lost the support of the majority of the army and even, it was said, feared that he would be physically attacked. In September 1240 he slipped away back to France.[44]

Within weeks the prisoners were freed; in the meantime Richard of Cornwall's force reached the Holy Land. Perhaps 600 knights strong, this contingent could have formed the basis for a more aggressive action, but like Thibaud he took a diplomatic approach. Thibaud's truce was confirmed and Richard also refortified the strategically important castle of Ascalon before he returned to the West in May 1241.[45]

Even though the Barons' Crusade saw little in the way of military success, it had managed to exploit the endemic divisions within the

Muslim Near East to build upon Frederick II's achievements and push
the kingdom of Jerusalem to its greatest extent since before the Battle
of Hattin, over fifty years earlier. Its leaders were frustrated further
by factional disunity amongst the Christians themselves. The poor
discipline at Gaza and the issue of the prisoners severely restricted
the crusaders' ability to launch a major assault on Egypt. In any case,
the Military Orders were bickering with one another and ongoing
troubles between representatives of the Italian city states, imperial
officers and the local nobility also drained the Christians' ability to
strike against their enemies. This rather weary poem conveys the
sense of wasted potential:

> How great and glorious a throng
> Set off from France, the flower
> Or so it seemed, of chivalry,
> Best in the world, all said.[46]

With the Barons' Crusade over, other sources of help would need to
take their turn. The chances of Frederick II visiting the Holy Land
again seemed remote. His conflict with Rome, in essence over papal
claims of superiority in the secular, as well as the religious, sphere
continued to ferment during the 1230s. At the end of the decade he
was excommunicated again, and in 1245 Pope Innocent IV declared
him deposed from the imperial throne.[47] Frederick, of course, ignored
both the decree and an attempt to launch a crusade against him. The
emperor seemed to be in a strong position when, in December 1250,
he died, just short of his fifty-sixth birthday. Frederick had continued
to enjoy, and to advertise, his good relations with Muslim powers. The
elephant given to him by al-Kamil carried a wooden tower that flew
the imperial standard in European campaigns (the beast lived until
1248), while in 1232 he entertained embassies from Damascus, Cairo
and the Assassins at his court. The Egyptians sent him a marvellous
jewelled astronomical tent in which images of the sun and moon were
moved by clockwork to tell the time both by day and by night; so
valuable was the machine that it had to be kept in the royal treasury.
Diplomacy continued at formal banquets where Sicilian bishops shared
tables with Egyptian emirs and envoys from the Assassins – a truly
remarkable guest list and, again, a testament to Frederick's open-minded

approach.[48] Truces and trade deals with Egypt showed his continued good relationship with al-Kamil, although such arrangements provided easy ammunition for papal attacks on him. Some in the West believed the emperor a man of immorality. One writer placed him in a most rarefied category of villain: 'worse than Herod, Judas and Nero', yet none of the major secular rulers were ever persuaded to oppose him openly. His vilification by the Church helps to explain why, unlike his contemporaries Louis IX of France and Fernando III of Castile and León, he was never canonised. Undeniably, however, he had experienced one of the most tumultuous reigns of the medieval period and his crusade, however unconventional in form, offered a glimpse of a different, and potentially more fruitful, way forwards for the Holy Land. As his officials prepared to lay their master to rest they wrapped Frederick in a silk garment embroidered with Arabic texts. He was buried in Palermo Cathedral in a fine porphyry tomb, still to be seen today. His epitaph, secular in tone, reads: 'If honesty, intelligence, the grace of manly virtues, wealth and noble birth, could death resist, Frederick who lies within, would not be dead.'[49]

'To kill the serpent, first you must crush the head': The Crusade of Louis IX and the Rise of the Sultan Baibars

Saladin's triumph at the Battle of Hattin is the most famous Muslim victory over the Franks, yet it was not – by a considerable margin – the most crushing. Fifty-seven years after Hattin, on 17 October 1244, the devastation inflicted upon the Christian army at the Battle of La Forbie marked a far heavier blow to the Frankish cause. In its bloody aftermath came the expedition of King (later St) Louis IX of France, the most zealous crusader king in history. His opponents included Baibars, a young Mamluk warrior who, in later decades, pushed the Christian presence in the Holy Land to the brink of extinction.

Events outside the Levant created the circumstances of La Forbie. The Khwarazmians were a group of nomadic Turkish tribesmen driven westwards by the Mongol invasion of Persia.[1] These Muslim warriors made contact with the sultan of Cairo who, in the early 1240s, promised them support for an invasion of the Holy Land. In the summer of 1244 the Khwarazmians tore through the Frankish Levant and slaughtered thousands of Christians; as one observer wrote: 'these people took no prisoners, all they wanted to do was kill'.[2] As they closed in on Jerusalem most of the inhabitants fled in the face of such a terrible danger; no one anticipated that this panic-stricken exodus signalled the end of Christian control over the holy city for more than six centuries. The priests of the Holy Sepulchre refused to abandon their church, a brave decision but one that would precipitate their martyrdom. As the clergy celebrated Mass the Khwarazmians broke into the building and began to butcher them; some were disembowelled while others were beheaded at the altars. Next, the invaders ripped open the tombs of the kings of Jerusalem and cast out the bones of crusading heroes such as Godfrey of Bouillon and King Baldwin I in their search for treasure. A northern French writer grimly summarised their deeds: 'they committed far more acts of shame, filth and destruction against Jesus Christ and the holy places and Christendom than all the unbelievers who had been in the land had ever done in peace or war.'[3]

The Khwarazmians' power prompted the Muslims of Damascus and Homs to join forces with the remaining Franks. The Levantine coalition met their enemy, who were reinforced by Egyptian troops, at La Forbie near Gaza. Faced by far superior forces, the Christians' allies were soon driven from the field and in spite of fighting bravely the Franks were doomed. The level of slaughter was stupefying: the Military Orders fared especially badly – of 348 Templars, thirty-six escaped; from 351 Hospitallers, twenty-one survived and of 400 Teutonic Knights, only three lived. Thousands of crossbowmen and foot soldiers perished and many of the Frankish nobility died too; the fighting strength of the kingdom of Jerusalem was all but erased.

Faced by this unprecedented crisis Patriarch Robert of Jerusalem dispatched an embassy to Europe to plead for help. So grave was the situation that envoys risked a midwinter sea voyage to convey their calamitous news and to urge a response. The interminable tension between the papacy and Frederick II ruled out German involvement, Henry III of England was too fearful of the French to co-operate and the Spanish were preoccupied with their own reconquest. Fortunately for the settlers, one monarch was prepared to act – Louis IX of France declared himself ready to lead the greatest crusade of the century as he tried to preserve and strengthen the Christian hold on the Holy Land.

The Crusade of Louis IX: Prayers and Preparations

Louis was an intriguing character, a man of immense piety for whom the crusade was the defining event of his reign; he would feel the most profound sense of personal responsibility for the failure of the 1248–54 campaign and died in a second attempt to capture Jerusalem in 1270.[4] Unlike men such as Richard the Lionheart or Frederick II, his desire to advance the Christian cause above all other considerations was conspicuously the dominant aspect of his life. Louis took the cross in late 1244, in part as a reaction to the news from the Levant, and in part to fulfil a vow made during his recovery from a near-fatal illness. Family honour also influenced him: Louis was from a long line of crusaders – his father, Louis VIII, had died returning from the Albigensian crusade in 1226; his grandfather, Philip, had fought on the Third Crusade; his great-grandfather, Louis VII, took part in the Second Crusade and his great-great-uncle, Hugh of Vermandois, was a senior figure on the First Crusade. It was inevitable that Louis responded to the weight of this immense crusading tradition.

Louis knew that it would cost a fortune to recover Jerusalem, and to gather the requisite funding he drew upon his kingdom's increasingly advanced administration. For the first time in crusading history we have a reasonably full set of accounts for an expedition, and we learn that it cost a total of 1.5 million livres.[5] The crown had an income of 250,000 livres per annum, with most of that taken up by ongoing expenses such as warfare, building projects and subsistence; some economies could be made but clearly extra funding would be needed. Louis turned to the towns and cities of his realm to raise 250,000 livres; the sums extracted varied: Paris gave 10,000 livres, the tiny settlement of Bonnevaux four livres, yet the point is clear – everyone, no matter how great or small, contributed. The king also pressured the French Church into providing a tenth of the revenue from its benefices, although the monastic orders claimed exemption. In spite of their grumbling the clergy eventually yielded 1 million livres over the course of the expedition, two-thirds of the total cost.

Louis was concerned to gain God's favour and he endeavoured to create an appropriate moral climate for his crusade; thus he sent out *enquêteurs* to resolve complaints against *baillis*, royal officials. The results were startling: between 1247 and 1249 the eighteen *bailliages* changed hands twenty times to mark a thorough purge of the corrupt. Aside from ending possible causes of disquiet, such a process demonstrated the king's interest in his people's welfare and also increased the efficiency of his administration.

Louis and his advisers tried to learn from the failure of previous crusading expeditions and noted that a breakdown in food provision had been a recurrent problem. While there were practical limits as to what was possible, some useful measures were feasible. With the capture of Cyprus in 1191 a safe forward base was available for westerners who planned to campaign in the East. The French sent huge supplies of grain and wine ahead: 'along the shore his people had laid out large stacks of wine barrels that had been bought two years before his [Louis'] arrival. They had been placed one on top of another so that when they were seen from the front they had the appearance of barns. The wheat and grain had been heaped in piles . . . rain that had fallen on the grain . . . made the outermost layer sprout so that all that could be seen was green grass . . . [but underneath] the wheat and barley were as fresh as if they had just been threshed.'⁶

The French monarch had to set his affairs in order; most importantly, he made peace with Henry III of England to prevent an invasion during his absence. Louis' choice of regent was easy; the natural candidate was his formidable mother, Blanche of Castile. Blanche had already managed to overcome the perceived handicaps of being both foreign and female to govern on Louis' behalf during his minority. So controlling was Blanche that she conceded little authority to her son until he was twenty-one, even though the age of majority was more usually fifteen. She is said to have disapproved of the king's affection for his young wife, Queen Margaret. At the royal castle of Pontoise the couple's bedrooms were in a tower, one above the other, but connected by a narrow staircase as well as the main flight of steps. If Blanche appeared unannounced, servants were to knock on the door and the couple could separate quickly and use the back staircase to avoid a scene. Once the coast was clear they might rejoin one another with ease.⁷ The arrival of eleven royal offspring indicates that their strategy succeeded. It has been suggested, perhaps a touch mischievously, that Louis went on crusade to escape from his mother. When, many years later, Blanche died, the news was broken to the queen thus: 'The woman who hated you most is dead.'⁸

As usual with the launch of a crusade, special spiritual preparations took place as well. Probably the most tangible manifestation of Louis' piety was (and remains) the beautiful, if restored, Sainte-Chapelle in Paris. Constructed between 1242 and 1247, it displays a dazzling combination of architectural brilliance and religious devotion.⁹ It was built on two levels, the lower floor for servants, the upper, a nonpareil reliquary for the religious and political hierarchy of France. In 1238 Louis had acquired the Crown of Thorns, worn by Christ during the crucifixion, pieces of the True Cross, the holy sponge and fragments of the Holy Lance, all purchased from the penniless Latin emperor of Constantinople. Given the momentous significance of such items

Louis deemed it proper to create a monument of appropriate splendour to house them, and he commissioned a building that blended beautiful coloured glass, dizzying vertical lines, frescoes, sculpture and metalwork. Sainte-Chapelle also emphasised Louis' role as a king in the biblical tradition, the legitimate heir to David and Solomon in the Holy Land. The relics themselves were placed within a structure of precious metals and gems. A fourteenth-century poet wrote:

> The refined colours of its paintings, the precious gilding of its images, the pure transparency of its windows which shimmer from all sides, the mystical power of its altars, the marvellous adornment of its shrines studded with precious stones, give to this house of prayer such a degree of beauty that on entering one would think oneself transported to heaven and one might, with reason, imagine oneself taken into one of the most beautiful rooms of paradise.[10]

We have a superb insight into Louis's personality through the account of John of Joinville, who, as he never tires from telling his reader, was a reasonably close companion of the king. He was also a man saturated in the chivalric and literary ideals of the age and his lively, gossipy style and acute observations constitute probably the most readable crusader narrative of all.[11] His writing was a product of the highly literate courtly culture of the county of Champagne, and there are moments when it takes very little effort to imagine an ageing Joinville (he lived to be ninety-two) sitting in front of a roaring fire, surrounded by young knights and squires, telling them (again and again) of his heroic deeds on the Nile. In Joinville we can see a vivid blend of the pilgrim and the holy warrior along with the status-conscious, honour-bound, secular knight.

Joinville offered his own version of the heartbreaking moment shared by all crusaders when, aged twenty-one, he had to set out for the Holy Land. In the period prior to his departure he had called together his household and, on a smaller scale than Louis' *enquête*, resolved any outstanding disputes. He went to Metz and mortgaged the greater part of his lands, perhaps to one of the Jewish moneylenders in the city. Then, before the hardships of the voyage began he organised several days of feasting. Finally came the day to leave; Joinville neatly captured the gnawing emotions of departure: 'I did not want to cast my eyes backwards towards Joinville at all, fearful that my heart would melt for the fine castle and the two children I was leaving behind.'[12] The startling omission of his wife may (just about) be explained by the fact that by the time he wrote this section of the work in the 1270s there was a second Madame Joinville (the first had died in 1260) and the author may have felt it inappropriate to include too emotional a tribute to the previous incumbent. On his way out of Champagne he also made a short pilgrimage – on foot, in his shirt and with legs bare – to local family shrines where he prayed for divine aid and was given relics and precious objects to help him on his journey. For Joinville at least, a pilgrim's devotion, so important to the First Crusaders over 150 years previously, formed a significant aspect of his own motivation as a crusader.

Louis' army numbered 2,500 knights, 5,000 squires and sergeants, 5,000 crossbowmen, 10,000 foot soldiers and 7,000–8,000 horses. Special vessels were constructed to transport the horses and Joinville was impressed when his animals were led through a door on the side of the boat and down into the hold; the entrance was then carefully sealed because when the ship was fully loaded and underway it would be below the waterline.[13]

Early Success: The Capture of Damietta

The king reached Cyprus in September 1248 although he needed to wait for the myriad of other French contingents to arrive. The stay over the winter was not a happy one; 250 knights died of illness; thus one-tenth of the prime fighting force was eliminated before it had seen action. Egypt was, again, to be the target for the crusade. The familiar strategic arguments remained valid – as Ibn Wasil, a contemporary Muslim writer, commented, Louis 'was a devoted adherent to the Christian faith and so his spirit told him that he should recover Jerusalem for the Franks . . . but he knew that he would achieve this only by conquering Egypt.'[14] A document said to be the last testament of Sultan Ayyub confirmed this point even more plainly: 'Know, my son, that Egypt is the seat of the empire and from it you can defy all other monarchs: if you hold it, you hold the entire East and they will mint coins and recite the *khutba* in your name.'[15]

The Seventh Crusade already had one stroke of good fortune: Sultan

Ayyub was suffering from a debilitating illness and the political situation in Cairo became increasingly tense as people positioned
themselves for the succession. Amongst the most important of the
factions to emerge were the Bahri Mamluks, a group created by Ayyub
to be his fighting elite. The Muslim rulers had long purchased slaves
from central Asia or the Crimea for their armies, and Ayyub decided
to separate the most promising of them and sent them to the island
of al-Rawda in the Nile (Bahr al-Nil may explain their name Bahri)
where they converted to Islam, lived in barracks and trained exceptionally hard. Conversion aside, in these other respects they bore some
similarities to the Christian Military Orders. After completing their
training they were emancipated and came to form the sultan's military household.

Bad weather and the need to fabricate special landing craft meant
the French ships could not set sail from Cyprus until May 1249. Just
like the Fifth Crusade they headed for the northern Egyptian port of
Damietta. A terrible storm scattered the boats and it took a while to
regroup; it was only on June 5 that Louis prepared to land. As the
vessels grounded, a detachment of Muslims charged the Christians
but a volley of crossbow fire forced them back. The crusaders poured
onto the beach, headed by the standard of St Denis, the patron saint
of France. The king saw the flag ahead of him and leapt into the
water up to his armpits, determined to follow the emblem of his
sovereignty; truly this was a French, royal crusade. The invaders
pursued the fleeing Muslims and their commander, Fakhr al-Din
(whom we met as an ambassador to Frederick II), simply fled. Ayyub
was furious because some Muslim writers judged the city to have been
so well provisioned that it could have held out for two years if properly defended. Thus the crusaders walked into Damietta – something
they could scarcely believe was possible given that their predecessors
on the Fifth Crusade (who included men such as Joinville's father) had
spent eighteen months outside it. The Muslim world was appalled: 'It
was a disaster without precedent . . . there was great grief and amazement, and despair fell on the whole of Egypt, the more so because
the sultan was ill, too weak to move, and without the strength to
control his army, which was trying to impose its will on him instead.'[16]

In one sense this unexpected turn of events completely baffled the
crusaders; nowhere in their plans had they catered for the prospect of

an immediate victory – what should they do next? A council of the
French nobles gathered; the options were either Alexandria or Cairo.
The former was the pre-eminent commercial port of the Mediterranean
and could act as an assembly point for crusader forces before they
headed up the Nile. The alternative was to go straight to Cairo (or
Babylon as it was often known) via Mansourah, just as the Fifth
Crusaders had tried. The arguments swung to and fro with most
favouring Alexandria; finally, however, one of Louis' brothers, Count
Robert of Artois, pressed the case for Cairo: 'to kill the serpent, first
you must crush the head.'[17] This pithy strategic metaphor won the day
and the assembly resolved to head southwards. First, however, they
decided to wait for the arrival of another royal brother, Alphonse of
Poitiers. More seriously, they were worried by the annual Nile flood
because it was only a month before the river would begin to rise. It is
possible that had the crusaders simply pressed on after taking Damietta
they could have got ahead of the flood, crossed the sections of the
Nile that caused them such problems later on, and exploited Ayyub's
frailty to devastating effect, yet – fatally – they were much more cautious.

An intriguing document survives to illuminate the French stay in
Damietta: the foundation charter of the Church of the Blessed Mary,
formerly the main mosque.[18] This was an official French government
charter, produced by Louis' chancery and confirmed by the royal seal.
It began with effusive thanks to God for his divine blessing in giving
the crusaders victory at Damietta and it stated that the city was now
'utterly purged of the pagans' filth'. It delineated the landholdings of
the church and exempted the clergy from tax. Numerous other rights
relating to mills, ovens, fisheries, salt springs, the bazaar and the
harbour were outlined too, all granted 'in perpetuity'; furthermore,
'when this land is liberated from the hand of the unbelievers' the archbishop was to receive the fiefs of ten knights who would do homage
to him and serve appropriately on his behalf. What all this really meant
was that Louis regarded Damietta as a permanent acquisition by the
Capetian monarchy. Unlike the Fifth Crusade when Damietta was
taken under the control of the kingdom of Jerusalem, the presence
of a dominant western ruler gave the Christian conquest a different
feel – that of the beginnings of a new empire.

Another writer, known as Rothelin, indicated that Louis handed
out property and revenues to the three great Military Orders, to the

Franciscans and the Dominicans, and to the nobles of the Latin East. Rothelin, a contemporary source, stated that the churches were endowed with 'chalices, censers, candelabras, seals, crosses, crucifixes, books, chasubles, albs, stoles, banners, altar cloths, silk hangings, images of Our Lady, choir surplices, tunics, dalmatics, reliquaries in gold, silver and crystal'; priests, chaplains and clerks were installed too. The completeness of this list is astonishing – all of these objects must have been brought over from France in clear anticipation of conquest and settlement. To travel with such a certainty of success offers a fascinating insight into the mentality of Louis and his army as they set out on the crusade.[19]

Meanwhile, Ayyub's illness continued its debilitating course. Fearful of the effect an announcement of his death might have on an already demoralised populace, those closest to the sultan conspired to hide his decline. Under the orders of his wife, Shajar al-Durr, and the emir, Fakhr al-Din, doctors enacted a freakish daily charade whereby they continued to enter his tent, take in food and issue pronouncements in his name. Given Ayyub's anger at Fakhr al-Din after the fiasco at Damietta, some officials doubted that the sultan would have given him any authority at all, but it seems that – as intended – the majority of people remained ignorant of the true condition of their ruler. Ayyub died on 22 November 1249 and his entourage needed to get a message to his surviving son, Turanshah, who was based far away in Mesopotamia, to come south because by now the Frankish advance was poised to begin. Ayyub's coffin was spirited away until it could be properly housed in Cairo where, tucked away next to his madrasa, it still remains. The shadow leadership dispatched letters to be read from the pulpit of the Great Mosque in Cairo which urged everyone to fulfil their duty, to come and join the jihad and to drive out the Franks.

The Battle of Mansourah: The Folly of Robert of Artois

By late November, once the Nile floods had subsided, the crusaders set out; they progressed in good formation with the fleet sailing close by the troops to provide supplies. The march to Cairo was said to take only a few days but Louis' progress was agonisingly slow. Fierce head-winds meant the crusader fleet could barely make any ground at all;

in addition, the crusaders had to cross countless small canals and to resist harassment from the Egyptians. By mid-December the Christians faced their first major obstacle when they had to traverse the Bahr as-Saghir, a branch of the Nile near the town of Mansourah, only about one-third of the way to their target. The Egyptian troops, led by Fakhr al-Din, barred their path as well; finding a place to ford an entire army proved extremely troublesome for the crusaders. The Muslims bombarded the Christian camp with Greek fire, a terrifying experience as Joinville described: 'These were the characteristics of Greek fire: the part that came foremost had the bulk of a vinegar barrel, while the flaming tail that shot from it extended as far as a long lance. It made such a noise as it came that it was as if the heavens thundered; it seemed as if a dragon was flying through the air. The great mass of the fire cast such a great light that one could see as clearly across the camp as if it were day.'[20] Louis' reaction to this fearsome episode reveals much about his religiosity; Joinville again provides the evidence: 'Each time our saintly king heard that they had launched Greek fire at us, he sat up in his bed, reached out his hands to Our Lord and said as he wept, "Sweet Lord God, protect my people for me!" And I truly believe his prayers served us well in our time of need.'[21]

In early 1250 the crusaders tried to build a series of pontoon bridges yet, in an almost farcical response, as quickly as the Christians' jetty extended into the river the Muslims dug away the opposite bank! The offer of a healthy reward eventually prompted a local peasant to indicate a suitable ford. As dawn broke on the morning of 8 February 1250 Robert of Artois and the master of the Templars led the vanguard over a narrow, treacherous causeway. A few men slipped off the side and drowned, but most made it across. Muslim resistance was minimal and the crusaders charged on towards the main camp. Their opponents were caught unawares – Fakhr al-Din was slaughtered in his bath – and many Muslims, including numerous women and children, were killed. Caught up in the adrenaline rush of victory, Robert of Artois made a cataclysmic misjudgement. In direct contradiction of Louis' orders, he did not stop and wait for the main army to cross the Nile and consolidate the victory, instead he led the cavalry onwards. This was a matter of great offence to the Templars who should have been at the head of the army and they asked Robert to let them past. Accounts differ as to what happened next; dubiously, Joinville blamed the deaf knight holding Robert's horse for his failure to hear and pass on the Templars' request. Thus, the count continued forwards and so, fearing dishonour, the Templars followed him into the town of Mansourah. Another report suggested the French crusaders taunted the Templars and accused them of cowardice for appearing hesitant: 'If the Templars and Hospitallers and the men who live here [the Levant] had really wanted it, the land would have been conquered long ago.' Another crusader allegedly asked Robert: 'Won't it be wicked and cowardly if we do not pursue our enemies?' Robert ignored further cautionary advice from the Templars, as well as a repeated command from the king; suffused with martial valour and a destructive sense of competitive honour, he urged his men to continue.[22] Recklessly, the crusader knights hurtled inside Mansourah, thus sealing their own fate and perhaps that of the entire expedition. The Muslims began to regroup and, led by the Bahri Mamluks, they realised the gravity of Robert's mistake; the town gates were closed and the crusaders were, de facto, entombed alive in the town. While the dense warren of streets prevented them charging at their enemy, the Muslims were able to kill the Christians' mounts and then pick off the stranded knights. By this stage of the struggle it was around midday and the Christians must have been thirsty and exhausted after hours of fighting. Sources tell of men pinned in houses, running up stairways and barricading themselves in rooms. One can imagine blows raining down on a door, the shouts and cries of attackers sensing victory – and revenge; the murmured prayers of crusaders expecting martyrdom, yet still fighting desperately in the vain hope that a relief force might arrive. Yet as time passed they must have realised that there was no prospect of escape and their fate was to be ripped apart by a hail of knife blows. Robert himself perished, along with 1,500 of the finest crusader knights, including 280 Templars, the men with most experience of war in the East. For the Bahri, this was a famous victory and one from which they made considerable political capital in later years.

Louis and part of the main army had also crossed the Nile and as the day wore on it became clear that the Muslims had recovered from the loss of their camp. Joinville himself was now in the thick of the fighting. He brilliantly conveys the confusion and noise of a battle-field, as well as the *esprit de corps* amongst his companions. He proudly related the bravery of particular individuals – and noted the cowardice of others, although out of courtesy to the dead, he refrained from mentioning names. At one stage Joinville and four of his friends were cornered. Erart of Sivry took a terrible blow to the face which left his nose hanging over his lips, while Frederic of Louppy 'had a lance thrust between his shoulders which made a wound so large that the blood came from his body as if from the bung-hole of a barrel.'[23] In this desperate situation memories of homelands and loved ones came to mind. As the struggle continued, the count of Soissons called out to Joinville 'Let this pack of hounds howl! By God's coif [a neck protector] – this was the oath he most often swore – we'll talk of this day again, you and I, in the ladies' chamber.'[24] Yet the Muslim archers took their toll. Joinville was relieved to have found a padded tunic which he used as a shield: 'It served me very well, since I was only wounded by their arrows in five places, and my horse in fifteen.'[25]

Louis himself was an inspirational leader who shared in the danger with his troops and did much to keep morale up: 'I never saw a man so finely armed; he could be seen from the shoulders up, set above the rest of his men, with a gilded helmet on his head and a German sword in his hand', eulogised Joinville.[26] This epic battle ended at night-fall and the two sides paused to regroup. Someone had to tell the king that his brother was dead. An officer of the Hospitallers volunteered that he was certain that Robert was in Paradise and, in any case, he urged the king to be proud of his army's achievements that day. 'God should be praised for all that He has given me', replied the king; only then, Joinville reports, did great tears begin to fall from his eyes.[27] Both armies pitched camp and began to dig in. For the crusaders this was disastrous; they had lost momentum in their march southwards and they still needed to get past Mansourah. The Muslims were jubilant after killing Count Robert and so many of the finest Christian knights; as Ibn Wasil wrote, 'This was the first battle in which the Turkish lions [the Mamluks] defeated the infidel dogs.'[28]

Starvation, Retreat and Defeat

In late February 1250 Turanshah arrived at Mansourah; Ayyub's death was formally announced and prayers were no longer said in his name. Turanshah was a controversial young man, destined to rule for only ninety-one days and to be the last of the Ayyubid sultans of Egypt. All accounts of his career were written under the subsequent regime and generally cast him in a hostile light. He was said to have been loathed by his father: while some sources report that he had an interest in *adab* and science, others claimed he was of low intelligence with a nervous twitch that affected his face and his left arm. Yet all this is with the benefit of hindsight – at the time, his presence provided a considerable boost to Muslim morale.

The two forces were now camped opposite each other; both sides made sporadic forays, but an epidemic in the Christian camp and the Muslims' successful blockade of the river caused the balance to tip decisively against the crusaders. The Egyptians had exploited their local knowledge to send camels carrying prefabricated boats overland to a canal. Once launched, this enabled them to bar the way to Christian shipping. In one engagement fifty-two ships were taken, in another, thirty-two; 'the Muslims had the upper hand and now nourished plans to attack', as Ibn Wasil commented.[29] Meanwhile, the physical and mental condition of the crusaders, ignorant of the blockade, plummeted. Joinville himself was afflicted with a tertian fever brought on by his wounds and was bedridden. Many of the army were struck by scurvy. Joinville provides another memorable description: 'people had so much dead flesh on their gums that the barbers had to remove it before they could chew their food and swallow it down. It was most pitiful to hear people throughout the camp howling as their dead flesh was cut away because they screamed like women in childbirth.'[30]

The crusaders began to worry that God no longer favoured their enterprise. When one small vessel eluded the blockade to bring news of what was happening it was obvious that there was little chance of escape and Turanshah swiftly rejected a half-hearted attempt to strike a bargain and exchange Damietta for Jerusalem. The crusaders decided to march back to Damietta. If they succeeded, the expedition would at least have a secure base in Egypt where they could regroup.

Slowly the French army started the retreat northwards, some moving by land, the others on the remaining boats. Louis himself suffered alongside his men – so bad was his dysentery that he frequently fainted and it was reported that the lower part of his drawers had to be cut away from the royal personage.[31] Constant harassment by the Egyptians hampered the Christians' progress, with the Mamluks – 'Islam's Templars', as Ibn Wasil proudly called them – the main source of danger.[32]

In the end, only about fifteen miles short of their target, the Christians were forced to surrender. Some of the king's advisers, such as his brother Charles of Anjou, had urged Louis to flee, believing that he could escape by taking ship, but their leader had no intention of deserting his men: 'Count of Anjou, if you think I am a burden to you, get rid of me; but I will never leave my people.'[33]

Joinville was one of those who travelled by water. Most of the men were suffering terribly from their wounds and sickness and could offer no resistance. Joinville's vessel was boarded and it seemed that the passengers would be butchered. Some crusaders prepared themselves for martyrdom, but Joinville, for all his piety, was more practical. He had managed to keep with him a box of personal possessions – relics and jewels – and, realising that he was going to be taken, he threw them into the Nile. On the advice of one of the sailors he then pretended to be a cousin of the king, in other words, even though wounded, he would be of value to ransom. Louis himself was captured and almost the entire Christian force fell into Muslim hands. The treatment of prisoners varied: Joinville's priest fainted and was duly killed and cast into the river, yet Joinville himself was allowed to keep a scarlet cloak lined with miniver (given to him by his mother), and was offered a remedy to cure a throat ailment. These small mercies aside, this proud crusade was in utter ruins; Ibn Wasil gloated:

You came to Egypt, thirsting to conquer it and reckoning the drumbeat but a gust of wind;

And so Time has carried you to a disaster which has made narrow what was broad in your eyes;

While through your fine strategy you have brought all your men to the inside of the tomb;

Of fifty thousand not one is to be seen who is not dead or a wounded prisoner.

God grant you [more] triumphs of this ilk, that Jesus may perhaps find relief from you.

If the pope was satisfied with this, perchance fraud has emanated from the counsellor!'[34]

A Sultan Slain: The Murder of Turanshah and the Rise of the Mamluks

Turanshah and Louis agreed on a ransom of 800,000 Saracen bezants and the release of all Christian prisoners, including the wounded, as well as the surrender of Damietta. Before the terms of the treaty could be implemented, however, the young sultan was murdered. It seems that he made the outsider's classic mistake – on his arrival in Egypt he had replaced many of his father's trusted advisers with his own men from the Jazira. This removed any sense of continuity and created a deep well of resentment amongst a powerful local hierarchy. It was rumoured he planned to eradicate the Bahri Mamluks, the stalwarts of Ayyub's regime. He was also criticised for being a drunkard; one writer claimed that when inebriated he would gather candles and slash at their heads with his sword, shouting 'thus I shall do with the Bahri'. Unsurprisingly, the Bahri decided to pre-empt any such action and kill the sultan. After dinner on 30 April 1250 one of them – possibly Baibars himself – attacked him; the blow was parried but the blade wounded his hand. 'Having wounded the snake there is no alternative to killing it', one of the Bahri shouted. Turanshah fled to his compound and its wooden tower. The Bahri set fire to it; the young man staggered to the door, desperate and begging for his life, he implored them, in God's name, to stop, but to no avail. He managed to flee to the river where, up to his neck in the water, he was finally dispatched; some writers claim that Baibars dealt him the fatal blow, others that it was Aqtay, the leader of the Bahri. His body was thrown into a pit on the riverbank, but after three days the water uncovered him and the corpse was taken over to the other bank where it was buried more securely; a truly ignominious end to the glorious Ayyubid dynasty in Egypt.

Ayyub's widow, Shajar al-Durr, became the head of government and coins were struck in her name. For a woman to rule a Muslim land was incredibly rare; she needed the close support of Aybek, another former slave who had once been Ayyub's chief food taster (testing for poison), but who was now head of the army. Her position was unacceptable to the caliph of Baghdad (amongst others) and she soon married Aybek and formally handed over power to him.[35]

For the crusaders, of course, such instability was a cause of great concern; their treaty was with Turanshah and it needed to be reconfirmed by the new regime. For a time things looked very bad indeed. Louis was threatened with the barnacle, a fiendish torture device that crushed a man's bones between two wooden levers. The king was, on the surface at least, unperturbed; he said that he was a prisoner and the Mamluks could do with him as they wished.[36] Here Joinville shows a serenity about Louis' bearing, almost as if he was a martyr-in-waiting. This was probably reflected in the later canonisation process, an issue towards which Joinville's writings contributed. Some, including Joinville himself, felt the king should have been rewarded with the elevated status of martyr-saint because he died during a crusade, but the fact that he perished from dysentery in 1270, rather than in battle, meant that he was not honoured in this way.

Fortunately for the crusaders the Mamluks reconfirmed the treaty and the crusaders handed over Damietta, along with the first half of the ransom. Queen Margaret, who had travelled to the East with Louis and had become pregnant, maintained command of the city. The crusade collapsed just after the birth of her son, known as John-Tristram, and such was her fear that the Muslims might arrive during her confinement that she had instructed a faithful old household knight to kill her if the city fell. 'Rest assured that I will do it readily, for I had already decided that I would kill you before they took us', was his reassuring response.[37]

By mid-May 1250 the king and most of his nobles were back at Acre. They had to decide whether to return home or to remain in the Levant. At this point, we see Joinville at his most self-important and perhaps introducing more poetic licence than usual into his story. He claimed that the entire nobility favoured leaving for France; they were ill, exhausted and penniless, yet only Joinville himself spoke up in favour of staying and it was this personal appeal, his lone voice, that carried the day with the king.[38]

Regardless of the accuracy of Joinville's report, the basic principles he expressed are echoed in a contemporary letter written by the king himself, an altogether more reliable source. This was a difficult piece for Louis to write – he had to explain the failure of the expedition and the losses he had suffered. He admitted to 'the folly' of the attack on Mansourah, but he also had to justify remaining away from France, and to call for reinforcements. The chief reason for staying in the East was to ensure the return of the Christian prisoners, probably around 12,000 in number. Louis felt deeply culpable for the fact that many had already been killed by the Muslims, or else forced to convert to Islam. He wrote that the emirs were 'openly violating the truce' and he also realised that the condition of the kingdom of Jerusalem had been drastically weakened by events on the Nile:

> our departure would simply leave it [the kingdom] exposed to the Saracens, particularly since at this time it was, alas, in such a weakened and wretched condition. In the wake of our departure the Christian prisoners . . . could be regarded as dead men, since all hope of release would have been removed . . . But if we stayed, some good, it was hoped, may come of our presence . . . although many urged us not to remain overseas, nevertheless in our pity on the miseries and adversities of the Holy Land, to whose aid we had come, and in our sympathy for the incarceration and sufferings of our prisoners, we have chosen to postpone our passage . . . rather than leave the Business of Christ in a state of such utter hopelessness.[39]

The tone of Louis' appeal for help was striking, a truly incendiary piece of polemic against the Muslims (the 'children of perdition' as he called them). A reading of even the most desperate of papal appeals yields nothing that transmits such real anger: 'For in addition to the blasphemies they uttered in the sight of Christian people, that most wicked race has offended the Creator by whipping the Cross, spitting upon it, and finally trampling it vilely underfoot, to the dishonour of the Christian faith. Come then, knights of Christ . . . make ready and prove yourselves mighty men in avenging these injuries and insults.'[40] The venom of his language is extreme; clearly the loss of so many Christian soldiers had struck the king hard.

While his surviving brothers and most of the nobility sailed home, Louis settled down to his work in the Levant; Joinville too had resolved to stay. The king would remain in the East for four years; in late 1252, his mother Blanche died, but he still refused to leave. Louis continued to use the money sent by the French Church to finance a series of major building projects in the Holy Land. He spent over 100,000 livres on strengthening the castles at Caesarea, Jaffa and Sidon, and some of this work remains visible today. At Acre he fortified the suburb of Montmusard to indicate that Christian presence there had a future. Louis also set up an institution that had been needed for many decades: a permanent regiment of French soldiers, financed by the crown and paid to help defend the Holy Land.[41] Finally, in April 1254 he set sail from Acre.

Overall his crusade was, of course, a failure. Given the superlative level of planning and resources, the feeble condition of the Muslim world and the scarcely believable victory at Damietta, it should have achieved so much more. The combination of Robert of Artois' foolishness, coupled with clever Muslim resistance, unpicked the king's best efforts. For Louis this represented God's judgement on the sins of the Christians and himself. To rectify this apparent moral failing he issued legislation that banned swearing, he renounced luxurious clothes and wore only a grey woollen cloak.[42] He discarded his feather bed in favour of a thin cotton mattress and a board, and simplified his diet; he even considered abdicating and becoming a monk. Queen Margaret had no wish to become a nun and managed to convince him that their son was too young to succeed; the king eventually concurred. Most pronounced of all was an obsessive performance of penitential acts. Louis was frequently flagellated (his flagellum is on display in Notre-Dame, Paris) and he repeatedly touched the diseased and the dirty, beginning with burying the rotting corpses of crusaders in the Levant with his own hands.[43] In short, a profound moral crisis had overcome the king: he felt that 'the whole of Christendom has been covered in confusion through me.'[44] It would take another crusade to begin to assuage such feelings.

Turmoil in the Muslim World: Mongol Invasions and the Triumph of the Mamluks

Over the next few decades – the final period of Frankish rule in the Levant – the settlers faced two particular threats: the Mongols and the Mamluks. The first of these dangers remained largely theoretical, although the Mongol presence undoubtedly influenced Christian policies. The Mamluks, however, emerged as an unrelentingly powerful military force that eventually pulverised the Franks into submission and defeat. The years immediately after the murder of Turanshah were, inevitably, a period of turbulence. Aybek and Shajar al-Durr remained in the centre of affairs but when, in April 1257, rumours reached the sultana that her husband was looking for a new chief wife, she had him slain by the bathhouse slaves. She appealed to the Bahri for support but they saw a chance to assert their own position and, in turn, had Shajar murdered. Later writers give graphic accounts of her demise: under threat, Shajar had fled to the citadel of Cairo and immured herself in the Red Tower where she spent several days grinding her jewels into dust so no other woman could wear them. Finally, on the verge of starving to death, she was forced to leave the tower but Aybek's concubines pounced on her, beat her to death with their clogs and left her body to be eaten by the dogs. Further political turmoil followed, but within a couple of years a Mamluk named Qutuz became the dominant man in the land and it was he who confronted the Mongols as they continued to push towards the eastern shores of the Mediterranean.[45]

By the late 1250s these nomadic tribesmen had constructed the largest land empire the world has ever known, stretching from China to the borders of Hungary. With a military operation of unprecedented efficiency they had ripped into the heartlands of Islam. Their rationale was simple: they had a divine mandate to rule the world; if people surrendered, they were spared, they paid tribute and were incorporated into the Mongol dominions. If someone resisted then, as an opponent of the word of God, they deserved annihilation. In February 1258 the Mongol armies entered Baghdad and in a sack of the most gargantuan proportions they obliterated centuries of culture and learning; the Mongols claimed 200,000 died, some Persian historians put the figure at 800,000. The caliph was trampled to death in a carpet, a fate that was regarded as an honourable end because it avoided the shedding of noble blood. This marked the end of five centuries of the caliphate in Baghdad – a severe blow to the Sunni community, although, as we will see, it presented an opportunity for others.[46]

In the face of the Mongol advance, the Seljuk Turks submitted, as did the Christian kingdoms of Armenia and Georgia. A Mongol army of 120,000 crossed the Euphrates in September 1259 and moved towards the Levant. Prince Bohemond VI of Antioch and Tripoli offered terms, the first of the crusader states to become a client of the invaders. The pope excommunicated him but, from Bohemond's perspective, he had no option. In January 1260, Aleppo fell to the Mongols and was heavily damaged; two months later, the horsemen took Damascus. As a point of comparison, neither of these cities – the most powerful in Muslim Syria – had ever been taken by the Franks in over 150 years . . .

The cumulative effect of their victories at Baghdad, Aleppo and Damascus meant that the Mongols appeared unstoppable. News of their brutal progress provoked panic in the kingdom of Jerusalem. Desperate appeals for help were dispatched to the West; the bishop of Bethlehem wrote that terrified Muslims had rushed to the Frankish coastal cities and surrendered to the Christians 'like birds fleeing a hawk'.[47] Yet the expected onslaught did not come. In August 1259 the Great Khan Mongke died and Mongol custom demanded the ruling clan return to their homelands in central Asia to choose a new leader. Thus, when Hulegu, Mongke's brother, learned of these events in March 1260 he departed eastwards, accompanied by large numbers of troops, intent upon the preservation of his own position in Persia and the Caucasus during the inevitable succession conflict. Another reason why he took so many men away with him may have been a lack of pasturage – the colossal size of his army had simply stripped the lands bare of grass and the Levant could not, unlike central Asia, sustain such a force. His general, Kitbuqa, was left with 20,000 men to hold on to the Mongol conquests.[48]

For this reason alone, the Mamluks may have felt they had a chance of victory. Unlike many other peoples or nations, Qutuz decided to respond aggressively to the Mongol threat. Given the latter's track record this may have seemed foolish, but Qutuz wanted to hold on to power and to justify his seizure of the throne. There was also a religious dimension to the conflict – a wish to defend the remaining independent Muslim lands in the Near East. In the summer of 1260 a Mongol embassy reached Cairo. It mocked the Mamluks for their origins as slaves and demanded immediate submission; the text shows the nomads' chilling self-belief, based upon their divine mandate:

We are the army of God on His earth. He created us from His wrath and urged us against those who incurred His anger . . . Be warned by the fate of others . . . we do not pity those who weep, nor are we tender to those who complain. You have heard that we have conquered the lands and cleansed the earth of corruption and killed most of the people. Yours to flee; ours to pursue. And what land will shelter you, what road save you; what country protect you? You have no deliverance from our swords, no escape from the terror of our arms. Our horses are swift in pursuit, our arrows piercing, our swords like thunderbolts, our hearts like rocks, our numbers like sand. Fortresses cannot withstand us; armies are of no avail in fighting us. Your prayers against us will not be heard ... If you resist you will be destroyed.[49]

Qutuz responded by cutting the four envoys in half and displaying their heads in public, one at each of the main gates of Cairo; an act of blatant provocation that made war inevitable. The Egyptians were joined by the Bahri Mamluks, now led by Baibars, who had based himself in Syria, far from the turmoil of Cairo. The kingdom of Jerusalem also needed to formulate a policy, and while the Franks openly assured Mongol envoys of their neutrality, in reality a council had decided to allow the Mamluks through their lands and to give them supplies. Because the Mamluks would later destroy the Latin settlements and, on account of sporadic hints of Mongol interest in Christianity (one of Hulegu's wives, for example, was an Eastern Christian), it might seem that the decision to favour the Egyptians rather than the Mongols meant the Franks missed a unique chance to destroy Islam in the Near East. In reality, the decade since the murder of Turanshah had offered little indication that the Mamluks would evolve into such a lethal military state. Likewise, the Mongols had done nothing serious to convince the Christians to work with them, and in 1260 and it was the steppe warriors that seemed to pose the greater threat.

Qutuz took the initiative when he led his men out of Egypt and chose to fight in Palestine; this gave the Mamluks the opportunity to fall back to their homelands in case of defeat. The sultan urged his warriors to fight bravely to protect their families, their property and, more importantly, to defend Islam: his troops vowed to resist. The two armies, probably numbering about 12,000 each, met at Ayn Jalut – the Springs of Goliath, an appropriate place for a supposedly weaker party to take on an allegedly invincible opponent.[50] Unlike a battle between Christians and Muslims, the forces here were very similar in make-up with both sides formed largely of mounted archers, rather than the heavy cavalry intrinsic to Frankish strategy. The battle took place on 3 September. At first the Mongols looked the stronger and they broke through the Mamluks' left wing. With a cry of 'Oh Islam! Help your servant Qutuz against his enemies', the Muslim general gathered his troops and pushed the Mongols back towards a marshy area; Baibars too was prominent; some of the enemy had climbed a slope and 'he stood facing the enemy all day long . . . people everywhere heard about his stand on the mountain . . . and he fought like one who staked his very life . . . the victory was due to [him].'[51] Some of the Mongols' Syrian Muslim allies deserted and when Kitbuqa was killed the Egyptians had won the day. The Mongols fled but they were pursued and soon driven out of Syria.

This was a magnificent achievement for Qutuz, but he did not get to enjoy the fruits of victory. Baibars had long been his rival and on the journey back to Egypt he murdered Qutuz near Gaza on 23 October 1260. Given his heroism during the battle, Baibars was able to claim much of the responsibility for the Mamluk victory; more importantly, Ayn Jalut allowed him to stand as the true defender of Islam, the saviour of the faith. Notwithstanding the Mongols' diminished resources, the battle also showed that the nomads could be defeated, something that had previously seemed unthinkable. With hindsight, Ayn Jalut marked the end of their advance westwards, although they threatened several further invasions.

While the Franks had favoured the winning side, in 1260 they were in no position to benefit. Their own affairs were in chaos. A detailed account of their troubles would be complex; in essence, however, conflicts such as the War of St Sabas (1256–8), a struggle that started between the Genoese and Venetian merchant communities of Acre and subsequently drew in the Levantine nobility, showed the settlers to be deeply riven by political troubles, aside from the threat of outside forces.[52] A series of absentee and minor kings of Jerusalem had opened the doors to faction and manipulation, and a lack of strong leadership was a feature of the final decades of Latin rule. By contrast, the dynamism and focus of Baibars and his successors gave the Mamluks the impetus to destroy the Christians.[53]

Baibars: From Slave to Sultan

Baibars himself was originally a Kipchak Turk, born on the southern Russian steppes *c.*1229. In the face of Mongol invasions his tribe fled to the Crimea where he was enslaved aged fourteen. A white mark in the iris of one of his eyes meant he fetched a low price when sold in the slave markets of Aleppo; after his master fell into political disfavour and lost his possessions, Baibars was sent to Ayyub's court in Cairo and then dispatched to join the Bahri. It was in the service of the revered Ayyub that Baibars claimed to acquire the nobility and the virtue necessary to rule. Given the brutal way that he took power there was an obvious need to justify himself; his biographer and head of chancery, Ibn Abd al-Zahir, claimed that it was a decree of fate: 'fortune made him king'. Baibars moved fast to capitalise on the victory at Ayn Jalut and began a clever propaganda push. Ibn Abd al-Zahir wrote: 'When God had granted him victory over the Tartars at Ayn Jalut, the sultan ordered the erection of the Mashhad al-Nasr to make plain the importance of this gift of God and the spilled blood of the enemy. He did this, furthermore, because the place was ennobled since God had mentioned it in the story of Talut and Jalut in his exalted book and the sultan acknowledged the rank of this site for which God had had this extraordinary victory in store.'[54]

Baibars brought a religious edge to the conflicts with both the Christians and the Mongols. Jihad sentiments had been notably low-key during the later decades of Ayyubid rule but, as we saw in the Mamluk approach at Ayn Jalut, this changed. Under Baibars the desire to rid the Levant of unbelievers formed a significant part of his approach and these lines from a letter to Prince Bohemond VI of Antioch after the capture of his city in 1268 give a flavour of his attitude: 'you should have seen your [Christian] knights prostrate beneath the horses' hooves . . . your women sold four at a time . . . the crosses in your churches smashed, the pages of false testaments scattered . . . fire running through your palaces, your dead burned in this world before going down to the fires of the next.'[55] Qutuz had discovered someone who claimed to be an uncle of the last caliph but when this individual proved too independent-minded for Baibars' taste he was disposed of. The sultan soon found another 'relative' of the caliph who was invested with the title in 1262. With the appropriate guidance this man provided Baibars with a source of supreme spiritual legitimacy, something that enabled him to tap into the traditions of Zengi, Nur ad-Din and Saladin as the leader of the jihad.

Perhaps Baibars' two most important personal characteristics were his energy and his uncompromising harshness. His reign was distinguished by an iron-fisted discipline – exemplary crucifixions or bisections were a familiar tactic. He made great use of spies and often turned up unannounced at government offices to check up on things; he would also venture out in disguise to reconnoitre enemy positions or to find out what his own people were thinking about him; deception was routine. There was a cruel edge to Baibars' career that marks him out as a particularly brutal – if effective – exponent of holy war. His personal physician described him as a short, barrel-chested man who slept only fitfully and was troubled by nightmares and frequent stomach upsets; given the number of enemies he had made such obvious manifestations of stress are hardly a surprise.[56]

Baibars' Campaigns Against the Franks

Once Baibars was established in Egypt and southern Syria, he turned his attention to the Franks. To confront the continued Mongol threat to Muslim Syria the sultan relied upon the support of Egyptian armies. To move quickly between his territories he needed to eradicate the Christians, and he also coveted the settlers' fertile lands on the coastal plain. Between 1261 and 1271 he mounted campaign after campaign against the Franks, who by this stage controlled little more than the coast from Jaffa northwards. Their authority was based upon fortified cities such as Caesarea and Acre, or massive castles such as the Templar fortress of Safad. Yet even these gigantic defences could not resist Baibars, whose ingenuity proved almost impossible to counter.[57] He approached Safad in June 1266 and, as usual, offered the defenders presents to try to induce them to surrender; much to his fury, however, the gifts were adopted as ammunition and hurled back by mangonels. The sultan brought up his own siege engines and soon took the barbican, although in doing so he suffered heavy losses. Worried by this he offered the Syrian Christians – but not the Templars – safe conduct; he then renewed the attack. Because the castle seemed about to fall, a Templar official went to negotiate with the sultan. Baibars still nursed a grievance over the diplomatic insult, and to revenge the slight to his honour he substituted a doppelganger of himself. This person was to offer safe conduct to everyone, while in reality the sultan intended to slay them all. Baibars told the Templar envoy his plan and gave him a simple set of alternatives – if he wanted to live and be rewarded, he was to go along with this stratagem, otherwise he would be killed most cruelly. The man picked the former option. The defenders duly made their agreement with the false sultan and surrendered on 22 July. The following night, as they made their way towards Acre, the Christians were seized and executed, and their bones and heads placed inside a small circular wall to be seen by travellers.

Baibars conducted annual raids, repeatedly ravaging crops and orchards near Acre to exert an unbearable pressure on the Franks. Again he employed various tricks: on one occasion his men carried captured Templar and Hospitaller banners so as not to alarm agricultural workers close to the city; only when it was too late did the defenceless peasants realise the deceit and 500 of them were killed and then scalped. The trophies were strung onto a cord and hung around a tower on the castle of Safad.

In 1268 he took Jaffa, although this time he allowed most of the defenders free passage to Acre. Once inside Jaffa he seized and burned relics from the churches as a mark of his hatred for Christianity. The same year, the Templar castle of Beaufort fell, as did Antioch, the latter accompanied by a huge massacre with up to 17,000 dead and tens of thousands taken captive. Around the same time, Baibars also brought the Assassins under his subjection. Like Saladin he claimed to defend Sunni orthodoxy against the heretical Shi'ite sect and thus justified his conflict with other Muslims.

The most celebrated castle of all, the mighty and majestic Krak des Chevaliers, fell in 1271.[58] While many crusader fortresses have been damaged or destroyed, Krak remains remarkably intact, still perched proudly on the edge of a ridge looking over a broad fertile valley towards the hills of the Lebanon. Krak was built to protect the towns and farms of the coastal region from Muslim raids. The Hospitallers acquired the castle in 1144, and over the years they developed it into one of the most sophisticated defensive sites of all time. In the early thirteenth century they erected the huge concentric walls and multiple towers that characterise castles of this period. The seemingly endless entry tunnel, complete with a 180-degree hairpin, ascends gently into the gloom, pierced only by shafts of dusty light from the murder holes. The high quality, neatly finished stonework shows the expense and care lavished upon this most sophisticated of defensive systems. At the core of Krak lies a surprisingly small courtyard – not the wide open areas familiar from contemporary Welsh castles, such as Caernarfon or Harlech, but a much more intimate space. Along the western side remains a façade of delicate Gothic tracery; looking at this, one could be in a western European monastery – which is exactly the point. It reminds us that the Military Orders were warrior-monks; both soldiers *and* religious men. Here was something akin to a cloister with a chapel also built on to the enclosure. Elsewhere, other features include immense stables and storerooms, vital to allow Krak to accommodate a garrison of 2,000. Yet in spite of this the castle could not hold out against Baibars – and once again, the sultan is suspected of using treachery. After the capture of the forward defences and the outer barbicans, he faced the muscular immensity of the main castle. To breach this structure would surely have cost him an intolerable number of men, and he therefore resorted to a trick. He sent the defenders a forged letter that claimed to be from the Hospitaller commander in Tripoli instructing them to surrender. Some historians believe the garrison was duped by this, others suggest that after two months of siege they had little chance of survival and saw this as a way to end their confinement; either way, this mighty stronghold capitulated for the first time in its history and Baibars had struck another weighty psychological blow for Islam.

The Second Crusade of Louis IX – The Death of a Crusader King

The Franks suffered a further setback in 1270. Louis IX had been determined to atone for the defeat of his first crusade.[59] In 1267 he began to organise another expedition, although this time he proposed to march through North Africa and approach Egypt from the west. By this time the king's health was poor and Joinville judged those who advised Louis to set out as having committed a mortal sin against the king and his people.[60] Another sizeable French army sailed for Africa on 2 July 1270. The king's profound religiosity meant the mendicant orders exerted a strong influence on this campaign; the idea of conversion had become an increasingly powerful theme during the thirteenth century and the desire to convince the Mongols, Muslims and the Eastern Christians to become Catholic was a highly prominent aspect of relations between Europe and the wider world. The main focus of Louis' attention was the ruler of Tunisia who had recently set up a rival claim to the caliphate in Cairo. In the event the French only reached Carthage. The Muslims showed little interest in conversion and, by contrast, harassed the Christian camp with arrows and projectiles. It was the height of summer and conditions for the crusaders quickly became deleterious. Louis' son, John-Tristram, born at the siege of Damietta in 1249, soon expired; after two weeks the king himself was struck down with dysentery and forced to his bed. By 24 August his death was imminent. As he lay in terminal decline the king called out 'O Jerusalem! O Jerusalem!' and prayed for his people; he died the following day. His bones were kept in a casket and brought to St Denis but his entrails and flesh were taken to the cathedral of Monreale on Sicily by his brother, Charles.

Louis had been determined to live as a true Christian monarch and crusading lay at the very heart of his thinking. The seven years he spent overseas between 1248 and 1254 represent an unmatched level of devotion to the Holy Land. Yet for all his prayers, suffering and financial outlay, he had, as he knew all too well, failed to turn around Christian fortunes in the Levant. His personal devotion in both France and Outremer was recognised in 1292 when he was canonised – the first crusader king to become a saint.

After Louis' death the French army soon broke up and returned home, although an important latecomer was to land in the Levant rather than North Africa. Louis had induced Lord Edward (soon to be King Edward I of England), eldest son of King Henry III, to join the crusade and after wintering in Sicily the prince set sail for the Holy Land in the spring of 1271.[61] The arrival of a powerful westerner was a cause for excitement and King Hugh I of Jerusalem and Cyprus (the two crowns were united at this time) came over to Acre. Edward, Hugh and the Military Orders executed several large raids into Muslim territory but their forces were nowhere near big enough to engage

Baibars. At Acre, Edward survived an assassination attempt. His entourage contained a convert from Islam whom the crusaders were using as a spy; he had given good information to the Christians and seemed to prove his loyalty during an earlier foray. One night he came to the royal chambers where Edward and his wife were sleeping and claimed to have urgent news for him. Dressed only in his undershirt and drawers, Edward opened the door and the traitor stabbed him deep in the hip; the prince was not felled, however; in one mighty punch, he knocked out his assailant, then grabbed a dagger and killed him. The prince's wound was sutured and luckily for him it remained free of infection; he recovered to leave the Levant in October 1272.

Baibars continued to squeeze the Christians closer to extinction – while at the same time he was also at war with the Seljuk Turks of Asia Minor and the Mongols of Persia. On occasion he made truces with the Franks to enable him to pursue these other opponents individually, although he tended to break these agreements when it suited him.[62] In 1277 he embarked upon a major campaign in Asia Minor and seemed poised to take control of the region only to return to Damascus to face a threatened Mongol invasion. There, on 20 June 1277, he fell ill while watching a polo match. He had consumed some *qumiz*, a highly alcoholic brew made from fermented mare's milk (not the wine so frowned upon by the sultan himself), a drink that can be lethal if it goes off; given Baibars' atrocious record of murder and deceit, rumours of poisoning abounded but no one was identified as responsible for his death. He was buried in Damascus, where his modified tomb remains in its original setting, the Zahiriyya madrasa, a couple of hundred metres from the resting place of Saladin. Few grieved the death of such a harsh ruler, yet he had maintained power for seventeen years and proved the most gifted and imaginative commander of the age. A carefully developed administration meant that by the time of his death his lands were immeasurably better organised for war than before. He had been a remorseless foe of the Franks and did much to break their hold on the Levantine coast. As his biographer wrote: 'The sultan stood among his comrades like a sun among the bright stars and like a lion amongst the cubs it protects. He trained to fight the unbelievers and continued to fight the holy war day and night.'[63]

Baibars' death did not mean the end of the Mamluk threat. In contrast to many previous successions in the Muslim world there was no civil war. After a brief reign by Baibars' son, the former sultan's chief emir, Qalawun, emerged in power. He was another former slave, nicknamed 'al-Alfi', the thousander, on account of the high price that he had fetched at auction. He served his master well and his daughter had married into the sultan's family; he was also a highly experienced soldier. Soon he had to confront the Mongols because in 1280 they plundered Aleppo. A year later, at the Battle of Homs, two huge armies met and practically obliterated each other; the carnage was immense but Qalawun held the field and so the victory went to him.

By the late 1280s the pattern familiar from Baibars' reign was repeating itself. Major Christian castles and cities fell with alarming regularity: Marqab in 1285, Latakia in 1287 and Tripoli in 1289. The Mamluks genuinely intended to erase the Frankish presence. Qalawun began to focus on Acre, the settlers' capital city; it would be a huge challenge to breach its massive defences, but if the sultan succeeded it would definitively break Christian power in the Holy Land. A truce was in operation but when a group of newly arrived crusaders killed Muslim farmers in Acre, the sultan had a *casus belli*. Since his success at Tripoli he had employed military inspectors to ensure that the castles near Acre were ready for war and he ordered the construction of special siege engines from Lebanese cedar wood. Before he could act, however, Qalawun was fatally poisoned. On his deathbed he was said to have urged his son, al-Ashraf, to take Acre and to avenge the blood of the Saracens slain by the crusaders.[64]

The End of the Frankish East: The Fall of Acre

In March 1291 al-Ashraf gathered a huge army, assembled from Egypt, Palestine and Syria; meanwhile any Franks who lived in the country-side fled behind the walls of Acre. The city was crammed with refugees; perhaps 30,000–40,000 men, women and children defended by around 800 knights and 13,000 footmen. Al-Ashraf sent a letter to the master of the Templars which conveyed unyielding menace:

> The Sultan of Sultans, King of Kings, Lord of Lords, al-Malik al-Ashraf, the Powerful, the Dreadful, the Scourge of Rebels, Hunter of Franks and Tartars and Armenians, Snatcher of Castles from the Hands of

Miscreants, Lord of the Two Seas, Guardian of the Two Pilgrim Sites
. . . We send you advance notice of our intentions, and give you to
understand that we are coming into your parts to right the wrongs
that have been done. We do not want the community of Acre to send
us any letters or gifts for we will by no means receive them.[65]

On 5 April 1291 the siege began when al-Ashraf pitched his red tent
with its entrance facing the city of Acre. Soon the Muslims brought
forward enormous siege engines, mighty machines that could fire
stones weighing about 50 kilograms each. One was called 'Furious';
another, 'the Victorious', took one hundred wagons to transport it (in
kit form) from its home at Krak des Chevaliers; two other huge
machines are also known to have been used.

Boldly, the Franks took the initiative and charged out of the city
gates to harass the Muslim camp. They also sent out ships from the
harbour and landed troops near the enemy lines to fire bows and
portable ballistas. One particularly heavy raid penetrated the Muslim
camp and caused panic – an emir fell into the latrine pit and drowned
– but a swift counter-attack drove back the Christians with heavy casualties. Over the weeks, however, the pressure on the Franks increased;
the Muslims hid behind huge padded wicker screens that deflected
artillery fire and, protected by these devices, they moved up to the
ditch outside the city. Such was their numerical superiority that they
could work four shifts a day and still remain fresh.

The Christians gained some relief from the arrival of King Henry
II of Cyprus and a ceasefire was declared. The king tried to negotiate
but al-Ashraf was not prepared to leave without taking the city and
would only offer free passage to the defenders and its inhabitants.
Henry could never agree to this 'because the people overseas would
hold us to be traitors'; he did not want to be the man who had surrendered the capital of the Christian presence in the Holy Land.[66] Under
the cover of a heavy bombardment the Muslims mined the outer wall
and the Tower of the King and created a breach of such dimensions
that the defenders panicked. More and more women and children
were evacuated to Cyprus – the dismal Mamluk navy meant that
Christian shipping was fairly safe.

The beating of a huge drum 'which had a horrible and mighty
voice', as one eyewitness characterised it, signalled a general onslaught.

The Muslims advanced on foot; first came shield-bearers, behind them men hurled Greek fire and next came javelin-throwers and archers. They spread out between Acre's inner and outer walls and concentrated on two gates that barred the city. William of Beaujeu, the master of the Templars, left his own tower and rushed towards the Gate of St Anthony. The Muslims continued their terrible bombardment of Greek fire, arrows and spears; when the knights charged at them 'it seemed as if they hurled themselves against a stone wall'.[67] In the middle of the engagement William was grievously wounded when a javelin hit him under the armpit. When the standard-bearer saw him turn his horse away he followed, assuming that William was leading a retreat, but others called out for the master not to leave or else the city would fall. William revealed his wound and collapsed forwards, almost falling from his mount. Men rushed to hold him in the saddle and then eased him onto a shield and carried him to the Templar headquarters inside the citadel. He lived one day longer, asking only to be left to die in peace.

The Muslims poured into the city and took tower after tower. The French regiment founded by Louis IX fought bravely but nothing could withstand the onslaught. King Henry and the master of the Hospital saw that all was lost, boarded boats and fled to Cyprus; 18 May 1291 was an inauspicious day for the Latin hierarchy. Not everyone was so fortunate; women and children remained and many were soon slaughtered. The Templar compound was the last place of refuge, the strongest location of all. At last an agreement of safe conduct was made. A group of Muslim horsemen came in and, according to Muslim and Christian sources, started to molest the female prisoners. Furious, the Franks attacked and killed them. Al-Ashraf claimed to accept responsibility for this incident and he asked to talk to the senior Templars. Once they were in his possession, however, he beheaded them all; in response, five Muslim prisoners were precipitated from the walls. For the surviving knights and citizens in the Templar tower there was no hope of escape. After ten days a corner in the complex was mined and as the defenders surrendered, it collapsed, killing Muslims and Christians alike. More carnage ensued – Franciscan and Dominican friars, female mendicants (the Poor Clares) were slain, while long lines of women and children were led off into slavery. Thus the city of Acre fell. The Christian capture of Jerusalem in 1099 and the Muslim victory at Acre in 1291 bookended the crusader presence in the Holy Land with massacres of exceptional savagery.

Within a short time Sidon, Beirut, Athlit, Jubail and Tyre capitulated as well. On 3 August 1291, when the last group of knights left Tortosa for the tiny isle of Ruad, just over a mile off the Syrian shore, it marked the end of Christian rule on the mainland. Almost 200 years after the First Crusaders had achieved an improbable victory at Jerusalem, their successors fled for their lives, or died. The Franks had fought hard but their penchant for ruinous political infighting, the failure of Louis' crusades and the lack of further meaningful help from the West, coupled with the focus and strength of their Mamluk opponents, meant the end of an era. Al-Ashraf had fulfilled Saladin's ambition at last. As the Muslim writer Ibn al-Furat wrote in a panegyric to his successful sultan:

> Because of you no town is left in which unbelief can repair, no hope for the Christian religion! Through al-Ashraf the lord sultan, we are delivered from the Trinity, and Unity rejoices in the struggle! Praise be to God, the nation of the Cross has fallen; through the Turks the religion of the chosen Arab has triumphed![68]

II

From the Trial of the Templars to Ferdinand and Isabella, Columbus and the Conquest of the New World

The Trial of the Templars

As dawn broke on Friday 13 October 1307 royal officials smashed their way into Templar priories and commanderies across France and arrested hundreds of knights.[1] The men were accused of a series of profane reception rituals that included: the denial of Christ's divinity, saying that he was a false prophet; spitting on the cross; kissing the officiating knight on the mouth, navel and genitals; worshipping false idols and engaging in further homosexual acts.[2] This was a very contentious move on the part of the French crown because the Templars were the most feared and formidable warriors in Christendom; in modern terms it would be comparable to a claim that the US Marines were disloyal to the American government and then, within years, disbanding them.

The crackdown was sudden and largely unexpected. The decision to persecute the Templars can, in part, be explained by the personality of their chief adversary, King Philip IV 'the Fair' (a reference to his good looks, rather than his character) of France (1285–1316). Philip was an austere man of high moral tone and it is possible that he saw some truth in the allegations and felt justified in moving to end the pollution of a religious order. Yet other, less lofty, ideals were in evidence too: expensive wars against England and Flanders meant that Philip owed the Templars massive sums of money and the need to repair his ailing finances was strongly rumoured to underlie his actions. Recent events had rendered the Order strangely susceptible to these accusations and to leap from the Templars' arrest to their complete destruction in only five years demonstrates peculiar vulnerability in a group hailed by many as the bravest of the brave. One trivial indication of the Templars' customary standing was their central role in *Parzival*, the popular story of the Holy Grail, composed in the first decade of the thirteenth century: who, other than the Templars, were fit to be the guardians of this most sacred object? Yet there had been complaints about the Templars' wealth, and sometimes their greed, for decades. Churchmen, in particular, grumbled about their substantial landholdings in western Europe (over 9,000 properties) and resented their exemptions from ecclesiastical taxes. Such corporate riches were a long, long way from the simple and rigorous path of founding father Hugh of Payns and his eight companions back in 1120, but this stupendous accumulation of property reflected their long-lasting popularity amongst lay donors, grateful for the Templars' protection during pilgrimages and their efforts in fighting the Muslims. In any case, these vast resources were vital because of the phenomenal cost of developing and holding spectacular castles such as Krak des Chevaliers. By 1307, however, the Templars' prime problem was one of perception. With the expulsion of the Christians from Acre in 1291 many felt that the Order had failed in its primary task, the defence of the Holy Land, and for this reason it became far more open to criticism than before. The Templar master, James of Molay, had a rather different perspective: to him, the Holy Land fell because of the indifference of western Europe and it was in an attempt to gather new crusading armies that he happened – fatefully for him – to be in France during late 1307.

Long before 1291 there had been discussions about a merger between the Templars and the other great Military Order, the Hospitallers. The latter's medical vocation gave them an additional and important *raison d'être*, and it was intimated that the united Order would follow a Rule closer to the Hospitallers' charitable way of life with less of the Templars' more militaristic focus. James vociferously opposed the plan because he feared his organisation would be absorbed into the Hospitallers and, more seriously, that the new entity would come under the dominance of one of the scheme's most enthusiastic advocates, Philip of France.[3] Crucially – and again, an issue of circumstance – one prime source of protection for any religious order was particularly feeble at this time: the frail Pope Clement V (1305–14) was based in Poitiers rather than Rome and there were times when he

seems to have been bullied by the same French churchmen responsible for his election to the papal crown.[4]

Once Philip had the Order in his sights he moved extremely fast:
Templar property was seized and the crown initiated a vicious and
wide-ranging propaganda campaign against the knights. The king gave
his officers a sweeping mandate to discover the 'truth'. He wrote of
'the strength of the presumptions and suspicions' raised and he
described the Templars as 'enemies of God, religion and nature, those
opponents of human society.' Philip acknowledged that some of the
men might be innocent, but argued that it was still appropriate they
'should be tested in the furnace like gold and cleared by due process
of judicial examination.'[5] The king had convinced himself of the
knights' guilt and he mandated torture as an entirely legitimate way
to extract a confession.[6] Inquisitors used a variety of horrific techniques, including the application of fire to a prisoner's feet; a process
accelerated by smothering the feet in fat before they were placed in
the flames. To allow further questioning a board could be placed
between the feet and the fire and on occasion the torture was so
extreme that some of the victim's foot bones dropped out. The rack,
a triangular-shaped frame onto which the detainee was tied, was
another option open to the interrogators. A windlass was attached to
the ropes that bound the prisoner's ankles and wrists and when it was
turned their joints dislocated. Finally, there was the strappado, a proce-
dure in which a prisoner's hands were tied behind his back and attached
to a rope passed over a ceiling beam. Weights could be attached to
his testicles or feet before the knight was hoisted high off the ground
and then allowed to plummet down, the rope stopping him inches
from the floor and the violent deceleration causing excruciating pain.
In October and November 1307 138 knights were questioned and in
the face of such a terrifying array of machinery only four failed to
confess to some or all of the crimes alleged. The testimony of James
of Molay was damning – he admitted to the denial of Christ (although
like many colleagues he claimed to have spoken such words without
meaning them in his heart) and spitting on the cross; other Templars
confessed to kissing on the mouth and stomach. James was made to
repeat his disclosure before the scholars of Paris University, thus
providing vital publicity for King Philip's case.[7]

By Christmas, however, Clement had begun to stand his ground a little, furious at Philip's uncompromising and extensive interference in Church matters. Soon he suspended the French Inquisition and sent his own cardinals to see the Templars; unsurprisingly they all retracted their statements and claimed they were given under extreme duress. By 1308 Clement established a papal commission and many of the knights continued to plead their innocence. Brother Ponsard of Gizy stated that 'if he continued to be tortured he would deny everything he was now saying and would say whatever any man wanted. While he was prepared to suffer death by decapitation, fire or boiling water for the honour of the Order, he was incapable of bearing such long torments as he had suffered in the more than two years he had been in prison.'[8] The recent discovery of a document hidden for centuries in the labyrinthine Vatican archives sheds fascinating new light on the ebb and flow of these proceedings. In spite of Philip's continued obstruction, a papal commission managed to meet the Templar leaders at the castle of Chinon on the River Loire in August 1308. In the presence of the pope's representatives the master and his companions denied the charges against them and were duly absolved of heresy – an intriguing development that showed, at this point, Clement's unwillingness to accept certain of the accusations directed at the Order.[9]

James of Molay began to make a positive case for his brethren: he emphasised their religiosity and frequent veneration of proper relics; he also noted their generosity to the poor in alms-giving and their willingness to risk life and limb in their vocation of fighting the Muslims.[10] While Molay's efforts were of limited effect, the defence mounted by Brother Peter of Bologna, a man trained in canon law, was considerably more powerful. He challenged the jurisdiction of Philip's churchmen and also raised what was, arguably, the most telling factor in this whole inquiry: the progress of other investigations across Christian Europe. As he indicated: 'Outside the kingdom of France no brother of the Temple can be found in whatever country on earth who tells or has told these lies; hence it is plainly obvious why these lies were told in the kingdom of France, namely because those who told them were corrupted by fear, persuasion or bribery when they made their depositions.'[11] In complete contrast to Philip the Fair, King Edward II of England and King James II of Aragon flatly refused to countenance the idea that the Templars were guilty and in Germany and Cyprus – without the use of torture – the inquisitors secured no confessions at all.[12] In fact, in the case of Cyprus, for which a manuscript of the trial hearings survives, numerous non-Templar witnesses testified to the good faith and charity of the brothers.[13] The only other areas where confessions were made were Navarre and Naples – both regions ruled by relatives of the Capetian royal house.

Philip's response to the Templars' show of defiance was swift and effective. In May 1310 the archbishop of Sens, a close associate of the crown, convoked a council to judge the individual charges against the Templars in his custody. He pushed aside objections from Peter of Bologna and rejected the idea that his process was running counter to the papal inquiry. On May 12 he ordered fifty-four knights, all hopelessly protesting their innocence, to be loaded onto carts and burned to death in a field near the convent of St Antoine outside Paris. By this brutal display of force Philip broke the resistance of many of the brothers and more began to make confession and seek absolution.[14]

For a while the papal commission stalled King Philip's momentum, but the weakening Clement was driven towards a definitive pronouncement at the Council of Vienne in March 1312. The arrival of King Philip and an armed force ensured that the pope made the 'correct' statement. On 22 March Clement held a secret meeting at which it was decided to suppress the Order and on 3 April a formal announcement was read out in public. In language saturated with biblical texts Clement made his position known: 'Not slight is the fornication of this house, immolating its sons, giving them up and consecrating them to demons and not to God, but to gods whom they do not know. Therefore this house will be desolate and in disgrace, cursed and uninhabited . . . let it not be lived in but reduced to a wilderness. Let everyone be astonished at it and hiss at all its wounds [Jeremiah 50:12–13]'.[15] The pope noted how, initially at least, he had been unwilling to believe the stories that circulated about the Order. He then spoke of Philip's 'zeal for the orthodox faith', and he was careful to distance the king from any hint of financial concerns. The absolution granted to the Templar leaders at Chinon was seemingly disregarded when Clement outlined the various confessions, including that of James of Molay, and he concluded that the brethren were guilty of apostasy, idolatry, sodomy and various other heresies. He added that his own officers had made further enquiries and claimed that these had unearthed more incriminating information. A majority of the council favoured giving the Order a chance to defend itself, but Clement adjudged that 'although legal process against the Order up to now does not permit its canonical condemnation as heretical . . . its good name has been largely taken away by the heresies attributed to it.' Because, he argued, so many individuals were guilty of heresy the Order as a whole remained suspect and for that reason no one of any calibre would wish to join it in future, thus it was rendered worthless in the task of recovering the Holy Land. Clement felt that further delay would only mean the final dilapidation of Templar property – land given to them in good faith to aid Christ's cause. 'Therefore, with a sad heart . . . we suppress the Order of Templars, and its rule and habit and name, by an inviolable and perpetual decree and we entirely forbid that anyone from now on enter the Order, or receive its habit or presume to behave as a Templar.'[16] Those brothers who had confessed and been absolved were to become Knights Hospitaller, while many of those who refused to recant were imprisoned. Templar lands were usually given over to other Military Orders, particularly the Hospitallers; within a couple of years, however, the rapacious King Philip had managed to acquire large amounts of this property in France.[17]

For the leading Templars, however, there was to be little mercy. They had languished in prison at Gisors since 1310 but were not brought to trial in Paris until December 1313.[18] James was to be tried on the basis of his initial confession, which he had retracted once, but since returned to. At a public gathering in front of the church of Notre-Dame he, along with three senior colleagues, was sentenced to life imprisonment. Two of the men remained silent, but James, along with Geoffrey of Charney, commander of the Templars in Normandy, stood up. Surely aware of the danger, once again they denied everything they had confessed, stubbornly refuted the charges against them and affirmed that they were good Christians. They argued passionately that they had never turned aside from their task and had suffered for God and justice. The presiding cardinals were taken aback and ordered the men to be kept under guard until the matter could be debated further. Calamitously for the prisoners, however, their custodian was a royal official who told the king. Philip snapped into action: he quickly consulted his advisers and, without any reference to the Church author-ities, he commanded the two men to be burned at the stake that very day. They were sent to the little island at the tip of the Île de la Cité, below the gardens of the king's palace (today known as the place du Vert-Galant; a memorial plaque marks the place of this shameful episode) where the stake was set up. A royal cleric, Geoffrey of Paris, witnessed the scene and wrote a verse chronicle of the event. James' serene bearing at this terrible moment profoundly moved those present:

> The master, who saw the fire ready,
> Stripped with no sign of fear.
> And, as I myself saw, placed himself
> Quite naked in his shirt
> Freely and with good appearance;
> Never did he tremble
> No matter how much he was pulled and jostled.
> They took him to tie him to the stake
> And without fear he allowed them to tie him.
> They bound his hands with a rope
> But he said to them: 'Gentlemen, at least
> Let me join my hands a little
> And make a prayer to God
> For now the time is fitting.
> Here I see my judgement
> When death freely suits me;
> God knows who is in the wrong and has sinned.
> Soon misfortune will come
> To those who have wrongly condemned us:
> God will avenge our death.
> Gentlemen,' he said, 'make no mistake,
> All those who are against us
> Will have to suffer because of us.
> In that belief I wish to die . . .'
> And so gently did death take him
> That everyone marvelled.[19]

Through his intimidation of the papacy and by his brutal and relentless persecution of the Templars, King Philip achieved something beyond the powers of the Muslims of the Near East: the destruction of a Military Order. With the benefit of hindsight, we can see that some of their difficulties were self-inflicted: for example, their reception ceremonies were arcane and secretive, yet in truth, they were a flawed, rather than a heretical organisation and had been the victims of a greedy and paranoid king. Nowhere other than France were they treated with such barbarity: elsewhere their membership simply dwindled and then expired; by the late fourteenth century the Templars were gone forever.[20] By coincidence – or fate, if you believed the Templars' supporters – James' final curse came true: one month later Pope Clement died and in November of the same year King Philip was killed in a riding accident.

The problems endured by the Templars help to illustrate the crisis that faced the crusading movement after the fall of Acre – but it would be wrong to suggest that there was no hope of recovering the Holy Land. The Christians still held Cyprus as a base in the eastern Mediterranean and for a short time there seemed the possibility of an alliance with the Ilkhan Mongols of Persia who, in 1299, had inflicted a heavy defeat on the Mamluks and then took Jerusalem. Rumours flashed across Europe that the Mongol khan Ghazan had handed over the Holy Sepulchre to local Christians. Pope Boniface VIII solemnly announced as much to Edward I of England in a letter of 7 April 1300, and the Christian West briefly regarded Ghazan as an instrument of divine will. The pope tried to fan enthusiasm for a new crusade but once the truth emerged this bubble of excitement quickly burst: Ghazan had not surrendered Jerusalem and it was soon under Mamluk rule again. Furthermore, the khan was not, as rumoured, a Christian (he was a Muslim), although in 1302 he sent an embassy to Edward I that sought co-operation against the Mamluks.[21]

An intriguing feature of this period of crusading – and really over the two generations after the fall of Acre – was the production of a large number of elaborate plans designed to hold on to, or regain, the Holy Land.[22] Often produced at papal request, these so-called 'Recovery Treatises' took two basic forms: either, a *passagium generale*, that is, a papally directed, pan-Christian enterprise – rather like the First Crusade; or, the use of a far more focussed, professional force that aimed to strike hard at a particular target. The latter would be prefaced by a blockade of the Mamluk ports (a reflection of Christian naval superiority) and, with calls for a general peace in Europe, was to be followed up by a larger, more traditionally constituted expedition. Perhaps the plan that came the closest to fruition was that of King Philip VI of France (1328–50) who in October 1332 announced his intentions to a splendid gathering of nobles in Sainte-Chapelle, the wondrous creation of his crusading predecessor, King (and by now St) Louis IX. The papacy tried hard to encourage this venture through clerical taxation and offers of generous spiritual rewards, yet public enthusiasm for the expedition was mixed. Twice in the fourteenth century (in 1309, known as the 'Crusade of the Poor' and 1320, the 'Shepherds' Crusade') there had been unauthorised popular movements in support of a new campaign to the Levant. Thousands of people – mainly from peasant stock – gathered in northern France and headed south to the Languedoc where they had massacred the Jewish populations and then hoped to set out for the Levant. Such anarchic bands posed an intolerable threat to civil order and the authorities had to suppress them, but anti-Semitism aside, they represented a fervent desire to recover the Holy Land.[23] By the time of Philip's planned crusade, however, a wider level of scepticism proved a serious barrier to recruitment. As one contemporary chronicler wrote of the royal project: 'fewer people than expected took the cross, for they had had their fingers burnt too often, and they suspected that the sermons being delivered in the name of the cross were only being given to get money.'[24] Outright resistance from the French towns brought Philip's enterprise to a halt; a year later, the beginning of the Hundred Years War compounded this and delivered a severe blow to crusades to the Holy Land. Other factors soon made their mark as well: in 1343, the Italian bankers, whose financial backing was vital to any new campaign, went into crisis; shortly afterwards the Black Death broke out, and thus crusading started to slip down the list of priorities of Christian Europe.

Chivalric Adventurers: Crusades to Egypt and to the Baltic

Even though major expeditions became less feasible, numerous manifestations of crusading, or an evolving form of the genre, were in evidence during the latter half of the fourteenth century. These were often channelled through, or alongside, notions of chivalry – in itself a theme that had become a dominant feature of European society; in fact, with its fusion of military, aristocratic and Christian mores, there were times when the boundary between chivalry and crusading became almost imperceptible.[25]

Holy wars continued to take place in the eastern Mediterranean, the Baltic and Iberia, and one – fictional – person who fought in all three of these arenas was the knight in the *Prologue* of Chaucer's *Canterbury Tales*, written *c.*1384. As has been argued elsewhere, this figure probably formed an accurate template of the aspirations and attitudes of leading men of the day:

> A knyght ther was, and that a worthy man,
> That fro the tyme that he first bigan
> To riden out, he loved chivalrie,
> Trouthe and honour, fredom and curteisie.
> Ful worthy was he in his lordes werre,
> And therto hadde he riden, no man ferre,
> As wel in cristendom as in hethenesse,
> And evere honoured for his worthynesse;
> At Alisaundre [Alexandria] he was whan it was wonne.
> Ful ofte tyme he hadde the bord bigonne
> Aboven all nacions in Pruce [Prussia];
> In Lettow [Lithuania] hadde he reysed and in Ruce [Russia],
> No Cristen man so ofte of his degree.
> In Gernade [Granada] at the seege eek hadde he be
> Of Algezir [Algeciras], and riden in Belmarye [Morocco].
> At Lyeys [Ayash] was he and at Satalye [Satalia],
> When they were wonne, and in the Grete See [Mediterrarean]
> At many a noble armee hadde he be.[26]

It seems likely that Chaucer's knight was a conflation of the crusading feats of the Scrope clan of Yorkshire, a family represented at all the episodes described above. But the Scropes were no aberration and their exploits were paralleled by numerous men from senior families across northern Europe (including royalty), as well as esquires and men of fortune.[27] This is not to say that military activity elsewhere, such as the recurrent conflicts of the Hundred Years War, was not the dominant concern of these people, but the point remains that all of these crusading outlets were deemed worthy of the risk and the expense. For the higher echelons of society the primary attraction of such escapades was simple: to gain an honourable reputation through great feats in battle, and the fact that this service was in the armies of God – the ultimate Lord – gave it particular prestige. For men-at-arms, unemployed during periods of peace between the major European wars, more basic motives operated and the lure of wages was paramount, but in the case of the nobility (who had to finance their own campaigns), repeated experience would have shown that most of these adventures – especially those in northern Europe – were physically arduous and rarely profitable. Yet that was not the point: the material outlay and personal hardship were more than compensated for by the boost to one's good name and the sense of belonging to an exclusive club, an elite group with shared values and experiences; the very pinnacle of chivalry. The escapades of two Englishmen can offer us a glimpse of this mentality: Sir Richard Waldegrave (an acquaintance of Chaucer), a well-to-do Suffolk knight from Bures Saint Mary, and Henry Bolingbroke, earl of Derby, later King Henry IV of England (1399–1413).

Over a five-year period, Richard took part in a trio of crusading enterprises: in southern Turkey in 1361, Prussia in 1363 and Egypt in 1365.[28] The first and third of these campaigns were under the leadership of King Peter I of Cyprus (1359–69), a man canny enough to note this contemporary enthusiasm for individuals to venture to the eastern Mediterranean. In 1361 Waldegrave, aged twenty-three, followed the trend when he fought in the capture the southern Turkish port of Satalia. Peter's motives were not simply to defeat the Mamluks but also to protect Cyprus from Turkish invasion and to boost his own economy. The presence at Satalia of westerners such as Richard encouraged the king to seek further help and in 1363, aided by a period of peace between England and France, he began a two-year tour of the West. Guillaume de Machaut's sympathetic account portrayed the king as a dynamic, persuasive leader determined to regain Jerusalem, but as we have just seen, other ideas were also in play.[29] Edward III of England was adamant that he would not join the crusade, although his subjects were free to do so. King John II of France was keen to follow in the crusading footsteps of St Louis but his death in 1364 left the crusade's leadership to King Peter. While much of the early preaching for the expedition was framed in terms of a broader recovery of the Holy Land, the target of the campaign was eventually revealed as the prosperous Mamluk port of Alexandria.

In spite of the enthusiastic advocacy of Pope Urban V, no crowned heads from the West took part, although a number of English and French nobles, including Richard Waldegrave, saw it as a worthy cause. Peter also employed European mercenaries (the notorious Free Companies), a measure supported by the pope who offered indulgences to these men as a means of steering their unruly presence away from France and Italy. Spiritual rewards for hired thugs might seem a little out of tune with Pope Urban II's original crusading ideas, but stipendiary troops had been employed on crusades for much of the thirteenth century and, in one sense, this echoed Urban's desire to export the lawless nobility of western Europe back in the eleventh century. Peter's crusade was also joined by the Knights Hospitaller who had been based on Rhodes since the fall of the Holy Land. The Hospitallers had developed an important naval function and Christian fleets worked hard to keep the seas free from Muslim raiders and to promote trade and pilgrimage. Thus – as with so many previous crusading expeditions – participants in this campaign had a plethora of interlocking, possibly contradictory, motives, and while it was endorsed by the papacy, European knights fought in a personal, rather than a national, capacity.

On Rhodes the legate 'piously preached to the king's little army on the mystery of the cross and the Lord's Passion and gave the venerable sign of the cross to all who were setting out.'[30] On 4 October 1365 the fleet departed for Alexandria – a formidable target and one that brought trepidation to the hearts of many. Peter encouraged them to be brave and he chose to blend a message of determination with the prospect of gaining fame and repute: 'you will defeat these men, you'll see it happen and you'll live to talk of it!' The shallow waters outside Alexandria made for a difficult landing because the galleys needed to hold just offshore. This meant the crusaders had to jump down from their ships and wade up the beach in the face of stern enemy resistance. Peter, of course, proved his courage – 'he excels them all' reported Machaut – and the king urged the troops forwards: 'Those are God's enemies . . . Forward my lords, let each man amaze his neighbour.' After successfully forcing their way onto dry land the Christians paused to consider their next move – again, expressed in terms suggestive of a spiritual and chivalric blend: 'Think of our Lord helping us to win such fame against the pagans.' After a vigorous effort the crusaders managed to set fire to one of the gates and then burst inside to take control of the city on 10 October 1365. Overnight, however, poor discipline briefly enabled the enemy to recover a gate before Peter rallied and drove the Muslims out. The visiting crusaders began to reflect on just how large a task they faced holding on to Alexandria and they started to comprehend the sheer scale of resources the Egyptians possessed. They became overwhelmed by fear of the Muslim response and demanded to depart, although Peter, of course, wanted to stay and secure the prosperity of his kingdom. He proclaimed his faith in God's support, the strong walls of Alexandria and the flood of people he believed would arrive from the West, inspired by his success. The legate pleaded with the Europeans to remain, couching his argument in spiritual terms: 'He [the legate] showed clearly how God's honour, the good of Christendom, and the acquisition of the city of Jerusalem hung on the retention of Alexandria . . . but by the Devil's work, the majority stood in his way . . . they had no trust in God . . . and entirely forgot His incredible victories.'[31] Machaut gave Peter's pleas a more chivalric spin: 'Honour, ladies and love, what are you going to say when you see these crowding to run away? They'll never win glory and honour, all are marked in shame!'[32] Yet the crusaders were adamant – they would leave. As they began to re-embark, the Muslims poured back into the city and, for the second time in just under 200 years (remembering Amalric of Jerusalem's brief tenure of the city in 1167), the Christian hold on Alexandria was over within a couple of days.

Peter soon renewed his attempts to recruit help from the West but he met with little success and the following year returned to Cyprus. In spite of the brevity of his conquest, this all-too-rare blow against the Mamluks had won him widespread renown and was reported in glowing terms across the Christian world, as far afield even as Russia. Yet the king's ultimate fate is hard to reconcile with this image of a gallant holy warrior. His attack had infuriated the Mamluks and thereby damaged the Cypriot economy and this, coupled with his own appalling temper, provoked a political crisis. Relations with his nobility deteriorated and Peter was frequently offensive towards their women-folk. Such was his level of irrationality that he is reported to have imprisoned his steward for failing to provide oil for his asparagus! These matters culminated in a decision to kill him and on 16 January 1369 he was attacked in his own bed. The murderers smashed his skull, cut his throat open, dressed him in a tramp's clothes and left the corpse in the palace hall.[33]

The siege of Alexandria represented one of the few high points of crusading warfare in the Mediterranean and, in effect, it came to mark the end of major conflict with the Mamluks. Richard Waldegrave survived the campaign and returned home, soon to venture into another field of war, the Baltic. Once more, he endured and in 1376 entered Parliament, and five years later he ascended the political hierarchy to become the Speaker of the House of Commons (one of his descendants, William Waldegrave, was a member of the Cabinet under Margaret Thatcher and John Major). Richard's days of long-distance travel were over and he settled down in England until his death in 1402. His career had overlapped with a much more influential figure, the future Henry IV of England, Henry Bolingbroke, and through him we can glimpse something of crusading in the Baltic region.

Henry was only twenty-four years old when he proposed to campaign against the infidel in, first, the Mediterranean and then the Baltic. His plans to join a crusade against Muslim pirates, based at al-Mahadia in Tunisia, foundered when promises of safe conduct through France failed to materialise, but he sustained his enthusiasm for holy war by going to north-eastern Europe in July 1390. After a second visit to the Baltic in 1392 he headed south to Venice and made a pilgrimage to Jerusalem in 1393. The survival of his household accounts permit an exceptionally vivid reconstruction of both these journeys: as the son of John of Gaunt, the wealthiest man in England, and as a cousin of King Richard II (1377–99), he was able, and expected, to travel in some considerable style.[34]

Henry became involved in the Teutonic Knights' continued attempts to defeat the Lithuanians, a fierce, pagan people who worshipped a panoply of Gods. Their rituals included the burial of leaders in full war regalia with their horses, while captured enemy commanders were asphyxiated to show their weakness. By this time they occupied lands in the river basins of a region known as the Wilderness, a hundred-mile stretch of territory characterised by dense forests, marshlands and lakes, as well as innumerable tributaries. This was an astoundingly hostile region in which to live and campaign. Experienced guides were vital to the crusaders and progress through the forests was inevitably slow, compounded by terrible rain and snow-storms. Freezing temperatures were the norm and daylight hours were minimal. Campaigns were only really possible twice a year: first, when it was cold enough to freeze the rivers and to solidify the bogs, yet not so bitter as to render movement dangerous; secondly, after the thaw when the sun had sufficiently dried out the marshes to permit safe passage.[35] The Teutonic Knights, based at Marienberg in Poland, had responsibility for the conversion and defeat of these pagans, although the morality of using warfare as a means of conversion provoked fierce debate in ecclesiastical circles. In the end, arguments that emphasised the untrustworthiness of the pagans – and hence the need to conquer them – prevailed and the Teutonics' role was reconfirmed. Not an especially convincing line of reasoning, perhaps, but sufficient for those contemporaries who fought for, and with, the Knights. Given the privilege of a perpetual crusade they could launch annual wars against the heathen, known as *Reisen* (jour-neys), for which spiritual rewards were merited, although there is little record of any ceremonial taking of the cross. The ebb and flow of local allegiances also intervened, most dramatically when, in 1386, the Lithuanian ruler Jogaila was baptised and, on his marriage to a Polish princess, he was elected to the throne of Poland as Wladislaus II. In consequence, the conversion of his lands looked likely and the morality of a crusade against Christians became ever more dubious.[36]

In the course of the fourteenth century, nobles from across Europe were drawn to these campaigns and during 1391 Henry Bolingbroke made his preparations. His expedition displayed all the hallmarks of a typical *Reise* with its potent combination of finery, feasting and fighting. He was accompanied by around seventy companions, including paid knights (plus their retainers), his own squires and domestic staff, as well as contingents of specialist miners and engin-eers, and maybe sixty bowmen. The actual expedition fell into two distinct elements: the military campaign (9 August to 22 October 1391) and the 'reward', laid on by the hosts (22 October 1391 to late March 1392). The first part saw steady progress through the dense forests towards Vilnius. A battle at the River Vilna saw the loss of one young

English knight but the Lithuanian Prince Skirgal (one of Wladislaus' brothers) suffered heavier casualties with three or four dukes taken prisoner and hundreds of his men slain. The town of Vilnius – an important trading centre – was quickly seized, a feat in which Henry played the prominent role that his position demanded. Thomas Walsingham's *Chronica Majora* recorded that 'the town was captured by the great abilities of the earl. For it was men of his own household who were the first to scale the town wall and to place his standard on its top, while the rest of the army were still drowsing.'[37] The main fortress resisted the efforts of miners and engineers and, after five weeks, the master of the Teutonic Knights decided, in the face of a lack of progress, sickness in the camp, and the oncoming winter, to abandon the attempt. Henry then headed back towards Königsberg, the usual base for campaigns against the Lithuanians; he also visited the nearby chapel of St Katharine, a place of pilgrimage. Over the next four months the tenor of the earl's stay changed: he was entertained by splendid tournaments and hunting trips; he was presented with hawks and horses (he was particularly careful to take the former home) and bears. Amongst his train were minstrels: two trumpeters, three pipers and a nakerer (drummer), as well as heralds, all of whom were kept busy during an intensive succession of feasts and social events. A particular highlight was the Ehrentisch, or Table of Honour, a feast usually held in Königsberg. This select gathering saw the leading knights on each campaign (the paid retainers were excluded) invited to a special ceremony at which they were seated according to their chivalric achievements and presented with a badge that bore the motto 'Honour conquers all' in golden letters. Such a highly esteemed award reflected immense prestige on the recipient and was borne with great pride at public events back home. Chaucer's imaginary knight often 'began the Board' which meant that he was seated in the place of honour at the feast. Such occasions added greatly to the allure of the *Reisen* and did much to seal bonds of appreciation between the hosts and their guests.[38] The spiritual aspect of Henry's journey did not disappear entirely because the earl made a variety of donations to churches and the poor during his stay in the north, including a gift to the Hospital of the Holy Spirit in Danzig, while in the same city his week of visits and gifts to four particular churches merited the award of an indulgence from Pope Boniface IX.[39] Thus,

we see the *Reisen* representing an overlapping blend of chivalry, spirituality and crusading.

Multiple tensions within the Polish-Lithuanian relationship offered
the Teutonic Knights chances to assert their strength, but the intellectual justification for their policies began to crumble. The University
of Cracow produced a polemical tract that demolished the Order's
claims to promote conversion. It said that the knights were only interested in land and not in people's souls: the Prussians still remained
semi-pagan after more than a century of the Order's rule, while the
convert Wladislaus and one of his subject tribes, the Samogitians,
were worthy of admiration; thus greed, rather than God's grace, motivated the knights.

In July 1410 events on the battlefield dealt another heavy blow to
the Order's standing. With the support of a number of German
crusaders the knights confronted Wladislaus' Polish-Lithuanian
invasion force at Tannenberg (now Grünwald), about seventy miles
south-east of Marienberg. Both sides implored the Virgin Mary for
help and by the end of the day she seemed to have favoured the Poles
and Lithuanians. At first, the Teutonics swept aside the Lithuanian
right wing, but in their triumphant pursuit a group of knights parted
company with their comrades and the larger contingent of Poles (with
Russian and Tartar Muslim auxiliaries) outflanked and swamped the
Grand Master and his men, killing most of the Order's leading officials and around 400 knights. The survivors rallied sufficiently well to
fight off a fifty-seven-day siege of Marienberg or else the Order might
have collapsed entirely. Of course, given the Lithuanian-Polish forces'
Catholicism this defeat could not be portrayed as a loss for
Christendom, unlike previous setbacks in the north.[40] Continued
debates about the validity of warfare against the Lithuanians and
various political and economic crises plagued the Order, and while it
struggled on to the Reformation and beyond, its heyday was long
past.[41]

Henry Bolingbroke had evidently enjoyed his *Reise* sufficiently to
repeat the experience in 1392; the political situation in England may
well have made it expedient for him to travel as well. Unfortunately,
by the time he had taken the trouble to reach Lithuania there was no
need for outside help, although the Teutonic Knights were sufficiently
grateful to offer him the considerable sum of £400 towards the cost

of his journey. Undeterred, Henry decided to make a pilgrimage to the Holy Land (contrary to the impression given by Shakespeare who suggested that he never went at all). Using the financial services of Lombard merchants he raised the money to march overland through Bohemia to Prague where he stayed with King Wenceslas, brother of Queen Anne of England; thence he went on to Moravia, Vienna and Venice. There, as befitted a man of his standing, he was accorded the honour of a public reception by the doge and together they gave oblations to St Mark's Basilica. On several occasions he visited the magnificent relic collections in the city, part of the haul taken by the Fourth Crusade from Constantinople in 1204. Huge supplies of food were laid in for Henry's voyage to the Orient, including 2,250 eggs, 450 kilograms of almonds, 2,000 dates, as well as fine wines; he also took the precaution of taking two doctors on the trip.[42] By this time, shipping could endure the Mediterranean in winter and Henry set sail from Venice on 23 December 1392. He spent Christmas Day in Zara, the site of so much contention during the Fourth Crusade, and then, via Corfu, he went on to Rhodes. Here Henry was entertained by the Hospitaller Grand Master before he pressed on to the port of Jaffa. In previous centuries Christian and Muslim rulers had permitted pilgrims to visit shrines and, given the lack of large-scale, open hostilities between the rulers of the Near East and the Catholic powers of the region, Henry was able to make his pilgrimage.

His stay in the Holy Land lasted only a few days, although the purchase of wax candles and records of offerings made at the Holy Sepulchre and the Mount of Olives signify conventional acts of devotion. En route home a stay on Lusignan Cyprus was accompanied by the usual festivities and the earl received a leopard to transport back to England, as well as a converted Muslim whose baptismal name was given as Henry. The earl then sailed to Venice before progressing through Milan, Burgundy, Champagne, Paris and thence to Dover and London.[43] This journey was, of course, a pilgrimage and a sign of devotion, rather than a crusade, although his travels – by no means unique amongst the English nobility – brought him into contact with those in the front line of holy war, such as the Hospitallers on Rhodes, and was a sign that interest in the holy places remained tangible amongst the elite of northern Europe.

Around the same time as Henry's adventures, upheavals within the

Catholic Church brought a controversial new kind of crusading to the fore. As European warfare grew increasingly costly, professional soldiers became the norm and the papacy used paid troops to try to shape the complex politics of northern and central Italy. Their aim was to end a period of exile at Avignon, a situation precipitated by disturbances in Rome. Although they returned to the holy city in 1376, within two years the outbreak of the Great Schism (1378–1417) damaged the reputation of the papacy even further. Disputes over the identity of the rightful occupant of the chair of St Peter meant that at times there were two, or even three, claimants – a corrosive state of affairs that inflicted considerable damage on the standing of, and respect for, the papacy. A series of overtly political crusades took place, most obviously when the agenda of a party in the papal schism coincided with that of someone in another conflict such as the Hundred Years War. In the early 1380s Pope Urban VI offered the English full crusade privileges to fight the French – the allies of his rival, Clement VII. The ebullient Bishop Hugh Despenser preached a crusade and sold large numbers of indulgences, although in the event Parliament granted a substantial sum to support the enterprise and approved the choice of commander. While officials tried to build up a case for the ʿcrusade in defence of the Holy Church and the realm of England', many contemporaries simply regarded this as a flimsy pretext to continue both the Great Schism and the Hundred Years War. National warfare was fast emerging as the major form of conflict within Europe, and while religious imagery and a sense of righteous cause was often writ large within it, this was not crusading. For example, in spite of the potent rhetoric that described King Henry V of England as a holy warrior, worthy of comparison with the Old Testament hero Judas Maccabeus – a figure who inspired the heroes of the First Crusade – in no sense was the Battle of Agincourt (1415) a papal crusade with full spiritual indulgences.[44]

Divisions of belief sparked another notable branch of crusading within Europe, although there was a contemporary whiff of nationalism. The first major crusade against heresy since the Albigensian crusade of 1209 was directed at the supporters of John Hus, a radical teacher at the University of Prague. He was a man scathing in his criticism of clerical vices, and he demanded that the clergy follow the example of the Bible and nothing else. Hus also dismissed various papal indulgences and stated that laymen could receive both bread and wine in the Eucharist, rather than just bread. The Bohemian monarchy reneged on promises of safe conduct and had Hus burned to death on 6 July 1415. His supporters, many of whom were members of the local nobility (shades of the situation in southern France 200 years earlier), turned to war and widespread social unrest followed. The king of Bohemia was (temporarily) deposed and the papacy authorised a series of crusades in 1420–2, although there was also a nationalist dimension in that the Hussites represented Czech identity in conflict with the crown's mainly German allies. The Hussites' anger towards the papacy cascades out of this manifesto published by the citizens of Prague in 1420: 'Most recently the Church acted not as a mother but as a stepmother. That most cruel snake has given birth to a malignant offspring ... and the entire poison has been poured out upon us when ... the Church raised the cruel cross against all of the faithful in our kingdom and with bloody hands announced a crusade ... All of this has been for nothing other than ... the truth of God. The pope has called from everywhere an unjust war, summoning our natural enemies, the Germans, and has invited them, with false indulgences from pain and sin, to fight us. Even though they have no reason they are always antagonistic to our language ... Who, faithful to the kingdom, would not grieve over the fact that the lying priest, full of iniquity, wished to ferment this pus in this golden and most Christian kingdom even to the point of exterminating within us the truth of God ... We pray that you, like brave knights, may remember our fathers, the old Czechs, and stand up willingly against this evil.'[45] On several occasions the Hussites roundly defeated the crusaders, often because of their innovative military skills. The use of wagons, sometimes drawn into a rectangular formation or else used as a mobile defensive barrier for infantry and cavalry, or even as a base for small cannon, was one element in their repertoire.[46] Hussite forces spread into neighbouring lands such as Poland, Hungary and Austria but local anti-Czech nationalism often blunted their religious message. Further crusades in 1427 and 1431 also failed; Hussite beliefs survived in Bohemia and in subsequent years a negotiated compromise was reached – a settlement in part engendered by increasing fear of the most powerful and dynamic force in south-eastern Europe, the Ottoman Turks.

The Rise of the Ottoman Empire and the Sack of Constantinople, 1453

In the course of the fourteenth century the main forum of crusading warfare in the eastern Mediterranean became Constantinople and the Balkans, a shift prompted by the remorseless rise of the Ottoman Empire. The Ottomans were a nomadic tribe from north-western Asia Minor who had emerged under the leadership of Osman, a frontier warlord, at the very start of the fourteenth century. Their origins are somewhat hazy but early on the presence of large numbers of *ghazis* (volunteers dedicated to the holy war who fought in the expectation of booty and who were treated as martyrs on their death) and Sufi mystics gave them a strong religious drive. A series of victories against Muslim and Byzantine Christian opponents convinced them that God was on their side. By the middle of the century they had established a strong territorial base in north-western Anatolia and begun to push through the Dardanelles and into south-eastern Europe. In 1389 the Ottomans destroyed a Serbian army at Kosovo, another battle that has remained strong in modern regional consciousness. The immensity of the Turkish threat began to concentrate minds in Catholic Europe in a way not seen for decades. Coupled with a rare window of peace in the Hundred Years War, and inflamed by the crusading enthusiasm of John of Nevers, son of the duke of Burgundy, and Marshal Boucicaut, this generated a substantial army ready to turn back the Ottoman menace. Boucicaut's biographer evoked the spirit in which the French nobility joined the crusade: 'he [John of Nevers] was then in the full flower of youth, and wanted to follow the path sought by the virtuous, that is to say, the honour of knighthood. He considered that he could not use his time better than in dedicating his youth to God's service, by bodily labour for the spreading of the faith . . . several young lords wanted to go along, to escape boredom and employ their time and energies on deeds of knighthood. For it really seemed to them that they could not go on a more honourable expedition or one more pleasing to God.'[47] The results of the expedition were, however, catastrophic.

In July 1396 the French linked up with King Sigismund of Hungary at Buda and a combined army of perhaps 15,000–20,000 men began to march down the Danube intent upon the recovery of Nicopolis, a strong defensive site in Bulgaria. After this the crusade planned to move on to Constantinople and relieve the city from a siege led by Sultan Bayezid I (1389–1402), known as Yilderim, or Thunderbolt. Early successes lulled the Christians into a sense of complacency and as they blockaded Nicopolis their camp became a scene of indiscipline and licentiousness; Bayezid, meanwhile, had gathered his troops and was approaching fast. On 25 September the two sides met in battle. The French impetuously hurled themselves against Bayezid's infantry and light cavalry who were carefully positioned at the top of a hill. Stakes in the ground tore the crusaders' horses to pieces, but although they fought on foot, so great was their momentum that they succeeded in cutting their way up past the Turkish infantry to face the light cavalry. At this point they discovered Bayezid's trap: waiting on the other side of the hill, fresh and rested, were his heavy cavalry. The Ottomans charged and the crusaders, from being convinced of their success, collapsed: 'the lion in them turned into a timid hare', commented one contemporary. Thousands of men were killed or taken prisoner, an earlier massacre of Turks was avenged by the summary execution of countless Christians, and Count John and Marshal Boucicaut were imprisoned. The debacle of Nicopolis was a massive blow to crusading morale in western Europe and it gave the Turks free access to continue their conquest of the Balkans.[48] In 1402 their momentum was briefly stalled by defeat at the hands the Turcoman ruler Timur (also known as Tamerlane) at the Battle of Ankara, and a period of dynastic infighting checked their progress further, but within a couple of decades they were looking to expand again.[49]

The Turks' prime target was clearly Constantinople, in part because of its immense wealth and importance to Christianity, in part because it lay directly between Ottoman lands in Anatolia and their possessions in the Balkans. The Greeks had regained the city from the Latins in 1261, but only a pale shadow of past glories survived; that said, it did survive blockades and sieges from 1394 to 1402 and in 1442. So great was the Ottoman menace that Emperor John VIII was persuaded to grasp the nettle of Church unity and in 1439 he led a delegation to Florence where, after centuries of division, the union of the Catholic and Orthodox – with the former as the senior partner – was finally proclaimed. This provoked outrage amongst some of the Greeks: 'We have betrayed our faith. We have exchanged piety for impiety.'[50] John, however, received the reward he was after with a new crusade in 1444. This saw another heavy defeat for the Christians at the town of Varna on the west coast of the Black Sea (in modern-day Bulgaria) when Ottoman troops, fighting under the banner of jihad, entirely crushed their opponents.[51]

In 1451, Mehmet II, known to posterity as Mehmet the Conqueror, became sultan at the age of seventeen (he had held the title briefly between 1444 and 1446). Two years later this remarkable character struck Christendom an enormous blow with the capture of Constantinople. He was a brave, secretive and utterly ruthless man; he was also a scholar and a superb strategist. He is described as having a hooked nose and fleshy lips, or 'a parrot's beak resting on cherries' as a poet so colourfully expressed it. Two actions early on in his sultanate – one a combination of the private and the political, the other strategic – give a sense of the man. First, as soon as he became ruler, he ordered his infant half-brother to be drowned in his bath (the perpetrator was then executed for murder); thus he enshrined fratricide as a means of preventing civil war. Secondly, he commissioned the construction of the castle of Bogaz Kesa, The Throat Cutter, a few miles east along the Bosphorus. This fine fortress (known today as Rumeli Hisari) has four large and thirteen smaller towers and was completed in a matter of months, testimony to the superbly efficient Ottoman war machine. As the name of the castle suggests, it was designed to block the passage of Christian shipping along the Bosphorus and thereby to close the net around Constantinople.

Within the city, Emperor Constantine IX (1449–53) viewed these developments with understandable trepidation.[52] He appealed to the West for help, but other than some support from the Venetians, who still retained an interest in Constantinople long after their part in the 1204 conquest, no major forces arrived. The Genoese held a colony at Galata, just across the Golden Horn, and while they professed neutrality, their men and shipping also came to play a vital role in the defence of the city. Even with such limited outside assistance the sheer strength of Constantinople's fortifications made it a formidable site. The emperor commanded ditches to be cleared while the dilapidated outer walls were restored and covered with huge bales of cotton and wool to try to cushion them from cannon-fire. He also ordered the fabrication of a huge boom, made from massive sections of wood and iron links, to span the Golden Horn and protect the more vulnerable walls on the inlet – the area where the Fourth Crusade had broken into the city. Contemporaries indicate the defenders' great faith in this construction and their confidence that, in conjunction with the mighty city walls, it would enable them to endure once more.[53] It is interesting to compare the two great sieges of 1204 and 1453. Aside from the obvious contrast of the latter episode being Muslim against Christian, rather than Catholics versus Orthodox, the size of the opposing forces was strikingly different. In 1204 the crusaders were massively outnumbered by the Byzantines; in 1453, however, the Christian troops in Constantinople totalled perhaps 10,000. Notwithstanding the defensive efforts of the citizenry – and even monks were pressed into service – in military terms, at over 80,000 men (plus tens of thousands of labourers) the Ottoman army was a vastly bigger fighting force, mighty enough for a Venetian eyewitness to describe the defenders as 'an ant in the mouth of a bear'.[54] The 1453 siege was also more multifaceted with a significant part of the fighting taking place on water. During the earlier campaign the besieging Venetians had enjoyed almost a free hand at sea, but in 1453 an Ottoman fleet of up to 400 ships frequently tussled with a small but powerful Genoese and Cretan force based around the defensive boom. Finally, technology had moved on: by 1453 the emergence of gunpowder (during the late thirteenth century) meant that cannon came to play a hugely prominent role in the later campaign.[55]

The siege began on 6 April. Mehmet's engineers had constructed a massive palisaded rampart that ran from the Sea of Marmara to the Golden Horn while a similar structure overlooked the city from the Galata side. With siege guns and catapults the Turks soon began to bombard the 'queen of cities'. Teams of workmen had strengthened roads and bridges to allow the transportation of several colossal cannon – one required sixty oxen to pull it – from their base at Edirne, 150 miles to the north-west. Most of the firepower concentrated on the gates of St Romanus (now known as the Topkapi Gate) and Charisus, both towards the middle of the land walls. The Turks' largest gun burst, but one of the others remained a monstrous piece of weaponry, capable of firing a shot of almost 550 kilograms. Mehmet had over fourteen batteries of cannon, most of which could launch balls of between 100 and 200 kilograms. Day after day these machines generated a lethal hail of stone that crashed and smashed against the walls of Constantinople, splintering its defences and demoralising the defenders. Mehmet was canny enough to continually reposition his cannon to best advantage, and at times he triangulated three guns on a single point to maximise their effect. The Byzantines had artillery of their own but these were far smaller devices and used mainly against troops and siege engines; lack of powder and shot were further restrictions on the Christians' firepower: by contrast, Mehmet's biggest cannon consumed 1,100 pounds of gunpowder a day! A contemporary noted: 'He devised machines of all sorts . . . especially of the newest kind, a strange sort, unbelievable when told of but, as experience demonstrated, able to accomplish everything.'[56]

Nicolò Barbaro, a Venetian eyewitness, described the debilitating effect of living in continuous anticipation of a major assault. Such tensions were increased by a series of night attacks, usually heralded by the harsh cracking and snapping of castanets, but all were successfully resisted. On 20 April, however, the Christians scored an unexpected victory. The appearance of three large Genoese vessels bearing papally sponsored troops and supplies prompted a sea battle. Mehmet's admiral engaged the galleys but the greater size of the Genoese boats gave them a crucial advantage over the oared Turkish ships and the Christians used their superior height to pour down arrows and small-arms fire onto their enemy. As Mehmet watched from the shore he grew increasingly enraged at the lack of progress and, famously, he mounted his horse and plunged into the sea to bellow inaudible advice to his admiral. Once the wind turned, the Christian vessels were able to reach the safety of the boom and this duly opened to bring them sanctuary. The defeat was a massive blow to Ottoman pride and caused consternation in the Muslim camp. Mehmet was beside himself with rage and summoned the admiral to answer for this failure – the sultan was said to have wanted to execute the man, but his colleagues persuaded their ruler that the loss of rank and a flogging would suffice.[57]

The Christians' continued trust in the boom seemed well placed, but Mehmet was not to be resisted. Because he could not break the barrier the sultan devised a quite brilliant way to – literally – get around it. As we saw with Reynald of Châtillon's transportation of kit-form ships from Kerak down to the Red Sea in 1182, it was possible to move vessels overland. Others had followed his example; more recently the Venetians had shifted galleys from the River Adige to Lake Garda. Mehmet accomplished something similar, although on a jaw-dropping scale. His engineers constructed a shallow trench that ran from the shore of the Bosphorus, up over the steep hill (through the modern Taksim square) and then down to the Golden Horn. This carefully crafted ditch was then covered in boards and greased, allowing ships to be laboriously hauled up the slope and then eased downhill behind the boom and into the heart of the Christian harbour. An incredible seventy-two vessels made this journey and once back in the water their sails were re-rigged and they could threaten the weakest walls of Constantinople. The creation of a pontoon bridge to link up the troops near Galata with those by the land walls was another sign of technical flair and a hint that a major assault was brewing.

On 28 April the Christians attempted to seize the upper hand with a bid to destroy the main Ottoman fleet. They filled transport ships with sacks of flammable materials – cotton and wool – to set the Turkish boats ablaze, but the flotilla's commander, 'a man eager to win honour in this world', raced ahead of the escort vessels and drew the full weight of enemy firepower. The Turks scored a direct hit on only their second shot and 'quicker than ten paternosters' the ship sank with all hands to ruin the Christian offensive.[58] Soon the Ottomans regained the initiative and in mid-May heavy bombardment of the gates of St Romanus and the Caligaria (near the Blachernae Palace in the north) called for the most desperate resistance. Around this time the Turks started to use yet another stratagem to break into the city – a contingent of specialist Serbian miners began to dig a series of shafts in a bid to get under the walls and to provide an entry point into Constantinople. As usual with Mehmet's armies the scale of these works was immense – one of the tunnels was over half a mile long – but one night the defenders heard the sound of digging and their own mining expert, a Scotsman named John Grant, located the shaft. He dug out a counter-mine, set fire to the Turks' supports and caused them to collapse and suffocate the attackers.[59]

Throughout the siege, the Turkish artillery continued to pound away at the walls, parts of which were now filled with a patchwork of earth, rubble and timber barricades. Barbaro noted the demoralising effect of the mighty cannon: 'One was of exceptional size . . . and when it fired the explosion made all the walls of the city shake and all the ground inside, and even the ships in the harbour felt the vibrations of it. Because of the great noise, many women fainted with the shock which the firing of it gave them. No greater cannon than this one was ever seen in the whole pagan world and it was this that broke down such a great deal of the city walls.'[60] A strange fog caused consternation in the Christian camp when what should have been a full moon appeared as a slim, three-day moon, an event seen as a dire omen because a famous prophecy foretold that Constantinople would fall when the planet gave a sign.[61]

Meanwhile Mehmet considered his next move. Some of his inner circle argued in favour of a peaceful solution and they suggested that Constantine could hand over his city in return for control of the Morea. The Byzantine emperor's response was curt: 'God forbid that I should live as an emperor without an empire. As my city falls, I will fall with it.' Rumours of an approaching Venetian fleet and plans for a Hungarian relief force to march to Constantinople probably underlay Constantine's continued resistance. By the same token, however, fear of this imminent crusade pushed Mehmet into action.[62] Like Saladin before the Battle of Hattin, the sultan's campaign had built up so much momentum that he needed to bring it all to the boil or else risk losing support amongst his own people. The danger of running out of supplies – his enormous army had been outside Constantinople for over fifty days and had utterly stripped the countryside of food – was another important consideration.

On 26 May the sultan ordered preparations to be made for the final assault. Huge fires were lit throughout the Turkish camp and the men fasted by day and feasted by night. Mehmet went amongst his men to raise morale and the imams told stirring stories of the jihad and of Islamic heroes of the past. The prospect of taking Constantinople had a profound spiritual resonance with Muslims because a well-known Hadith promised the capture of the city. The prophecy had powerful eschatological overtones and claimed this would be a definitive Muslim victory, surpassing all others and representing the penultimate defeat of Christianity before the final Armageddon. Here, then, was a chance to fulfil that centuries-old destiny – and with a leader named Mehmet, the Turkish form of Muhammad. Encouraged by these portents, the Ottoman encirclement of Constantinople grew ever tighter. The troops brought up 2,000 scaling ladders, they filled in the ditches and the bombardment intensified further until, in Barbaro's words, 'it was a thing not of this world'.[63] The defenders knew their supreme test was about to come and while Emperor Constantine deployed his troops as best he could, the clergy paraded relics and led prayers and processions around the city. A couple of hours before daybreak on 29 May a volley of artillery fire announced the start of the attack. The principal focus was the damaged area near the St Romanus Gate, although in the course of the day Ottoman forces also engaged the remainder of the land walls and the defences along the Golden Horn. First to be sent forward were Christian prisoners and subject peoples – the most expendable of all Mehmet's troops. The defenders' crossbowmen and light artillery duly slaughtered most of these hapless souls – in any case, had they retreated, then Mehmet's Janissaries, his crack troops, had orders to kill them. A second, more organised division made a further foray although they too were driven back. All of this drained the defenders' energy and resources – it also left the Janissaries fresh and rested, waiting for their turn to move. As Mehmet himself watched, these professional warriors advanced with disconcerting slowness towards the St Romanus Gate and, unusually for Muslim armies, without musical accompaniment. This sinister new assault was fiercer than ever – they were 'not like Turks, but like lions', related Barbaro. Still the Christians held them off, but the city resounded with the chaos of battle, the Turks 'firing cannon again and again, with so many other guns and arrows without number and shouting from these pagans, that the very air seemed to be split apart.' For all the Christians' valour they were doomed, 'since God had made up his mind that the city should fall into the hands of the Turks.'[64] The Janissaries at last got a foothold in the St Romanus barbican but their determination was coloured with good fortune too. Several accounts describe the Genoese commander, John Giustiniani Longo, being wounded, although reports of his reaction vary. Some claim that he sought medical help, although in doing so, he caused the emperor to believe he was deserting his post. Barbaro, admittedly a hostile Venetian, suggested that Longo had retreated, shouting 'The Turks have got into the city!' which made everyone abandon hope. This panic, in turn, gave the Janissaries the chance to make a proper opening in the main walls and from there they poured into the city.

In the early morning light the flags of Venice and the emperor were torn down and Ottoman banners began to appear on the skyline of Constantinople. As the Christians lost heart, the Genoese and the Venetians attempted to fight through to their vessels on the Golden Horn and flee. While the Italians rushed out, Ottoman troops poured in from every side and for one day the city was given over to the sack. Across Constantinople, the Turks wrought havoc, killing indiscriminately, whether young or old, male or female, healthy or infirm. Women, girls and nuns were ravaged and many thousands of Christians were captured to be ransomed or sold as slaves. Barbaro luridly conveys the savagery of the moment: 'The blood flowed in the city like rainwater in the gutters after a sudden storm, and the corpses of Turks and Christians were thrown into the Dardanelles, where they floated out to sea like melons on a canal.' They tore an inestimable amount of booty from the great religious institutions, as well as from private houses and from merchants.[65] Just as in 1204, the mighty sanctuary of the Hagia Sophia was ripped open and plundered, and Leonard of Chios claimed the Turks 'showed no respect for the sacred altars or holy images, but destroyed them, and gouged the eyes from the saints . . . and they stuffed their pouches with gold and silver taken from the holy images and sacred vessels.'[66] Crucifixes were paraded in a mocking procession through the Muslim camp and very soon the Hagia Sophia was turned from a church into a mosque. The death of Constantine himself is shrouded in mystery. Some writers claimed that as the final onslaught began the emperor begged his courtiers to kill him and when they refused he charged into the fray and died under a hail of scimitars and daggers. Muslim sources indicate that he was close to the walls on the Sea of Marmara, looking to escape by boat, when he was slain by troops unaware of his true identity. Yet once the battle was over Sultan Mehmet did not try to eradicate a Christian presence from his new capital; for a start he realised that the city needed its local population to survive and prosper and soon Muslims, Christians and Jews mingled freely enough, although the latter two remained subject groups who paid a poll tax according to Islamic law. The sultan even appointed a new Orthodox patriarch, which shows a broad sense of tolerance too.

The loss of Christendom's greatest city provoked outrage in the West, not least because of the apparent indifference of the major ruling powers. Aeneas Sylvius Piccolomini (later Pope Pius II) wrote: 'For what calamity of the times is not laid at the door of the princes? All troubles are ascribed to the negligence of rulers. "They might", said the populace, "have aided perishing Greece before she was captured. They were indifferent. They are not fit to rule."'[67]

A New Crusade? The Feast of the Pheasant

Within a year of Mehmet's triumph, Duke Philip the Good of Burgundy, one of the most powerful men in Europe, made lavish promises to launch a crusade to recover Constantinople and to drive back the infidel. The forum for this was the Feast of the Pheasant (February 1454), an event saturated with chivalric behaviour and another superb, if slightly late, example of the intimate connection between noble display and crusading.[68] The year 1453 had also marked the end of the Hundred Years War and this seemed the perfect moment to respond to the catastrophe in the East. Philip's father had led the forces defeated at Nicopolis in 1396 and although held prisoner for six months he had received a hero's welcome on his return. Philip summoned the Burgundian nobility to the city of Lille in northern France to attend a sumptuous banquet and to hear his plans. Thirty-five artists were employed to decorate the chamber and, to ensure that the world knew of this splendid occasion, the duke ordered official accounts of the feast to be distributed. The report noted:

There was even a chapel on the table, with a choir in it, a pasty full of flute players. A figure of a girl, quite naked, stood against a pillar . . . she was guarded by a live lion who sat near her. My lord duke was served by a two-headed horse ridden by two men sitting back to back, each holding a trumpet . . . Next came an elephant . . . carrying a castle in which sat the Holy Church, who made piteous complaint on behalf of the Christians persecuted by the Turks, and begged for help. Then two knights of the Order of the Golden Fleece brought in two damsels . . . these ladies asked my lord duke to make his vow. It was understood that if the king of France would go on the crusade, the duke would go.[69]

Philip's vow was made 'to God my creator and to the most virgin His mother, and to the ladies, and I swear on the pheasant . . . If the Grand Turk would be willing to do battle with me in single combat, I shall fight with him with the aid of God and the Virgin mother in order to sustain the Christian faith.'[70] This entrancing combination of revelry and unrestrained excess shows an almost total absorption of crusading into the chivalric ethos. The contrast between the cavorting of naked women and the impassioned preaching of a man such as Bernard of Clairvaux is self-evident, yet the Holy Church was said to be delighted by Philip's promise – as well it might, given that many of the guests soon followed his example and assumed the cross too.

Two months later Philip repeated his intention at Regensburg where he spoke of his Christian duty and of 'the crisis in which Christianity finds itself. If we wish to keep our faith, our liberty, our lives, we must take the field against the Turks and crush their power before it becomes any stronger.' Centuries of crusading hyperbole had preceded this statement, but it was a rare occasion when the gravity of the threat seemed to match the claims being made. Philip pushed ahead with his plans and engaged in serious and extensive preparations that included the manufacture of new pennons and banners, as well as signing up over 500 gunners: an indication that Mehmet's use of heavy artillery had been noticed in the West. Mehmet heard about the crusade and riled the duke with use of his spectacular title: 'true heir of King Alexander and Hector of Troy, sultan of Babylon', and he promised to do to Philip's army the same as his predecessor had done to the duke's father at Nicopolis.[71] By the summer of 1456, however, the duke's enthusiasm had begun to wane. His stipulation that the king of France should crusade remained unfulfilled as national rivalries became ever more important in frustrating the chances of holy war.

Mehmet, meanwhile, inspired by his triumph, advanced towards the Balkan town of Belgrade. In spite of his recent successes the determined resistance of Hungarian troops led by John Hunyadi and the seventy-year-old Franciscan friar John of Capistrano held off the Turks for three weeks and then, in a pitched battle, utterly defeated them.[72] This feat of virtuosity, achieved without the crowned heads of western Europe, did much to stem the Ottoman advance for the next fifty years at least. As the fifteenth century drew to a close, the final large-scale crusading campaign of the medieval period was about to take place in Iberia.

Ferdinand and Isabella: The Conquest of Granada and the Voyages of Christopher Columbus

Chaucer's fictional knight had campaigned in Iberia during the late fourteenth century. A burst of crusading energy during the reign of Alfonso XI of Castile (1325–50) brought the capture of Algeciras in 1344, but this was not really a period of substantial progress for the reconquest and more one of consolidation and immigration as the Christians sought to confirm the gains of previous generations. Decades of political infighting also slowed the process, and the rule of Henry IV of Castile (1454–74) saw a man drawn to Islamic customs, clothing and company. Some disapproved of this dubious behaviour and continued unrest saw him cede the succession to his half-sister, Isabella, and her husband the Aragonese Prince Ferdinand. Thus two of the great Spanish dynasties joined together and their profound personal devotion to the crusading cause was a vital factor in the Christians' eventual victory. This aggressive mood chimed in with the feelings of their people too. *Convivencia*, that is the toleration of other peoples, had been a striking feature of Iberian culture for centuries but a new sense of hostility now emerged. The first groups to experience this were the Jews and the *conversos* (converts from Judaism) and pogroms began during the 1390s. In the aftermath of Henry IV's reign, Ferdinand and Isabella stepped up the antagonism towards non-Catholics with the launch of the Inquisition in 1478, once again targeted largely at the *conversos*.

Ferdinand and Isabella's eventual triumph was also the product of a good, if at times tense, relationship with the papacy. National and religious interests coalesced and successive popes legislated vital financial support for the enterprise. Increasingly generous offers of spiritual rewards – not just for those who went on crusade, but also to individuals who paid for someone to go in their place – were augmented by the full indulgence for people who gave as little as two silver reales. Legislation that allowed payment for spiritual benefits for deceased relatives was another recent – and highly lucrative – development. Taken

together, and actively promoted by the Church hierarchy, these measures produced immense sums of money without which the reconquest
could not have happened. As well as creating a fiscal framework for
this new offensive Pope Sixtus IV also offered spiritual encouragement,
and in 1482 he sent the two monarchs a great silver crucifix to be carried
at the front of the crusader army as a battle standard. These new expeditions were important to the pope, and indeed to Christendom in
general, because the Ottoman triumph at Constantinople had generated a fear that the Turks might move through North Africa and
penetrate Europe from the west. Ferdinand and Isabella played upon
this sentiment to some extent and a letter from the king to his envoy
in Rome in 1485 is generally taken as a fair representation of his crusading
fervour: 'We have not been moved nor are we moved to this war by
any desire to enlarge our realms and seigniories, not by greed to obtain
greater revenues than we possess, not by any wish to pile up treasures;
for should we wish to we could do it with much less danger and expen-
diture . . . But our desire to serve God and our zeal for His holy Catholic
faith, make us put all other interests aside.'[73]

Thousands of people journeyed to Spain to expel the Moors from
Iberia – men from England (sent on the orders of King Henry VII
himself, who commanded prayers for the crusade's success to be said
across the land), Germany, Switzerland, Ireland, Poland and France
came to fight under the silver standard, although the bulk of the
armies were of Spanish origin. Annual campaigns began in 1483 and
within a few years they took Ronda and Malaga. The size of the
Christian forces was immense and we have reliable evidence that an
army of 52,000 besieged Baza for six months in 1489. By way of
comparison, the *combined* sides at the Battle of Hattin in 1187 had
numbered no more than 40,000. By the summer of 1491 the Muslims
were pinned back to the stronghold of Granada, on the edge of the
Sierra Nevada mountains, deep in southern Andalusia. The royal
family led a huge army, well supported by artillery, to besiege this
formidable site which was defended by the emir Boabdil. This was
not the most intense of conflicts, and once it became plain that the
Muslims were not going to get help from their co-religionists in North
Africa a negotiated surrender was always likely. On 2 January 1492
Granada capitulated and the great silver cross was raised on the highest
tower. Ferdinand and Isabella received Boabdil's submission (the

doffing of his hat to Ferdinand), leaving the Muslim to a tearful, if probably apocryphal, return to his mother, who allegedly scolded him for crying like a woman for what he could not defend like a man.

The entire Iberian peninsula was back in Christian hands and the king sent an ecstatic report to Rome: 'Your Holiness has such good fortune, after many travails, expenditures and deaths, and outpouring of the blood of our subjects and citizens, this kingdom of Granada which for 780 years was occupied by the infidels, that in your day and with your aid the victory has been won ... to the glory of God and the exaltation of our holy Catholic faith.'[74] A special Mass celebrated this landmark victory – and the Spanish legate held a bullfight for the citizens of Rome as his way of marking the moment.

In the decades immediately after Granada the Spanish started to make inroads into North Africa, in part to gain economic benefits but also to progress eastwards in the stated hope of reaching Jerusalem. Back in the 1120s Bishop Diego Gelmírez of Compostela had argued that the holy city could be reached via North Africa and, almost four centuries later, it seemed a possibility. In 1510, however, a Spanish defeat at Tripoli marked the end of this plan.[75] The wish to recover Jerusalem had been a powerful idea in the court of Ferdinand and Isabella and the same year that Granada fell one notable individual made his contribution to this aim: Christopher Columbus. Given his fame as the man who discovered the Americas, Columbus may not be the most obvious character to be heralded as a crusader but the capture of Granada had generated a fevered atmosphere of religious renewal. Within months the Spanish monarchs had signed and sealed documents to authorise his first great voyage, and Columbus' own diaries show that his ultimate intention was to lay the ground for the recovery of Jerusalem itself. On 26 December 1492 he wrote of his wish to secure gold and spices to finance an expedition 'to conquer the Holy Sepulchre, for thus I urged Your Highnesses to spend all the profits of this, my enterprise, on the conquest of Jerusalem.' His desire for riches was driven by spiritual as well as earthly reasons. By 1501–2 Columbus came to see himself as an agent of divine will, encouraged by the Holy Spirit. Stirred by apocalyptic ideas in the writings of contemporary Franciscans, he hoped to create the conditions for the Second Coming of Christ by the conversion of all peoples to

Christianity and the recapture of the holy city. He also wanted to form an alliance with the Great Mongol Khan to fight Islam. By this time, however, while the Mongols might offer patronage to Nestorian monks, they had no interest in a war against the Muslims. Even more damagingly, Columbus' conviction that such an alliance was possible was founded on a misunderstanding that the distance westwards to the Orient was far smaller than in reality.[76]

The political and religious climate of the sixteenth century effectively brought to an end crusading's formal ties with its medieval origins. Struggles between the mighty Habsburg Empire of Charles V (1519–56) and the Ottoman Sultan Suleyman the Magnificent (1520–66) still represented Christianity at war with Islam and in 1529 the relief of Vienna repulsed a Turkish thrust at the heart of Europe. While this was indeed a fully fledged crusade, such clashes were more akin to an imperial-led defence of Habsburg lands, rather than a holy war. In northern Europe, meanwhile, the Reformation swept away Catholic beliefs, national churches emerged to cast aside papal authority, and crusading became increasingly irrelevant: indulgences had become a debased and discredited idea. Too many false preachers had extracted money for their own ends and spiritual rewards were seen as a commercial, rather than a holy transaction. A vast range of causes were eligible for these benefits and many people – often including secular princes – had taken a cut from the funding. As Pius II lamented, 'People think our sole object is to amass gold. No one believes what we say. Like insolvent tradesmen, we are without credit.'[77] What had happened at Granada represented a combination of crusading fervour and national interests, combined with effective papal support, efficient government control over crusade taxes, and a well-oiled publicity machine. This had helped to generate widespread popular enthusiasm but elsewhere in Europe it became almost impossible to draw together all these factors simultaneously, and this too explains the broader decline of crusading in this period. On rare occasions, fear of the Turks induced the Christians to act together, most notably with the epic sea victory of a Venetian-Spanish fleet at the Battle of Lepanto in 1571. Perhaps the last crusade of any real size was the Spanish Armada where the agendas of the papacy and Philip II coincided and the *curia* blessed the expedition as a crusade. When God's will – or the tenacity of the English navy, combined with devastating storms off Ireland – rebuffed the campaign, the holy war seemed spent. Other than the Knights Hospitaller, boldly holding on to their island fortress of Malta, this most prominent feature of the medieval age appeared, finally, to have run its course.

The jihad spirit was in decline too – at least with regard to its use against the Christian West. In fact, the Ottomans spent much of the sixteenth century fighting Muslims rather than Christians. The Safavids of Iran, a powerful Shi'ite group, emerged as a serious danger and, just as Nur ad-Din and Saladin had called jihads in the name of orthodoxy, so the Turks vigorously pursued holy war against these enemies of the Sunni. Another opponent was, however, orthodox; namely, the Mamluks of Egypt, and in 1516–17 further Ottoman success brought an enormous area of land (plus a massive increase in revenue) under their control. From Egypt much of North Africa fell under Turkish authority. To the West, the armies of Suleyman the Magnificent prevailed at Belgrade in 1521, although defeat at Vienna eight years later marked the fullest extent of Ottoman expansion. The Turks also picked off surviving outposts of the crusades: the Hospitallers were expelled from Rhodes in 1522 (which prompted their move to Malta) and by 1571, Venetian-ruled Cyprus was conquered as well. Notwithstanding the famous defeat at the Battle of Lepanto the Ottomans dominated the eastern Mediterranean. By the seventeenth century, jihad sentiments and the drive of the *ghazis* had, like the zeal of the crusaders, largely given way to an imperialist agenda and the need to sustain the ruling institution. As the century drew to a close, the mighty Ottoman Empire began, ever so slowly, to decline – and in doing so it became ever more tempting to the expanding monarchies of Christian Europe.[78]

New Crusaders? From Sir Walter Scott to Osama Bin Laden and George W. Bush

In the emotional aftermath of the terrorist attacks of 9/11 President George W. Bush began to articulate his response: 'This crusade . . . this war on terror is going to take a while.' Thus, unwittingly or not, he offered up one of the most incendiary remarks of recent years. His choice of the word 'crusade' was a propaganda gift to Osama Bin Laden who could claim that, just as crusader forces had unleashed death and destruction on the medieval Muslim world, now Bush called for the repeat of such a phenomenon. While the validity of bin Laden's analogy can be questioned it is worth considering how and why the idea of a 'crusade' – whatever it now means – has survived into the twenty-first century. As we have seen already, crusading – in its various forms – continued to be a potent concept long after Frankish control of the Holy Land had ended in 1291.

The Post-Medieval Reputation of Crusading

In post-Reformation Europe, the disdain of Enlightenment thinkers, ignoring the brutality of their own era, did much to relegate the crusades to a distant and discredited past. Criticism of crusading during the medieval period had been sporadic and short-lived. It was usually provoked by the collapse of an expedition or when the target of a particular campaign, such as the Albigensian crusade, was especially controversial. With the advent of Protestantism, judgements on the Catholic holy war became far harsher. The failure of the majority of the crusades to the Holy Land made the movement a particularly tempting target and writers such as Thomas Fuller (who wrote c.1639) launched vitriolic attacks on the immorality of the papacy as the promoter of such a worthless bloodbath. He also claimed that the Catholic Church had made an immense profit from the crusades: 'Some say purgatory fire heateth the pope's kitchen; they may add, the holy war filled his pot, if not paid for all of his second course.'[1] Equally culpable were the gullible, sinful participants: 'Many a whore was sent thither to find her virginity; many a murderer was enjoined to fight the holy war, to wash off the guilt of Christian blood by shedding the blood of Turks.' In any case, Fuller believed little of value had emerged from the medieval period at all: 'One may wonder that the world should see most visions when it was blind; and that age, most barren in learning, should be most fruitful in revelation.'[2]

William Robertson dismissed crusading as 'a singular monument of human folly' in 1769, while several decades later Edward Gibbon argued that 'the principle of the crusades was a savage fanaticism' which 'had checked rather than forwarded the maturity of Europe.' In mid-eighteenth century France, Voltaire described crusading as an outbreak of blind religious zealotry and gave it the ironic label 'une maladie épidémique'. Taking the sickness metaphor further he insisted that the only thing that Europeans gained from the crusades was leprosy; he also decried the leaders' arrogance and derided their military failings.[3] In 1780 the German Wilhelm Friedrich Heller thundered: 'Urban and Peter [the Hermit]! The corpses of two millions of men lie heavy on your graves and will fearfully summon you on the day of judgement.'[4] In the United States, Ralph Waldo Emerson observed that the crusades were perceived as 'a monument of folly and tyranny' and that claims to be the voice of God were 'shrill and evil'.[5]

Sir Steven Runciman echoed some of these damning judgements in his hugely influential three-volume *History of the Crusades,* first published 1951–4 and still in print over fifty years later. By faith Runciman was a Calvinist, and by academic inclination a Byzantinist; two reasons why the crusades were never likely to emerge with much credit from his writings. The closing lines of his work convey a lacerating final judgement: 'There was so much courage and so little honour, so much devotion and so little understanding. High ideals were besmirched by cruelty and greed, enterprise and endurance by a blind and narrow self-righteousness; and the Holy War itself was nothing more than a long act of intolerance in the name of God,

which is a sin against the Holy Ghost.'[6] In more modern parlance
Runciman described the crusades as 'a tool of unscrupulous western
imperialism'.[7] Through sheer ubiquity Runciman's work has done
much to form attitudes to the crusades, in the English-speaking world
at least. It has created the impression that a primitive idea, born of
superstition and barbarity, was stone dead by the end of the medieval
period and was worthy, at most, of a place in Romantic literature. In
reality, across much of nineteenth-century Europe, particularly those
areas that had remained Catholic, the concept and legacy of crusading
provided rulers and policymakers with a remarkably accessible short-
hand to a series of powerful ideas. The international nature of the
medieval crusades gave these lands a collective or, if required, a selec-
tive past to draw upon. Self-evidently papal appeals, preaching tours
and offers of indulgences were, in most cases, inappropriate; the
modern age highlighted the more secular principles of morality and
heroism. Thus it was no longer the papacy that called for, or invoked,
crusades but often royalist governments or particular groups –
frequently nationalist in tone. As the historian Marc Bloch wrote:
'Once an emotional chord has been struck, the limit between past and
present is no longer regulated by a mathematically measurable
chronology.'[8] Crusading history was a rich store of ideals and images
that could be made relevant and appropriate to a variety of contemporary events. Colonial expansion into North Africa and the Middle
East, coupled with nascent nationalism in, for example, Italy, offered
potent outlets for the revival of some form of crusading mentality.
There are, of course, several fundamental differences between colonialism and crusading: the latter was originally conceived as defensive
in nature, while colonial empires were quintessentially expansionist.
Plus, while one can suggest that the crusades to the Holy Land were,
in a broad sense, a form of religious colonisation on behalf of the
Catholic Church, a conventional understanding of colonialism with
the organised dispatch of governing representatives and the passing
of money and resources back to a homeland was, with the exception
of the enclaves of the Italian trading states, absent during the medieval
age. With nineteenth-century conquests coterminous with the energy
of the emerging Romantic movement and the stimulus of an ongoing
interest in the culture of the East (orientalism), crusading – or a
mutated subspecies of the genre – found a relevance that it had lacked

for centuries. Contrary, therefore, to the impression offered by Gibbon, Robertson et al., crusading was not dead but remained a vigorous and evolving phenomenon. This nineteenth-century reawakening is, in turn, the prime reason why the idea has carried over into the present and explains why the word and the concept continue to be used in both secular and political arenas today.

The Crusades in Literature

The emergence of the Romantic movement did much to restore interest in and respect for the Middle Ages after the dismissive and condescending treatment it had received in the preceding period. Above all else, the writings of Sir Walter Scott proved crucial in generating enthusiasm for the medieval world and the crusades.[9] The nineteenth century was an era when reading and literary culture expanded dramatically, and Scott's exotic adventures sold in astounding numbers and were translated all across Europe. His perspective of the crusades was, broadly speaking, a positive one, yet as a Calvinist he strongly disapproved of their 'intolerant zeal'.[10] On the other hand, crusading presented a perfect stage for chivalric values to shine forth and it was through this prism that he forged an association with the glamour and the excitement of great deeds in the mysterious Orient. The crusades were the setting for four of his novels: *Ivanhoe* (1819), *The Betrothed* (1825), *The Talisman* (1825) and *Count Robert of Paris* (1831). In *The Talisman* he set Richard and Saladin up as opposites: the king of England was 'a pattern of chivalry, with all its extravagant virtues, and its no less absurd errors'; he 'showed all the cruelty and violence of an eastern sultan. Saladin, on the other hand, displayed the deep policy and prudence of a European sovereign.'[11] As one recent commentator wrote, the sultan 'was patently a modern liberal European gentleman, beside whom medieval westerners would always have made a poor showing.'[12] In the story, Sir Kenneth of the Leopard, a (seemingly) poor Scottish crusader, befriended a Muslim emir; this man (eventually shown to be Saladin himself) came to the crusader camp and healed King Richard of sickness. Religious motives are not, however, entirely absent from *The Talisman*; Sir Kenneth considers 'his good sword as his safest escort and devout thoughts his best companion'.[13] Yet faith must compete with love and the Knight of the Leopard was transfixed by his feelings for the lady Edith: 'A Christian soldier, a devoted lover, he could fear nothing, think of nothing, but his duty to heaven and his devoir to his lady.'[14] The hero fell into disgrace when he failed to guard the royal standard, drawn away by a message supposedly sent by Edith. In Scott's depiction of chivalric virtues, Sir Kenneth 'thought of her as a deity' and believed that his 'sole object in life was to fulfil her commands.'[15] He narrowly escaped execution when a furious Richard learnt of his neglect but recovered his standing when, disguised as a Nubian slave, he saved the king's life and revealed himself as the brother of the king of Scotland. Saladin then gave an amulet with healing powers (the talisman) to his Christian friend. The sultan shared in the chivalric values so important to Scott: 'let us leave to mullahs and monks to dispute about the divinity of our faith, and speak on themes which belong to youthful warriors – upon battles, upon beautiful women, upon sharp swords, and upon bright armour.'[16] A strong supporting cast included the master of the Templars – a brave man, but one anachronistically described by King Richard as 'a worse pagan [than Saladin], an idolator, a devil-worshipper, a necromancer, who practises crimes the most dark and unnatural in the vaults and secret places of abomination and darkness.'[17]

This intriguing, if historically challenged, plot was propelled by Scott's narrative powers into a major bestseller. It was outstripped, however, by *Ivanhoe* which, in turn, inspired a vast number of poets, artists, sculptors and other authors. This was an international success with translations into French (where perhaps 2 million of Scott's novels were sold by 1840), German, Italian, Spanish, Dutch, Danish, Norwegian and Swedish. Its influence was immense: 290 *Ivanhoe*-derived dramas have been produced; in 1820, no less than sixteen versions of the story were staged across England, and various operas, including one by Rossini, were performed. A further manifestation of the cultural impact of Scott's creation was the popularity of his characters in the costume balls held by the royalty of the day. In short, he had produced a compelling and noble tableau which the public devoured. Other artists and composers took crusading figures as their primary actors: Edvard Grieg composed *Sigurd Jorsalfar* (Sigurd the Crusader, after the Norwegian king who visited the Holy Land in 1110);

crusade-themed operas by Verdi, Schubert and Spohr were also performed across Europe during the nineteenth century.[18]

The combination of European colonial power and an interest in the Orient prompted many to visit the Levant to see the world of the crusaders and the Holy Land for themselves; incidentally, this was a practice that caused Walter Scott to worry that people might fault the authenticity of his descriptions of the region given that he had not travelled to the East in person.[19] Tellingly, perhaps, almost all of his settings in *The Talisman* feature desert landscapes as if he was unaware of the more fertile districts. Travellers were as diverse as the writer Anthony Trollope, future prime minister Benjamin Disraeli (later the author of the Young England Trilogy, subtitled 'The New Crusader'), and Mark Twain. The latter wrote *The Innocents Abroad* (1869) about his travels and in Jerusalem he viewed the sword of Godfrey of Bouillon (it can still be seen today, although closer inspection reveals it to be a thirteenth-century weapon), and he delighted in the 'visions of romance' such an object stirred up. For him 'no blade in Christendom wields such enchantment as this . . . it stirs within a man every memory of the holy wars.' The Prince of Wales visited Jerusalem in 1862, as did his sons two decades later. Another prominent royal, Prince Albert, made a more public contribution to the preservation of the crusading ideal with his commission to Baron Carlo Marochetti for a splendid equestrian statue of Richard the Lionheart. First shown at the Great Exhibition in 1851, a bronze replica was erected in front of the House of Commons in 1860 where it remains today, standing proudly outside the heart of the national government. This majestic figure, defiantly brandishing a sword, vividly conveys the nineteenth-century devotion to chivalry and pride in British achievements overseas, values much heralded in the literature of the day.

The Crusades in the Age of Nationalism and Imperialism

Napoleon's invasion of Egypt and Syria (1798–1802) marked a starting point for Europe's revived interest in the history of the Near East. Ironically, it began with the capture of Malta from the surviving Knights Hospitaller, effectively ending their standing as an independent political body after centuries of power in the central Mediterranean.

The literature produced at this time began to stir interest in orientalism and thence the crusades. In 1806 the Institut de France offered a prize for an essay concerning 'the influence of the crusades on the civil liberty of the peoples of Europe, upon their civilisation, and upon the progress of their culture, commerce and industry' – a series of categories that betrayed a far more enthusiastic view of the crusades than that of the Enlightenment age.

The Romantic writer, Chateaubriand, visited the Levant and his works became enormously influential in France. To him the crusades represented an idealised Christian past: 'In modern times, there are only two noble subjects for epic poetry: the crusades and the discovery of the new world.'[20] Chateaubriand encouraged others to write about the subject. In post-Revolutionary France, Joseph Michaud's *Histoire des croisades* set the tone by providing a ringing endorsement of the crusades as a source of glory and achievement for the French people and the French nation.[21] Nineteen editions were published between 1808 and 1899 and there was a special children's version too (the book was also translated into Russian, English, Italian and German). Michaud was, however, careful to deplore the massacre at Jerusalem in 1099 and he was extremely guarded in his comments on the efficacy of miracles and visions. To him, the crusades had a positive aspect in that they created a sense of unity amongst the participants and they reduced internal warfare – both appropriate to his desires for contemporary France; they also stimulated chivalry and trade. Michaud regarded the crusades as especially 'French', although, as we saw earlier, in medieval times this was recognised in ethnic terms alone.[22] The nationalistic pulse at the heart of Michaud's viewpoint is revealed here: 'If many scenes from this great epoch excite our imagination or our pity, how many events fill us with admiration and surprise! How many names made illustrious in this war are still today the pride of families and of the nation! What is most positive of the results of the First Crusade is the glory of our fathers, this glory which is also a real achievement for a nation. These great memories establish the existence of peoples as well as that of families, and are, in this respect, the noblest source of patriotism.'[23] St Louis loomed large in Michaud's thoughts too. He wrote: 'the memory of the saint-king has been, for me, like a spirit encouraging the pilgrims to set out for Palestine.'[24]

King Charles X (1825–30) highlighted several traditions from the

medieval age; for example, he chose to be crowned in Rheims
Cathedral, thereby emulating the Capetian crusading monarchs; he
also identified himself particularly closely with the crusader-saint Louis
IX. In 1830 Charles initiated an invasion of Algeria and the leader of the
campaign, General Bourmont, explicitly recalled the memory of
St Louis as he set out on his new crusade. Charles had ordered the
expedition to help generate a sense of national unity, as well as to
reduce the threat of piracy in the Mediterranean. He claimed that
the enterprise was 'for the benefit of Christianity', although Bourmont's
capture of Algiers on 3 July 1830 failed to save Charles' line from defeat
by King Louis-Philippe and the Orleans dynasty.

While Louis-Philippe's continued involvement in North Africa had
more of an imperialist hue compared to the actions of his predecessor,
the age of the crusades remained prominent in his thinking. The king's
desire to recall a magnificent past – and to legitimise the present
regime – was most dramatically revealed by his commission of a historical museum for the royal palace at Versailles.[25] This was an attempt
to reconcile the Revolutionary and the Napoleonic eras with the July
Monarchy and, in Louis-Philippe's words, to assimilate 'all the glories
of France' in one place. The crusades were designated the first stage
of French history: as a formative influence on 'national' unity and,
with their purportedly positive effect on the peoples of the East, they
dovetailed well with the contemporary political climate. Five entire
rooms were devoted to the crusades and over 120 pictures were
commissioned, collected and displayed, including Emile Signol's
Capture of Jerusalem by the Crusaders on 15 July 1099; Jean-Baptiste
Mauzaisse's *Louis VII taking the banner of the cross for the Second Crusade
at Saint-Denis, 11 June 1147* and Eugène Delacroix's *Entry of the Crusaders
into Constantinople, 12 April 1204* (now in the Louvre Museum, Paris),
along with works closely connected to the ongoing North African
wars, such as *The Death of St Louis before Tunis on 25 August 1270*; other
rooms at Versailles included images of the conflict in Algeria, thereby
memorialising these events in the national consciousness.[26] One visitor
to these latter rooms gave voice to this sense of continuity:

We there find again, after an interval of 500 years, the French nation
fertilising with its blood the burning plains studded with the tents of
Islam. These are the heirs of Charles Martel, Godfrey of Bouillon,

Robert Guiscard and Philip Augustus, resuming the unfinished labours of their ancestors. Missionaries and warriors, they every day extend the boundaries of Christendom.[27]

The rooms also displayed the coats of arms of families with crusading ancestors. When the gallery opened 316 arms were shown, but so great was the perceived importance of such a heritage that protests from families not included caused it to close within a year. People 'found' documents attesting to their lineage and in 1843 the rooms reopened with a further sixty-two families represented. In fact, a trio of master forgers had set up a lucrative business to generate fully convincing 'medieval' charters, often complete with seals, to sate the demands of those desperate to be honoured. The full extent of these forgeries was only revealed in 1956, understandably a matter of genuine dismay to some of the surviving families.[28] While the July Monarchy fell in 1848, the impetus provided by Louis-Philippe and his Bourbonist predecessor Charles X caused crusading to remain prominent in the mindset of French efforts overseas for decades to come.

As the Ottoman Empire slid into decay during the nineteenth century, so French involvement in the Middle East intensified; one consequence of this was an increased standing for the various Christian communities across the region, a change in the status quo that provoked serious discontent amongst the Muslims.[29] In the summer of 1860 violence engulfed the eastern Lebanon and an estimated 11,000 Christians were killed. By July the trouble had extended to Damascus and a mob tore through the Christian quarter pillaging, raping and killing the inhabitants. One eyewitness wrote of seeing hundreds of dogs who had died of a surfeit of human flesh; the district, which included churches, a monastery and consulates, was utterly devastated. A writer in Le Correspondant suggested that this had been part of a Muslim conspiracy that planned to 'exterminate all Christians' and that it was necessary for 'a new crusade of Christendom and civilisation' (by which he largely meant the French) to set up an independent Christian state in the region; a proposal that bears an uncanny resemblance to the boundaries of the modern state of the Lebanon.[30] Napoleon III dispatched a French fleet to fight the Ottomans and as they set out he urged the men to prove themselves 'worthy descendants of those heroes who had gloriously carried the banner of Christ to those lands'.[31] Several pamphlets connected the medieval and modern periods; one compared the current pope, Pius IX, to Urban II and another called for a new crusade.[32]

While little came of this 'crusade', Ottoman rule in Syria finally collapsed in 1918. The next two years saw a short-lived Arab government before the League of Nations mandated French rule. Paul Pic, professor of law at the University of Lyons, regarded Syria as 'a natural extension of France', a view shared by many of his countrymen.[33] Historians enthusiastically reinforced this sense of national pride and placed the contemporary occupation of the area in a continuum with their medieval territories in the Levant; in 1929 the historian Jean Longnon wrote that 'The name of Frank has remained a symbol of nobility, courage and generosity . . . and if our country has been called on to receive the protectorate of Syria, it is the result of that influence.'[34] This proud memory of the medieval past effectively reinforced and recapitulated the essence of mid-nineteenth-century nationalist rhetoric to produce a positive perception of the crusading period.

At the same time as the French invasions of Algeria the notion of crusading became visible in another nationalist movement, although on this occasion the focus was inward-looking: namely the effort to create a united Italy. A leading figure amongst the democratic patriots was Giuseppe Mazzini who derived huge inspiration from Francesco Hayez's painting *Peter the Hermit Preaches the Crusade*, first exhibited to great acclaim in 1829.[35] Mazzini was attracted to the alluring combination of religion and politics represented by crusading and he used it as a symbol or concept to draw people together in his bid for progress. He wrote that the picture showed everyone 'driven on by a single, true and binding force, the thought that pervades each mind: "God wills it, God wills it" . . . Unity is *felt* here without being *seen*.'[36] His Young Italy group, a secret society (albeit one with 50,000 members), had an overt religious dimension: God desired Italy to become unified and independent, and if believers had to sacrifice their lives in the holy struggle, then so be it. This cause would have a national, ethical faith, rather than a religion channelled through the papacy – a particularly radical concept in the homeland of St Peter's Church.[37] Mazzini's planned insurrections failed miserably and in 1837 he was forced to go into exile in London; eventually, however, he returned to Italy to play a part in the unification process and he continued to use the image of the crusade in his calls for liberty, nationalism and, eventually, internationalism.[38]

Mazzini was not the only nationalist to invoke the medieval past in Italy. In 1848, during an attempt to drive out the ruling Austrians and to secure the liberation of Italy, King Carlo Alberto launched a half-hearted invasion of Lombardy. Other Italian rulers joined his campaign and Pope Pius IX, who had been reluctant to fight another Catholic country, dispatched an expeditionary force led by General Giovanni Durando. In his determination to push Pius into outright support for the nationalist cause, Durando hoped to convince the public that his undertaking had complete papal – and therefore divine – sanction. His men advanced dressed as crusaders, complete with crosses sewn on their uniforms; he also issued a strident press release: 'Soldiers! . . . The Holy Father has blessed your swords, which, united now with those of Carlo Alberto, must move in concord to annihilate the enemies of God, the enemies of Italy, and those who have insulted Pius IX . . . such a war of civilisation against barbarism is accordingly not just a national war but also a supremely Christian one . . . Let our battle cry be: God wills it!' Pius was, predictably, furious at this arrogation of his authority; he promptly repudiated the war and reminded everyone that he was the head of all Christendom and not just Italy alone.[39]

In this century of the birth of nations another new arrival, in 1831, was the state of Belgium. Ideas of crusading played little part in its actual formation but as the Belgians began to establish a sense of the past they seized upon Godfrey of Bouillon, the first ruler of Jerusalem, and a man whose family hailed from the Ardennes region (although some believe that he was born in Boulogne, which means that he can be a French hero as well). Godfrey was also pious (and Catholic, of course), fearless and successful, and his fame as the conqueror of Jerusalem had assured him of a place in history and literature throughout the ages; the huge equestrian statue standing in the Place de Brussels demonstrates Godfrey's centrality to this nineteenth-century sense of self.[40]

As we saw earlier, the Iberian peninsula had a long and ultimately successful history of crusading. This, coupled with the immense residual authority of the Catholic Church, meant crusading ideas were often revived at times of turbulence and crisis. Napoleon's invasion

of 1808 and his subsequent disestablishment of the Catholic Church
provoked huge resistance from traditionalists.[41] One royal polemicist
compared Napoleon to Sultan Mehmet II and some pressmen claimed
that the war with the French was as holy as the struggle against the
Prophet Muhammad. Ironically, therefore, the French, the nation with
the greatest crusading heritage, became equivalent to Muslims in the
developing struggle to preserve Spanish identity.

Later in the century the restored monarchy under Don Carlos
emphasised the country's Catholic past and laid heavy stress upon the
reconquista. The eleventh-century warrior El Cid was frequently
invoked as a defender of Spain and Christianity. The fact that El Cid
was a hired hand who sometimes fought for Muslim paymasters and
that Christian Spain had several rival monarchs during his lifetime was
irrelevant. From the early twelfth century the legend of El Cid had
developed to satisfy the need for a national Christian hero.[42] In 1859–60
the Spanish attempted to emulate the French by conquering part of
North Africa, in this case, Morocco. While some disliked giving the
campaign a religious edge, many pressmen enthusiastically revived
past glories and called upon the spirit of their ancestors who had made
'the Moorish multitude bow before the sacred sign of the cross and
bite the dust.' Several poets and dramatists also made explicit references to earlier crusaders. The Spaniards' heavy losses in Morocco
and the subsequent decline of their overseas empire began to limit
their enthusiasm for crusading imagery, but in 1921 the clergy described
the war in North Africa as a crusade and two years later, King Alfonso
XIII made a speech at the Vatican in which he offered to lead a new
crusade if the pope was to call one.[43] These were, however, relatively
isolated instances of such language and ideology but, as the tensions
between traditionalists and the modern world reached breaking point,
the early twentieth century saw one further opportunity to recall the
medieval age.

In 1936 the Spanish Civil War broke out and in their struggle
against the Republican government the Catholic Church soon found
common ground with the Nationalists, led by General Francisco
Franco. As the conflict intensified the Catholic hierarchy formed a
vital pillar in the rise and legitimisation – at home and abroad – of
Francoism. While his ideological appeal had many different dimensions there is little doubt that he enthusiastically engaged with the

Church's representation of himself and his cause as a holy crusade.[44] In August 1936 a canon of Salamanca Cathedral gave a radio broadcast titled 'The lawfulness of the armed rising', which concluded with a stirring call to arms: 'Our war is holy. Our battle-cry that of the crusades: God wills it. Long live Catholic Spain.'[45] On 30 September the bishop of Salamanca built upon a recently issued papal endorsement for the nationalists and published a text – approved by Franco himself – which presented the rebel cause as 'a crusade against communism to save religion, the fatherland and the family.'[46] Within weeks the archbishop of Toledo had made the same point, again calling the war a crusade and providing a further moral buttress for Franco's party. Republican attacks on religious institutions gave the idea of fighting to save the Church a special currency because crusading tapped into a deep well of historical memory as well as giving a moral imperative to the rebels' actions. Unlike a medieval crusade, spiritual rewards were not on offer simply for participation, although death in the Nationalist army was treated as martyrdom and the fallen were often memorialised as crusaders. Franco was careful – in contrast to his German and Italian allies – not to submit the Church to the authority of the state and thereby to jeopardise the backing of an institution so valuable to his fight and so vital to his self-image. In November 1937 he spoke to a French journalist about contemporary matters: 'our war is not a civil war . . . but a crusade . . . we who fight, whether Christian or Muslim, are soldiers of God.'[47] The caveat about Christians and Muslims is an interesting point. In spite of his identification as a crusader Franco saw no irony in employing thousands of Moroccan Muslims in his forces and it was these men who perpetrated many of the worst excesses of the war. The next month, the ceremonial swearing in of the first Consejo Nacional was an occasion heavy with historical symbolism.[48] The venue was the medieval monastery of Santa Maria de Real de las Huelgas, near Burgos. The fifty incoming committee members swore loyalty to Franco in front of a statue of Christ and the battle standard from Las Navas de Tolosa – an immensely potent symbol of Spanish crusading success – which, as we saw earlier, had proved a seminal moment in the advance of medieval Spain.

In April 1940, arguably at the height of his powers, and in celebration of the first anniversary of his victory in the Civil War, Franco presided over the construction of a colossal monument to dead Nationalists: the Valley of the Fallen. Once again his words reveal religious and moral justification as being at, or near, the top of his thoughts: 'The dimension of our Crusade, the heroic sacrifices involved in the victory and the far-reaching significance this epic has for the future of Spain cannot be commemorated by a simple monument . . .'[49] The general himself was also depicted as a crusader in a mural entitled *Franco: Victor of the Crusade* placed in the Military Historical Archive in Madrid.

In the aftermath of World War II Franco's ambitions had to be less grandiose although in 1955, as he unveiled a statue of El Cid at Burgos (the region where El Cid had grown up and where his tomb lies), he reflected on his own achievements and his place in history. He argued that 'the great service of our Crusade, the virtue of our *movimiento* is to have awakened an awareness of what we were, of what we are and what we can be.' He presented El Cid as the symbol of a new Spain: 'in him is enshrined all the mystery of the great Spanish epics: service in noble undertakings; duty as a norm; struggle in the service of the true God.' Thus, implicitly, he set out both his own definition of a crusade and offered himself as the modern-day Cid.[50]

Britain made some use of crusading imagery during the nineteenth century; hardly a surprise given the impetus from literature, drama and art we noted above. Not every conflict, however, was appropriate to such ideas, or produced a significant outburst of crusade-connected comment. The Crimean War (1854–6), fought between Russia and a coalition of the Ottomans, British, French and the kingdom of Sardinia, was one such scenario. It was a matter of some irony that the 'crusading' lands of Britain (itself Protestant, of course) and France fought on behalf of the Muslim Ottomans against another Christian power, Russia.[51] By contrast, events in Bulgaria during May 1876 produced a surge of crusading rhetoric. The Ottomans suppressed an insurrection in which perhaps 12,000 Christians were slaughtered. In spite of this Prime Minister Disraeli continued his alliance with Turkey and in doing so he provoked the anger of many, including the former prime minister and recently resigned leader of the Liberal Party, Gladstone. The latter wrote a pamphlet entitled *Bulgarian Horrors and the Question of the East* that sold 200,000 copies. 'Vindictive and ill-written – in that respect, of all the Bulgarian horrors, perhaps the greatest', was Disraeli's tart response.[52] In contrast, Gladstone's magnificent rhetoric condemned 'a murderous harvest from soil soaked and reeking with blood.' He claimed that the Turks were responsible for scenes 'at which Hell itself might blush', and he concluded that 'no Government ever has so sinned; none has proved itself so incorrigible or, which is the same, so impotent for reformation.'[53] A group of clerics and men of letters formed the Eastern Question Association and held over 500 public meetings to deplore the moral detachment of the government. High Churchmen and Catholics alike thundered against the government policy. William Stead, a northern newspaper editor, felt the 'clear call of God's voice' and did much to inflame the agitation. He wrote that the crusades were no longer an enigma to him; the historian Edward Freeman was accused of 'crusading bluster' and several contemporaries such as the MPs Joseph Chamberlain, John Bright and George Russell (nephew of former prime minister John Russell) described Gladstone's efforts as a crusade.[54] A young Oscar Wilde, then at Oxford, wrote a sonnet on the massacres and lamented 'Over thy Cross the Crescent moon I see' and urged Christ to return 'Lest Mahomet be crowned instead of thee.'[55]

For crusading – a creation of the papacy – to survive in a Protestant country required more than an occasional resonance in foreign affairs. There was, of course, a substantial Catholic minority in Britain, but the perceived tie between crusading and Rome was partially dismantled through the cult of Christian militarism. In the course of the nineteenth century the manly virtues of fighting to extend the empire were linked to Protestant teaching – the notion of 'muscular Christianity' so integral to the English public-school system. Warrior-saints were important in the teachings of the Church and the heroes of history – including Richard the Lionheart – became popular material for stories of great deeds; hymns such as 'Onward, Christian Soldiers', composed in 1864, set out a similar message.[56]

The most obvious contemporary candidate to be labelled a crusader was General Charles Gordon, killed by Muslims at Khartoum in 1885. Even before his death he had been identified as a Christian knight and his 'martyrdom' only confirmed this. In 1909 he featured in a book of *Heroes of Modern Crusades: True Stories of the Undaunted Chivalry of Champions of the Down-Trodden in Many Lands*. Links between the spirit of the empire and the higher purpose of the crusades were explicitly set out by Professor Cramb of the University of London in 1909: 'This ideal of Imperial Britain – to bring to the peoples of the earth beneath her sway the larger freedom and the higher justice – the world has known none fairer, none more exalted, since that for which Godfrey and Richard fought, for which Barbarossa and St Louis died.'[57]

When it came to World War I, it was almost inevitable that the emotive pull of a crusade came to form a *part* (and one must keep a due perspective on this) of the Allies' propaganda effort, although the Germans made a particular play on holy war too. In spite of the apparent paradox of Anglican clergy using the ideology of Catholic holy war, several churchmen wholeheartedly adopted the language of crusading. Presumably they felt that the moral force of their case was an appropriate parallel to that of the medieval age and this, combined with its demonstrable currency in popular and political culture over the previous hundred years, meant that it was a potent and recognisable theme.[58]

Lord Halifax called for a formal declaration of holy war against Germany, and Anglican clergy such as the bishop of London spoke of 'a great crusade . . . to save the world'. Lloyd George made a speech at Conway in May 1916 in which he claimed men were flocking to join 'a great crusade' for justice and right and his collected speeches were entitled *The Great Crusade*. Others drew parallels of martyrdom and compared the sacrifice and the fears of soldiers leaving their families to those of the medieval crusaders. A young Harold Macmillan, fighting at Ypres in May 1916, described both the devastation of war and 'the thrill of battle'; he reminded the reader (his mother) that it was easy to lose sight of the moral and spiritual strength of the Allies: 'Many of us could never stand the strain and endure the horrors which we see every day, if we did not feel that this was more than a war – a Crusade. I never see a man killed but think of him as a martyr. All the men (tho' they could not express it in words) have the same conviction – that our cause is right and certain in the end to triumph. And because of this unexpected and almost unconscious faith, our allied armies have a superiority in morale which will be (some day) the deciding factor.'[59] Austen Chamberlain, then president of the Liberal Unionist Association, sketched out a detailed concept of the crusading cause, covering chivalry, morality, justice and economic and political advantage: '[We should be wrong] if we thought we are merely embarked in a chivalrous crusade on behalf of another nation, without our interests being engaged . . . it is not for Belgium only we are fighting. It is not merely a crusade for right and for law against wrong and brute force – though it is all of that – but it is a struggle for the vital interests of this country.'[60] Aside from directly invoking God, these points are all shared with the medieval crusades and represent an idealised, secular version of its forerunner.

Other countries employed the crusading theme too. When the Americans entered the war their troops were led by General 'Black Jack' John Pershing and the first official Government War Picture, filmed by the US Signal Corps as a report of his activities, was titled *Pershing's Crusaders*. The advertisement showed the general riding at the head of his troops with the Stars and Stripes fluttering beside him; in the background ride two ghostly medieval crusaders, both clearly bearing the cross upon their shields as they watch over the American troops.[61]

In France, perhaps unsurprisingly, the idea was invoked as well: one recruiting poster proclaimed: '*Pour achever la croisade au droit*' ('To finish the crusade for right'); Germany also called upon a medieval and crusading past, and victory over the Poles in August 1914 was seen as revenge for the defeat of the Teutonic Knights at the Battle of Tannenberg in 1410. The Germans created a massive memorial on the battlefield and this came to be the burial place of the revered German commander of the day, General Hindenburg, who was depicted as a medieval knight. In later decades Hitler and the Nazis adopted these concepts and staged nationalist ceremonies at the site.[62]

Poetry, such an integral part of the public conduct of World War I, made reference to the crusades. The Irish poet, Katharine Tynan, believed in the cause:

Your son and my son, clean as new swords
Your man and my man, now the Lord's
Your son and my son for the Great Crusade
With the banner of Christ over them – our new knights made.[63]

Frederick Orde-Ward, St John Adcock and Gordon Alchin all composed poems with crusading themes, with the third of these authors included in the very popular anthology *The Muse in Arms*. Some poetry criticised the Germans, rather than simply extolling the virtues of the

Allied troops; an idea that can be found beyond the leading poets of the age and amongst schoolchildren too. In June 1916 a pupil at Charterhouse compared the nobility and valour of Godfrey of Bouillon with the ambitions of the kaiser in the East:

> Would-be protector of the Muslim power,
> And Over-Lord of the whole rolling world,
> Ambition-led, o'er all men else he'd tower;
> But grasping all, will from his Throne be hurled.[64]

Probably the most famous poet to invoke crusading imagery, albeit in a letter rather than verse, was Rupert Brooke, who died of blood poisoning in April 1915 as he travelled to Gallipoli. In a somewhat naive expression of enthusiasm, he wrote to a friend: 'This is probably the first letter you ever got from a crusader. The early crusaders were very jolly people. I've been reading about them. They set out to slay the Turks and very finely they did it when they met them.'[65]

In the public perception, by far the most appropriate episode to be clothed in crusading imagery was General Allenby's Palestine campaign which culminated in the recovery of Jerusalem on 9 December 1917. A famous *Punch* cartoon showed Richard the Lionheart gazing at Jerusalem with the caption 'At last my dreams come true'; a reference to the king's failed attempts to take the city on the Third Crusade (1189–92).[66] In March 1918 the Department of Information released a forty-minute film called *The New Crusaders: With the British Forces on the Palestine Front*.[67] Victory in the Near East provided a real opportunity to celebrate an Allied success and to distract public attention from domestic economic problems and the horrors of the Western Front. Officials sensed a chance to play upon the 'sentimental, romantic and religious' connections of the Holy Land; the director of government propaganda was the author John Buchan, no less. Yet in spite of this seemingly propitious moment there were compelling reasons not to stress the 'Last Crusade' theme too heavily. Britain's nearest ally in the region was the Muslim ruler of the Hejaz, and panicked officials insisted how utterly 'ill-advised' it would be to label the campaign a crusade. Allenby himself was acutely aware of this sensitivity because some of his troops were Muslims who refused to fight their co-religionists.[68] Even more serious, perhaps, was the legacy of German encouragement for the proclamation of a jihad against the British and their allies, an effort to arouse a holy war across India and the Middle East. As we will see below, this was largely a failure, but it remained, in theory at least, a terrifying prospect. In consequence of these concerns the Department of Information issued a D notice to the press on 15 November 1917: 'The attention of the Press is again drawn to the undesirability of publishing any article, paragraph or picture suggesting that military operations against Turkey are in any sense a Holy War, a modern Crusade, or have anything whatever to do with religious questions. The British Empire is said to contain 100 million Muhammadan subjects of the king and it is obviously mischievous to suggest that our quarrel with Turkey is one between Christianity and Islam.'[69] From an official perspective, therefore, a crusading comparison was erased.

Once Allenby had secured Jerusalem there was a need to strike a balance between a military triumph and the wider political and religious agenda; this explains Allenby's modest entrance into the city. He marched in through the Jaffa Gate – a carefully considered contrast to the staged splendour of Kaiser Wilhelm II's arrival on horseback through a special breach in the walls in 1898. Allenby's approach was meant to highlight the kaiser's immense arrogance rather than trumpet an act of Christian symbolism. The general emphasised free access to Jerusalem for all faiths and showed overt respect to Muslim interests; perhaps, in part, as a way of trying to soften the impact of the Balfour Declaration (2 November 1917) that marked a major step towards the creation of a Zionist state, Israel.[70] The press drew parallels with a metaphorical crusade against the Germans, rather than the Muslims: 'In its essence it is a vindication of Christianity. At a moment when Christendom is torn by strife, let loose through the apostate ambitions of those who have returned in practice to the sanguinary worship of their "Old German God", it stands forth as a sign that the righteousness and justice that are the soul of Christian ethics guide Christian victors even in the flush of triumph.'[71]

Yet the more obvious ties to the medieval age, combined with a sense of national pride, soon surfaced as well: 'During the British occupation of Palestine we have been very sedulous in considering the feelings of others . . . some have wondered whether we had any religion of our own. This Easter in Jerusalem has been the answer.

The British Army has celebrated the greatest festival of the Church in a place where the English under arms have never before prayed at Easter. King Richard never reached the Holy City but King George's men communicated and sang the Easter hymns.'[72] For the troops in Palestine it seems that a sense of biblical culture rather than a crusading ethos drew them onwards, but in the wider popular memory the label of a crusade became firmly attached.

In the aftermath of the campaign this would be heavily reinforced. One of Allenby's troops, the actor Vivian Gilbert, embarked upon a North American lecture tour in 1923 and published his account of the war entitled *The Romance of the Last Crusade: With Allenby to Jerusalem*. To modern eyes this is a peculiar blend of a travelogue populated by music-hall cockneys, combined with genuinely harrowing descriptions of warfare, particularly the terrible moment when the legs of Gilbert's servant were blown off, leaving his master to comfort the dying man and to compose a letter home to his family.[73] Gilbert was certain that he had taken part in something with a medieval analogue: 'were we not descendants of those same crusaders?' He imagined sharing identical hardships in the same lands as his forefathers; after the capture of Jerusalem he concluded: 'In all, ten crusades [were] organised and equipped to free the Holy City, only two were really successful – the first led by Godfrey of Bouillon, and the last under Edmund Allenby.'[74] Allenby, however, continued to try his utmost to dislodge the connection; in 1933 he argued: 'Our campaign has been called "The Last Crusade". It was not a crusade. There is still a current idea that our object was to deliver Jerusalem from the Muslims. Not so. Many of my soldiers were Muslims. The importance of Jerusalem lay in its strategic position. There was no religious impulse in this campaign.'[75] Such protestations aside, the appellation had stuck and, as we will see below, percolated into the Muslim world as well.

In the aftermath of the war the word 'crusade' sometimes came to take on a generic meaning for the conflict as a whole. Perhaps the best example of this was the tomb of the Unknown Soldier in Westminster Abbey, created in 1920 and adorned with a medieval sword donated by King George V. The committee in charge of the burial fretted over public interpretation of the weapon and, as they feared, the popular press duly labelled it a 'crusader's sword'. In 1923 the Order of Crusaders, a group imitating the Military Orders, held a service in the abbey and, with the Duke of York amongst their number, laid a wreath at the tomb of the Unknown Soldier and honoured him as their Principal Knight and Supreme Head. Other memorials made reference to the notion of crusading: British Imperial war cemeteries were adorned with a Cross of Sacrifice, a design viewed 'as a mark of symbolism of the present crusade' by the Imperial War Graves Commission architects; a significant number of local commemorative windows and statues made reference to the war in comparable terms. Images of King Richard – sometimes alongside St Louis of France to symbolise the Anglo-French alliance – and St George were used in places as diverse as Eton Chapel and the parish church of Hadlow in Kent. Crusading was defined as 'freedom, mercy, righteousness and truth' in the fine memorial 'The Spirit of the Crusaders' erected at Paisley, Scotland; this recognised a kindred spirit with the medieval warriors, although it noted that the ideal the contemporary soldiers strove for was similar, rather than identical, to that of their predecessors.[76]

The Great War had brought horror on a scale unprecedented in human history and, in tandem with the stirring rhetoric, there was understandable criticism of the terrible losses and suffering. Again, one can find references to crusading, although in the case noted here, a specific parallel was drawn between the Children's Crusade and the slaughter of young soldiers. Archibald Jamieson wrote a pamphlet called *Holy Wars in the Light of Today* and observed of the Children's Crusade: 'rightly do we condemn the "hallucination" of 1212, why, therefore, did we recruit the boy-life of our nation, and organise our youth in school and church for military purposes in the sacred name of "patriotism"?'[77] Siegfried Sassoon was less than impressed with the use of crusading motifs: 'Bellicose politicians and journalists were fond of using the word crusade. But the chivalry (which I have seen in epitome at the Army School) had been mown down and blown up in July, August and September and its remnant finished the year's crusade in a morass of torment and frustration.'[78]

During World War II fewer links were made between crusading imagery and contemporary warfare. In the first instance, the utter carnage of World War I had, to a great extent, shattered any notions of warfare as a chivalric exercise. Between 1939 and 1945, genocides, mass civilian casualties and the displacement of millions moved the scale of the conflict even further beyond previous reference points. The idea of the crusade did, however, appear on occasion, sometimes in a positive sense, on other occasions, most certainly not. Probably the best example of the former was Eisenhower's speech on D-Day, June 1944 when the Order of the Day read: 'Soldiers, sailors and airmen of the Allied Expeditionary Forces, you are about to embark upon a Great Crusade, towards which you have striven these many months . . . Let us beseech the blessing of Almighty God upon this great and noble undertaking'; his account of the war was entitled *Crusade in Europe* (1948). War memorials did not look to the medieval period as they had done decades before, although one lasting edifice from the aftermath of the war, the ultra-modernist Coventry Cathedral, was envisaged to represent a form of crusading ideology, albeit one meant to gather people together and to heal the wounds of war. Basil Spence wrote: 'The Chapel's shape represents Christian Unity; in elevation it is shaped like a Crusader's tent, as Christian unity is a modern Crusade.'[79] For the American writer Kurt Vonnegut, however, the connection to be drawn with the crusades was negative; the subtitle of his bestselling *Slaughterhouse 5* (1969) is *The Children's Crusade: A Duty Dance with Death*, an ironic recognition of the youth of so many of the US troops sent to Europe. As one character remarked when his new recruits arrived: 'My God, it's the Children's Crusade.'[80] The Allies' wartime approach was in contrast to that of the Germans. While the latter had used elements of imagery derived from the crusades in World War I, the Nazis extended this substantially, albeit in a strictly secular and ritualistic form and usually in connection with the Teutonic Knights who, as we saw earlier, had conquered large areas of northern Europe. In *Mein Kampf* Hitler urged Germans once again to set out 'on the march of the Teutonic Knights of old' to Russia.[81] Himmler was fixated on the ceremonies and hierarchy of this venerable organisation and he drew links between the SS and the history of the Teutonic Knights in various chambers of his castle of Wewelsberg, along with other spurious ties to, for example, the legend of the Holy Grail. Fortunately, his plans for the castle were never completed and the surviving parts of the fortress now house a museum to the bishops of Paderborn.

Crusading as a Metaphor

With the revival of the idea of crusading as a force for good during the
nineteenth and the early twentieth centuries, the word 'crusade', with
its complex legacy of moral justification, was taken out of a military
and cultural context and also became used in a looser, more metaphorical sense, albeit one that could have a high profile. To give but two
examples: the Women's Temperance Crusade in the USA during the
1870s and the Jarrow Crusade in England of 1936. Both movements
closely engaged with the language and imagery of the medieval period.
In the case of the former, the religious zeal of its advocates was easily
comparable to the medieval preachers. A founder of the Temperance
Crusade, Mrs Mildred Carpenter, wrote of 'a fight against organised
evil' and argued passionately that 'it is a glorious heritage to leave our
children, to be able to say "I was a crusader in Washington Court
House."' She described one of the preachers as an 'Apostle of
Temperance', his followers as being 'aflame with the Master's zeal' and
the whole episode as 'a whirlwind of the Lord'.[82]

The Jarrow Crusade has some interesting parallels with medieval
crusading, not least because it had a sense of a pilgrimage – although
in this case the destination was a very secular one: the Houses of
Parliament, rather than the Holy Sepulchre. The march was a protest
against the government's closure of the local shipyard and the refusal
to construct a new steelworks; it was designed to create a wave of
popular support across the country and to save the jobs of the people
of Jarrow. It began with a non-religious character but the marshal of
the march decided the metaphor was appropriate and photographs
of the campaign show people carrying banners proclaiming 'Jarrow
Crusade'. Once underway a religious dimension started to emerge
because the 'crusaders' received the blessing of the bishop of Jarrow
and many Church of England clergy offered their backing too.[83] By
a neat irony, five years earlier Pope Pius XI had linked crusading and
unemployment with a call to Catholics to ameliorate the effects of
this rising problem.[84] Given Franco's almost exactly contemporaneous
use of crusading – with a far more deadly purpose – the preferred
term of one Tyneside newspaper of 'pilgrimage' may have been more
apt. In the event, in spite of considerable publicity and a rousing

reception on their return home, the marchers entirely failed in their purpose.[85]

Islam, Jihad and the Crusades

While an idea of crusading – in real or metaphorical form – has survived and, in some respects, flourished in the West over the last 200 years, its status and perception in the Muslim world has been less clear cut: sometimes almost invisible, at others, a stridently proclaimed byword for hatred and oppression. As we have seen, some in the West, regardless of accuracy, have looked to the crusading era for parallels to their own situation; Muslims too have sought exemplars or to legitimise their actions. Comparisons to Saladin often provide our most illuminating insight into many contemporary understandings of the past and also the agendas of the present day. As the victor at Hattin, the man who recovered Jerusalem for Islam and then resisted the might of Richard the Lionheart and the Third Crusade, he is an alluring figure across the Muslim world. Saladin's achievements have been matched to the aspirations of a remarkable variety of individuals, countries and causes. His legacy has been interpreted and appropriated by figures as diverse as the pan-Arabist President Nasser of Egypt, the totalitarian dictatorship of Saddam Hussein, and the Islamist Osama Bin Laden and his al-Qaeda organisation.

Muslim relations with the West, from an Arab nationalist or an Islamist perspective, have had a disturbing tone over the last 200 years or so. Prior to this, in the form of the Maghrebi Muslims, the Mamluks and most especially the Ottomans, Muslim rulers had been of comparable, or greater, power than many of their western contemporaries. In contrast, beginning with Napoleon's invasion of Egypt in 1798 and, the following year, the defeat of Mysore, the last important Muslim barrier to British power in India, the next 120 years saw the majority of the Islamic community (*umma*) brought under the direct control, or close authority, of the West.[86] Only the Yemen, Afghanistan, the Hejaz region (western edge of the Arabian peninsula) and central Arabia remained free; Iran had a form of independence and Ataturk founded the state of Turkey. After World War I the Middle East was divided between the British and the French, and western initiatives created conditions for the emergence of the state of Israel. From the 1920s to the 1960s, the majority of Muslim societies escaped from direct western rule (except Mongolia and central Asia which had to wait for the fall of the USSR in the 1990s), although western intervention has been prominent in the political affairs of Iran, Pakistan, Egypt and Algeria, amongst others. Furthermore, the USA continues to influence the countries of the Arabian peninsula, home to the sacred cities of Mecca and Medina. Russian involvement in Afghanistan and Chechnya, the British and the French in Egypt and the British and US invasion of Iraq have represented acts of aggression by the West and in the course of these struggles many, many thousands of Muslims have died. Alongside these geopolitical events there is a recognition that the rise of capitalism and science have helped to propel the West forwards at a considerably faster rate than the Muslim world. Colonialism, imperialism, economics and technology have all been of immense significance in relations between Islam and the West, and in the cases of trade, capitalism and the media, western values continue to flow into the Islamic world. Within this complex mesh the idea of crusading emerges as a factor of some note, although *in no way* the dominant one. More importantly, the crusade–jihad prism should not distort a situation whereby the majority of the Islamic world has been at peace with the West. Koranic verses attest to this desire, for example: 'And if they incline to peace, do thou incline to it; and put thy trust in God.' (K.8:61). Since the terror attacks of 9/11, representations of bellicose western crusaders have once more been propelled towards the centre stage. It is, therefore, interesting to offer a few broad brushstrokes to trace the history of the crusades in the Muslim world and to follow Saladin's reincarnation as an Islamic role model.

For many centuries the Ottoman Empire stood as the major power in the Islamic world; jihad imagery was prominent in the conquest of Constantinople in 1453 and the Ottomans assumed the role of *ghazis* as they extended the lands of Islam. Victory over the Mamluks in 1517 brought the caliphate – the spiritual head of Islam – under their control, a point emphasised when the sultan ordered relics of the Prophet to be transported to Istanbul where some remain in the Topkapi Museum. The Ottoman Empire was not, however, a strictly Islamic state and it operated on a combination of secular laws for government and finance and sharia law in other matters. Jihads continued to be proclaimed but their targets were usually the heterodox Safavids of Iran and Iraq, rather than the Christian powers. Suleyman the Magnificent's wars against the Habsburgs in the sixteenth century had more of an imperial rather than a religious edge and there was a decline in the *ghazi* ethic.[87]

Examples of jihad against western powers in the seventeenth and eighteenth centuries are comparatively rare. From around 1800 onwards there was an intensification of European intervention and involvement in North Africa, the eastern Mediterranean and India. The Egyptians briefly regarded Napoleon's invasion of 1798 as a crusade but the French soon made plain their secular, imperialist agenda and managed to convince the locals of their good intentions towards Islam. Bonaparte's proclamation (translated into Arabic when originally published) also delighted in his victory over the Knights Hospitaller on Malta: 'I honour . . . God, his Prophet and the Koran . . . Is it not we who destroyed the pope, the Christian enemy of the Muslims? It was this army who destroyed the Chevaliers of Malta, the ancient enemies of your faith.'[88]

There was no Arabic word for 'crusades' until the mid-nineteenth-century; in the medieval period the western invasions were simply referred to as 'The Wars of the Franks', or as jihads by contemporaries – reasonable enough analogues in the circumstances. In the course of the nineteenth century, perhaps in response to the westerners' self-perception as crusaders, some Muslims began to call for a holy war; the Algerians fighting the French and the Indians against the British being but two examples.[89]

In the eastern Mediterranean, however, another approach began to emerge, prompted by the Ottoman Empire's efforts to survive and encouraged by the expansionist agenda of Germany. In 1898 Kaiser Wilhelm II courted the Muslim world with his visit to Jerusalem and Damascus (a trip organised by Thomas Cook's travel company, an arrangement which earned him the nickname 'Cook's Crusader'). Dressed in a white uniform with his helmet surmounted by a golden imperial eagle and riding a splendid black stallion, Wilhelm processed into Jerusalem on 29 October through a specially made gap in the city walls. Frederick II of Germany, almost seven centuries earlier, had been the previous Christian monarch to enter the city, a connection

Wilhelm deliberately emphasised; indeed his presence in the holy city was announced from the pulpits of Berlin and became the subject of many publications, including illustrated books and children's stories.[90] In November the kaiser reached Damascus where he visited Saladin's tomb and laid a wreath with the message 'from one great emperor to another'; clearly Wilhelm saw no irony in the fact that he had recently portrayed himself as a crusader. He also paid for the restoration of the mausoleum, an incongruous intervention by western imperialism in the burial chamber of one of Islam's greatest heroes. Until this visit Saladin had been a figure of limited interest to the people of the Muslim Near East and it was the deeds of Baibars that continued to attract far greater attention; in fact, in Cairo in the 1830s no less than thirty street performers earned a living reciting a verse account of the Mamluk sultan's life. It is ironic that the kaiser, presumably indoctrinated by Saladin's prominent place in western art and literature – and we know that he had read or heard works by Walter Scott as a child – appeared as familiar with the sultan as his hosts, and that it was a western monarch who brought the medieval hero back to prominence and reminded the rulers of the Middle East of his great achievements.[91]

While acknowledging the importance of this external stimulus in a revival of the memory of the crusades, especially in the elite levels of Muslim society, the enduring position of the crusades through popular culture should not be underestimated. The genre of the epic narrative has been largely ignored in any analysis of this subject, in part because the language used in them was far less polished than the fine literary texts produced in courts, and also by reason of the immense difficulties in finding definitive texts.[92] Coupled with this, as one writer notes, these epics 'tread gingerly along the shoreline of historical fact'. This distortion of the historical record can be shown by Saladin's alleged recovery of Baghdad from the Mongols, or Baibars' relief of Damascus from the Franks, neither of which ever happened. Yet public storytelling was, certainly down to the later twentieth century, an extremely important aspect of Middle Eastern culture, and western visitors to Aleppo in the 1790s and Cairo in the 1830s provide significant evidence of this. As noted, the *Sirat al-Zahir Baibars* was very popular, as was the *Sirat Bani Hilal* and the *Sirat Antar*. Yet these texts are surely worth consideration as long-term transmitters of opinion, prejudices and preoccupations, rather than descriptions of actual events. While the crusaders do not take a dominant role in these stories, they are presented as a menace to the Muslims. They are huge, clean-shaven men, who carry broad-headed lances and whose archers never miss, led by an unnamed but wicked and guileful man. Such tales helped provide a seedbed of memory that political and religious leaders could tap into whether they were Islamists or Arab nationalists. In conjunction with this, as Muslim empires began to decline during the nineteenth century, the concept of looking to the past to learn lessons for the present also emerged.[93] Through this variety of channels, therefore, the history of the crusading age began to appeal to a variety of religious and political movements across the Muslim community.

Bolstered by German support, Abdulhamid II chose to enter World War I against Britain, France and Russia. Over previous decades the sultan had developed the concept of pan-Islamism, a response to his declining power as Ottoman sultan and a sincere reflection of his conception of his religious responsibilities as leader of the *umma*. He issued a call for Muslims across the world to defend Islam from western Christian powers (whom he often termed crusaders) and to rally around their spiritual leader.[94] On 11 November 1914 he issued a fatwa to all Muslims, including those who lived outside Ottoman lands, which proclaimed a jihad against these enemies of Islam. This call was the ultimate expression of Ottoman pan-Islamic aspirations and the document's impact was enhanced by translation into Arabic, Persian, Urdu and Turkic. The fatwa stated that it was 'incumbent on all Muslims in all parts of the world, be they old or young, on foot or mounted, to hasten to take part in the jihad.' It enjoined a responsibility on Muslims in lands ruled by Britain, France, Russia and their allies to resist their overlords, all of whom were trying 'to extinguish and annihilate the exalted light of Islam'. It argued that it was a terrible sin to fight against Germany and Austria (the allies of the Supreme Islamic Government).[95] Although no large-scale uprising took place, a substantial new corpus of jihad literature began to emerge and one strand of the Muslim community's challenge to the West was formed.

While religion provided a cornerstone for confrontation with the

West, for several decades during the twentieth century Arab nationalism emerged centre stage. This was a credo concerned to promote
a shared cultural and ethnic identity across Arab lands in the Levant
(principally Egypt, Syria and Palestine), as opposed to the broader
Muslim consciousness; groups such as the Ottoman Turks, for example,
would not have fallen into this category. The concept did not exclude
Islam – far from it, the leadership were Muslims and could wage jihad
– but it was defined as an Arab community and as a people, rather
than by faith alone.

An early instance of the fusion of nationalism with both jihad rhetoric and the memory of Saladin took place in Damascus between the
end of Ottoman control in 1918 and the start of the French protectorate
in July 1920. In the interim, Syria was ruled by an Arab government
under Emir (later King) Faisal. As a part of their Independence Day
celebrations the authorities looked to gather support through cultural
events and they encouraged theatre productions; unsurprisingly, perhaps,
the victories of Saladin over the kingdom of Jerusalem proved a popular
reminder of nationalist virtues.[96] As the French threatened to impose
their military authority Faisal directly invoked crusading imagery when
he claimed that the pope wanted the conquest to succeed, and he called
upon his people to anticipate death in a jihad.[97] In the event the French
army did prevail, a victory that prompted General Gouraud's triumphant
comment on entering Damascus: 'Behold, Saladin, we have returned',
a statement that only acted to confirm the belief that a new crusade
was underway. The contrast with Allenby's attempts to stage a
diplomatically sensitive takeover of Jerusalem just three years earlier is
striking.

Several other Arab nationalists chose to identify themselves with
Saladin and their reasons for doing so illuminate fascinating parallels
– and contrasts – between their own agendas and the life of the
medieval hero. The individual who drew the closest ties between his
own career and that of Saladin was Gamal Abdel Nasser, president of
Egypt between 1954 and 1970, and a man whose vision of pan-Arabism
embraced modernisation and technology, while simultaneously
making links with Egypt's history. His decision to nationalise the Suez
Canal in 1956 pitted Egypt against Israel, France and Britain and was,
in his terms, a blow for Arab standing against western colonial powers
and their Zionist allies. While his troops were soon driven away from

the strategically vital waterway, by the following year international pressure (including support from the United States) brought a United Nations force into play and triggered a terminal decline of British and French influence in the region. In 1958, Nasser built upon this advance to become the head of the United Arab Republic, a confederation of Syria and Egypt – the same lands that Saladin himself had ruled. His speeches made frequent references to his illustrious predecessor and in February 1958 he planned a formal visit to the sultan's tomb in Damascus.[98]

Around the same time, Nasser emphasised that the Arab nation had always striven for unity; intriguingly, he extended his sense of an eastern Mediterranean community to include its indigenous Christian population (presumably the Copts, a significant minority of the Egyptian population, were at the forefront of his thoughts). He drew an explicit connection to the age of the crusades when he stated that 'the whole region was united for reasons of mutual security to face an imperialism coming from Europe and bearing the cross in order to disguise its ambitions behind the façade of Christianity. The meaning of unity was never clearer than when the Christianity of the Arab Orient joined the ranks of Islam to battle the crusaders until victory.'[99] A year later, in speeches at Katana in Syria and Alexandria in Egypt, he reiterated the importance of a strong Syria and the need for Egypt and Syria to work together: 'the Syrian army, when it was united with the Egyptian, was able to liberate the Arab nation from the crusaders' occupation and colonisation . . . Today our forces are united to protect the Arab fatherland. We shall not be impeded by the conspiracies of imperialist lackeys or agents.' Nasser also emphasised the Arab victory over the Mongols at Ayn Jalut (1260) as another momentous episode in history, although his claim that 'the united armies pursued the retreating Tartar forces across the Euphrates until they liberated Iraq' stretched the truth somewhat.[100]

Another theme that he developed was the historical roots of Arab nationalism. For him these lay back in the medieval period when 'the Arab armies achieved their victory only when they felt that their unity brought them strength and that Arab nationalism was their shield of protection.'[101] In strict terms this point was highly anachronistic because most commentators believe Arab nationalism came into being in the early twentieth century – on the other hand, it is undeniable that

the basic parallels were there for Nasser to exploit. The president also
fixed upon particularly favourable historical precedents. He argued
that the western crusaders had used the cross as a slogan for imperialism, and in a speech of August 1959 he dwelt in some detail on the
capture of Louis IX in 1250, a previous occasion when the French had
been crushed.[102] On 7 May 1960 Nasser led celebrations to mark the
710th anniversary of the defeat of St Louis at the Battle of Mansourah
in 1250 and unveiled a new painting of Turanshah's victory. Nasser
saw this as an 'epoch-making' event that showed 'nothing can stand
in the way of a unified Arab nation'. Louis' humiliation represented
a triumph for Arab nationalism and the president made reference to
the crucial arrival of Turanshah's troops from Syria, because during
the Suez Crisis western forces (including, he claimed, French descendants of the crusaders) had again been turned back when Syria and
Egypt acted together.[103] He also spoke of the Third Crusade of 1189–92:
'Fanatic crusaders attacked us in Syria, Palestine and Egypt. Arab
Muslims and Christians fought side by side to defend their Motherland
against this aggressive, foreign domination. They all rose as one man,
unity being the only means of safety, liberty and the expulsion of the
aggressors. Saladin was able to take Richard . . . as prisoner of war
and was able to defeat his forces.'[104] Once again this last point is pure
fabrication, but the reason for this manipulation was to compare it to
the Egyptian victory in the Suez Crisis: 'We had the honour of beating
Britain and France together [at Suez] after we had beaten each of
them before separately.'[105] To hammer home the connections between
the medieval and modern periods Nasser pointedly crushed the sentiments of Allenby's celebrated, if fictional, phrase of 1917. He boasted
that the westerners 'had never forgotten their defeat [by Saladin]' and
wanted revenge in another 'fanatical, imperialist, crusade'. Nasser then
'quoted' the general: 'when he entered Jerusalem during World War
I he [Allenby] said: "Today, we end the fight of the Crusaders who
were defeated 700 years ago."' The president's use of this statement
shows exactly why Allenby tried so hard to disavow this phrase – and
it demonstrates just how unsuccessful he had been in doing so.[106]

Closely in tune with the president's aspirations was an epic product
of the Egyptian film industry, Youssef Chahine's *Saladin* (1963).[107] The
narrative follows the crusaders' murder of innocent Muslim pilgrims,
through to the Battle of Hattin, the fall of Jerusalem and the Third

Crusade. As a product of its times it takes certain liberties with strict historical accuracy; it also offered a manifesto for pan-Arabism; for example, early on in the film Saladin says: 'my dream is to see an Arab nation united under one flag.'[108] The Arabs only fought the Christians because the latter had attacked them; Saladin asked: 'Since when do aggressors impose conditions on the legitimate owners? You started this war; if you want peace truly, leave my country.' A crusader responded by asking if this was a declaration of war, to which the emir replied: 'I hate war. Islam and Christianity condemn bloodshed. Yet we shall fight if necessary to save our land.' By the end of the film there was a clear message: Saladin and his trustworthy allies presided over a cosmopolitan and humane society, they were worthy guardians of Jerusalem and would freely welcome outsiders to visit. Saladin explained: 'Christianity is respected here; you know that. Jerusalem belongs to the Arabs. Stop this bloodshed. That would satisfy God and Christ.'[109] The film closed with a wholly imagined scene in which Richard and Saladin hold a night-time pageant with the former invited into Jerusalem (even though in reality he never entered the holy city). As snow falls, a choir sings 'Come all ye faithful', interspersed with a muezzin's call: peace reigns supreme. What takes only a limited role in the film, interestingly, is religion. As we saw earlier, there was a strong spiritual dimension to Saladin's jihad against the Christians, but for Chahine and pan-Arabism in the early 1960s this was of secondary importance behind the issue of Arab identity. Nonetheless, the history of the crusading age and the importance of Saladin, Egypt and Syria in resisting the westerners was now clearly established in the public consciousness.

Nasser's successor, President Anwar Sadat, forged close links with the West, particularly with the US. Ultimately, this was to cost him his life, but in 1977 when he became the first Muslim leader to address the Knesset (the Israeli parliament), he too invoked the legacy of Saladin. Presumably based on the sultan's decision to release Christian prisoners after the capture of Jerusalem, Sadat suggested a positive approach: 'Instead of awakening the hatreds of the crusades, we should revive the spirit of . . . Saladin, the spirit of tolerance and respect for rights.'[110]

Nasser and Saladin were the heroes of another Arab nationalist leader – the self-proclaimed 'Lion of Syria', Hafiz al-Asad, president of the country from 1971 until his death in 2000.[111] He was also keen to develop Arab unity and to defeat the 'neo-crusaders' in Israel. While he chose to portray himself as a devout Sunni Muslim, some high in the regime shared his roots in the minority heterodox clan of the Alawites, regarded by many Sunnis as heretics. Indeed, in 1983, Asad brutally crushed the potential challenge of the Islamist Muslim Brotherhood by killing around 30,000 of their supporters in the city of Hama. He also encouraged a tremendous cult of personality. On the main coast road north a monumental statue of him welcomes visitors to his home district and countless banners and pictures of him adorned the shops and offices (now often found alongside the image of his son and successor, Bashar). Given this level of self-promotion the creation of other statuary was rare, although a notable exception stands proudly in front of the citadel of Damascus. First set up in 1992 this monument shows a triumphant Saladin on horseback, preceded by a Sufi holy man and a jihad warrior, while trailing behind him slump disconsolate, defeated crusaders.[112] The message is clear: just as Saladin defeated the West, so will Asad. He could invoke jihad rhetoric too – in the run-up to the 1973 struggle with Israel he called the conflict a holy war. Saladin's achievements were of prime interest, however; the anniversary of his death was usually marked with public ceremonies and the castle named Saone (Zion) in the north of the country was renamed Qal'at Saladin in honour of the medieval hero. Visitors to the president were reminded of history because his office was adorned with a massive picture of Saladin's victory at Hattin. Former US Secretary of State Henry Kissinger went to Damascus in the aftermath of the 1973 Arab–Israeli war and he reflected: 'The symbolism was plain enough: Asad frequently pointed out that Israel would sooner or later suffer the same fate.'[113] Former US president Jimmy Carter visited Asad in 1984 and wrote: 'As Asad stood in front of the brilliant scene [the picture] and discussed the history of the crusaders and the other ancient struggles for the Holy Land, he took particular pride in retelling tales of Arab successes, past and present. He seemed to speak like a modern Saladin, feeling that it was his dual obligation to rid the region of all foreign presence, while preserving Damascus as the only focal point for Arab unity today.'[114]

One further example of a nationalist leader who embraced the legacy of Saladin and also invoked jihad is Saddam Hussein.[115] The Iraqi president made much of the fact that he shared Saladin's birthplace, the village of Takrit. Given Saddam's persecution of the Kurds, presumably no one felt inclined to point out that Saladin himself had been of Kurdish stock but, that historical inconvenience aside, the president emphasised the emir's recovery of Jerusalem and his resistance to the West. Saddam's methods of making these connections ranged from a colloquium – 'The Battle for Liberation – from Saladin to Saddam Hussein' – to a children's book on the two men (although Saladin's career was dealt with in a perfunctory fashion) in which the modern-day leader was called Saladin II Saddam Hussein. A mural on his palace wall depicted the medieval sultan watching his horsemen, while next to him Saddam admired his tanks rolling forwards – in both cases, the onlooker imagines, to victory against the West. In the course of the First Gulf War and the coalition invasion of Iraq Saddam was able to argue that – like Saladin – he was engaged in a defensive jihad. In the context of Muslim history and culture, this was understandable, although to the West it may have seemed cynical for such a secular ruler as Saddam to invoke religion. Even after his defeat in Kuwait Saddam was able to claim that, in *ghazi* tradition, he had attacked Israel and had managed to hold on to power, showing he possessed some aspects of *baraka* (divine blessing).[116] The liberation of Palestine was a prominent motif in Saddam's political discourse and in 2001 he announced the creation of a 'Jerusalem army' to take back the city and claimed that huge numbers of recruits had been trained for this purpose. In the build-up to the Second Gulf War he again brought up the defeat of the crusaders, although a mention of the Mongols – who devastated Baghdad in 1258 – proved prescient if, from his perspective, ultimately inappropriate.

If the predominantly secular principles of Arab nationalism dominated relations with the West during the latter decades of the twentieth century, in the new millennium, religion and jihad have stepped up the agenda considerably. Jihad is a concept with a wide spectrum of interpretations and meanings. As we saw earlier, its origins lie in the Koran and it stands, therefore, as a fundamental tenet of Islam. There is the greater jihad for purity of the soul and the lesser jihad to fight in the world, although some fundamentalists dispute this hierarchy. Just as crusading can be used in a more secular sense, jihad can also be linked to good causes; thus a *jihad al-tarbiya* for education. An emphasis on the defensive aspect of the jihad formed an integral part of Islamic holy war. Saladin used such ideas in the medieval age and this defensive duty, as stated in the Koran, has been frequently invoked by nationalists and Islamists alike. If Muslim lands and/or Islamic belief were attacked then it is a religious duty to resist – if too few of the faithful are present to do so, then neighbours should assist: 'Yet if they ask you for help, for religion's sake, it is your duty to help them.' (K.8:72)

More radical Muslims, however, hold that jihad should be expansionist and, at its most extreme, must bring the entire world under sharia law; jihad is a permanent revolutionary struggle for the sake of mankind. This would not require forced conversion, but would topple regimes that were un-Islamic and followed man-made laws. If there was a situation in which Muslims were endangered it would be justifiable to remove such an authority and to bring about a moral regeneration from within. Some Islamists fear that one day their lands will become secularised and their faith as marginalised as Christianity has become in Europe. They argue that proper religious practice will bring God's blessing, military success and a change for good.

One country where such a drastic programme surfaced was Egypt, where radical thinkers, such as Sayyid Qutb, exerted a huge influence – hence his execution by the government in 1966. Egyptian defeat in the 1967 Arab–Israeli war advanced the fundamentalist cause and, to some extent, discredited the ruling nationalist and socialist regimes because it was possible to argue that poor religious observance had brought about divine disfavour. After the 1973 war a paradox emerged: more religious imagery was used to encourage a sense of Muslim fraternity in Egypt, yet for wider political reasons President Sadat engaged ever more closely with the USA. One consequence of this was President Carter's Camp David agreement, a peace accord between Israel and Egypt, which marked the most serious attempt to date to bring lasting solution to the troubles in the Middle East.[117] Sadat persuaded religious scholars to issue fatwas that declared the agreement legitimate in Islamic law to try to assuage concern over a deal with Israel and the West. Yet wealth within Egypt was increasingly concentrated in the hands of a small elite and western culture had become ever more invasive; fertile ground for radicals. Islamic groups had, to some extent, been tolerated because they offered ties with other Arab countries (the oil states in particular) but in the circumstances outlined here, several of the Islamist parties became radicalised.[118] Some groups were outlawed but the Jihad Organisation set out to assassinate President Sadat. Their aims were laid out in a document, *The Neglected Duty*, in which they argued that while the Jews were the more distant enemy, the rulers of Egypt were closer and, in accordance with the Koran, should be dealt with first.[119] Egypt needed an Islamic ruler rather than an impious one, and the existence of Israel was the fault of bad Muslim rulers. The text used the writings of Ibn Taymiyya (1263–1328), a Syrian theologian and jurist whose fundamentalist views brought him into trouble during his own lifetime. Ibn Taymiyya stressed the moral duty of the jihad and the need for a ruler to govern according to sharia law. He had issued fatwas against the Mongol rulers of Persia who, although they professed to be Muslims, continued, he believed, to venerate Chinggis Khan, their world-conquering ancestor; they also made alliances with unbelievers and preferred the Mongol legal code, the *yasa*, to sharia law. *The Neglected Duty* drew attention to the similarity between Mongol rule and modern Egypt: 'Therefore the rulers of these days are apostates. They have been brought up at the tables of colonialism, no matter whether of the crusading, the communist or the Zionist variety. They are Muslims only in name, even if they pray, fast and pretend to be Muslims.'[120] Sadat was an apostate and according to sharia law had to be killed; thus the deed was justified and in October 1981 the assassins struck, although they proved mistaken in their belief that his murder would be followed by a popular revolt.

In recent times Osama Bin Laden's pronouncements have emerged as the most powerful, notorious and strident condemnations of what he regards as anti-Islamic policies by the West. He has reached out to the *umma*, the Islamic community across the world, particularly in Palestine and Kashmir (and briefly in Chechnya too), and urged Muslims to stand up to the humiliations he claims have been imposed by Israel, the USA and Britain. Other targets of his anger are the Saudi authorities whom he regards as having 'desecrated their own legitimacy' through the 'suspension of Islamic law and replacement thereof with man-made laws . . . and allowing the enemies of God to occupy it in the form of the American crusaders who have become the principal reason for all aspects of our land's disastrous predicament.'[121]

Bin Laden is a polemicist of the first order whose canny use of

Internet and satellite television technology has enabled him to reach an audience no previous antagonist of the West could have dreamt of.[122] His language is laced with texts from the Koran, with Hadith, and statements by authoritative scholars, including Ibn Taymiyya.[123] Bin Laden's allure is also based upon his personal piety, generosity and the sharing of hardships with his men – qualities that, as the former head of the CIA unit hunting him wrote, make him 'an Islamic hero, as the faith's ideal type, and almost as a modern-day Saladin.'[124] For many years Bin Laden has consistently referred to a Judaeo-Crusader alliance against Islam, or a fight between the people of Islam and the global crusaders.[125] The religious edge this language provides is important to him and, crucially, signposts the ultimate failure of his enemies – and a parallel to the defeat of the medieval crusaders. Bin Laden has viewed the struggle as a war of religion, rather than one of imperialism, which is a concept rarely mentioned in his speeches. When President Bush so disastrously used the word 'crusade' in his unscripted response to the 9/11 atrocities he simply fulfilled the claims Bin Laden had been making for years: 'So Bush has declared in his own words: "crusader attack". The odd thing about this is that he has taken the words right out of our mouth.'[126] He neatly turned Bush's words against him: 'So the world today is split into two parts, as Bush said: either you are with us, or you are with terrorism. Either you are with the crusade or you are with Islam. Bush's image today is of him being in the front of the line, yelling and carrying his big cross.'[127] Quite what President Bush really understood by his remarks will never be clear – given the intimate relationship between religion and politics during his presidency, a holy war could have formed part of his meaning. On the other hand, while such a statement may have gained currency amongst far-right constituencies at home, to make such a comment to the world's media in his position as commander-in-chief of the US forces would have been imprudent to say the least. Perhaps Bush was thinking of a crusade in the more secular sense that is so frequently invoked in modern society (the good cause of cutting a hospital waiting list, or of cleaning streets); or maybe he was drawing upon the notion of a morally worthwhile struggle such as rights for workers, or against corruption. A blurred combination of all the above is, of course, possible. Whatever the answer, it is plain that he had absolutely no inkling of the toxic quality of the word

'crusade' in the Muslim world. White House spokesmen issued statements to clarify the president's words but it was too late. Bin Laden
gleefully noted: 'people make apologies for him and they say that he
didn't mean to say that the war is a crusade, even though he himself
said it was!'[128]

Bin Laden's appeal has taken root in terror cells across the world
and in the wider consciousness of millions of Muslims. The invasion
of Iraq only served to refresh his arguments and the destruction and
devastation of that land have given his ideas even greater currency.
Countries which supported the war became leading targets and in
March 2004 Spain, with its long history of Christian–Muslim conflict,
was hit by a series of train bombs that claimed 201 lives; subsequent
al-Qaeda statements duly made reference to the crusader legacy in
the peninsula. Likewise, although the British presence in Iraq was the
key factor precipitating the 7 July 2005 bombs in London, links were
made with the crusading period in subsequent propaganda. To those
who take part in such appalling acts, Bin Laden holds out the prospect
of martyrdom, although as commentators have noted, unlike Islamic
polemicists of the past such as Sayyid Qutb, he offers no social
programme for the future; similarly, the compassion and tolerance so
central to Islam are conspicuously absent from his words.[129]

Conclusion:
In the Shadow of the Crusades

In one of Winston Churchill's characteristically pithy observations he declared: 'The further back you look, the farther forward you can see.' In the case of the crusades, one might add the (unfair and obvious) rider that the clarity of your foresight depends upon how closely you examine the past. What, on the surface, appears a simple clash between two faiths is, as we have seen, far more complex and contradictory.

In the early medieval period the Islamic conquest of the Middle East, Spain and Sicily brought the two faiths into conflict but it was the launch of the First Crusade in 1095 that transformed the situation because it gave the entire Catholic West reasons to engage in, or to support, holy war. The imperative to free Jerusalem and the desire to secure unprecedented spiritual rewards meant that crusading emerged as an inspirational blend of penitential activity and religious warfare. The polyglot armies of the First Crusade demonstrated the near-universal appeal of Pope Urban's idea and the capture of Jerusalem startled and exhilarated Christendom. From then on, crusading evolved quickly, both in theory and practice.

Prompted largely by the success of the First Crusade, kings – themselves becoming ever more powerful in the medieval West – began to take part. The launch of the First Crusade had required a partnership between the nobility and the Church, but once kings were involved their military and financial strength changed the dynamic and the papacy started to lose control over its creation. Papal legate Adhémar of Le Puy had exerted some influence over the First Crusade but in many subsequent campaigns the presence of royal power rendered most legates all but invisible. Church authority remained centred upon the preaching of the crusade, and the spellbinding rhetoric of Urban II, Bernard of Clairvaux and James of Vitry echo down the ages and their efforts did much to convince thousands of men and women to set out for the Holy Land. They generated intense belief in the moral right of the crusaders' actions, and evoked tremendous faith in the sign of the cross: 'the last plank for a shipwrecked world', as James of Vitry so eloquently claimed. The popular appeal of Jerusalem, Christ's own city and the place of mankind's salvation, should never be underestimated and, as we saw during the Third Crusade, the army's desire to march to the holy city compelled even King Richard to follow their wishes. Papal legislation produced much of the money to finance the crusades, but once underway, there was relatively little the *curia* could do to steer its prodigy in the manner it desired. The most glaring example of this was the Fourth Crusade's diversion to Constantinople, but Pope Innocent's deep disquiet at Simon de Montfort's territorial acquisitions during the Albigensian Crusade and, most of all, the recovery of Jerusalem by the excommunicate Frederick II in 1229, amply demonstrate the Church's problem. The secular powers had, quite naturally, their own agendas and while devotion to the crusading cause was manifest in their taking of the cross and setting out on campaign they could not always put other matters aside, no matter how worthy the cause. Thus long-standing Anglo-French rivalry caused Richard the Lionheart and Philip to spar and bicker during the Third Crusade, and when the latter departed for home his behaviour undoubtedly compromised Richard's actions in the Levant. Similarly, tensions between the German and French armies were said to have hampered the march of the Second Crusade. Of course, the papacy and the lay powers usually shared the same ultimate aim – to recover the Holy Land – but the former felt morally better equipped to direct a holy war and believed that they were less likely to allow it to be distracted by matters displeasing to God.

Kings and nobles from the Baltic and Iberia asked for the extension of crusading privileges to their homelands and the flexibility and willingness of the papacy to accommodate this proved vital in the wider attraction and longevity of the movement. Along with a wish to fight the enemies of God, it was the territorial ambitions of the Spanish and Baltic nobility, along with the commercial drive of the Italian mercantile cities, that gave the crusades an energy that faith alone could not provide. Similarly, the chivalric aspects of holy war did much to invigorate crusading across Europe and the Near East and, as the Feast of the Pheasant so vividly demonstrated, it remained an important theme well into the fifteenth century. While this variety gave crusading an extra vitality, it could also cause difficulties. People were unclear where their priorities should lie; in the mid-thirteenth century, for example, Matthew Paris – a strong critic of the papacy – observed: 'the papalists . . . shamelessly harassed people who had taken the cross, urging them under the penalty of excommunication now to set out for the Holy Land, now for the Byzantine Empire, and now suggesting that they attack Frederick . . . and they extorted the necessary funds for an expedition on whatever pretext.'[1] In other words, as far as Matthew Paris was concerned, the diversity of crusading had diluted its impact and opened the way to corruption and vice.

In contrast to Christianity's evolution of holy war and crusading theory, Islam was already equipped with such an ideology through the presence of jihad in the Koran and Hadith. Unfortunately for the Muslims the First Crusade arrived in the Levant at a time when jihad was in abeyance and the political authority of the Seljuk Turks had just fractured; few, therefore, were motivated to fight the latest invaders of the Near East, as the Damascene preacher al-Sulami discovered. The vital mutual interest in holy war on the part of the clerical and the ruling classes only emerged under Nur ad-Din and Saladin. Such a simple picture, however, is complicated by the dynastic conflict between these two men and it was only the former's death in 1174 that prevented civil war. In other words, wholly secular actions are visible even in those held up as heroes of the jihad. The idea waned under Saladin's successors and it was not until the Mamluk Baibars seized power in 1260 that holy war returned to the top of the agenda, leading to the expulsion of the Christians from Acre in 1291. Likewise, after another period of relatively low profile, the *ghazi* zeal of the early Ottomans brought jihad back to the fore once more.

For all the high-profile focus on Christian (by which we really mean just Catholic) and Muslim conflict, it is worth remembering that a significant proportion of holy war – *on both sides* – was directed against people of their own faith, or rival groups therein. Crusades were sent to defeat the Cathars of southern France (a rather radical form of Christianity, admittedly) and the Hussites of Bohemia; and although the Fourth Crusade was not originally aimed at the Orthodox Greeks of Constantinople, the papal legate offered its participants spiritual rewards in April 1204. The sack of Constantinople remains an immensely sensitive issue even now. When Pope John Paul II visited Athens in May 2001 the city's Orthodox archbishop made his anger abundantly clear: 'Understandably a large part of the Church of Greece opposes your presence here . . . [we] demand . . . a formal condemnation of injustices committed against them by the Christian West . . . The Orthodox Greek people sense more intensely in its religious consciousness and national memory the traumatic experiences that remain as open wounds on its vigorous body, as is known by all, by the destructive mania of the Crusaders and the period of Latin rule . . .'[2] Crusades were also called against the political enemies of the papacy such as Frederick II and, at the time of Bishop Despenser's crusade (1390), the French. In the Islamic world the fundamental divide between Sunni and Shi'a was an obvious fault line and leaders of the former made much of their efforts to wage jihad against the so-called heresy of their opponents in the centuries before, and during, the crusades. This desire to purge lands of religious enemies was a prominent aspect of the spiritual case put forward by Nur ad-Din and Saladin in their efforts to unify the Near East. It follows, therefore, that the Sunni–Shi'a split explains why Saladin is no role model for modern Shi'ite regimes because he was the man who destroyed their caliphate in Cairo in 1169–71.

Notwithstanding the powerful rhetoric of holy war there was not a constant state of conflict between Christianity and Islam in the Near East and Iberia. We have seen numerous truces and diplomatic engagements – although in some cases these were impelled by reason of expediency and practicality, rather than mutual regard. There was a further complication in the Levant with the need to distinguish between most crusaders – western knights who came to the Holy Land, desperate to slay the infidel – and the Frankish settlers – those who were born and lived in the Levant. The priority of a group of men, inspired by preachers, who had travelled thousands of miles at great cost and risk, and were intent upon great deeds – but who would then go home – was different to those who existed in the Middle East day after day. Usama ibn Munqidh's encounter with a bullying western crusader during his prayers in the al-Aqsa Mosque vividly demonstrated this and, as we saw earlier, the contrast between this newcomer's aggression and the restraint shown by the indigenous Templar knight was marked. The Frankish settlers had to bear in mind longer-term strategies and without the permanent presence of large western armies (the Military Orders notwithstanding), peace was sometimes preferable. This inherent tension between crusaders and settlers was a fundamental fault line in the practice of crusading because without a single over-arching authority to direct or pull together the Christians, even the greater benefit of the Holy Land could be subsumed under the contrasting interests of either settlers of crusaders. In consequence, there was often considerable mutual mistrust between the Franks and the crusaders, as the aftermath of the failed Second Crusade exposed.

In contrast to this expectation of mutual antipathy we have seen situations where the protaganists seek treaties across religious lines; the deal between Damascus and Jerusalem to resist Zengi of Aleppo and Mosul was but one example of a Christian–Muslim alliance against a common opponent. Usama described part of this particular process taking place during a hunting party, which also reminds us of the shared cultural values of two heavily equestrian societies. Count Raymond of Tripoli's arrangement with Saladin in 1186–7 was perhaps the most nakedly self-serving of all cross-religious treaties, especially given the fevered atmos-phere of holy war at the time. The most dramatic feat of diplomacy by a crusader was Frederick II's recovery of Jerusalem. This was accom-plished in part because of his political and military strength, in part on account of rivalries within the contemporary Muslim world, but also because of his skills as a linguist and a diplomat, along with his prepared-ness to engage wholeheartedly with the etiquette and culture of his opponents. His approach was not unique and again, in contrast to the familiar bellicose images of Richard and Saladin, we have seen that both were accomplished diplomats and, in fact, Frederick's settlement was quite similar to ideas discussed by these men thirty years earlier.

Crusading imagery and metaphor have survived, and indeed blos-somed over the centuries. They have emerged in common, if diverse, use across many aspects of the cultural and political life of the West; the blend of historical resonances and a feeling of moral right are a heady mixture. The combination of epic confrontation, the clash of faiths, the sense of defending one's own culture, a unified cause, and above all, the sense of moral right, have helped to keep the idea alive. Added to that, the deeds and desires of compelling characters, such as those covered here, also explain why the subject retains such an allure in popular culture; for example, the Knights Templar were promin-ent in Umberto Eco's *Foucault's Pendulum* (1988) and Dan Brown's

The Da Vinci Code (2002) while the fall of Jerusalem was the centre-piece of Ridley Scott's major 2005 movie *Kingdom of Heaven* (although the film had a very secular idea at its heart with chivalry, rather than faith, being held up as the true belief). In the contemporary Muslim world Saladin is now starring as a children's cartoon character, displaying his appeal in a less polemical form than usual.

As we have seen, some sensed the troubles the crusading legacy might cause, and General Allenby's determination to disconnect the medieval from the modern in Jerusalem in 1917 stands as a stark contrast to General Gouraud's triumphal behaviour in Damascus three years later ('Saladin, we have returned!'). Encouraged by such expression of superiority and, in the face of widespread western conquests of Islamic lands during the nineteenth century, many Muslims recalled both the traumas of the medieval age and also their ultimate success in defeating the crusaders. By tapping into their own history and folklore, as well as using the modern western constructs provided by men such as Kaiser Wilhelm II, they found a very potent set of images. The cumulative effect of the use of 'crusade' by leaders as ideologically diverse as Sultan Abdulhamid II, Nasser of Egypt, Saddam Hussein and Osama Bin Laden, has given it a wholly abhorrent meaning to the Islamic world and one that reflects western imperialist aggression, rather than Christian zeal.

What took place across so many theatres of war and involved so many millions of people has embedded itself into the consciousness of the Christian West and the Muslim Near East. Given the intrinsic nature of jihad to Islam it will never disappear, yet crusading has ended. The failure of the Christians to hold on to the Holy Land, the conversion of the pagans of the Baltic, the successful reconquest of Iberia, rising distaste for the sale of indulgences, plus a growing sense of national identity and the Reformation, brought about its demise. What has survived is an immensely rich body of terminology, sentiment and imagery. Crusading was, in many ways, initially conceived and justi-fied as a defensive idea, but its later successors, such as colonialism, were unashamedly aggressive and share few elements of the same DNA. For centuries we have actually seen just shadows of the crusades, not true shapes. While many of these phantoms can guide us and – as Churchill implied – offer us warnings, the medieval and modern contexts are wholly different and for that reason such shadows need to be treated with real care – from all sides – to avoid disaster.

Illustrations and Maps

Notes

Introduction

1. N. Housley, *Contesting the Crusades* (Oxford, 2006); *The Oxford Illustrated History of the Crusades*, ed. J. S. C. Riley-Smith (Oxford, 1995). • 2. My thanks to Thomas Phillips for his research on this point: *Batman and Robin: The Complete 1949 Movie Serial Collection*. • 3. J. P. Phillips, 'Why a Crusade will lead to a Jihad', *Independent*, 18 September 2001. • 4. E. Sivan, 'The Crusades Described by Modern Arab Historiography', in *Asian and African Studies* 8 (1972), pp. 104–49; C. Hillenbrand, *The Crusades: Islamic Perspectives* (Edinburgh, 1999). • 5. C. Hillenbrand, *Turkish Myth and Muslim Symbol: The Battle of Manzikert* (Edinburgh, 2007).

1 'Deus vult!': The First Crusade and the Capture of Jerusalem, 1095–1099

1. Robert of Rheims, account of Urban II's speech at Clermont taken from L. and J. S. C. Riley-Smith, *The Crusades: Idea and Reality, 1095–1274* (London, 1981), pp. 42–5. For the full text of Robert's chronicle, see *Robert the Monk's History of the First Crusade*, tr. C. Sweetenham (Aldershot, 2005). • 2. C. J. Tyerman, *God's War: A New History of the Crusades* (London, 2006), pp. 1–24 elegantly sketches out the situation in Europe and the Mediterranean during the eleventh century. • 3. J. S. C. Riley-Smith, *What were the Crusades?*, third edition (Basingstoke, 2002), pp. 5–9; *idem, The First Crusade and the Idea of Crusading* (London, 1986), pp. 5–8; Tyerman, *God's War*, pp. 27–51. In a broader context see F. H. Russell, *The Just War in the Middle Ages* (Cambridge, 1975). • 4. See the accounts of Robert of Rheims, Baldric of Bourgueil, Fulcher of Chartres and Guibert of Nogent, all translated in Riley-Smith, *Crusades: Idea and Reality*, pp. 41–53. • 5. Both the tympanum at Conques and at Autun are especially vivid. • 6. Guibert of Nogent, *The Deeds of God through the Franks: Gesta Dei per Francos*, tr. R. Levine (Woodbridge, 1997),

p. 28. • 7. *Gesta Francorum et aliorum Hierosalimitanorum: The Deeds of the Franks and the other Pilgrims to Jerusalem*, ed. R. Hill, tr. R. A. B. Mynors (London, 1962), p. 1; Guibert of Nogent, *Deeds of God*, p. 45. • 8. C. Hillenbrand, *Turkish Myth and Muslim Symbol*; idem, 'The First Crusade: The Muslim Perspective', in *The First Crusade: Origins and Impact*, ed. J. P. Phillips (Manchester, 1997), pp. 130–41. • 9. J. Shepard, 'Cross-Purposes: Alexius Comnenus and the First Crusade', in *The First Crusade: Origins and Impact*, pp. 107–29. • 10. Riley-Smith, *The First Crusaders, 1095–1131* (Cambridge, 1999), pp. 55–60. • 11. R. Chazan, *European Jewry and the First Crusade* (Berkeley, CA, 1987). • 12. *Ibid.*, p. 66. • 13. *Ibid.*, p. 234. • 14. Albert of Aachen, *Historia Ierosolimitana: History of the Journey to Jerusalem*, ed. and tr. S. B. Edgington (Oxford, 2007), pp. 52–3. • 15. Chazan, *European Jewry*, p. 69. • 16. Albert of Aachen, *Historia Ierosolimitana*, pp. 56–9. • 17. M. G. Bull, 'The Diplomatic of the First Crusade' in *The First Crusade: Origins and Impact*, pp. 35–56. • 18. Charter from Riley-Smith, *The First Crusaders*, p. 114. • 19. *Ibid.*, pp. 67–8. • 20. Fulcher of Chartres, *A History of the Expedition to Jerusalem, 1095–1127*, tr. F. R. Ryan, ed. H. S. Fink (Knoxville, TN, 1969), p. 88. • 21. Riley-Smith, *The First Crusade*, p. 43. • 22. A. V. Murray, 'Money and Logistics in the Forces of the First Crusade: Coinage, Bullion, Service, and Supply, 1096–1099', in *Logistics of Warfare in the Age of the Crusades*, ed. J. H. Pryor (Aldershot, 2006), pp. 229–50. • 23. Letter of Urban II to the congregation of Vallombrosa, 7 October 1096, tr. Riley-Smith, *Crusades: Idea and Reality*, pp. 39–40. • 24. A. V. Murray, *The Crusader Kingdom of Jerusalem: A Dynastic History, 1099–1125* (Oxford, 2000), pp. 1–93. • 25. For the letters see H. Hagenmeyer, *Die Kreuzzugsbriefe aus den Jahren 1088–1100* (Innsbruck, 1901), pp. 138–42, 149–52. The latter is translated in 'Letter of Stephen of Blois to Adela of Blois', in *The First Crusade: 'The Chronicle of Fulcher of Chartres' and Other Source Materials*, ed. E. Peters, second edition (Philadelphia, PA, 1998), pp. 287–8. See also K. LoPrete, 'Adela of Blois: Familial Alliances and Female Lordships' in *Aristocratic Women in Medieval France*, ed. T. Evergates (Philadelphia, PA, 1999), pp. 7–43. • 26. J. H. and L. L. Hill, *Raymond IV, Count of Toulouse* (Syracuse, NY, 1962). • 27. R. B. Yewdale, *Bohemond I, Prince of Antioch* (Princeton, NJ, 1924); *Gesta Francorum, passim*. • 28. Fulcher of Chartres, *History of the Expedition to Jerusalem*, p. 74. • 29. G. T. Dennis, 'Defenders of the Christian People: Holy War in Byzantium', in *The Crusades from the Perspective of the Byzantine and Muslim World*, eds. A. E. Laiou and R. P. Mottahedeh (Washington, DC, 2001), pp. 31–40; Shepard, 'Cross-Purposes', pp. 108–13; J. Harris, *Byzantium and the Crusades* (London, 2003), pp. 53–60; Anna Comnena, *The Alexiad*, tr. E. R. A. Sewter (London, 1969), p. 319. • 30. J. France, *Victory in the East: A Military History* (Cambridge, 1994), p. 105. • 31. Anna Comnena, *The Alexiad*, p. 323. • 32. J. Harris, *Constantinople* (London, 2006). • 33. Albert of Aachen, *Historia Ierosolimitana*, pp. 84–5. • **34**. *Ibid.*, pp. 90–1; Harris, *Byzantium and the Crusades*, pp. 60–7. • **35**. Hillenbrand, 'The First Crusade: The Muslim Perspective', pp. 130–41. • **36**. *Ibid.*, p. 132. • **37**. Fulcher of Chartres, *History of the Expedition to Jerusalem*, p. 85. • **38**. *Gesta Francorum*, p. 19. • **39**. *Ibid.*, pp. 20–1. • **40**. J. B. Segal, *Edessa: The Blessed City* (Oxford, 1970); C. MacEvitt, *The Crusades and the Christian World of the East: Rough Tolerance* (Philadelphia, PA, 2008), pp. 50–73. • **41**. *Gesta Francorum*, pp. 44–7. • **42**. *Ibid.*, p. 62. • **43**. R.-J. Lilie, *Byzantium and the Crusader States, 1096–1204*, trs. J. C. Morris and J. E. Ridings (Oxford, 1993), pp. 31–60; Harris, *Byzantium and the Crusades*, pp. 64–71. • **44**. *Gesta Francorum*, pp. 59–60. • **45**. *Ibid.*, p. 68. • **46**. *Ibid.*, p. 69. • **47**. France, *Victory in the East*, pp. 278–96. • **48**. *Ibid.*, pp. 303, 323–4; Ralph of Caen, *The Gesta Tancredi of Ralph of Caen: A History of the Normans on the First Crusade*, trs. B. S. and D. S. Bachrach (Aldershot, 2005), pp. 113–14. • **49**. For a general context see R. Bartlett, *Trial by Fire and Water* (Oxford, 1984), esp. pp. 70–102. • **50**. T. S. Asbridge, 'The Holy Lance of Antioch: Power, Devotion and Memory on the First Crusade', in *Reading Medieval Studies*, 33 (2007), pp. 3–36. • **51**. O. Figes, *A People's Tragedy: The Russian Revolution, 1891–1924* (London, 1996), pp. 777–8. • **52**. Ralph of Caen, *Gesta Tancredi*, pp. 129–30. • **53**. The best account of the siege is to be found in France, *Victory in the East*, pp. 325–66. • **54**. Raymond of Aguilers, *Historia Francorum qui ceperunt Iherusalem*, trs. J. H and L. L. Hill (Philadelphia, PA, 1968), pp. 127–8. • **55**. *Ibid.*, p. 128. • **56**. Albert of Aachen, *Historia Ierosolimitana*, pp. 428–9. • **57**. Raymond of Aguilers, *Historia Francorum*, p. 127. • **58**. B. Z. Kedar, 'The Jerusalem Massacre of July 1099 in the Western Historiography of the Crusades', in *Crusades* 3 (2004), pp. 15–76. • **59**. *Gesta Francorum*, p. 92. • **60**. William of Tyre, *A History of Deeds Done Beyond the Sea*, trs. E. A. Babcock and A. C. Krey, 2 vols. (New York, 1943) 1.372–3; Latin text in *Chronicon*, ed. R. B. C. Huygens, 2 vols. (Turnhout, 1986). • **61**. Pope Paschal II, in Hagenmeyer, *Die Kreuzzugsbriefe*, p. 178. • **62**. Raymond of Aguilers, *Historia Francorum*, p. 128. • **63**. Murray, *Crusader Kingdom of Jerusalem*, pp. 63–77. • **64**. J. P. Phillips, *The Second Crusade: Extending the Frontiers of Christendom* (London, 2007), pp. 17–36.

2 'May God's curse be upon them!': Relations Between Muslims and Franks in the Levant, 1099–1187

1. Translated by C. Hillenbrand, in Phillips, *Crusades*, p. 169. • **2**. Hillenbrand, *The Crusades: Islamic Perspectives*, pp. 83–109. • **3**. Al-Sulami, *Kitab al-Jihad*, tr. N. Christie, published online at http:// www.arts.cornell.edu/prh3/447/texts/Sulami.html; see also N. Christie, 'Motivating Listeners in the *Kitab al-Jihad* of Ali ibn Tahir al-Sulami (d.1106)', in *Crusades* 6 (2007), pp. 1–14. The seminal article on this topic is

E. Sivan, 'La génèse de la contre-croisade: un traité damasquin du début du XIIe siècle', in *Journal Asiatique* 254 (1966), pp. 197–224. • 4. Al-Sulami, f. 179b (references follow the manuscript numbering in Christie's translation). • 5. *Ibid.*, f. 176b. • 6. *Ibid.*, f. 175a. • 7. *Ibid.*, f. 177a. • 8. Bernard of Clairvaux and Raol, author of *The Conquest of Lisbon*, were two mid-twelfth-century Christian writers who used this theme. See Phillips, *Second Crusade*, pp. 72–3, 154. • 9. Usama ibn Munqidh, *The Book of Contemplation. Islam and the Crusades*, tr. P. M. Cobb (London, 2008); P. M. Cobb, *Usama ibn Munqidh: Warrior Poet of the Age of Crusades* (Oxford, 2005); *idem*, 'Infidel Dogs: Hunting Crusaders with Usama ibn Munqidh', in *Crusades* 6 (2007), pp. 57–68; R. Irwin, 'Usama ibn Munqidh: An Arab-Syrian Gentleman at the Time of the Crusades Reconsidered', in *The Crusades and their Sources: Essays Presented to Bernard Hamilton*, eds. J. France and W. G. Zajac (Aldershot, 1998), pp. 71–87. • 10. M. G. S. Hodgson, *The Secret Order of the Assassins: The Struggle of the Early Nizari Isma'ilis Against the Islamic World* (Philadelphia, PA, 1955). • 11. Usama ibn Munqidh, *Book of Contemplation*, pp. 208–10. • 12. Excerpts in *ibid.*, pp. 254–9. • 13. Irwin, 'Usamah ibn Munqidh', pp. 83–5. • 14. Usama ibn Munqidh, *Book of Contemplation*, pp. 245–54. • 15. For this anecdote, see Irwin, 'Usamah ibn Munqidh', p. 86. • 16. Usama ibn Munqidh, *Book of Contemplation*, p. 144. • 17. *Ibid.*, p. 149. • 18. Koran, 17.1. • 19. Usama ibn Munqidh, *Book of Contemplation*, p. 147. • 20. *Ibid.*, pp. 205–6; Phillips, *Second Crusade*, pp. 217–18. • 21. Fulcher of Chartres, *History of the Expedition to Jerusalem*, p. 271. • 22. Usama ibn Munqidh, *Book of Contemplation*, pp. 122, 138, 208. • 23. *Ibid.*, p. 25. • 24. *Ibid.*, pp. 59–62. • 25. Irwin, 'Usamah ibn Munqidh', pp. 73–5. • 26. Usama ibn Munqidh, *Book of Contemplation*, pp. 145–6. • 27. *Ibid.*, p. 146. • 28. P. D. Mitchell, *Medicine in the Crusades: Warfare, Wounds and the Medieval Surgeon* (Cambridge, 2004). • 29. Usama ibn Munqidh, *Book of Contemplation*, p. 179. • 30. *Ibid.*, pp. xxxiii–xxxiv. • 31. *Ibid.*, p. 178. • 32. Ibn Jubayr, *The Travels of Ibn Jubayr*, tr. R. J. C. Broadhurst (London, 1952); I. R. Netton, 'Ibn Jubayr: Penitent Pilgrim and Observant Traveller', in *Seek Knowledge: Thought and Travel in the House of Islam* (Richmond, 1996), pp. 95–102. • 33. Ibn Jubayr, *Travels*, p. 20. • 34. *Ibid.*, p. 15. • 35. *Ibid.*, p. 60. • 36. *Ibid.*, p. 67. • 37. *Ibid.*, pp. 166–7. • 38. *Ibid.*, p. 66. • 39. *Ibid.*, p. 71. • 40. *Ibid.*, p. 138. • 41. *Ibid.*, p. 271. • 42. *Ibid.*, p. 279. • 43. *Ibid.*, p. 311. • 44. *Ibid.*, pp. 311–14. • 45. *Ibid.*, p. 312. • 46. For example, see Beha ad-Din Ibn Shaddad, *The Rare and Excellent History of Saladin*, tr. D. S. Richards (Aldershot, 2001), esp. pp. 22–6. • 47. Ibn Jubayr, *Travels*, p. 316. • 48. *Ibid.*, pp. 300–1. • 49. *Ibid.*, pp. 316–17. • 50. *Ibid.*, p. 318. • 51. *Ibid.*, pp. 320–1. • 52. S. A. Epstein, *Genoa and the Genoese, 958–1528* (Chapel Hill, NC, 1996); T. F. Madden, *Enrico Dandolo and the Rise of Venice* (Baltimore, MD, 2003); W. Heywood, *A History of Pisa: Eleventh and Twelfth Centuries* (Cambridge, 1921). • 53. Ibn Jubayr, *Travels*, p. 325. • 54. *Ibid.*, p. 331.

3 'A woman of unusual wisdom and discretion': Queen Melisende of Jerusalem

1. N. R. Hodgson, *Women, Crusading and the Holy Land in Historical Narrative* (Woodbridge, 2007), p. 107; D. Gerish, 'Gender Theory', in *Palgrave Advances: The Crusades*, ed. H. J. Nicholson (Basingstoke, 2005), pp. 130–47. • **2.** MacEvitt, *Rough Tolerance*, pp. 70–1; Murray, *Crusader Kingdom of Jerusalem*, p. 182. • **3.** Murray, *Crusader Kingdom of Jerusalem*, pp. 115–27; Hodgson, *Women, Crusading and the Holy Land*, pp. 141–4; MacEvitt, *Rough Tolerance*, pp. 75–8. • **4.** J. P. Phillips, *Defenders of the Holy Land: Relations between the Latin East and the West, 1119–1187* (Oxford, 1996), pp. 19–35. • **5.** Hodgson, *Women, Crusading and the Holy Land*, pp. 57–60, 71–90, 159–60, 181–90; see also William of Tyre, 2.135. • **6.** William of Tyre, 2.45–6, contrasts with 50–1 to give the crucial difference in terms. • **7.** *Ibid.*, 2.38. • **8.** Orderic Vitalis, *The Ecclesiastical History*, ed. and tr. M. Chibnall, 6 vols. (Oxford, 1969–80), 6.390–1. • **9.** J. Prawer, *The Latin Kingdom of Jerusalem: European Colonialism in the Middle Ages* (London, 1972), pp. 96–101. • **10.** J. S. C. Riley-Smith, 'King Fulk of Jerusalem and "The Sultan of Babylon"', in *Montjoie: Studies in Crusade History in Honour of Hans Eberhard Mayer*, eds. B. Z. Kedar, J. S. C. Riley-Smith and R. Hiestand (Aldershot, 1997), pp. 55–66. • **11.** *Le cartulaire du chapitre du Saint-Sépulcre de Jérusalem*, ed. G. Bresc-Bautier (Paris, 1984), no. 92, p. 209. • **12.** B. F. Reilly, *The Kingdom of León-Castilla under Queen Urraca, 1109–1126* (Princeton, NJ, 1982). • **13.** H. E. Mayer, 'Studies in the History of Queen Melisende of Jerusalem', in *Dumbarton Oaks Papers* 26 (1972), pp. 95–182; Phillips, *Crusades*, pp. 106–8; Hodgson, *Women, Crusading and the Holy Land*, pp. 134–5. • **14.** William of Tyre, 2.71–2. • **15.** H. E. Mayer, *Varia Antiochena: Studien zum Kreuzfahrerfürstentum Antiochia im 12. und frühen 13. Jahrhundert* (Hanover, 1993), no. 2, p. 114; Phillips, *Defenders of the Holy Land*, pp. 44–52. • **16.** William of Tyre, 2.72. • **17.** Bartlett, *Trial by Fire and Water*, pp. 103–26, esp. 111. • **18.** William of Tyre, 2.72. • **19.** *Ibid.*, 2.73–4 • **20.** Ibn al-Qalanisi, *The Damascus Chronicles of the Crusades*, tr. H. A. R. Gibb (London, 1932), p. 215. • **21.** William of Tyre, 2.73–4. • **22.** J. H. Pryor, *Geography, Technology and War: Studies in the Maritime History of the Mediterranean, 649–1571* (Cambridge, 1988), pp. 3–4. • **23.** A. J. Boas, *Crusader Archaeology: The Material Culture of the Latin East* (London, 1999), pp. 13, 25–30. • **24.** William of Tyre, 2.74–6. • **25.** B. Z. Kedar, 'A Twelfth-Century Description of the Jerusalem Hospital'; S. B. Edgington, 'Medical Care in the Hospital of St John in Jerusalem', both in *The Military Orders Volume 2: Welfare and Warfare*, ed. H. J. Nicholson (Aldershot, 1994), pp. 3–26, 27–33; Mitchell, *Medicine in the Crusades*, pp. 60–85. • **26.** William of Tyre, 2.75–6. • **27.** Mayer, 'Studies in the History of Queen Melisende', pp. 107, 109. • **28.** William of Tyre, 2.76. • **29.** H. E. Mayer, 'Angevins versus Normans:

The New Men of King Fulk of Jerusalem', in *Proceedings of the American Philosophical Society* 133 (1989), pp. 1–25. • **30**. Orderic Vitalis, *Ecclesiastical History*, 6.390–3. • **31**. Ibn al-Qalanisi, *Damascus Chronicles of the Crusades*, p. 208. • **32**. *Regesta regni Hierosolymitani, 1098–1291*, ed. R. Röhricht (Innsbruck, 1893), nos. 163–4, pp. 40–1. • **33**. Phillips, *Defenders of the Holy Land*, pp. 46–52, 59–61. • **34**. J. Folda, *The Art of the Crusaders in the Holy Land, 1098–1187* (Cambridge, 1995), pp. 137–63; B. Kühnel, *Crusader Art of the Twelfth Century: A Geographical, an Historical, or an Art-Historical Notion?* (Berlin, 1994), pp. 67–125. • **35**. Folda, *Art of the Crusaders in the Holy Land*, pp. 130–7, 246–9. • **36**. William of Tyre, 2.132–4; Folda, *Art of the Crusaders in the Holy Land*, pp. 131–6. • **37**. Boas, *Crusader Archaeology*, p. 25. • **38**. William of Tyre, 2.134–5. • **39**. Bernard of Clairvaux, *The Letters of St Bernard of Clairvaux*, new edition, tr. B. S. James, introduction B. M. Kienzle (Stroud, 1998), no. 274, p. 347. • **40**. *Ibid.*, no. 273, p. 346. • **41**. *Gesta Stephani (The Deeds of Stephen)*, ed. and tr. K. R. Potter (London, 1955), p. 81; M. Chibnall, *The Empress Matilda* (Oxford, 1996). • **42**. Orderic Vitalis, *Ecclesiastical History*, 5.324–5; Hodgson, *Women, Crusading and the Holy Land*, pp. 109–10, 114–15, 236–8. • **43**. William of Tyre, 2.283, 291. • **44**. Folda, *Art of the Crusaders in the Holy Land*, pp. 324–8. • **45**. William of Tyre, 2.139–40, 283.

4 The 'blessed generation': St Bernard of Clairvaux and the Second Crusade, 1145–1149

1. On the Second Crusade generally, see Phillips, *Second Crusade*, and the seminal article by G. Constable, 'The Second Crusade as Seen by Contemporaries', in *Traditio* 9 (1953), pp. 213–79. • **2**. C. Hillenbrand, '"Abominable Acts": The Career of Zengi', in *The Second Crusade: Scope and Consequences*, eds. J. P. Phillips and M. Hoch (Manchester, 2001), pp. 111–32, text here from p. 123. • **3**. Nersēs Šnorhali, 'Lament on Edessa', tr. T. Van Lint, in *East and West in the Crusader States II: Context, Contacts, Confrontations*, eds. K. Ciggaar and H. Teule, Orientalia Lovaniensia Analecta 92 (Leuven, 1999), pp. 49–105, text here from p. 75. • **4**. Phillips, *Second Crusade*, pp. 1–16. • **5**. *Ibid.*, pp. 37–60. • **6**. William of Malmesbury, *Gesta Regum Anglorum: The Deeds of the Kings of England*, eds. and trs. R. A. B. Mynors, R. M. Thomson and M. Winterbottom, 2 vols. (Oxford, 1998–9), 2.655. • **7**. Translation in Riley-Smith, *Crusades: Idea and Reality*, p. 91; also in Phillips, *Second Crusade*, pp. 280–2. • **8**. Odo of Deuil, *The Journey of Louis VII to the East: De profectione Ludovici in Orientem*, ed. and tr. V. G. Berry (Columbia, 1948), pp. 8–9. • **9**. Phillips, *Second Crusade*, pp. 99–100. • **10**. Bernard of Clairvaux, *Letters*, p. 399. • **11**. *Ibid.*, p. 462. • **12**. *Ibid.* • **13**. B. Ward, *Miracles and the Medieval Mind*, second edition (Aldershot, 1987), p. 182. • **14**. R. Chazan, 'From the First Crusade to the Second: Evolving Perceptions of the Christian-Jewish Conflict', in *Jews and Christians in Twelfth-Century Europe*, eds. M. A. Singer and J. Van Engen (Notre Dame, IN, 2001), pp. 46–62; *The Jews and the Crusaders*, ed. S. Eidelberg (Madison, WI, 1977); R. Chazan, *European Jewry and the First Crusade* (Berkeley, CA, 1987); Bernard of Clairvaux, *Letters*, pp. 46–66; Otto of Freising, *The Deeds of Frederick Barbarossa*, tr. C. C. Mierow (New York, 1953), pp. 74–5. • **15**. Otto of Freising, *Deeds of Frederick Barbarossa*, p. 70. • **16**. Phillips, *Second Crusade*, pp. 94–5. • **17**. W. J. Purkis, *Crusading Spirituality in the Holy Land and Iberia, c.1095–c.1187* (Woodbridge, 2008); J. F. O'Callaghan, *Reconquest and Crusade in Medieval Spain* (Philadelphia, PA, 2003). • **18**. Translated in Riley-Smith, *Crusades: Idea and Reality*, p. 40. • **19**. Phillips, *Second Crusade*, pp. 244–68; S. A. Epstein, *Genoa and the Genoese, 958–1528* (Chapel Hill, NC, 1996), pp. 49–53. • **20**. Phillips, *Second Crusade*, pp. 228–43; E. Christiansen, *The Northern Crusades*, second edition (Harmondsworth, 1997), pp. 1–49; K. Lotter, 'The Crusade Idea and the Conquest of the Region East of the Elbe', in *Medieval Frontier Societies*, eds. R. Bartlett and A. Mackay (Oxford, 1989), pp. 267–85. • **21**. Phillips, *Second Crusade*, p. 235. • **22**. Bernard of Clairvaux, *Letters*, p. 467. • **23**. K. Villads Jensen, 'Denmark and the Second Crusade: The Formation of a Crusader State?', in *The Second Crusade: Scope and Consequences*, eds. J. P. Phillips and M. Hoch (Manchester, 2001), pp. 164–79. • **24**. Phillips, *Second Crusade*, pp. xxviii–ix, 238. • **25**. *Ibid.*, pp. 136–67; idem, 'Ideas of Crusade and Holy War in *The Conquest of Lisbon (De expugnatione Lyxbonensi)*', in *The Holy Land, Holy Lands and Christian History*, ed. R. N. Swanson, *Studies in Church History* 36 (2000), pp. 123–41. • **26**. J. P. Huffman, *The Social Politics of Medieval Diplomacy: Anglo-German Relations (1066–1307)* (Ann Arbor, MI, 2000), pp. 46–56. • **27**. *The Conquest of Lisbon (De expugnatione Lyxbonensi)*, ed. and tr. C. W. David, with a new foreword and bibliography by J. P. Phillips (New York, 2001), pp. 56–7. • **28**. *Ibid.*, pp. 68–9; Phillips, *Second Crusade*, pp. 145–6. • **29**. *Conquest of Lisbon*, pp. 78–9. • **30**. *Ibid.*, pp. 90–3. • **31**. H. Kennedy, *Muslim Spain and Portugal: A Political History of al-Andalus* (Harlow, 1996), pp. 179–203. • **32**. *Conquest of Lisbon*, pp. 120–3. • **33**. *Ibid.*, pp. 152–5. • **34**. Phillips, *Second Crusade*, pp. 99–103. • **35**. E. A. R. Brown and M. W. Cothren, 'The Twelfth-Century Crusading Window of the Abbey of Saint-Denis', in *Journal of the Warburg and Courtauld Institutes* 49 (1986), pp. 1–40. • **36**. Odo of Deuil, *Journey of Louis VII*, pp. 16–19. • **37**. Harris, *Byzantium and the Crusades*, pp. 94–101; Phillips, *Second Crusade*, pp. 168–77. • **38**. Otto of Freising, *Deeds of Frederick Barbarossa*, pp. 80–1. • **39**. J. Roche, 'Conrad III and the Second Crusade: Retreat from Dorylaion?', in *Crusades* 5 (2006), pp. 85–94. • **40**. Phillips, *Second Crusade*, pp. 188–95. • **41**. John Kinnamos, *The Deeds of John and Manuel Comnenus by John Kinnamos*, tr. C. M. Brand (New York, 1976), p. 69; Odo of Deuil, *Journey of Louis VII*, pp. 56–61. • **42**. Odo of Deuil, *Journey of Louis VII*, pp. 114–21; William of Tyre, 2.175–7; Phillips, *Second Crusade*, pp. 198–202. • **43**. Phillips, *Second Crusade*, pp. 207–9. • **44**. Michael the Syrian, *Chronique de Michel* *le Syrien, patriarche jacobite d'Antioche (1166–1199)*, ed. and tr. J.-B. Chabot, 4 vols. (Paris, 1899–1910), 3.272. • **45**. William of Tyre, 2.193–5. • **46**. John of Salisbury, *Historia Pontificalis*, ed. and tr. M. Chibnall (London, 1956), p. 52. • **47**. Phillips, *Second Crusade*, pp. 210–12. • **48**. M. Hoch, 'The Choice of Damascus as the Objective of the Second Crusade: A Re-evaluation', in *Autour de la Première Croisade*, ed. M. Balard, *Byzantina Sorboniensia* 14 (Paris, 1996), pp. 359–69; Phillips, *Second Crusade*, pp. 215–18. • **49**. Phillips, *Second Crusade*, pp. 218–23. • **50**. Sibt Ibn al-Jawzi, 'Mirror of the Times', in *Arab Historians of the Crusades*, tr. F. Gabrieli (Berkeley, CA, 1969), p. 62; see also Ibn al-Qalanisi, *Damascus Chronicles of the Crusades*, p. 284; Phillips, *Second Crusade*, pp. 222–7. • **51**. Phillips, *Second Crusade*, pp. 269–71; John of Salisbury, *Historia Pontificalis*, pp. 11–12. • **52**. R. Hiestand, 'The Papacy and the Second Crusade', in *The Second Crusade: Scope and Consequences*, pp. 32–53. • **53**. William of Tyre, 2.196. • **54**. Phillips, *Defenders*, pp. 100–18; G. Constable, 'The Crusading Project of 1150', in *Montjoie: Studies in Crusade History in Honour of Hans Eberhard Mayer*, eds. B. Z. Kedar, J. S. C. Riley-Smith and R. Hiestand (Aldershot, 1997), pp. 67–75; T. Reuter, 'The non-crusade of 1149–1150', in *The Second Crusade: Scope and Consequences*, pp. 150–63. • **55**. Phillips, *Second Crusade*, pp. 239–41. • **56**. Helmold of Bosau, *The Chronicle of the Slavs*, tr. F. J. Tschan (New York, 1935), pp. 180–1. • **57**. Phillips, *Second Crusade*, pp. 241–3. • **58**. *Ibid.*, pp. 253–9. For a contemporary source see the 'Poem of Almeria', in *The World of El Cid*, trs. S. Barton and R. A. Fletcher (Manchester, 2000), pp. 250–63. • **59**. *Ibid.*, p. 251. • **60**. N. Jaspert, 'Capta est Dertosa: clavis Christianorum. Tortosa and the Crusades', *The Second Crusade: Scope and Consequences*, pp. 90–110. • **61**. For the contemporary writings of the Genoese consul Caffaro see J. B. Williams, 'The Making of a Crusade: The Genoese anti-Muslim Attacks in Spain, 1146–1148', in *Journal of Medieval History* 23 (1997), pp. 29–53, Caffaro's text at pp. 48–53, charter cited at pp. 38–9. • **62**. C. Di Fabio, *La cattedrale di Genova nel medioevo, secoli vi–xiv* (Genoa, 1998), pp. 88–91.

5 Saladin, the Leper King and the Fall of Jerusalem in 1187

1. Folda, *Art of the Crusaders in the Holy Land*, pp. 175–245. • **2**. Mayer, 'Queen Melisende', pp. 117–25; Hodgson, *Women, Crusading and the Holy Land*, pp. 183–5; William of Tyre, 2.204–7. • **3**. *Ibid.*, 2.196–8; Ibn al-Qalanisi, *Damascus Chronicles of the Crusades*, pp. 291–2. • **4**. N. Elisséeff, 'Les monuments de Nur ad-Din: inventaire, notes archéologiques et bibliographiques', in *Bulletin des Études Orientales* 12 (1949–51), pp. 5–43. • **5**. William of Tyre, 2.225. • **6**. Y. Tabbaa, 'Propagation of Jihad under Nur al-Din (1146–1174)', in *The Meeting* *of Two Worlds: Cultural Exchange between East and West during the Period of the Crusades*, ed. V. P. Goss (Kalamazoo, MI, 1986), pp. 223–40; H. Dajani-Shakeel, '*Al-Quds*: Jerusalem in the Consciousness of the Counter-Crusader', *idem*, pp. 201–22; Hillenbrand, *Crusades: Islamic Perspectives*, pp. 150–67; D. Talmon-Heller, *Islamic Piety in Medieval Syria: Mosques, Cemeteries and Sermons under the Zangids and Ayyubids (1146–1260)* (Leiden, 2007); S. A. Mourad and J. E. Lindsay, 'Rescuing Syria from the Infidels: The Contribution of Ibn Asakir of Damascus to the Jihad Campaign of Sultan Nur ad-Din', in *Crusades* 6 (2007), pp. 37–56; N. Elisséeff, 'The Reaction of Syrian Muslims after the Foundation of the First Latin Kingdom of Jerusalem', in *Crusaders and Muslims in Twelfth-Century Syria*, ed. M. Shatzmiller (Leiden, 1993), pp. 162–72. • **7**. Ibn Jubayr, *Travels*, p. 262. • **8**. Cited in Hillenbrand, *Crusades: Islamic Perspectives*, p. 161. • **9**. William of Tyre, 2.273–5, 288–90; Phillips, *Defenders*, pp. 132–4, 142. • **10**. William of Tyre, 2.212–14, 224; Hodgson, *Women, Crusading and the Holy Land*, pp. 221–4. • **11**. B. Hamilton, 'The Elephant of Christ: Reynald of Châtillon', in D. Baker, ed., *Studies in Church History* 15 (Oxford, 1978), pp. 97–108; J. Richard, 'Aux origines d'un grand lignage: des Paladii Reynald de Châtillon', in *Media in Francia: Recueil de mélanges offerts à Karl F. Werner* (Paris, 1989), pp. 409–18. • **12**. William of Tyre, 2.235–6. • **13**. For a fine analysis of William's writings and career see P. W. Edbury and J. G. Rowe, *William of Tyre: Historian of the Latin East* (Cambridge, 1988). • **14**. William of Tyre, 2.300. • **15**. *Ibid.*, 2.313. • **16**. Louis VII, 'Epistolae', in *Recueil des historiens des Gaules et de la France*, ed. M. Bouquet et al., 24 vols. (Paris, 1737–1904), 16.28. • **17**. By far the most comprehensive biography of Saladin is M. C. Lyons and D. E. P. Jackson, *Saladin: The Politics of the Holy War* (Cambridge, 1982); see pp. 1–29 for his early years. Note also D. S. Richards, 'The Early Life of Saladin', in *Islamic Quarterly* 17 (1973), pp. 140–59. See also H. Möhring, *Saladin: The Sultan and His Times*, tr. D. S. Bachrach (Baltimore, MD, 2008); Hillenbrand, *Crusades: Islamic Perspectives*, *passim*. For a more hostile view of his early career, see A. Ehrenkreutz, *Saladin* (Albany, NY, 1972). • **18**. Imad ad-Din, tr. Richards, 'Early Life', p. 146. On this author, see also D. S. Richards, 'Imad ad-Din al-Isfahani: Administrator, Litterateur and Historian', in *Crusaders and Muslims in Twelfth-Century Syria*, ed. M. Shatzmiller (Leiden, 1993), pp. 133–46. • **19**. Ibn Abi Tayy, tr. Richards, 'Early Life', p. 147. • **20**. Y. Lev, *Saladin in Egypt* (Leiden, 1999). • **21**. *Ibid.*, pp. 81–4. • **22**. Beha ad-Din, *The Rare and Excellent History of Saladin*, tr. D. S. Richards (Aldershot, 2001), pp. 47–9; Ibn al-Athir, *The Chronicle of Ibn al-Athir for the Crusading Period from al-Kamil fi'l-ta'rikh, Part 2: The Years 541–589/1146–1193: The Age of Nur al-Din and Saladin*, tr. D. S. Richards (Aldershot, 2007), pp. 198–200. • **23**. William of Tyre, 2.360. • **24**. Phillips, *Defenders of the Holy Land*, pp. 168–208. • **25**. William of Tyre, 2.377–83. • **26**. John Kinnamos, *Deeds of John and Manuel Comnenus*, p. 209. • **27**. Folda, *Art of the Crusaders in the Holy Land*, pp. 347–78; Phillips, *Defenders of the Holy*

Land, pp. 156–7; A. Jotischky, 'Manuel Comnenus and the Reunion of the Churches: The Evidence of the Conciliar Mosaics in the Church of the Nativity in Bethlehem', in *Levant* 26 (1994), pp. 207–23. • **28**. William of Tyre, 2.394. • **29**. Imad ad-Din, translation from Hillenbrand, *Crusades: Islamic Perspectives*, p. 166. • **30**. P. D. Mitchell, 'An Evaluation of the Leprosy of King Baldwin IV of Jerusalem in the Context of the Medieval World', in B. Hamilton, *The Leper King and his Heirs: Baldwin IV and the Crusader Kingdom of Jerusalem* (Cambridge, 2000), pp. 245–58. • **31**. William of Tyre, 2.398, 417. • **32**. Hamilton, *Leper King*, pp. 84–94. • **33**. William of Tyre, 2.402–4. • **34**. Ibn Jubayr, *Travels*, p. 324. • **35**. P. W. Edbury, 'Propaganda and Faction in the Kingdom of Jerusalem: The Background to Hattin', in *Crusaders and Muslims in Twelfth Century Syria*, ed. M. Shatzmiller (Leiden, 1993), pp. 173–89. • **36**. William of Tyre, 2.460. • **37**. Hamilton, *Leper King*, pp. 150–8. • **38**. Lyons and Jackson, *Saladin*, pp. 109–10. • **39**. *Anonymi auctoris chronicon ad A.C. 1234 pertinens*, tr. A. Abouna (Louvain, 1974), p. 141. • **40**. Hamilton, *Leper King*, pp. 135–6; Lyons and Jackson, *Saladin*, pp. 123–4. • **41**. P. D. Mitchell, *Medicine in the Crusades: Warfare, Wounds and the Medieval Surgeon* (Cambridge, 2004), pp. 61–75. • **42**. Letter of Louis VII, translation from Hamilton, *Leper King*, p. 140. • **43**. Hamilton, *Leper King*, pp. 150–8. • **44**. 'The Old French Continuation of William of Tyre', in *The Conquest of Jerusalem and the Third Crusade*, tr. P. W. Edbury (Aldershot, 1996), pp. 43–4; B. Z. Kedar, 'The Patriarch Heraclius', in *Outremer: Studies in the History of the Crusading Kingdom of Jerusalem*, eds. B. Z. Kedar, H. E. Mayer and R. C. Smail (Jerusalem, 1982), pp. 177–204. • **45**. William of Tyre, 2.461. • **46**. Lilie, *Byzantium and the Crusader States*, pp. 220–30. • **47**. Ibn Jubayr, *Travels*, pp. 51–3; Ibn al-Athir, *Chronicle, Part 2*, pp. 289–90; Hamilton, *Leper King*, pp. 178–85; A. Mallett, 'A Trip Down the Red Sea with Reynald of Châtillon', *Journal of the Royal Asiatic Society* 18 (2008), pp. 141–53. • **48**. Ibn Jubayr, *Travels*, p. 52. • **49**. Hamilton, 'Elephant of Christ', p. 97. • **50**. Letter of Imad ad-Din, in Abu Shama, 'Le livre des deux jardins', *Recueil des historiens des croisades: Historiens orientaux*, 5 vols. (Paris, 1872–1906), 4.231–5. • **51**. B. Z. Kedar, 'The General Tax of 1183 in the Crusader Kingdom of Jerusalem', *English Historical Review* 89 (1974), pp. 339–45; D. M. Metcalf, *Coinage of the Crusades and the Latin East* (London, 1995), pp. 44, 46–7. • **52**. Hamilton, *Leper King*, pp. 193–6. • **53**. William of Tyre, 2.498–501. • **54**. 'Eracles Continuation of William of Tyre', translation, *ibid.*, p. 205; see also 'Old French Continuation of William of Tyre', p. 14. • **55**. Alexander III, 'Epistolae et privilegia', *Patrologia Latina*, ed. J. P. Migne, vol. 200, cols. 1294–6. • **56**. Phillips, *Defenders*, pp. 253–63; C. J. Tyerman, *England and the Crusades, 1095–1588* (Chicago, 1988), pp. 50–4. • **57**. *Records of the Templars in England in the Twelfth Century. The Inquest of 1185*, ed. B. A. Lees (London, 1935), p. 163. • **58**. Imad ad-Din, *Conquête de la Syrie et de la Palestine par Saladin*, tr. H. Massé (Paris, 1972), pp. 18–19. • **59**. 'Lyon Eracles', translated in *The Conquest of Jerusalem*, pp. 154–5. • **60**. Roger of Wendover, *The Flowers of History*, tr. J. A. Giles, 2 vols. (London, 1849), 2.59. • **61**. 'Old French Continuation of William of Tyre', p. 46. • **62**. Ibn al-Athir, *Chronicle, Part 2*, pp. 315–16. • **63**. *Ibid.*, p. 316. • **64**. For an account of the battle see *The Conquest of Jerusalem*, pp. 156–7; M. Barber, *The New Knighthood: A History of the Order of the Temple* (Cambridge, 1994), pp. 111–13. • **65**. Ibn al-Athir, *Chronicle, Part 2*, p. 320. • **66**. The best summary and analysis of the battle is B. Z. Kedar, 'The Battle of Hattin Revisited', in *The Horns of Hattin*, ed. B. Z. Kedar (Jerusalem, 1992), pp. 190–207. See also Beha ad-Din, *Rare and Excellent History*, pp. 72–5; the documents collected in *The Conquest of Jerusalem and the Third Crusade*, tr. P. W. Edbury (Aldershot, 1996), pp. 158–63. • **67**. Ibn al-Athir, *Chronicle, Part 2*, p. 321. • **68**. 'Old French Continuation of William of Tyre', pp. 38–9. • **69**. C. P. Melville and M. C. Lyons, 'Saladin's Hattin Letter', in *The Horns of Hattin*, ed. B. Z. Kedar, p. 211. • **70**. Beha ad-Din, *Rare and Excellent History*, p. 73. • **71**. Imad ad-Din, *Conquête*, pp. 25–6. • **72**. R. Lewis of the Hebrew University of Jerusalem is conducting a detailed topographical study of the Battle of Hattin. • **73**. Ibn al-Athir, *Chronicle, Part 2*, p. 322. • **74**. *Ibid.*, p. 323. • **75**. Imad ad-Din, *Conquête*, pp. 29–30. • **76**. Beha ad-Din, *Rare and Excellent History*, pp. 74–5; 'Old French Continuation of William of Tyre', pp. 47–8. • **77**. Peter of Blois, 'Passio Reginaldi', in *Tractatus Duo*, ed. R. B. C. Huygens, CCCM 194 (Turnhout, 2002). • **78**. Z. Gal, 'Saladin's Dome of Victory at the Horns of Hattin', in *The Horns of Hattin*, ed. B. Z. Kedar, pp. 213–15. • **79**. Imad ad-Din, *Arab Historians of the Crusades*, p. 147. • **80**. N. Jaspert, 'Zwei unbekannte Hilfsersuchen des Patriarchen Eraclius vor dem Fall Jerusalems (1187)', *Deutsches Archiv* 60 (2005), pp. 515–16. • **81**. Ibn al-Athir, *Chronicle, Part 2*, p. 332. • **82**. There is some disagreement in the sources on the precise sums agreed, but the outline scale is consistent. See Ibn al-Athir, *Chronicle, Part 2*, p. 333; Beha ad-Din, *Rare and Excellent History*, p. 228; 'Old French Continuation of William of Tyre', pp. 59–63. • **83**. Ibn al-Athir, *Chronicle, Part 2*, p. 334. • **84**. Al-Maqrizi, *A History of the Ayyubid Sultans of Egypt*, tr. R. J. C. Broadhurst (Boston, MA, 1980), pp. 89–90. • **85**. Talmon-Heller, *Islamic Piety in Medieval Syria*, pp. 101–2; Hillenbrand, *Crusades: Islamic Perspectives*, pp. 189–91. • **86**. *The Minbar of Saladin*, ed. L. Singer (London, 2008). • **87**. 'Old French Continuation of William of Tyre', p. 64. • **88**. *Ibid.*, pp. 77–8.

6 'Nowhere in the world would ever two such princes be found': Richard the Lionheart, Saladin and the Third Crusade

1. Beha ad-Din, *Rare and Excellent History of Saladin*, p. 153. • **2**. *Itinerarium peregrinorum et gesta regis Ricardi*, tr. H. J. Nicholson (Aldershot, 1997), p. 378.

• **3.** *Ibid.*, p. 367. • **4.** Beha ad-Din, *Rare and Excellent History of Saladin*, p. 216. • **5.** Gregory VIII, *Audita tremendi*, in Riley-Smith, *Crusades: Idea and Reality*, pp. 64–5. • **6.** Bertrand de Born, 'Nostre seigner somonis el mezeis', in *The Poems of the Troubadour Bertran de Born*, eds. and trs. W. D. Paden Jr., T. Sankovitch and P. H. Stäblein (Berkeley, CA, 1986), no. 36, pp. 384–7. • **7.** J. B. Gillingham, *Richard I* (London, 1999), pp. 140–1, 254–68. This is an excellent – and generally very favourable – biography of the king. Similarly positive in tone, and with more of an emphasis on the chivalric context, is J. Flori, *Richard the Lionheart: King and Knight*, tr. J. Birell (Edinburgh, 2006). More critical voices are those of R. V. Turner and R. R. Heiser, *The Reign of Richard the Lionheart: Ruler of the Angevin Empire, 1189–1199* (Harlow, 2000), although this, as the subtitle suggests, is not especially concerned with events on the crusade. • **8.** Chrétien de Troyes, *Arthurian Romances*, tr. W. W. Kibler (London, 1991). • **9.** J. B. Gillingham, 'Richard I and the Science of War', in *Richard Coeur de Lion: Kingship, Chivalry and War in the Twelfth Century* (London, 1984), pp. 211–26. • **10.** Richard's preparations are expertly covered in C. J. Tyerman, *England and the Crusades, 1095–1588* (Chicago, 1988), pp. 59–84. • **11.** D. Jacoby, 'Conrad of Montferrat and the Kingdom of Jerusalem, 1187–92', in *Atti del Congresso internazionale 'Dai feudi monferrine e dal Piemonte ai nuovi mondi oltre gli Oceani'*, Alessandria, 2–6 aprile 1990, Biblioteca della Società di storia, arte e archeologia per le province di Alessandria e Asti, 27 (Alessandria, 1993), pp. 187–238. • **12.** *Itinerarium peregrinorum*, p. 42. • **13.** *Ibid.*, p. 73. • **14.** Lyons and Jackson, *Saladin*, pp. 298–330; for the details of the Muslim camp, see p. 329; Gillingham, *Richard I*, pp. 155–71. • **15.** Ibn Jubayr, *Travels*, pp. 54–5; Lyons and Jackson, *Saladin*, pp. 97–253. • **16.** 'The Old French Continuation of William of Tyre', p. 89. • **17.** Beha ad-Din, *Rare and Excellent History of Saladin*, p. 106. • **18.** Al-Fadil quoted in Lyons and Jackson, *Saladin*, p. 313. • **19.** Beha ad-Din, *Rare and Excellent History of Saladin*, pp. 100–1. • **20.** *Itinerarium peregrinorum*, p. 122. • **21.** Abu Shama, 'Le livre des deux Jardins', *Recueil des historiens des croisades: Historiens orientaux*, 5 vols. (Paris, 1872–1906), vol. 4, p. 436. • **22.** Beha ad-Din, *Rare and Excellent History of Saladin*, pp. 144–5. • **23.** *Ibid.*, pp. 147–8. • **24.** Roger of Howden, *Gesta*, tr. Gillingham, *Richard I*, p. 131. • **25.** Beha ad-Din, *Rare and Excellent History of Saladin*, p. 146. • **26.** Flori, *Richard the Lionheart*, pp. 401–6 discusses Richard and the Arthur legend. • **27.** Roger of Howden, *Gesta*, pp. 146–7. • **28.** Letter of Richard to the justiciar of England, August 1191, *The Conquest of Jerusalem*, p. 179. • **29.** 'Eracles Continuation of William of Tyre', *The Conquest of Jerusalem*, p. 178. • **30.** Ambroise, *The History of the Holy War*, p. 95. • **31.** Richard of Devizes, *The Chronicle of Richard of Devizes of the Time of King Richard the First*, ed. and tr. J. T. Appleby (London, 1963), p. 39. • **32.** Beha ad-Din, *Rare and Excellent History of Saladin*, p. 150. • **33.** Ambroise, *The History of the Holy War*, pp. 95–102. • **34.** *Ibid.*, p. 102. • **35.** Beha ad-Din,

Rare and Excellent History of Saladin, p. 161; *Itinerarium peregrinorum*, pp. 218–20.
• **36**. *Ibid.*, p. 161. • **37**. Richard of Devizes, *Chronicle of Richard of Devizes*,
pp. 46–7. • **38**. Rigord, *Histoire de Philippe Auguste*, eds. and trs. E. Carpentier,
G. Pon and Y. Chauvin (Paris, 2006), pp. 303–7; J. Bradbury, *Philip Augustus:
King of France 1180–1223* (London, 1998), pp. 76–97. • **39**. *Itinerarium peregrinorum*, p. 223. • **40**. See, for example, the comments by Tariq Ali in *Richard
the Lionheart and Saladin: Holy Warriors*, BBC2, 26 March 2005. • **41**. Beha
ad-Din, *Rare and Excellent History of Saladin*, pp. 164–5. • **42**. Gillingham,
Richard I, pp. 167–71. See also Richard's own letter, *The Conquest of Jerusalem*,
pp. 179–81. This issue is discussed by Flori, *Richard the Lionheart*, pp.
360–1. • **43**. Beha ad-Din, *Rare and Excellent History of Saladin*, pp. 168–70.
• **44**. Ambroise, *The History of the Holy War*, p. 110. • **45**. *Ibid.* • **46**. *Ibid.*,
p. 117; see also Beha ad-Din, *Rare and Excellent History of Saladin*, p. 170.
• **47**. *Ibid.*, p. 175. • **48**. Ambroise, *The History of the Holy War*, p. 120; Beha
ad-Din, *Rare and Excellent History of Saladin*, p. 223. • **49**. Ambroise, *The
History of the Holy War*, p. 120. • **50**. *Ibid.*, p. 127. • **51**. Beha ad-Din, *Rare and
Excellent History of Saladin*, p. 193. • **52**. Ambroise, *The History of the Holy
War*, p. 135. • **53**. P. W. Edbury, *The Kingdom of Cyprus and the Crusades,
1191–1374* (Cambridge, 1991), pp. 27–9. • **54**. Ambroise, *The History of the Holy
War*, pp. 153–4. • **55**. *Ibid.*, p. 162. • **56**. Beha ad-Din, *Rare and Excellent History
of Saladin*, p. 210. • **57**. Ambroise, *The History of the Holy War*, p. 172. • **58**.
Beha ad-Din, *Rare and Excellent History of Saladin*, pp. 222–3. • **59**. *Itinerarium
peregrinorum*, p. 355. • **60**. *Ibid.*, p. 367. • **61**. Beha ad-Din, *Rare and Excellent
History of Saladin*, pp. 226–34. • **62**. Ambroise, *The History of the Holy War*,
pp. 187–91. • **63**. *Ibid.*, p. 193. • **64**. Gillingham, *Richard I*, pp. 222–53. • **65**.
Ibn al-Athir, *The Chronicle of Ibn al-Athir, Part 2*, p. 387. • **66**. *Itinerarium
peregrinorum*, p. 382. • **67**. Abd al-Latif, cited in Ibn Abi Usay'bia, translated
in B. Lewis, *Islam: From the Prophet Muhammad to the Capture of Constantinople*
(New York, 1974), pp. 66–7.

7 'An example of affliction and the works of hell':
The Fourth Crusade and the Sack of Constantinople, 1204

1. Innocent III, 'Epistolae et privilegia', Innocent to the patriarch of Antioch,
June 1211, in *Patrologia Latina*, ed. J. P. Migne, vol. 216, cols. 435–6. • **2**. C.
Maier, 'Mass, the Eucharist and the Cross: Innocent III and the Relocation
of the Crusade', in *Pope Innocent III and His World*, ed. J. C. Moore (Aldershot,
1999), pp. 351–60. • **3**. E. N. Johnson, 'The Crusades of Frederick Barbarossa
and Henry VI', in *A History of the Crusades*, ed. K. M. Setton, 6 vols. (Wisconsin,
1969–89), 2.87–122. • **4**. E. Kennan, 'Innocent III and the First Political
Crusade', in *Traditio* 27 (1971), pp. 231–49; N. Housley, 'Crusades against

Christians: Their Origins and Early Development, *c*.1000–1216', in *Crusade and Settlement*, ed. P. W. Edbury (Cardiff, 1985), pp. 17–36. See also *The Deeds of Pope Innocent III by an Anonymous Author*, ed. and tr. J. M. Powell (Washington, DC, 2004), pp. 19–49. • **5**. Innocent III, *Register*, ed. O. Hageneder et al. (Vienna, 1964), 2.413–14. • **6**. *Deeds of Pope Innocent III*, p. 46, translating 'remissione' as 'indulgence' rather than Powell's 'blessing'. • **7**. For overviews of the Fourth Crusade see J. P. Phillips, *The Fourth Crusade and the Sack of Constantinople* (London, 2004); D. E. Queller and T. F. Madden, *The Fourth Crusade: The Conquest of Constantinople*, second edition (Philadelphia, PA, 1997); M. Angold, *The Fourth Crusade: Event and Context* (Harlow, 2003). • **8**. Innocent III, *Sources for the History of the Fourth Crusade*, tr. A. Andrea (Leiden, 2000), pp. 10–11. • **9**. Phillips, *Fourth Crusade*, pp. 39–47. • **10**. Geoffrey of Villehardouin (henceforth GV), 'The Conquest of Constantinople', in *Joinville and Villehardouin: Chronicles of the Crusades*, tr. C. Smith (London, 2008). • **11**. J. Longnon, *Les Compagnons de Villehardouin: Recherches sur les croisés de la quatrième croisade* (Geneva, 1978). • **12**. Madden, *Enrico Dandolo*, pp. 63–8, 90–116. • **13**. Gunther of Pairis, *The Capture of Constantinople*, ed. and tr. A. J. Andrea (Philadelphia, PA, 1997), p. 97. • **14**. See the comments on this figure by Smith in GV, 'Conquest', pp. 350–1, n. 14. • **15**. GV, 'Conquest', p. 9. • **16**. *Ibid*., p. 10. • **17**. D. E. Queller and T. F. Madden, 'Some Further Arguments in Defence of the Venetians on the Fourth Crusade', in *Byzantion* 62 (1992), pp. 433–73. • **18**. GV, 'Conquest', pp. 9–11. • **19**. Phillips, *Fourth Crusade*, p. 66. • **20**. *Ibid*., pp. 67–72. • **21**. GV, 'Conquest', p. 12. • **22**. H. de Jubainville, *Histoire des ducs et des comtes de Champagne*, 8 vols. (Paris, 1859–69), 4.96. • **23**. Phillips, *Fourth Crusade*, pp. 81–7. • **24**. *Ibid*., pp. 90–5. • **25**. Robert of Clari, *The Conquest of Constantinople*, tr. E. H. McNeal (New York, 1936), p. 40. • **26**. Madden, *Enrico Dandolo*, p. 16. • **27**. GV, 'Conquest', p. 20. • **28**. Robert of Clari, *Constantinople*, p. 42. • **29**. GV, 'Conquest', p. 24. • **30**. Peter of les Vaux-de-Cernay (henceforth PVC), *The History of the Albigensian Crusade*, trs. W. A. and M. D. Sibly (Woodbridge, 1998), p. 58. • **31**. Innocent III, *Sources*, pp. 41–5. • **32**. Phillips, *Fourth Crusade*, pp. 120–3. • **33**. GV, 'Conquest', p. 26. • **34**. Phillips, *Fourth Crusade*, pp. 130–4. • **35**. GV, 'Conquest', p. 27; Robert of Clari, *Constantinople*, p. 66. • **36**. Innocent III, *Sources*, p. 48. • **37**. GV, 'Conquest', p. 34. • **38**. *Ibid*., p. 38. • **39**. Phillips, *Fourth Crusade*, pp. 165–8. • **40**. GV, 'Conquest', pp. 42–3. • **41**. *Ibid*., p. 46. • **42**. Letter of Hugh of Saint-Pol, *Sources*, p. 197. • **43**. GV, 'Conquest', p. 48. • **44**. Niketas Choniates, *O City of Byzantium: Annals of Niketas Choniates*, tr. H. J. Magoulias (Detroit, MI, 1984), p. 299. • **45**. GV, 'Conquest', p. 50. • **46**. Letter of Hugh of Saint-Pol, *Sources*, pp. 187–9; Phillips, *Fourth Crusade*, pp. 193–6. • **47**. *Ibid*., p. 199. • **48**. *Ibid*., pp. 199–200. • **49**. Letter of Alexius IV to Innocent III, *Sources*, p. 79. • **50**. Niketas Choniates, *Annals*, p. 302. • **51**. GV, 'Conquest', p. 52. • **52**. Phillips, *Fourth Crusade*, pp. 197–205. • **53**. *Ibid*., pp. 206–10. • **54**. GV, 'Conquest', p. 57.

• **55**. Robert of Clari, *Constantinople*, p. 84. • **56**. GV, 'Conquest', p. 58. • **57**. Niketas Choniates, *Annals*, p. 307. • **58**. Robert of Clari, *Constantinople*, p. 89. • **59**. Niketas Choniates, *Annals*, p. 312. • **60**. Phillips, *Fourth Crusade*, pp. 233–6. • **61**. Robert of Clari, *Constantinople*, pp. 91–2. • **62**. Innocent III, *Sources*, pp. 140–4; Phillips, *Fourth Crusade*, pp. 237–40. • **63**. *Ibid.*, pp. 240–7. • **64**. GV, 'Conquest', p. 64. • **65**. Robert of Clari, *Constantinople*, p. 95. • **66**. *Ibid.*, pp. 96–8. • **67**. GV, 'Conquest', pp. 66–7. • **68**. Letter of Baldwin of Flanders, *Sources*, p. 107. • **69**. Gunther of Pairis, *The Capture of Constantinople*, p. 111. • **70**. *Ibid.*, pp. 122–8; 'The Anonymous of Soissons', *Sources*, pp. 230–8; 'The Deeds of the Bishops of Halberstadt', *Sources*, pp. 260–3. • **71**. Nicholas Mesarites, translated in C. M. Brand, *Byzantium Confronts the West, 1180–1204* (Cambridge, MA, 1968), p. 269. • **72**. Niketas Choniates, *Annals*, p. 317. • **73**. Phillips, *Fourth Crusade*, pp. xi–xii, 270–5. • **74**. Innocent III, *Sources*, p. 147. • **75**. Phillips, *Fourth Crusade*, pp. 281–91; P. Lock, *The Franks in the Aegean, 1204–1500* (Harlow, 1995); N. Chrissis, *Crusading in Romania: A Study of Byzantine-Western Relations and Attitudes*, unpublished PhD thesis, Royal Holloway, University of London, 2007. • **76**. Phillips, *Fourth Crusade*, pp. 298–303. • **77**. Innocent III, *Sources*, p. 114. • **78**. *Ibid.*, p. 135. • **79**. *Ibid.*, p. 166. • **80**. *Ibid.*, p. 173. • **81**. *Ibid.*, p. 176.

8 From 'little foxes in the vines' and the Children's Crusade to the Greatest Church Council of the Age

1. Several excellent books on this subject exist: R. I. Moore, *The Birth of Popular Heresy* (London, 1975); M. Lambert, *Medieval Heresy*, third edition (Oxford, 2002). On the Cathars and the Albigensian Crusade more broadly, see M. Barber, *The Cathars: Dualist Heretics in Languedoc in the High Middle Ages* (Harlow, 2000); M. G. Pegg, *A Most Holy War: The Albigensian Crusade and the Battle for Christendom* (Oxford, 2008); M. Costen, *The Cathars and the Albigensian Crusade* (Manchester, 1997); L. W. Marvin, *The Occitan War: A Military and Political History of the Albigensian Crusade, 1209–1218* (Cambridge, 2008); J. Sumption, *The Albigensian Crusade* (London, 1978); A. P. Roach, *The Devil's World: Heresy and Society 1100–1300* (Harlow, 2005). • **2**. R. I. Moore, *The Formation of a Persecuting Society*, second edition (Oxford, 2007). • **3**. William of Tudela in *The Song of the Cathar Wars: A History of the Albigensian Crusade*, tr. J. Shirley (Aldershot, 1996), p. 13. • **4**. Barber, *Cathars*, pp. 71–106. • **5**. Decrees of the Third Lateran Council, 1179, in *Decrees of the Ecumenical Councils*, ed. N. Tanner, 2 vols. (Washington, DC, 1990), 1.224–5. • **6**. Henry of Marcy, abbot of Clairvaux, mission to Languedoc 1178, translated in Moore, *The Birth of Popular Heresy*, pp. 116–22. • **7**. Pegg, *Most Holy War*, pp. 59–60. • **8**. William of Tudela, *Song*, p. 12. • **9**. There is an account of the murder in PVC, pp. 31–4. • **10**. William of Tudela, *Song*, p. 14. • **11**. Innocent III to

French provinces, in PVC, pp. 303–4. • **12**. *Ibid.*, p. 45. • **13**. *Ibid.*, p. 24. • **14**. Innocent III to Raymond VI of Toulouse, May 1207, in PVC, pp. 304–5. • **15**. *Ibid.*, pp. 633–44. • **16**. William of Tudela, *Song*, p. 123. • **17**. C. F. O'Meara, *The Iconography of the Façade of Saint-Gilles-du-Gard* (New York, 1977). • **18**. William of Tudela, *Song*, pp. 15–16; PVC, pp. 42–5. • **19**. For accounts of the siege see SCW, pp. 19–23; PVC, pp. 47–51; Marvin, *Occitan War*, pp. 37–45. • **20**. William of Tudela, *Song*, p. 20. • **21**. For a discussion of this evidence see PVC, Appendix B, pp. 289–93. It should be noted that the source for this comment was not present at the siege. Even if, however, it is not accurate, the sentiment conveyed shows the Church attitude towards the Cathars. • **22**. PVC, pp. 56–7; Marvin, *Occitan War*, pp. 45–62. • **23**. William of Tudela, *Song*, p. 74. • **24**. PVC, pp. 78–9. • **25**. William of Tudela, *Song*, p. 116. • **26**. *Ibid.*, p. 172. • **27**. *Ibid.*, p. 176. • **28**. R. Kay, *The Council of Bourges, 1225: A Documentary History* (Aldershot, 2002). • **29**. Barber, *Cathars*, pp. 139–44. • **30**. B. Hamilton, *The Medieval Inquisition* (London, 1981); J. B. Given, *Inquisition and Medieval Society: Power, Discipline and Resistance in Languedoc* (Ithaca, NY, 1997); W. L. Wakefield, *Heresy, Crusade and Inquisition in Southern France, 1100–1250* (London, 1974); Barber, *Cathars*, pp. 144–52, 169–75; Costen, *Cathars and the Albigensian Crusade*, pp. 161–74. • **31**. William of Puylaurens, *Chronicle: The Albigensian Crusade and its Aftermath*, tr. W. A. and M. D. Sibly (Woodbridge, 2003), pp. 82–6. • **32**. The Manual for Inquisitors is translated in Wakefield, *Heresy, Crusade and Inquisition in Southern France*, pp. 250–8. See also William of Puylaurens, *Chronicle*, pp. 91–8. • **33**. Good accounts of the siege are in Costen, *Cathars and the Albigensian Crusade*, pp. 159–60; Sumption, *Albigensian Crusade*, pp. 236–41. • **34**. William of Puylaurens, *Chronicle*, p. 108. • **35**. G. Dickson, *The Children's Crusade: Medieval History, Modern Mythistory* (Basingstoke, 2007). • **36**. *Ibid.*, pp. 131–57. • **37**. *Ibid.*, p. 126. • **38**. Translation in *ibid.*, p. 55. • **39**. 'Laon Anonymous', translation in *ibid.*, p. 76. • **40**. Innocent III, *Quia maior*, translated in Riley-Smith, *Crusades: Idea and Reality*, pp. 118–24. • **41**. O'Callaghan, *Reconquest and Crusade in Medieval Spain*, pp. 50–77; D. J. Smith, *Innocent III and the Crown of Aragon: The Limits of Papal Authority* (Aldershot, 2004). • **42**. Kennedy, *Muslim Spain and Portugal*, pp. 200–36. • **43**. O'Callaghan, *Reconquest and Crusade in Medieval Spain*, pp. 61, 63, 142, 179–83; Kennedy, *Muslim Spain and Portugal*, pp. 244–7. • **44**. Kennedy, *Muslim Spain and Portugal*, pp. 249–56. • **45**. O'Callaghan, *Reconquest and Crusade in Medieval Spain*, pp. 72–3, 142–3. • **46**. The letter is translated in *The Crusades: A Reader*, eds. S. J. Allen and E. Amt (Peterborough, Ontario, 2003), pp. 309–13. • **47**. D. J. Smith, '"Soli Hispani?" Innocent III and Las Navas de Tolosa', in *Hispania Sacra* 51 (1999), pp. 487–513. • **48**. The best discussions of crusading in northern Europe are I. Fonnesberg-Schmidt, *The Popes and the Baltic Crusades, 1147–1254* (Leiden, 2007); Christiansen, *Northern Crusades*; *Jerusalem in the North: Denmark and the Baltic Crusades, 1100–1522*, eds. A. Bysted, C. S. Jensen and K. Villads Jensen

(Turnhout, 2009). • **49**. From Fonnesberg-Schmidt, *Baltic Crusades*, p. 93. • **50**. *Ibid.*, pp. 133–86. • **51**. Morton, *Teutonic Knights in the Holy Land*. • **52**. W. L. Urban, *The Baltic Crusade*, second edition (Chicago, IL, 1994). • **53**. Housley, 'Crusades against Christians', p. 30. • **54**. Translated in Riley-Smith, *Crusades: Idea and Reality*, pp. 118–24. See also P. J. Cole, *The Preaching of Crusades to the Holy Land, 1095–1270* (Cambridge, MA, 1991), pp. 104–9. • **55**. Moore, *Pope Innocent III*, pp. 228–52; S. Kuttner and A. Garcia y Garcia, 'A New Eyewitness Account of the Fourth Lateran Council', in *Traditio* 20 (1964), pp. 115–78; translated in C. Fasolt, in *Readings in Western Civilisation: Medieval Europe*, eds. J. Kishner and K. F. Morison (Chicago, IL, 1986), pp. 369–76. • **56**. This decree of the Fourth Lateran Council is translated in Riley-Smith, *Crusades: Idea and Reality*, pp. 124–9. The full set of these decrees are edited and translated in *Decrees of the Ecumenical Councils*, 1.227–71. • **57**. James of Vitry, see: Jacques de Vitry, *Lettres*, ed. R. B. C. Huygens, new edition (Turnhout, 2000), pp. 551–2. • **58**. Comment observed by Moore, *Pope Innocent III*, p. 289.

9 'Stupor mundi' – *The Wonder of the World: Frederick II, the Fifth Crusade and the Recovery of Jerusalem*

1. Sibt Ibn al-Jawzi, *Arab Historians of the Crusades*, p. 275. • **2**. D. Abulafia, *Frederick II: A Medieval Emperor* (London, 1988). • **3**. J. Johns, *Arabic Administration in Norman Sicily: The Royal Diwan* (Cambridge, 2002). • **4**. The best monograph on the Fifth Crusade is J. M. Powell, *Anatomy of a Crusade, 1213–1221* (Philadelphia, PA, 1986). • **5**. C. N. Johns, *Pilgrims' Castle (Atlit), David's Tower (Jerusalem) and Qal'at ar-Rabad (Ajlun)* (Aldershot, 1997). • **6**. Oliver of Paderborn, 'Capture of Damietta', in *Christian Society and the Crusades, 1198–1229*, tr. E. Peters (Philadelphia, PA, 1971), pp. 63–9. • **7**. Letter of Robert Aboland, in R. Röhricht, *Testimonia minora de Quinto bello sacro* (Geneva, 1882), p. 83. • **8**. James of Vitry, *Lettres*, p. 510. • **9**. For a striking analysis of this famous meeting and its consequences, see J. V. Tolan, *Saint Francis and the Sultan: The Curious History of a Christian-Muslim Encounter* (Oxford, 2009). • **10**. James of Vitry, *Lettres*, p. 576. • **11**. B. Hamilton, 'Continental Drift: Prester John's progress through the Indies', in *Prester John, the Mongols and the Ten Lost Tribes*, eds. C. F. Beckingham and B. Hamilton (Aldershot, 1996), pp. 237–69. • **12**. *Ibid.*, pp. 243–6. • **13**. D. M. Metcalf, *Coinage of the Crusades and the Latin East*, second edition (London, 1995), pp. 80–6. • **14**. Ibn al-Athir, *The Chronicle of Ibn al-Athir for the Crusading Period, Part 3: The Years 589–629/1193–1231: The Ayyubids after Saladin and the Mongol Menace*, tr. D. S. Richards (Aldershot, 2008), p. 179. • **15**. James of Vitry, *Lettres*, pp. 663–44. • **16**. D. O. Morgan, *The Mongols*, second edition (Oxford, 2007), pp. 60–2. • **17**. Oliver of Paderborn gives the dates of the Nile flood, 'Capture of

Damietta', p. 85. • **18**. Ibn al-Athir, *Chronicle, Part 3*, p. 180. • **19**. *Ibid*. • **20**. William the Clerk, *Le bezant de Dieu*, translated in P. Throop, *Criticism of the Crusade: A Study of Public Opinion and Crusade Propaganda* (Amsterdam, 1940), p. 32. • **21**. S. C. Aston, *Peirol, Troubadour of Auvergne* (Cambridge, 1953), p. 163. • **22**. J. H. Pryor, 'The Crusade of Emperor Frederick II, 1220–1229: The Implications of the Maritime Evidence', in *The American Neptune* 52 (1992), pp. 123–7. • **23**. On this issue, see T. C. Van Cleve, *The Emperor Frederick II of Hohenstaufen: Immutator Mundi* (Oxford, 1972), pp. 165–7. • **24**. N. E. Morton, *The Teutonic Knights in the Holy Land* (Woodbridge, 2009). • **25**. Roger of Wendover, *Flowers of History*, 2.499. • **26**. *Ibid*., 2.507. • **27**. *Ibid*., 2.493. • **28**. *Ibid*., 2.511. • **29**. Ibn Wasil, *Arab Historians of the Crusades*, pp. 268–9. • **30**. Pryor, 'Crusade of Emperor Frederick II', pp. 131–2. • **31**. Sibt Ibn al-Jawzi, *Arab Historians of the Crusades*, pp. 273–4. • **32**. Ibn Wasil, *Arab Historians of the Crusades*, p. 272. • **33**. Sibt Ibn al-Jawzi, *Arab Historians of the Crusades*, p. 275. • **34**. Abulafia, *Frederick II*, pp. 186–8. • **35**. Frederick II to Henry III of England, from Roger of Wendover, *Flowers of History* 2.522–4; translated in *Christian Society and the Crusades*, pp. 162–3. • **36**. Patriarch Gerold to the Christian faithful, from Matthew Paris, *Chronica Majora*, translated in *Christian Society and the Crusades*, pp. 165–70, here, p. 166. • **37**. Abulafia, *Frederick II*, pp. 191–201. • **38**. M. Lower, *The Barons' Crusade: A Call to Arms and its Consequences* (Philadelphia, PA, 2005) is by far the best study of this crusade. • **39**. N. Vincent, *The Holy Blood: King Henry III and the Westminster Blood Relic* (Cambridge, 2001). See also M. Reeve, 'The Painted Chamber at Westminster, Edward I and the Crusade', in *Viator* 37 (2006), pp. 189–221 • **40**. M. Barber, 'Western Attitudes to Frankish Greece in the Thirteenth Century', in *Latins and Greeks in the Eastern Mediterranean after 1204*, eds. B. Arbel, B. Hamilton and D. Jacoby (London, 1989), pp. 111–28. • **41**. Rothelin, *Crusader Syria in the Thirteenth Century*, tr. J. Shirley (Aldershot, 1999), p. 48. • **42**. Lower, *Barons' Crusade*, pp. 167–71. • **43**. Rothelin, *Crusader Syria in the Thirteenth Century*, p. 54. • **44**. *Ibid*., p. 57. • **45**. Lower, *Barons' Crusade*, pp. 175–7. • **46**. Rothelin, *Crusader Syria in the Thirteenth Century*, p. 54. • **47**. B. Weiler, 'Gregory IX, Frederick II and the Liberation of the Holy Land', in *Holy Land and Holy Lands*, ed. R. L. Swanson, Studies in Church History 36 (2000), pp. 192–206. • **48**. N. Barbour, 'Frederick II's Relations with the Muslims', in *Orientalia Hispanica: Sive studia F. M. Pareja octogenario dictata*, ed. J. M. Barral, 2 vols. (Leiden, 1974), 1.89–90. • **49**. *Ibid*., p. 80.

10 *'To kill the serpent, first you must crush the head':*
The Crusade of Louis IX and the Rise of the Sultan Baibars

1. Morgan, *Mongols*, pp. 60–2; Ibn al-Athir, *Chronicle, Part 3*, pp. 204–31;

al-Maqrizi, *A History of the Ayyubid Sultans of Egypt*, tr. R. J. C. Broadhurst, pp. 273–5. • **2.** 'The Eracles Continuation of William of Tyre', in *Crusader Syria in the Thirteenth Century*, tr. J. Shirley (Aldershot, 1999), p. 132. • **3.** Rothelin, *Crusader Syria in the Thirteenth Century*, p. 64. • **4.** For accounts of Louis' life see J. Richard, *Saint Louis, Crusader King of France*, ed. S. Lloyd, tr. J. Birell (Cambridge, 1992); W. C. Jordan, *Louis IX and the Challenge of the Crusade* (Princeton, NJ, 1979); J. Le Goff, *Saint Louis*, tr. G. E. Gollrad (Notre Dame, IN, 2009). For Louis' legacy see M. C. Gaposchkin, *The Making of Saint Louis: Kingship, Sanctity and Crusade in the Later Middle Ages* (Ithaca, NY, 2008). • **5.** Jordan, *Louis IX and the Challenge of the Crusade*, pp. 35–133. • **6.** John of Joinville, 'The Life of Saint Louis', in *Joinville and Villehardouin: Chronicles of the Crusades*, tr. C. Smith (London, 2008), p. 178. • **7.** John of Joinville, 'Life of Saint Louis', pp. 296–7. • **8.** *Ibid.*, p. 296. • **9.** D. Weiss, *Art and Crusade in the Age of Saint Louis* (Cambridge, 1998). • **10.** Jean de Jandun, cited in Weiss, *Art and Crusade in the Age of Saint Louis*, p. 33. • **11.** C. Smith, *Crusading in the Age of Joinville* (Aldershot, 2006). • **12.** John of Joinville, 'Life of Saint Louis', p. 176. • **13.** *Ibid.*, p. 177. • **14.** Ibn Wasil, in P. Jackson, *The Seventh Crusade: Sources and Documents* (Aldershot, 2007), pp. 129–30. • **15.** The Testament of Ayyub, unpublished translation by P. Jackson. See also C. Cahen and I. Chabbouh, 'Le testament d'al-Malik as-Salih Ayyub', in *Bulletin d'Études Orientales de l'Institut Français de Damas* 29 (1977), pp. 97–114. • **16.** Ibn Wasil, *Arab Historians of the Crusades*, p. 286. • **17.** John of Joinville, 'Life of Saint Louis', p. 190. • **18.** Foundation Charter of the Church of Damietta, in Jackson, *Seventh Crusade*, pp. 95–7. • **19.** Rothelin, *Crusader Syria in the Thirteenth Century*, p. 89. • **20.** John of Joinville, 'Life of Saint Louis', p. 196. • **21.** *Ibid.* • **22.** Rothelin, *Crusader Syria in the Thirteenth Century*, pp. 95–6. • **23.** John of Joinville, 'Life of Saint Louis', p. 201. • **24.** *Ibid.*, p. 206. • **25.** *Ibid.*, pp. 205–6. • **26.** *Ibid.*, p. 202. • **27.** *Ibid.*, p. 206. • **28.** Ibn Wasil, *Arab Historians of the Crusades*, p. 292. • **29.** *Ibid.* • **30.** John of Joinville, 'Life of Saint Louis', p. 220. • **31.** *Ibid.*, p. 221. • **32.** Ibn Wasil, *Arab Historians of the Crusades*, p. 294. • **33.** Deposition by Charles of Anjou during the canonisation process of Saint Louis, in Jackson, *Seventh Crusade*, p. 116. • **34.** Ibn Wasil in Jackson, *Seventh Crusade*, p. 149. • **35.** *Ibid.*, pp. 150–53; Joinville, *Life of Saint Louis*, pp. 231–33. • **36.** *Ibid.*, pp. 229–30. • **37.** *Ibid.*, p. 243. • **38.** *Ibid.*, pp. 249–54. • **39.** Louis IX to his subjects in France, before 10 August 1250, in Jackson, *Seventh Crusade*, p. 113. • **40.** *Ibid.*, p. 114. • **41.** C. J. Marshall, *Warfare in the Latin East, 1191–1291* (Cambridge, 1992). • **42.** On this period of his rule see Jordan, *Louis IX and the Challenge of the Crusade*, pp. 135–213. • **43.** *Ibid.*, pp. 127–8. • **44.** Matthew Paris, *The Chronicles of Matthew Paris: Monastic Life in the Thirteenth Century*, tr. R. Vaughan (Gloucester, 1984), pp. 248–9. • **45.** R. Irwin, *The Middle East in the Middle Ages: The Early Mamluk Sultanate 1250–1382* (Beckenham, 1986), pp. 26–9. • **46.** Morgan, *Mongols*, pp. 130–7; Ibn

Kathir in Lewis, *Islam: From the Prophet Muhammad to the Capture of Constantinople*, pp. 80–4. • **47**. P. Jackson, 'The Crisis in the Holy Land in 1260', in *English Historical Review* 95 (1980), pp. 481–513. For a broader study of Mongol–Christian relations see the same author's splendid *The Mongols and the West, 1221–1405* (Harlow, 2005). • **48**. R. Amitai-Preiss, *Mongols and Mamluks* (Cambridge, 1995), pp. 27–35; letter of Hulegu Khan to Saint Louis, 1262, P. Meyvaert, 'An Unknown Letter of Hulegu, Ilkhan of Persia to King Louis IX of France', in *Viator* 11 (1980), pp. 252–9. • **49**. Al-Maqrizi in Lewis, *Islam: From the Prophet Muhammad to the Capture of Constantinople*, pp. 84–5. • **50**. Amitai-Preiss, *Mongols and Mamluks*, pp. 35–45; M. Piana, *Burgen und Städte der Kreuzzugszeit* (Petersberg, 2008), pp. 44–6; Irwin, *The Middle East in the Middle Ages*, pp. 32–4. • **51**. Ibn Abd al-Zahir, *Baybars I of Egypt*, tr. F. Sadeque (Dacca, 1956), p. 93. • **52**. D. Jacoby, 'New Venetian Evidence on Crusader Acre', *The Experience of Crusading*, 2 vols. (Cambridge, 2003), vol. 2, eds. P. W. Edbury and J. P. Phillips, pp. 240–56. • **53**. The best modern biography of Baibars is P. Thorau, *The Lion of Egypt: Sultan Baibars I and the Near East in the Thirteenth Century*, tr. P. M. Holt (Harlow, 1992); see also Irwin, *Middle East in the Middle Ages*, pp. 37–61. • **54**. Ibn Abd al-Zahir, *Baybars I*, pp. 115–16. On Baibars' legitimacy and good rule, see pp. 96–121. • **55**. Ibn al-Furat, *Ayyubids, Mamluks and Crusaders: Selections from the Tarikh al-Duwal wa'l- Muluk of Ibn al-Furat*, eds. and trs. U. and M. C. Lyons and J. S. C. Riley-Smith, 2 vols. (Cambridge, 1971), 1.124. • **56**. Ibn al-Nafis, *The Theologus autodidactus*, eds. and trs. M. Meyerhof and J. Schacht (Oxford, 1968), pp. 68–9. • **57**. Kennedy, *Crusader Castles*, pp. 120–79; Marshall, *Warfare in the Latin East*, pp. 233–6, 244; Ibn al-Furat, *Ayyubids, Mamluks and Crusaders*, 1.88–96. • **58**. Kennedy, *Crusader Castles*, pp. 145–63; Thorau, *Lion of Egypt*, pp. 204–5; D. J. Cathcart King, 'The Taking of Le Krak des Chevaliers in 1271', in *Antiquity* 23 (1949), pp. 83–92. • **59**. Richard, *Saint Louis*, pp. 329–35; Jordan, *Louis IX and the Challenge of the Crusade*, pp. 214–18. • **60**. John of Joinville, 'Life of Saint Louis', p. 329. • **61**. S. D. Lloyd, *English Society and the Crusade, 1216–1307* (Oxford, 1988). • **62**. Thorau, *Lion of Egypt*, pp. 220–50; P. M. Holt, *Early Mamluk Diplomacy (1260–1290): Treaties of Baibars and Qalawun with Christian Rulers* (Leiden, 1995). • **63**. Ibn Abd al-Zahir, *Baibars I*, pp. 77–8. • **64**. D. P. Little, 'The Fall of Akka in 690/1291: The Muslim Version', in *Studies in Islamic History and Civilisation in Honour of Professor David Ayalon*, ed. M. Sharon (Jerusalem and Leiden, 1986), pp. 159–81; Marshall, *Warfare in the Latin East*, pp. 232–8, 244–55; Irwin, *Middle East in the Middle Ages*, pp. 62–76; Amitai-Preiss, *Mongols and Mamluks*, pp. 179–201. • **65**. *The 'Templar of Tyre': Part III of the 'Deeds of the Cypriots'*, tr. P. Crawford (Aldershot, 2003), pp. 104–5. • **66**. *Ibid.*, p. 109. • **67**. *Ibid.*, p. 111. • **68**. Ibn al-Furat in Little, 'The Fall of Akka in 690/1291', p. 181.

11 From the Trial of the Templars to Ferdinand and Isabella, Columbus and the Conquest of the New World

1. M. Barber, *The Trial of the Templars*, second edition (Cambridge, 2006), pp. 59–61. This is by far the best account of the end of the Templars, although see also the arguments of J. S. C. Riley-Smith, 'Were the Templars Guilty?', and 'The Structures of the Orders of the Temple and the Hospital in *c*.1291', both in *The Medieval Crusade*, ed. S. Ridyard (Woodbridge, 2004). • 2. *The Templars*, trs. M. Barber and K. Bate (Manchester, 2002), pp. 244–8; • 3. A. Demurger, *The Last Templar: The Tragedy of Jacques de Molay, Last Grand Master of the Temple* (London, 2002), pp. 144–52; S. Menache, 'The Last Master of the Temple: James of Molay', in *Knighthoods of Christ: Essays on the History of the Crusades and the Knights Templar, Presented to Malcolm Barber*, ed. N. Housley (Aldershot, 2007) pp. 229–40. • 4. S. Menache, *Clement V* (Cambridge, 1998), pp. 13–34. • 5. *The Templars*, p. 246. • 6. Barber, *Trial of the Templars*, pp. 67–87. • 7. *Ibid.*, pp. 79–80, 88–90. • 8. *The Templars*, p. 290. • 9. B. Frale, 'The Chinon Chart: Papal Absolution to the Last Templar, Master Jacques de Molay', in *Journal of Medieval History* 30 (2004), pp. 109–34. • 10. *The Templars.*, pp. 292–5. • 11. *Ibid.*, p. 299. • 12. Barber, *Trial of the Templars*, pp. 217–58; A. Gilmour-Bryson, *The Trial of the Templars in Cyprus: A Complete English Edition* (Leiden, 1998), pp. 40–1. • 13. *Ibid.*, pp. 30–1. • 14. Barber, *Trial of the Templars*, pp. 141–201. • 15. *Decrees of the Ecumenical Councils*, 1.331–49, here at p. 336; Barber, *Trial of the Templars*, pp. 267–70. • 16. *Decrees of the Ecumenical Councils*, 1.341–2. • 17. *The Templars*, pp. 323–8. • 18. Demurger, *Last Templar*, pp. 194–200. • 19. Translation from *ibid.* pp. 197–8. • 20. Barber, *New Knighthood*, pp. 314–34. • 21. S. Schein, '*Gesta Dei per Mongolos* 1300. The Genesis of a Non-Event', in *English Historical Review* 94 (1979), pp. 805–19; P. Jackson, *The Mongols and the West, 1221–1410* (Harlow, 2005), pp. 165–95. • 22. A. Leopold, *How to Recover the Holy Land: The Crusade Proposals of the Late Thirteenth and Early Fourteenth Centuries* (Aldershot, 2000); S. Schein, *Fideles Crucis: The Papacy, the West, and the Recovery of the Holy Land, 1274–1314* (Oxford, 1991). • 23. For 1309 see N. Housley, 'Pope Clement V and the Crusades of 1309–1310', in *Journal of Medieval History* 8 (1982), pp. 29–42; for 1320, see M. Barber, 'The *Pastoureaux* of 1320', in *Journal of Ecclesiastical History* 32 (1981), pp. 143–66. • 24. *Documents on the Later Crusades, 1274–1580*, ed. and tr. N. Housley (Basingstoke, 1996), p. 67. • 25. M. Keen, *Chivalry* (London, 1984), pp. 44–63; N. Housley, 'The Crusading Movement, 1274–1700', in *The Oxford Illustrated History of the Crusades* p. 272. • 26. M. Keen, 'Chaucer's Knight, the English Aristocracy and the Crusade', in *English Court Culture in the Later Middle Ages*, eds. V. J. Scattergood and J. W. Sherborne (London, 1983), pp. 45–61. • 27. Tyerman, *England and the Crusades*, pp. 259–75. • 28. J. S. Roskell, 'Sir Richard de

Waldegrave of Bures Saint Mary, Speaker in the Parliament of 1381–1382', in *Proceedings of the Suffolk Institute of Archaeology* 27 (1957), pp. 154–75. • **29**. Edbury, *The Kingdom of Cyprus and the Crusades*, pp. 161–79; S. Bliznyuk, 'A Crusader of the Later Middle Ages: King Peter I of Cyprus', in *The Crusades and the Military Orders: Expanding the Frontiers of Medieval Latin Christianity*, eds. Z. Hunyadi and J. Laszlovsky (Budapest, 2001), pp. 51–7; Philip of Mézières, 'Account of the Alexandria Crusade', in *Documents on the Later Crusades*, p. 86; Guillaume de Machaut, *The Capture of Alexandria*, tr. J. Shirley and P. W. Edbury (Aldershot, 2001), p. 56. • **30**. Philip of Mézières, 'Account of the Alexandria Crusade', p. 86. • **31**. *Ibid.*, pp. 87–8. • **32**. Guillaume de Machaut, *Capture of Alexandria*, p. 86. • **33**. *Ibid.*, pp. 186–91. • **34**. *The Earl of Derby's Expeditions to Prussia and the Holy Land, 1390–1391 and 1392–1393*, ed. L. Toulmin Smith, Camden Society 52 (London, 1894); F. R. H. Du Boulay, 'Henry of Derby's Expeditions to Prussia, 1390–1391 and 1392', in *The Reign of Richard II: Essays in Honour of May McKisack*, eds. F. R. H. Du Boulay and C. M. Barron (London, 1971), pp. 153–72; I. Mortimer, *The Fears of Henry IV: The Life of England's Self-Made King* (London, 2007), pp. 84–115. • **35**. Christiansen, *Northern Crusades*, pp. 167–76. • **36**. *Ibid.*, pp. 139–46; 164–7. • **37**. Thomas Walsingham, *Chronica Majora*, trs. D. Preest and J. G. Clark (Woodbridge, 2005), pp. 278–9. • **38**. A. S. Cook, 'Beginning the Board in Russia', in *Journal of English and German Philology* 14 (1915), pp. 375–88. • **39**. *Earl of Derby's Expeditions*, pp. 116–17. • **40**. Christiansen, *Northern Crusades*, pp. 227–31. • **41**. *Documents on the Later Crusades*, pp. 351–75. • **42**. *Earl of Derby's Expeditions*, pp. lx–lxiii; 222, 275–6. • **43**. *Ibid.*, pp. lxiii–lxxi; 226, 277–8. • **44**. Tyerman, *England and the Crusades*, pp. 332–42. • **45**. Hussite Manifesto from Prague, 1420, in T. A. Fudge, *The Crusade against Heretics in Bohemia, 1418–1437: Sources and Documents for the Hussite Crusades* (Aldershot, 2002), pp. 59–60 – part of an exemplary collection of documents to study these events. See also F. G. Heymann, 'The Crusades against the Hussites', in *History of the Crusades*, ed. K. M. Setton, 6 vols. (Madison, WI, 1969–89), 3.586–646; *Documents on the Later Crusades*, pp. 249–59. • **46**. Fudge, *Crusade against Heretics in Bohemia*, pp. 24–5. • **47**. Biography of Marshal Boucicaut, cited in *Documents on the Later Crusades*, pp. 105–6. • **48**. A. S. Atiya, *The Crusade of Nicopolis* (London, 1936); V. Laszlo, 'Some Remarks on Recent Historiography of the Crusade of Nicopolis (1396)', in *The Crusades and the Military Orders: Expanding the Frontiers of Medieval Latin Christianity*, eds. Z. Hunyadi and J. Laszlovsky (Budapest, 2001), pp. 223–30. • **49**. C. Imber, *The Ottoman Empire, 1300–1481* (Istanbul, 1990); *idem, The Ottoman Empire, 1300–1650: The Structure of Power* (Basingstoke, 2002), pp. 5–27; H. Inalcik, *The Ottoman Empire: The Classical Age* (London, 1973), pp. 5–22; D. Goffman, *The Ottoman Empire and Early Modern Europe* (Cambridge, 2002), pp. 29–54. • **50**. Michael Doukas, *The Decline and Fall of Byzantium to the Ottoman Turks*, tr. H. J. Magoulias (Detroit, 1984), p. 181. • **51**. C. Imber, *The Crusade* *of Varna, 1443–1445* (Aldershot, 2006), p. 51. • **52**. A splendid account remains that of S. Runciman, *The Fall of Constantinople, 1453* (Cambridge, 1965). Another accessible account is R. Crowley, *1453: The Holy War for Constantinople and the Clash of Islam and the West* (London, 2005). See also the fine analysis of D. Nicolle, *Constantinople 1453* (Oxford, 2000). • **53**. Nicolò Barbaro, *Diary of the Siege of Constantinople, 1453*, tr. J. R. Melville-Jones (New York, 1969), pp. 29–30. • **54**. Leonard of Chios, in *The Siege of Constantinople 1453: Seven Contemporary Accounts*, tr. J. R. Melville-Jones (Amsterdam, 1972), p. 26. • **55**. K. DeVries, 'Gunpowder Weapons at the Siege of Constantinople, 1453', in *War and Society in the Eastern Mediterranean, 7th–15th Centuries*, ed. Y. Lev (Leiden, 1997), pp. 343–62. • **56**. Michael Kritovoulos, *History of Mehmet the Conqueror*, tr. C. T. Riggs (Princeton, NJ, 1954), p. 37. • **57**. H. Inalcik, 'Mehmet the Conqueror (1432–1481) and His Time', in *Speculum* 35 (1960), pp. 411–12. • **58**. Nicolò Barbaro, *Diary*, p. 40; Leonard of Chios, p. 24. • **59**. Nicolò Barbaro, *Diary*, pp. 50–1. • **60**. *Ibid.*, p. 54. • **61**. *Ibid.*, p. 56. • **62**. Inalcik, 'Mehmet the Conqueror', pp. 411–12. • **63**. Nicolò Barbaro, *Diary*, p. 60. • **64**. *Ibid.*, p. 64. • **65**. *Ibid.*, p. 67. • **66**. Leonard of Chios, *The Siege of Constantinople*, p. 38. • **67**. Pius II, *The Commentaries of Pius II*, tr. F. A. Gragg (Northampton, 1937), p. 69. • **68**. R. Vaughan, *Philip the Good: The Apogee of Burgundy* (London, 1970); K. DeVries, 'The Failure of Philip the Good to Fulfil his Crusade Promise of 1454', in *The Medieval Crusade*, ed. S. J. Ridyard (Woodbridge, 2004), pp. 157–70. • **69**. Letter of J. De Pleine concerning the Feast of the Pheasant, translated in Vaughan, *Philip the Good*, pp. 144–5. • **70**. *Ibid.*, p. 297. • **71**. *Ibid.*, pp. 358–72, text at pp. 366–7. • **72**. R. N. Bain, 'The Siege of Belgrade by Muhammad II, July 1–23, 1456', in *English Historical Review* 7 (1892), pp. 235–45. • **73**. J. Goni Gaztambide, 'The Holy See and the Reconquest of the Kingdom of Granada (1479–1492)', in *Spain in the Fifteenth Century*, ed. R. Highfield (London, 1972), p. 361. • **74**. *Ibid.*, p. 371. See also P. K. Liss, *Isabel the Queen* (Oxford, 1992). • **75**. Purkis, *Crusading Spirituality in the Holy Land and Iberia*, pp. 130–2; *Documents on the Later Crusades*, pp. 304–8. • **76**. C. Delaney, 'Columbus' Ultimate Goal: Jerusalem', in *Comparative Studies in Society and History* 48 (2006), pp. 260–92; A. Hamdani, 'Columbus and the Recovery of Jerusalem', in *Journal of the American Oriental Society* 99 (1979), pp. 39–48. • **77**. Pius II cited in *Documents on the Later Crusades*, p. 107. For the conflict between Charles and Suleyman, see the summary in Goffman, *Ottoman Empire*, pp. 98–112. • **78**. V. H. Aksan, *Ottoman Wars 1700–1870: An Empire Besieged* (Harlow, 2007).

12 New Crusaders? From Sir Walter Scott to Osama Bin Laden and George W. Bush

1. Thomas Fuller quoted in R. Ellenblum, *Crusader Castles and Modern Histories*

(Cambridge, 2007), p. 5. • **2.** Ibid., pp. 5–6. • **3.** Voltaire, taken from K. Munholland, 'Michaud's History of the Crusades and the French Crusade in Algeria under Louis-Philippe', in The Popularisation of Images: Visual Culture under the July Monarchy, eds. P. ten-Doesschate Chu and G. P. Weisberg (Princeton, NJ, 1994), p. 145; Dickson, Children's Crusade, pp. 233–4; R. Irwin, For Lust of Knowing: The Orientalists and their Enemies (London, 2006), p. 117. • **4.** Heller in Ellenblum, Crusader Castles, p. 8. • **5.** Ralph Waldo Emerson cited in Constable, 'Historiography of the Crusades', p. 8. • **6.** S. Runciman, History of the Crusades (London, 1951–4), 3.480. • **7.** Ibid., 2.48. • **8.** M. Bloch, The Historian's Craft, fifth edition (Paris, 1964). • **9.** This paragraph is drawn from E. Siberry, The New Crusades: Images of the Crusades in the 19th and 20th Centuries (Aldershot, 2000), pp. 112–30. On Scott see also M. Girouard, The Return to Camelot: Chivalry and the English Gentleman (London, 1981), pp. 29–54. • **10.** Siberry, New Crusaders, pp. 114–15. • **11.** W. Scott, The Talisman, edition used here (London, 1832), p. 2. • **12.** J. S. C. Riley-Smith, 'Islam and the Crusades in History', in Crusades 2 (2003), p. 154. • **13.** Scott, The Talisman, p. 18. • **14.** Ibid., p. 75. • **15.** Ibid., p. 70. • **16.** Ibid., p. 35. • **17.** Ibid., p. 89; see also p. 125. • **18.** Siberry, New Crusaders, pp. 175–87. • **19.** E. Bar-Yosef, The Holy Land in English Culture 1799–1917: Palestine and the Question of Orientalism (Oxford, 2005), pp. 18–181; Siberry, New Crusaders, pp. 64–72; Scott, The Talisman, pp. 1–2. • **20.** Dickson, Children's Crusade, pp. 173–4. • **21.** Munholland, 'Michaud's History of the Crusades', pp. 144–65; Ellenblum, Crusader Castles, pp. 18–23. See the similar comments of M. Jubb, The Legend of Saladin in Western Literature and Historiography (Lewiston, NY, 2000), pp. 197–206. • **22.** For a sophisticated demolition of 'ethnic nationalism' in the medieval period and a view on the construction of modern 'national' identities, see P. J. Geary, The Myth of Nations: The Medieval Origins of Europe (Princeton, NJ, 2002), pp. 15–40. • **23.** Michaud, Histoire des croisades (1825), 1.510, 522–4, taken from Munholland, 'Michaud's History of the Crusades', p. 150. • **24.** J.-F. Michaud and J.-J. Pujoulet, Correspondance d'Orient, 7 vols. (Paris, 1833–5), 1.2. At times Michaud's letters are an almost endless list of excited reports of sites he has seen that were connected to the history of the crusades; ibid., 1.23–5, 28, 67, 69, etc. • **25.** Munholland, 'Michaud's History of the Crusades', pp. 159–64; Siberry, New Crusaders, pp. 169–70, 208–11. • **26.** C. Constans, Musée national du château de Versailles: Les peintures, 3 vols. (Paris, 1995). • **27.** Taken from Munholland, 'Michaud's History of the Crusades', p. 164. • **28.** Siberry, New Crusaders, p. 52; R.-H. Bautier, 'La collection de chartes de croisade dite "Collection Courtois"', in Comptes-rendus des séances de l'Académie des Inscriptions et Belles-Lettres (1956), pp. 382–5. • **29.** G. Degeorge, Damascus (Paris, 2004), pp. 218–27. • **30.** Cited in ibid., p. 224. • **31.** A. Knobler, 'Holy Wars, Empires, and the Portability of the Past: The Modern Uses of Medieval Crusades', in Comparative Studies in Society and History 48 (2006), p. 296; Siberry, New Crusaders, p. 83. • **32.** Siberry,

New Crusaders, p. 83. • **33**. P. Pic, *Syrie et Palestine* (Paris, 1924), p. vii. • **34**. Cited by Riley-Smith, 'Islam and the Crusades in History', p. 158. In this connection see also E. Sivan, 'Modern Arab Historiography of the Crusades', in *Asian and African Studies* 8 (1972), pp. 117–19. • **35**. C. Duggan, *The Force of Destiny: A History of Italy since 1796* (London, 2007), esp. pp. 125–33. • **36**. *Ibid.*, p. 126. • **37**. J. Mazzini, *Mazzini's Letters*, tr. A. De Rosen Jervis (London, 1930), pp. x–xi, 172–3. • **38**. Siberry, *New Crusaders*, pp. 135–6. • **39**. Duggan, *Force of Destiny*, pp. 171–2. • **40**. Ellenblum, *Crusader Castles*, pp. 26–7; for Godfrey's status as a crusading hero see Siberry, *New Crusaders*. • **41**. Knobler, 'Holy Wars', pp. 297–8. • **42**. R. A. Fletcher, *The Search for El Cid* (London, 1989). • **43**. J. M. Sanchez, *The Spanish Civil War as a Religious Tragedy* (Notre Dame, IN, 1987), pp. 152–3. • **44**. P. Preston, *Franco: A Biography* (London, 1993); M. Vincent, 'The Martyrs and the Saints: Masculinity and the Construction of the Francoist Crusade', in *History Workshop Journal* 47 (1999), pp. 69–98; S. G. Payne, *The Franco Regime, 1936–1975* (London, 2000), esp. pp. 197–208; N. Cooper, 'The Church: From Crusade to Christianity', in *Spain in Crisis: The Evolution and Decline of the Franco Regime*, ed. P. Preston (Hassocks, 1976), pp. 48–81; Sanchez, *The Spanish Civil War as a Religious Tragedy*, pp. 91, 152–6. • **45**. M. Vincent, *Catholicism in the Second Spanish Republic: Religion and Politics in Salamanca, 1930–1936* (Oxford, 1996), pp. 248–9. • **46**. Preston, *Franco*, pp. 184–5; Vincent, 'The Martyrs and the Saints', p. 72. • **47**. Preston, *Franco*, p. 290. • **48**. *Ibid.*, p. 291. • **49**. *Ibid.*, p. 351. • **50**. *Ibid.*, pp. 640–1; Fletcher, *Quest for El Cid*, pp. 201–5. • **51**. O. Anderson, 'The Reactions of Church and Dissent towards the Crimean War', in *Journal of Ecclesiastical History* 16 (1965), pp. 209–20; Siberry, *New Crusaders*, pp. 83–4. • **52**. R. Jenkins, *Gladstone* (London, 1995), p. 400. • **53**. *Ibid.*, p. 403. • **54**. R. T. Shannon, *Gladstone and the Bulgarian Agitation 1876*, second edition (Hassocks, 1975), pp. 80–1, 187–8, 213, 217. • **55**. *Ibid.*, p. 187, n. 2 • **56**. Knobler, 'Holy Wars', pp. 310–13. • **57**. Cramb cited in Knobler, 'Holy Wars', p. 315. • **58**. A. Marrin, *The Last Crusade: The Church of England in the First World War* (Durham, NC, 1974); Girouard, *Return to Camelot*, pp. 275–93. • **59**. A. Horne, *Macmillan: 1894–1956* (London, 1988), pp. 39–40; see also pp. 131, 307. Grateful thanks to my father for finding these references. • **60**. Siberry, *New Crusaders*, p. 91. • **61**. Note that Pershing himself did not describe his campaign in France in such terms, although he did refer to it as 'this great war for civilisation'. See J. J. Pershing, *My Experiences in the World War*, 2 vols. (New York, 1931), 1.45. • **62**. S. Goebel, *The Great War and Medieval Memory: War, Remembrance and Medievalism in Britain and Germany, 1914–1940* (Cambridge, 2006), pp. 127–47. • **63**. *Ibid.* • **64**. R. F. Eldridge, 'The Crusaders' Monument', in *The Carthusian* (June 1916), p. 608. I am grateful to Revd William Lane for this reference. • **65**. Siberry, *New Crusaders*, p. 92. • **66**. *Ibid.*, pp. 94–7; Knobler, 'Holy Wars', pp. 315–16. • **67**. Bar-Yosef, *The Holy Land in English Culture*, p. 249. • **68**. *Ibid.*, pp. 251–3. • **69**.

Ibid., p. 249. • **70**. *Ibid.*, pp. 251–64. • **71**. *Ibid.*, p. 264. • **72**. *Ibid.*, p. 267.
• **73**. V. Gilbert, *The Romance of the Last Crusade: With Allenby to Jerusalem* (New York, 1923), the scene mentioned here at pp. 204–16. • **74**. *Ibid.*, pp. 116, 171. • **75**. Bar-Yosef, *The Holy Land in English Culture*, p. 293. • **76**. Siberry, *New Crusaders*, pp. 99–100; Goebel, *Great War and Medieval Memory*, p. 91. • **77**. Dickson, *Children's Crusade*, p. 194. • **78**. Siberry, *New Crusaders*, p. 103. • **79**. Goebel, *Great War and Medieval Memory*, pp. 300–1. • **80**. K. Vonnegut, *Slaughterhouse 5: The Children's Crusade: A Duty Dance with Death* (New York, 1969), p. 77. • **81**. Cited in M. Burleigh, *Germany Turns Eastwards* (Cambridge, 1988), p. 6. • **82**. M. G. Carpenter, *The Crusade: Its Origins and Development at Washington Court House and its Results* (Columbus, OH, 1893), p. 20. • **83**. M. Perry, *The Jarrow Crusade: Protest and Legend* (Sunderland, 2005), esp. pp. 153–7. • **84**. *Ibid.*, p. 154. • **85**. *Ibid.*, pp. 171–82. • **86**. This paragraph is a summary of F. C. R. Robinson, 'Other-Worldly and This-Worldly Islam and the Islamic Revival. A Memorial Lecture for Wilfred Cantwell Smith', in *Journal of the Royal Asiatic Society*, Series 3 (2004), pp. 50–1. • **87**. R. Irwin, 'Islam and the Crusades, 1096–1699', in *The Oxford Illustrated History of the Crusades*, pp. 250–7. • **88**. J. Miot, *Memoirs of my Service in the French Expedition to Egypt and Syria* (Paris, 1997), p. 13. • **89**. J. T. Johnson, *The Holy War Idea in Western and Islamic Traditions* (Pennsylvania, 1997), p. 165. • **90**. J. C. G. Röhl, *Wilhelm II: The Kaiser's Personal Monarchy, 1888–1900* (Cambridge, 2004), pp. 944–54. • **91**. J. S. C. Riley-Smith, *The Crusades, Christianity and Islam* (New York, 2008), pp. 63–4. • **92**. M. C. Lyons, 'The Crusading Stratum in the Arabic Hero Cycles', in *Crusaders and Muslims in Twelfth-Century Syria*, ed. M. Shatzmiller (Leiden, 1993), pp. 147–61; *idem*, *The Arabic Epic: Heroic and Oral Storytelling*, 3 vols. (Cambridge, 1995), esp. 1.1–28, 105–7. For a vivid background to storytelling see R. Irwin, *The Arabian Nights: A Companion* (London, 1994), pp. 103–19; for the western travellers, see A. Russell, *The Natural History of Aleppo*, 2 vols. (London, 1794), 1.148–9; E. W. Lane, *An Account of the Manners and Customs of the Modern Egyptians* (London, 1860), pp. 360–91. For the *Sirat al-Zahir Baibars*, see M. C. Lyons, 'The *Sirat Baibars*', in *Orientalia Hispanica*, ed. F. Pareja Casanas (Leiden, 1974), pp. 490–503. • **93**. Sivan, 'Modern Arab Historiography of the Crusades', pp. 109–49. • **94**. A. Özcan, *Pan-Islamism: Indian Muslims, the Ottomans and Britain (1877–1924)* (Leiden, 1997), pp. 61–3. • **95**. R. Peters, *Jihad in Classical and Modern Islam: A Reader* (Princeton, NJ, 1996), pp. 56–7. • **96**. J. L. Gelvin, *Divided Loyalties: Nationalism and Mass Politics in Syria at the Close of Empire* (Berkeley, CA, 1998), pp. 254–5. • **97**. *Ibid.*, pp. 2–3. • **98**. *President Gamal Abdel-Nasser's Speeches and Press Interviews 1958* (Cairo, 1959), p. 63. • **99**. *Ibid.*, p. 18; *President Gamal Abdel-Nasser's Speeches and Press Interviews 1959* (Cairo, 1960), p. 382. • **100**. *President Gamal Abdel-Nasser's Speeches and Press Interviews 1959*, pp. 140–1, 217–18. • **101**. *Ibid.*, pp. 217–18. • **102**. *Ibid.*, pp. 382–3, 427–8. • **103**. N. Rejwan, *Nasserist Ideology:*

Its Exponents and Critics (Jerusalem, 1974), pp. 21–2. • **104**. *President Gamal Abdel-Nasser's Speeches and Press Interviews 1959*, pp. 428–9. • **105**. *Ibid.*, p. 429. • **106**. *Ibid.* • **107**. J. Aberth, *A Knight at the Movies: Medieval History on Film* (London, 2003), pp. 91–107; J. M. Ganim, 'Reversing the Crusades: Hegemony, Orientalism, and Film Language in Youssef Chahine's *Saladin*', in *Race, Class and Gender in 'Medieval' Cinema*, eds. L. T. Ramey and T. Pugh (Basingstoke, 2007), pp. 45–58. P. B. Sturtevant, 'SaladiNasser: Nasser's Political Crusade in *El Naser Salah Ad-Din*', in *Hollywood in the Holy Land: Essays on Film Depictions of the Crusades and Christian–Muslim Clashes*, eds. N. Haydock and E. L. Risden (Jefferson, NC, 2009), pp. 123–46. • **108**. Aberth, *Knight at the Movies*, p. 104. • **109**. *Ibid.*, p. 103. • **110**. *Speech by President Anwar el Sadat to the Knesset, 20 November 1977* (Cairo, 1978), p. 20. • **111**. M. Ma'oz, *Asad: The Sphinx of Damascus – A Political Biography* (New York, 1988). • **112**. Hillenbrand, *Crusades: Islamic Perspectives*, pp. 595–600. • **113**. Ma'oz, *Asad: The Sphinx of Damascus*, p. 45. • **114**. *Ibid.*, pp. 44–5. • **115**. O. Bengio, *Saddam's Word: Political Discourse in Iraq* (Oxford, 1998), pp. 171–5. • **116**. Johnson, *Holy War Idea*, p. 166. • **117**. J. E. Carter, *Keeping Faith: Memoirs of a President* (New York, 1982), pp. 267–409. • **118**. Peters, *Jihad*, p. 158. • **119**. J. J. G. Jansen, *The Neglected Duty: The Creed of Sadat's Assassins and the Islamic Resurgence in the Middle East* (New York, 1986). • **120**. *Ibid.* • **121**. Osama Bin Laden, *Messages to the World: The Statements of Osama Bin Laden*, ed. B. Lawrence, tr. J. Howarth (London, 2005), p. 28. • **122**. A. Awan, 'Virtual Propagation of Jihadist Media and its Effects' *RUSI Journal* 152 (2007) pp. 76–81. • **123**. Osama Bin Laden, *Messages to the World*, pp. 5, 9, 11, 26, 42, 61, 80, 118, 229, 249–50. • **124**. *Ibid.*, p. xvii. • **125**. *Ibid.*, for example, pp. 25, 108. • **126**. *Ibid.*, p. 121. • **127**. *Ibid.*, pp. 121–2. • **128**. *Ibid.*, p. 121. • **129**. *Ibid.*, pp. xxi–xxiii.

Conclusion

1. Matthew Paris, *The Illustrated Chronicles of Matthew Paris: Observations of Thirteenth-Century Life*, tr. R. Vaughan (Stroud, 1993). • **2**. Cited in *The Fourth Crusade: Event, Aftermath and Perceptions*, ed. T. F. Madden (Aldershot, 2008), pp. vii–viii.

Primary Bibliography

Note: In line with the general readership at which this book is aimed I have, wherever possible, cited an English translation of the source. If the reader wishes to track down a version in the original language these works will signpost such a text. If no English translation exists, I have cited a foreign language original or translation.

Abu Shama, 'Le livre des deux jardins', *Recueil des historiens des croisades: Historiens orientaux*, 5 vols. (Paris, 1872–1906), 4.

Aguilers, Raymond of: See Raymond of Aguilers.

Albert of Aachen, *Historia Ierosolimitana: History of the Journey to Jerusalem*, ed. and tr. S. B. Edgington (Oxford, 2007).

Alexander III, 'Epistolae et privilegia', in *Patrologia Latina*, ed. J. P. Migne, 221 Vols. (Paris, 1844–64), vol. 200.

Allen, S. J. and Amt, E. (eds.), *The Crusades: A Reader* (Peterborough, Ontario, 2003).

Al-Maqrizi, *A History of the Ayyubid Sultans of Egypt*, tr. R. J. C. Broadhurst (Boston, MA, 1980).

Al-Sulami, *Kitab al-Jihad*, tr. N. Christie, published online at http://www.arts.cornell.edu/prh3/447/texts/Sulami.html

Ambroise, *The History of the Holy War: Ambroise's Estoire de la Guerre Sainte*, ed. and tr. M. Ailes and M. C. Barber, 2 vols. (Woodbridge, 2003).

Andrea, A., *Sources for the History of the Fourth Crusade* (Leiden, 2000).

Anna Comnena, *The Alexiad*, tr. E. R. A. Sewter (London, 1969).

Anonymi auctoris chronicon ad A.C. 1234 pertinens, tr. A. Abouna (Louvain, 1974).

Barbaro, Nicolò: see Nicolò Barbaro.

Beha ad-Din, *The Rare and Excellent History of Saladin*, tr. D. S. Richards (Aldershot, 2001).

Bernard of Clairvaux, *The Letters of St Bernard of Clairvaux*, new edition, tr. B. S. James, introduction B. M. Kienzle (Stroud, 1998).

Bertrand de Born, *The Poems of the Troubadour Bertrand de Born*, ed. and tr. W. D. Paden Jr., T. Sankovitch and P. H. Stäblein (Berkeley, CA, 1986).

The Birth of Popular Heresy, tr. R. I. Moore (London, 1975).

Blois, Peter of: see Peter of Blois.

Bosau, Helmold of: see Helmold of Bosau.

Bresc-Bautier, G. (ed.), *Le cartulaire du chapitre du Saint-Sépulcre de Jérusalem* (Paris, 1984).

Caen, Ralph of: see Ralph of Caen.

Caffaro: see J. B. Williams, 'The Making of a Crusade: The Genoese anti-Muslim Attacks in Spain, 1146–1148', *Journal of Medieval History* 23 (1997), pp. 29–53, Caffaro's text at pp. 48–53.

Carter, J. E., *Keeping Faith: Memoirs of a President* (New York, 1982).

Chartres, Fulcher of: see Fulcher of Chartres.

Chios, Leonard of: see Leonard of Chios.

Choniates, Niketas: see Niketas Choniates.

Chrétien de Troyes, *Arthurian Romances*, tr. W. W. Kibler (London, 1991).

Christian Society and the Crusades, 1198–1229, tr. E. Peters (Philadelphia, PA, 1971).

Chronicle of the Third Crusade: Itinerarium peregrinorum et gesta regis Ricardi, tr. H. J. Nicholson (Aldershot, 1997).

Clairvaux, Bernard of: see Bernard of Clairvaux.

Comnena, Anna: see Anna Comnena.

The Conquest of Jerusalem and the Third Crusade, tr. P. W. Edbury (Aldershot, 1996).

The Conquest of Lisbon (De expugnatione Lyxbonensi), ed. and tr. C. W. David, with a new forword and bibliography by J. P. Phillips (New York, 2001).

The Crusade against Heretics in Bohemia, 1418–1437: Sources and Documents for the Hussite Crusades, tr. T. A. Fudge (Aldershot, 2002).

The Crusade of Varna, 1443–1445, tr. C. Imber (Aldershot, 2006).

Crusades: Idea and Reality, 1095–1274, trs. J. S. C. and L. Riley-Smith (London, 1981).

Decrees of the Ecumenical Councils, ed. and tr. N. J. Tanner, 2 vols. (London, 1990).

Deuil, Odo of: See Odo of Deuil.

Devizes, Richard of: see Richard of Devizes.

Doukas, Michael: see Michael Doukas.

Eldridge, R. F., 'The Crusaders' Monument', in *The Carthusian* (June 1916).

Eracles, 'The Eracles Continuation of William of Tyre', in *Crusader Syria in the Thirteenth Century*, tr. J. Shirley (Aldershot, 1999).

Freising, Otto of: see Otto of Freising.

Fulcher of Chartres, *A History of the Expedition to Jerusalem, 1095–1127*, tr. F. R. Ryan, ed. H. S. Fink (Knoxville, TN, 1969).

Geoffrey of Villehardouin, 'The Conquest of Constantinople', translated in *Joinville and Villehardouin: Chronicles of the Crusades*, tr. C. Smith (London, 2008).

Gesta Francorum et aliorum Hierosolimitanorum: the Deeds of The Franks and the other Pilgrims to Jerusalem, ed. R. Hill, tr. R. A. B. Mynors (London, 1962).

Gesta Stephani (The Deeds of Stephen), ed. and tr. K. R. Potter (London, 1955).

Gilmour-Bryson, A. (ed.), *The Trial of the Templars in Cyprus: A Complete English Edition* (Leiden, 1998).

Guibert of Nogent, *The Deeds of God through the Franks: Gesta Dei per Francos*, tr. R. Levine (Woodbridge, 1997).

Guillaume de Machaut, *The Capture of Alexandria*, trs. J. Shirley and P. W. Edbury (Aldershot, 2001).

Gunther of Pairis, *The Capture of Constantinople*, ed. and tr. A. J. Andrea (Philadelphia, PA, 1997).

Hagenmeyer, H., *Die Kreuzzugsbriefe aus den Jahren 1088–1100* (Innsbruck, 1901).

Helmold of Bosau, *The Chronicle of the Slavs*, tr. F. J. Tschan (New York, 1935).

Holt, P. M. (ed. and tr.), *Early Mamluk Diplomacy (1260–1290): Treaties of Baybars and Qalawun with Christian Rulers* (Leiden, 1995).

Housley, N. (ed. and tr.), *Documents on the Later Crusades, 1274–1580* (Basingstoke, 1996).

Hulegu Khan, letter to St Louis, 1262, P. Meyvaert, 'An Unknown Letter of Hulegu, Ilkhan of Persia to King Louis IX of France', *Viator* 11 (1980), pp. 252–9.

Ibn Abd al-Zahir, *Baybars I of Egypt*, tr. F. Sadeque (Dacca, 1956).

Ibn al-Athir, *The Chronicle of Ibn al-Athir for the Crusading Period, Part 2: The Years 541–589/1146–1193: The Age of Nur al-Din and Saladin*, tr. D. S. Richards (Aldershot, 2007); *The Chronicle of Ibn al-Athir for the Crusading Period, Part 3: The Years 589–629/1193–1231: The Ayyubids after Saladin and the Mongol Menace*, tr. D. S. Richards (Aldershot, 2008).

Ibn al-Furat, *Ayyubids, Mamluks and Crusaders: Selections from the Tarikh al-Duwal wa'l-Muluk of Ibn al-Furat*, ed. and trs. U. and M. C. Lyons and J. S. C. Riley-Smith, 2 vols. (Cambridge, 1971).

Ibn al-Nafis, *The Theologus autodidactus*, ed. and tr. M. Meyerhof and J. Schacht (Oxford, 1968).

Ibn al-Qalanisi, *The Damascus Chronicles of the Crusades*, tr. H. A. R. Gibb (London, 1932).

Ibn Jubayr, *The Travels of Ibn Jubayr*, tr. R. J. C. Broadhurst (London, 1952).

Imad ad-Din, *Conquête de la Syrie et de la Palestine par Saladin*, tr. H. Massé (Paris, 1972).

Innocent III, 'Epistolae et privilegia', *Patrologia Latina*, ed. J. P. Migne, 221 vols. (Paris, 1844–64), vol. 216; *Die Register Innocenz' III*, ed. O. Hageneder et al. (Vienna, 1964); *The Deeds of Pope Innocent III by an Anonymous Author*, tr. J. M. Powell (Washington, DC, 2004).

Itinerarium peregrinorum et gesta regis Ricardi, tr. H. J. Nicholson (Aldershot, 1997).

Jacques de Vitry, *Lettres*, ed. R. B. C. Huygens, new edition (Turnhout, 2000).

James of Vitry: see Jacques de Vitry.

The Jews and the Crusaders, ed. and tr. S. Eidelberg (Madison, WI, 1977).

John of Joinville, 'The Life of Saint Louis', in *Joinville and Villehardouin: Chronicles of the Crusades*, tr. C. Smith (London, 2008).

John Kinnamos, *The Deeds of John and Manuel Comnenus by John Kinnamos*, tr. C. M. Brand (New York, 1976).

John of Salisbury, *Historia Pontificalis*, ed. and tr. M. Chibnall (London, 1956).

Joinville, John of: see John of Joinville.

Kay, R., *The Council of Bourges, 1225: A Documentary History* (Aldershot, 2002).

Kinnamos, John: see John Kinnamos.

Kritoboulos, Michael: see Michael Kritoboulos.

Kuttner, S. and Garcia y Garcia, A. (eds.), 'A New Eyewitness Account of the Fourth Lateran Council', *Traditio* 20 (1964), pp. 115–78; translated in C. Fasolt, in *Readings in Western Civilisation: Medieval Europe*, eds. J. Kishner and K. F. Morison (Chicago, IL, 1986), pp. 369–76.

Lane, E. W., *An Account of the Manners and Customs of the Modern Egyptians* (London, 1860).

Lees, B. (ed.), *Records of the Templars in England in the Twelfth Century. The Inquest of 1185*, (London, 1935).

Leonard of Chios, in *The Siege of Constantinople 1453: Seven Contemporary Accounts*, tr. J. R. Melville-Jones (Amsterdam, 1972).

Lewis, B. (ed. and tr.), *Islam: From the Prophet Muhammad to the Capture of Constantinople. Volume 1: Politics and War* (Oxford, 1987).

Louis VII, 'Epistolae', *Recueil des historiens des Gaules et de la France*, ed. M. Bouquet et al., 24 vols. (Paris, 1737–1904), vol. 16.

Machaut, Guillaume de: see Guillaume de Machaut.

Malmesbury, William of: see William of Malmesbury.

Matthew Paris, The Chronicles of Matthew Paris: Monastic Life in the Thirteenth Century, tr. R. Vaughan (Gloucester, 1984); The Illustrated Chronicles of Matthew Paris: Observations of Thirteenth-Century Life, tr. R. Vaughan (Stroud, 1993).

Mazzini, J., Mazzini's Letters, tr. A. De Rosen Jervis (London, 1930).

Michael Doukas, The Decline and Fall of Byzantium to the Ottoman Turks, tr. H. J. Magoulias (Detroit, 1984).

Michael Kritoboulos, History of Mehmed the Conqueror, tr. C. T. Rigg (Princeton, NJ, 1954).

Michael the Syrian, Chronique de Michel le Syrien, patriarche jacobite d'Antioche (1166–1199), ed. and tr. J.-B. Chabot, 4 vols. (Paris, 1899–1910).

Michaud J.-F. and Pujoulet, J.-J., Correspondance d'Orient, 7 vols. (Paris, 1833–5).

Miot, J., Memoirs of my Service in the French Expedition to Egypt and Syria (Paris, 1997).

Nasser, G., President Gamal Abdel-Nasser's Speeches and Press Interviews 1958 (Cairo, 1959); President Gamal Abdel-Nasser's Speeches and Press Interviews 1959 (Cairo, 1960).

Nersēs Šnorhali, 'Lament on Edessa', tr. T. Van Lint, in East and West in the Crusader States II: Context, Contacts, Confrontations, eds. K. Ciggaar and H. Teule, Orientalia Lovaniensia Analecta 92 (Leuven, 1999), pp. 49–105.

Nicolò Barbaro, Diary of the Siege of Constantinople, 1453, tr. J. R. Melville-Jones (New York, 1969).

Niketas Choniates, O, City of Byzantium: Annals of Niketas Choniates, tr. H. J. Magoulias (Detroit, MI, 1984), p. 299.

Nogent, Guibert of: see Guibert of Nogent.

Odo of Deuil, The Journey of Louis VII to the East: De profectione Ludovici in Orientem, ed. and tr. V. G. Berry (Columbia, 1948).

Oliver of Paderborn, in Christian Society and the Crusades, 1198–1229, tr. E. Peters (Philadelphia, PA, 1971).

Orderic Vitalis, The Ecclesiastical History, ed. and tr. M. Chibnall, 6 vols. (Oxford, 1969–80).

Osama Bin Laden, Messages to the World: The Statements of Osama Bin Laden, ed. B. Lawrence, tr. J. Howarth (London, 2005).

Otto of Freising, The Deeds of Frederick Barbarossa, tr. C. C. Mierow (New York, 1953).

Paderborn, Oliver of: see Oliver of Paderborn.

Pairis, Gunther of: see Gunther of Pairis.

Paris, Matthew: see Matthew Paris.

Pershing, John J., *My Experiences in the World War*, 2 vols. (New York, 1931).

Peter of Blois, 'Passio Reginaldi', in *Tractatus Duo*, ed. R. B. C. Huygens CCCM 194 (Turnhout, 2002).

Peter of les Vaux-de-Cernay, *The History of the Albigensian Crusade*, trs. W. A. and M. D. Sibly (Woodbridge, 1998).

Peters, E. (ed.), *The First Crusade: 'The Chronicle of Fulcher of Chartres' and Other Source Materials*, second edition (Philadelphia, PA, 1998).

Pius II, *The Commentaries of Pius II*, tr. F. A. Gragg (Northampton, 1937).

'Poem of Almeria', translated in *The World of El Cid*, trs. S. Barton and R. A. Fletcher (Manchester, 2000), pp. 250–63.

Puylaurens, William of: see William of Puylaurens.

Ralph of Caen, *The Gesta Tancredi of Ralph of Caen: A History of the Normans on the First Crusade*, trs. B. S. and D. S. Bachrach (Aldershot, 2005).

Raymond of Aguilers, *Historia Francorum qui ceperunt Iherusalem*, trs. J. H and L.L.Hill (Philadelphia, PA, 1968).

Richard of Devizes, *The Chronicle of Richard of Devizes of the Time of King Richard the First*, ed. and tr. J. T. Appleby (London, 1963).

Rigord, *Histoire de Philippe Auguste*, ed. and tr. E. Carpentier, G. Pon and Y. Chauvin (Paris, 2006).

Robert of Clari, *The Conquest of Constantinople*, tr. E. H. McNeal (New York, 1936).

Robert of Rheims, *Robert the Monk's History of the First Crusade*, tr. C. Sweetenham (Aldershot, 2005).

Roger of Wendover, *The Flowers of History*, tr. J. A. Giles, 2 vols. (London, 1849).

Röhricht, R. (ed.), *Testimonia minora de Quinto bello sacro* (Geneva, 1882); *Regesta regni Hierosolymitani, 1098–1291* (Innsbruck, 1893).

Rothelin, *Crusader Syria in the Thirteenth Century*, tr. J. Shirley (Aldershot, 1999).

Russell, A., *The Natural History of Aleppo*, 2 vols. (London, 1794).

Sadat, A., *Speech by President Anwar el Sadat to the Knesset, 20 November 1977* (Cairo, 1978).

Salisbury, John of: see John of Salisbury.

Scott, Walter, *The Talisman* (London, 1832).

The Seventh Crusade: Sources and Documents, tr. P. Jackson (Aldershot, 2007).

Sibt al-Jawzi, 'Mirror of the Times', translated in *Arab Historians of the Crusades*, tr. F. Gabrieli (Berkeley, CA, 1969).

Šnorhali, Nersēs: see Nersēs Šnorhali.

Syrian, Michael the: see Michael the Syrian.

The 'Templar of Tyre': Part III of the 'Deeds of the Cypriots', tr. P. Crawford (Aldershot, 2003).

The Templars, trs. M. Barber and K. Bate (Manchester, 2002).

The Testament of Ayyub, unpublished translation by P. Jackson. See also C. Cahen and I. Chabbouh, 'Le testament d'al-Malik as-Salih Ayyub', in *Bulletin d'Études Orientales de l'Institut Français de Damas* 29 (1977), pp. 97–114.

Thomas Walsingham, *Chronica Majora*, trs. D. Preest and J. G. Clark (Woodbridge, 2005).

Toulmin-Smith, L. (ed.), *The Earl of Derby's Expeditions to Prussia and the Holy Land, 1390–1391 and 1392–1393, Camden Society* 52 (London, 1894).

Troyes, Chrétien de: see Chrétien de Troyes.

Tudela, William of: see William of Tudela.

Tyre, William of: see William of Tyre.

Usama ibn Munqidh, *The Book of Contemplation. Islam and the Crusades*, tr. P. M. Cobb (London, 2008).

les Vaux-de-Cernay, Peter of: see Peter of les Vaux-de-Cernay.

Villehardouin, Geoffrey of: see Geoffrey of Villehardouin.

Vitalis, Orderic: see Orderic Vitalis.

Vitry, James of: see James of Vitry.

Vonnegut, K., *Slaughterhouse 5: The Children's Crusade: A Duty Dance with Death* (New York, 1969).

Walsingham, Thomas: see Thomas Walsingham.

Wendover, Roger of: see Roger of Wendover.

William of Malmesbury, *Gesta Regum Anglorum: The Deeds of the Kings of England*, ed. and tr. R. A. B. Mynors, R. M. Thomson and M. Winterbottom, 2 vols. (Oxford, 1998–99).

William of Puylaurens, *Chronicle: The Albigensian Crusade and its Aftermath*, trs. W. A. and M. D. Sibly (Woodbridge, 2003).

William of Tudela, in *The Song of the Cathar Wars: A History of the Albigensian Crusade*, tr. J. Shirley (Aldershot, 1996).

William of Tyre, *A History of Deeds done beyond the Sea*, trs. E. A. Babcock and A. C. Krey, 2 vols. (New York, 1943); Latin text in *Chronicon*, ed. R. B. C. Huygens, 2 vols. (Turnhout, 1986).

Secondary Bibliography

Aberth, J., *A Knight at the Movies: Medieval History on Film* (London, 2003).

Abulafia, D., *Frederick II: A Medieval Emperor* (London, 1988).

Aksan, V. H., *Ottoman Wars 1700–1870: An Empire Besieged* (Harlow, 2007).

Amitai-Preiss, R., *Mongols and Mamluks* (Cambridge, 1995).

Anderson, O., 'The Reactions of Church and Dissent towards the Crimean War', in *Journal of Ecclesiastical History* 16 (1965), pp. 209–20.

Angold, M., *The Fourth Crusade: Event and Context* (Harlow, 2003).

Asbridge, T. S., 'The Holy Lance of Antioch: Power, Devotion and Memory on the First Crusade', in *Reading Medieval Studies* 33 (2007), pp. 3–36.

Aston, S. C., *Peirol, Troubadour of Auvergne* (Cambridge, 1953).

Atiya, A. S., *The Crusade of Nicopolis* (London, 1936).

Awan, A., 'Virtual Propagation of Jihadist Media and its Effects', in *RUSI Journal* 152 (2007), pp. 76–81.

Bain, R. N., 'The Siege of Belgrade by Muhammad II, July 1–23, 1456', in *English Historical Review* 7 (1892), pp. 235–45.

Barber, M., 'The *Pastoureaux* of 1320', in *Journal of Ecclesiastical History* 32 (1981), pp. 143–66; 'Western Attitudes to Frankish Greece in the Thirteenth Century', in *Latins and Greeks in the Eastern Mediterranean after 1204*, eds. B. Arbel, B. Hamilton and D. Jacoby (London, 1989), pp. 111–28; *The Cathars: Dualist Heretics in Languedoc in the High Middle Ages* (Harlow, 2000); *The New Knighthood: A History of the Order of the Temple* (Cambridge, 1994); *The Trial of the Templars*, second edition (Cambridge, 2006).

Barbour, N., 'Frederick II's Relations with the Muslims', in *Orientalia Hispanica: Sive studia F. M. Pareja octogenario dictata*, ed. J. M. Barral, 2 vols. (Leiden, 1974), I.77–95.

Bartlett, R., *Trial by Fire and Water* (Oxford, 1984).

Bar-Yosef, E., *The Holy Land in English Culture 1799–1917: Palestine and the Question of Orientalism* (Oxford, 2005).

Bautier, R.-H., 'La collection de chartes de croisade dite "Collection

Courtois"', in *Comptes-rendus des séances de l'Académie des Inscriptions et Belles-Lettres* (1956), pp. 382–5.

Bengio, O., *Saddam's Word: Political Discourse in Iraq* (Oxford, 1998).

Bliznyuk, S., 'A Crusader of the Later Middle Ages: King Peter I of Cyprus', in *The Crusades and the Military Orders: Expanding the Frontiers of Medieval Latin Christianity*, eds. Z. Hunyadi and J. Laszlovsky (Budapest, 2001), pp. 51–7.

Bloch, M., *The Historian's Craft*, fifth edition (Paris, 1964).

Boas, A. J., *Crusader Archaeology: The Material Culture of the Latin East* (London, 1999).

Bradbury, J., *Philip Augustus: King of France 1180–1223* (London, 1998).

Brand., C. M., *Byzantium Confronts the West, 1180–1204* (Cambridge, MA, 1968).

Brown, E. A. R. and Cothren, M. W., 'The Twelfth Century Crusading Window of the Abbey of St Denis', in *Journal of the Warburg and Courtauld Institutes* 49 (1986), pp. 1–40.

Bull, M. G., 'The Diplomatic of the First Crusade', in *The First Crusade: Origins and Impact* (Manchester, 1997), pp. 35–56.

Burleigh, M., *Germany Turns Eastwards* (Cambridge, 1988).

Bysted, A., Jensen, C. S. and Jensen K. V., *Jerusalem in the North: Denmark and the Baltic Crusades, 1100–1522* (Turnhout, 2009).

Carpenter, M. G., *The Crusade: Its Origins and Development at Washington Court House and its Results* (Columbus, OH, 1893).

Cathcart King, D. J., 'The Taking of Le Krak des Chevaliers in 1271', in *Antiquity* 23 (1949), pp. 83–92.

Chazan, R., *European Jewry and the First Crusade* (Berkeley, CA, 1987); 'From the First Crusade to the Second: Evolving Perceptions of the Christian–Jewish Conflict', in *Jews and Christians in Twelfth-Century Europe*, eds. M. A. Singer and J. Van Engen (Notre Dame, IN, 2001), pp. 46–62.

Chibnall, M., *The Empress Mathilda* (Oxford, 1996).

Chrissis, N., 'Crusading in Romania: A Study of Byzantine–Western Relations and Attitudes', unpublished PhD thesis, Royal Holloway, University of London, 2007.

Christiansen, E., *The Northern Crusades*, second edition (Harmondsworth, 1997).

Christie, N., 'Motivating Listeners in the *Kitab al-Jihad* of Ali ibn Tahir al-Sulami (d.1106)', in *Crusades* 6 (2007), pp. 1–14.

Cobb, P. M., *Usama ibn Munqidh: Warrior Poet of the Age of Crusades* (Oxford, 2005); 'Infidel Dogs: Hunting Crusaders with Usama ibn Munqidh', in *Crusades* 6 (2007), pp. 57–68.

Cole, P. J., *The Preaching of Crusades to the Holy Land, 1095–1270* (Cambridge, MA, 1991).

Constable, G., 'The Second Crusade as Seen by Contemporaries', in *Traditio* 9 (1953), pp. 213–79. 'The Crusading Project of 1150', in

Montjoie: Studies in Crusade History in Honour of Hans Eberhard Mayer, eds. B. Z. Kedar, J. S. C. Riley-Smith and R. Hiestand (Aldershot, 1997), pp. 67–75; 'The Historiography of the Crusades', in *The Crusades from the Perspective of the Byzantine and Muslim World*, eds. A. E. Laiou and R. P. Mottahedeh (Washington, DC, 2001), pp. 1–22.

Constans, C., *Musée national du château de Versailles: Les peintures*, 3 vols. (Paris, 1995).

Cook, A. S.,'Beginning the Board in Russia', in *Journal of English and German Philology* 14 (1915), pp. 375–88.

Cooper, N., 'The Church: From Crusade to Christianity', in *Spain in Crisis: The Evolution and Decline of the Franco Regime*, ed. P. Preston (Hassocks, 1976), pp. 48–81.

Costen, M., *The Cathars and the Albigensian Crusade* (Manchester, 1997).

Crowley, R., *1453: The Holy War for Constantinople and the Clash of Islam and the West* (London, 2005).

Dajani-Shakeel, H., 'Al-Quds: Jerusalem in the Consciousness of the Counter Crusader', in *The Meeting of Two Worlds: Cultural Exchange between East and West during the Period of the Crusades*, ed. V. P. Goss (Kalamazoo, MI, 1986), pp. 201–22.

Degeorge, G., *Damascus* (Paris, 2004).

Delaney, C., 'Columbus's Ultimate Goal: Jerusalem', in *Comparative Studies in Society and History* 48 (2006), pp. 260–92.

Demurger, A., *The Last Templar: The Tragedy of Jacques de Molay, Last Grand Master of the Temple* (London, 2002).

Dennis, G. T., 'Defenders of the Christian People: Holy War in Byzantium', in *The Crusades from the Perspective of the Byzantine and Muslim World*, eds. A. E. Laiou and R. P. Mottahedeh (Washington, DC, 2001), pp. 31–9.

DeVries, K., 'Gunpowder Weapons at the Siege of Constantinople, 1453', in *War and Society in the Eastern Mediterranean, 7th–15th Centuries*, ed. Y. Lev (Leiden, 1997), pp. 343–62; 'The Failure of Philip the Good to Fulfil his Crusade Promise of 1454', in *The Medieval Crusade*, ed. S. J. Ridyard (Woodbridge, 2004), pp. 157–70.

Dickson, G., *The Children's Crusade: Medieval History, Modern Mythistory* (Basingstoke, 2007).

Di Fabio, C., *La cattedrale di Genova nel medioevo, secoli vi–xiv* (Genoa, 1998).

Du Boulay, F. R. H.,'Henry of Derby's Expeditions to Prussia, 1390–1 and 1392', in *The Reign of Richard II: Essays in Honour of May McKisack*, eds. F. R. H. Du Boulay and C. M. Barron (London, 1971), pp. 153–72.

Duggan, C., *The Force of Destiny: A History of Italy since 1796* (London, 2007).

Edbury, P. W., *The Kingdom of Cyprus and the Crusades, 1191–1374* (Cambridge, 1991); 'Propaganda and Faction in the Kingdom of Jerusalem: The Background to Hattin', in *Crusaders and Muslims in Twelfth-Century Syria*, ed. M. Shatzmiller (Leiden, 1993), pp. 173–89; *The Conquest of Jerusalem and the Third Crusade* (Aldershot, 1996).

Edbury P. W., and Rowe, J. G., *William of Tyre: Historian of the Latin East* (Cambridge, 1988).

Edgington, S. B., 'Medical Care in the Hospital of St John in Jerusalem', in *The Military Orders' Volume 2: Welfare and Warfare*, ed. H. J. Nicholson (Aldershot, 1994), pp. 27–33.

Ehrenkreutz, A., *Saladin* (Albany, NY, 1972).

Elisséeff, N., 'Les monuments de Nur ad-Din: inventaire, notes archéologiques et bibliographiques', in *Bulletin des Études Orientales* 12 (1949–51), pp. 5–43; 'The Reaction of Syrian Muslims after the Foundation of the First Latin Kingdom of Jerusalem', in *Crusaders and Muslims in Twelfth-Century Syria*, ed. M. Shatzmiller (Leiden, 1993), pp. 162–72.

Ellenblum, R., *Crusader Castles and Modern Histories* (Cambridge, 2007).

Epstein, S. A., *Genoa and the Genoese, 958–1528* (Chapel Hill, NC, 1996).

Figes, O., *A People's Tragedy: The Russian Revolution, 1891–1924* (London, 1996).

Fletcher, R. A., *The Search for El Cid* (London, 1989).

Flori, J., *Richard the Lionheart: King and Knight*, tr. J. Birell, (Edinburgh, 2006).

Folda, J., *The Art of the Crusaders in the Holy Land, 1098–1187* (Cambridge, 1995).

Fonnesberg-Schmidt, I., *The Popes and the Baltic Crusades, 1147–1254* (Leiden, 2007).

Frale, B., 'The Chinon Chart: Papal Absolution to the Last Templar, Master Jacques de Molay', in *Journal of Medieval History* 30 (2004), pp. 109–34.

France, J., *Victory in the East: A Military History* (Cambridge, 1994).

Gal, Z., 'Saladin's Dome of Victory at the Horns of Hattin', in *The Horns of Hattin*, ed. B. Z. Kedar (Jerusalem, 1992), pp. 213–15.

Ganim, J. M., 'Reversing the Crusades: Hegemony, Orientalism and Film Language in Youssef Chahine's *Saladin*', in *Race, Class and Gender in 'Medieval' Cinema*,' eds. L. T. Ramey and T. Pugh (Basingstoke, 2007), pp. 45–58.

Gaposchkin, M. C., *The Making of St Louis: Kingship, Sanctity and Crusade in the Later Middle Ages* (Ithaca, NY, 2008).

Geary, P. J., *The Myth of Nations: The Medieval Origins of Europe* (Princeton, NJ, 2002).

Gelvin, J. L., *Divided Loyalties: Nationalism and Mass Politics in Syria at the Close of Empire* (Berkeley, CA, 1998).

Gerish, D., 'Gender Theory', in *Palgrave Advances: The Crusades*, ed. H. J. Nicholson (Basingstoke, 2005), pp. 130–47.

Gilbert, V., *The Romance of the Last Crusade: With Allenby to Jerusalem* (New York, 1923).

Gillingham, J. B., 'Richard I and the Science of War', in *Richard Cœur de Lion: Kingship, Chivalry and War in the Twelfth Century* (London, 1984), pp. 211–26; *Richard I* (London, 1999).

Girouard, M., *The Return to Camelot: Chivalry and the English Gentleman* (London, 1981).

Given, J. B., *Inquisition and Medieval Society: Power, Discipline and Resistance in Languedoc* (Ithaca, NY, 1997)

Goebel, S., *The Great War and Medieval Memory: War, Remembrance and Medievalism in Britain and Germany, 1914–1940* (Cambridge, 2007).

Goffman, D., *The Ottoman Empire and Early Modern Europe* (Cambridge, 2002).

Goni Gaztambide, J., 'The Holy See and the Reconquest of the Kingdom of Granada (1479–1492)', in *Spain in the Fifteenth Century*, ed. R. Highfield (London, 1972), pp. 354–79.

Hamdani, A., 'Columbus and the Recovery of Jerusalem', in *Journal of the American Oriental Society* 99 (1979), pp. 39–48.

Hamilton, B., 'The Elephant of Christ: Reynald of Châtillon', in *Studies in Church History* 15 (Oxford, 1978), pp. 97–108; *The Medieval Inquisition* (London, 1981); 'Continental Drift: Prester John's progress through the Indies', in *Prester John, the Mongols and the Ten Lost Tribes*, eds. C. F. Beckingham and B. Hamilton (Aldershot, 1996), pp. 237–69; *The Leper King and his Heirs: Baldwin IV and the Crusader Kingdom of Jerusalem* (Cambridge, 2000).

Harris, J., *Byzantium and the Crusades* (London, 2003); *Constantinople* (London, 2006).

Heymann, F. G., 'The Crusades against the Hussites', in *History of the Crusades*, ed. K. M. Setton, 6 vols. (Madison, WI, 1969–89), 3.586–646.

Heywood, W., *A History of Pisa: Eleventh and Twelfth Centuries* (Cambridge, 1921).

Hiestand, R., 'The Papacy and the Second Crusade', in *The Second Crusade: Scope and Consequences*, eds. J. P. Phillips and M. Hoch (Manchester, 2001), pp. 32–53.

Hill, J. H. and L. L., *Raymond IV, Count of Toulouse* (Syracuse, NY, 1962).

Hillenbrand, C., 'The First Crusade: The Muslim Perspective', in *The First Crusade: Origins and Impact*, ed. J. P. Phillips (Manchester, 1997), pp. 130–41; *The Crusades: Islamic Perspectives* (Edinburgh, 1999); '"Abominable Acts": The Career of Zengi', in *The Second Crusade: Scope and Consequences*, eds. J. P. Phillips and M. Hoch (Manchester, 2001), pp. 111–32; *Turkish Myth and Muslim Symbol: The Battle of Manzikert* (Edinburgh, 2007).

Hoch, M., 'The Choice of Damascus as the Objective of the Second Crusade:

A Re-evaluation', in *Autour de la Première Croisade*, ed. M. Balard, Byzantina Sorboniensia 14 (Paris, 1996), pp. 359–69.

Hodgson, M. G. S., *The Secret Order of the Assassins: The Struggle of the Early Nizari Isma'ilis Against the Islamic World* (Philadelphia, PA, 1955).

Hodgson, N. R., *Women, Crusading and the Holy Land in Historical Narrative* (Woodbridge, 2007).

Horne, A., *Macmillan, 1894–1956, Volume 1* (London, 1988).

Housley, N., 'Pope Clement V and the Crusades of 1309–10', in *Journal of Medieval History* 8 (1982), pp. 29–42; 'Crusades against Christians: Their Origins and Early Development, c.1000–1216', in *Crusade and Settlement*, ed. P. W. Edbury (Cardiff, 1985), pp. 17–36; 'The Crusading Movement, 1274–1700', in *The Oxford Illustrated History of the Crusades* (Oxford, 1995), pp. 258–90; *Contesting the Crusades* (Oxford, 2006).

Huffman, J. P., *The Social Politics of Medieval Diplomacy: Anglo-German Relations (1066–1307)* (Ann Arbor, MI, 2000).

Imber, C., *The Ottoman Empire, 1300–1481* (Istanbul, 1990); *The Ottoman Empire, 1300–1650: The Structure of Power* (Basingstoke, 2002).

Inalcik, H., 'Mehmed the Conqueror (1432–1481) and His Time', in *Speculum* 35 (1960), pp. 408–27; *The Ottoman Empire: The Classical Age* (London, 1973).

Irwin, R., *The Middle East in the Middle Ages: The Early Mamluk Sultanate 1250–1382* (Beckenham, 1986); *The Arabian Nights: A Companion* (London, 1994); 'Islam and the Crusades, 1096–1699', in *The Oxford Illustrated History of the Crusades*, ed. J. S. C. Riley-Smith (Oxford, 1995), pp. 211–57; 'Usamah ibn Munqidh: An Arab-Syrian Gentleman at the Time of the Crusades Reconsidered', in *The Crusades and Their Sources: Essays Presented to Bernard Hamilton*, eds. J. France and W. G. Zajac (Aldershot, 1998), pp. 71–87; *For Lust of Knowing: The Orientalists and their Enemies* (London, 2006).

Jackson, P., 'The Crisis in the Holy Land in 1260', in *English Historical Review* 95 (1980), pp. 481–513; *The Mongols and the West, 1221–1410* (Harlow, 2005).

Jacoby, D., 'Conrad of Montferrat and the Kingdom of Jerusalem, 1187–92', in *Atti del Congresso internazionale 'Dai feudi monferrine e dal Piemonte ai nuovi mondi oltre gli Oceani', Alessandria, 2–6 aprile 1990*, Biblioteca della Società di storia arte e archeologia per le province di Alessandria e Asti, 27 (Alessandria, 1993), pp. 187–238; 'New Venetian Evidence on Crusader Acre', in *The Experience of Crusading*, eds. P. W. Edbury and J. P. Phillips, 2 vols. (Cambridge, 2003), 2.240–56.

Jansen, J. J. G., *The Neglected Duty: The Creed of Sadat's Assassins and the Islamic Resurgence in the Middle East* (New York, 1986).

Jaspert, N., 'Capta est Dertosa: clavis Christianorum. Tortosa and the Crusades', in *The Second Crusade: Scope and Consequences*, eds. J. P. Phillips and M. Hoch (Manchester, 2001), pp. 90–110; 'Zwei unbekannte Hilfsersuchen des Patriarchen Eraclius vor dem Fall Jerusalems (1187)', in *Deutsches Archiv* 60 (2005), pp. 483–516.

Jenkins, R., *Gladstone* (London, 1995).

Jensen, K. V., 'Denmark and the Second Crusade: the Formation of a Crusader State?', in *The Second Crusade: Scope and Consequences*, eds. J. P. Phillips and M. Hoch (Manchester, 2001), pp. 164–79.

Johns, C. N., *Pilgrims' Castle (Atlit), David's Tower (Jerusalem) and Qal'at ar-Rabad (Ajlun)* (Aldershot, 1997).

Johns, J., *Arabic Administration in Norman Sicily: The Royal Diwan* (Cambridge, 2002).

Johnson, E. N., 'The Crusades of Frederick Barbarossa and Henry VI', in *A History of the Crusades*, ed. K. M. Setton, 6 vols. (Wisconsin, 1969–89), 2.87–122.

Johnson, J. T., *The Holy War Idea in Western and Islamic Traditions* (Pennsylvania, 1997).

Jordan, W. C., *Louis IX and the Challenge of the Crusade* (Princeton, NJ, 1979).

Jotischky, A., 'Manuel Comnenus and the Reunion of the Churches: The Evidence of the Conciliar Mosaics in the Church of the Nativity in Bethlehem', in *Levant* 26 (1994), pp. 207–23.

de Jubainville, H., *Histoire des ducs et des comtes de Champagne*, 8 vols. (Paris, 1859–69).

Jubb., M., *The Legend of Saladin in Western Literature and Historiography* (Lewiston, NY, 2000).

Kedar, B. Z., 'The General Tax of 1183 in the Crusader Kingdom of Jerusalem', in *English Historical Review* 89 (1974), pp. 339–45; 'The Patriarch Heraclius', in *Outremer: Studies in the History of the Crusading Kingdom of Jerusalem*, eds. B. Z. Kedar, H. E. Mayer and R. C. Smail (Jerusalem, 1982), pp. 177–204; 'The Battle of Hattin Revisted', in *The Horns of Hattin*, ed. B. Z. Kedar (Jerusalem, 1992), pp. 190–207; 'A Twelfth Century Description of the Jerusalem Hospital', in *The Military Orders Volume 2: Welfare and Warfare*, ed. H. J. Nicholson (Aldershot, 1994), pp. 3–26; 'The Jerusalem Massacre of July 1099 in the Western Historiography of the Crusades', in *Crusades* 3 (2004), pp. 15–76.

Keen, M., 'Chaucer's Knight, the English Aristocracy and the Crusade', in *English Court Culture in the Later Middle Ages*, eds. V. J. Scattergood and J. W. Sherborne (London, 1983) pp. 45–61; *Chivalry* (London, 1984).

Kennan, E., 'Innocent III and the First Political Crusade', in *Traditio* 27 (1971), pp. 231–49.

Kennedy, H., *Muslim Spain and Portugal: A Political History of al-Andalus* (Harlow, 1996).

Knobler, A., 'Holy Wars, Empires, and the Portability of the Past: The Modern

Uses of Medieval Crusades', in *Comparative Studies in Society and History* 48 (2006), pp. 293–325.

Kühnel, B., *Crusader Art of the Twelfth Century: A Geographical, an Historical, or an Art-Historical Notion?* (Berlin, 1994).

Lambert, M., *Medieval Heresy*, third edition (Oxford, 2002).

Laszlo, V., 'Some Remarks on Recent Historiography of the Crusade of Nicopolis (1396)', in *The Crusades and the Military Orders: Expanding the Frontiers of Medieval Latin Christianity*, ed. Z. Hunyadi and J. Laszlovsky (Budapest, 2001), pp. 223–30.

Le Goff, J., *Saint Louis*, tr. G. E. Gollrad (Notre Dame, IN, 2009).

Leopold, A., *How to Recover the Holy Land: The Crusade Proposals of the Late Thirteenth and Early Fourteenth Centuries* (Aldershot, 2000).

Lev, Y., *Saladin in Egypt* (Leiden, 1999).

Lilie, R.-J., *Byzantium and the Crusader States, 1096–1204*, trs. J. C. Morris and J. E. Ridings (Oxford, 1993).

Liss, P. K., *Isabel the Queen* (Oxford, 1992).

Little, D. P., 'The Fall of Akka in 690/1291: The Muslim Version', in *Studies in Islamic History and Civilisation in Honour of Professor David Ayalon*, ed. M. Sharon (Jerusalem and Leiden, 1986), pp. 159–81.

Lloyd, S. D., *English Society and the Crusade, 1216–1307* (Oxford, 1988).

Lock, P., *The Franks in the Aegean, 1204–1500* (Harlow, 1995).

Longnon, J., *Les Compagnons de Villehardouin: Recherches sur les croisés de la quatrième croisade* (Geneva, 1978).

LoPrete, K., 'Adela of Blois: Familial Alliances and Female Lordships', in *Aristocratic Women in Medieval France*, ed. T. Evergates (Philadelphia, PA, 1999), pp. 7–43.

Lotter, K., 'The Crusade Idea and the Conquest of the Region East of the Elbe', in *Medieval Frontier Societies*, eds. R. Bartlett and A. Mackay (Oxford, 1989), pp. 267–85.

Lower, M., *The Barons' Crusade: A Call to Arms and its Consequences* (Philadelphia, PA, 2005).

Lyons, M. C., 'The *Sirat Baybars*', in *Orientalia Hispanica*, ed. F. Pareja Casanas (Leiden, 1974), pp. 490–503; 'The Crusading Stratum in the Arabic Hero Cycles', in *Crusaders and Muslims in Twelfth Century Syria*, ed. M. Shatzmiller (Leiden, 1993), pp. 147–61; *The Arabic Epic: Heroic and Oral Story-Telling*, 3 vols. (Cambridge, 1995).

Lyons M. C. and Jackson, D. E. P., *Saladin: The Politics of the Holy War* (Cambridge, 1982).

MacEvitt, C., *The Crusades and the Christian World of the East: Rough Tolerance* (Philadelphia, PA, 2008).

Madden, T. F., *Enrico Dandolo and the Rise of Venice* (Baltimore, MD, 2003);

(ed.), *The Fourth Crusade: Events, Aftermath and Perceptions* (Aldershot, 2008).

Maier, C., 'Mass, the Eucharist and the Cross: Innocent III and the Relocation of the Crusade', *Pope Innocent III and His World*, ed. J. C. Moore (Aldershot, 1999), pp. 351–60.

Mallett, A., 'A Trip Down the Red Sea with Reynald of Châtillon', in *Journal of the Royal Asiatic Society* 18 (2008), pp. 141–53.

Ma'oz, M., *Asad: The Sphinx of Damascus – A Political Biography* (New York, 1988).

Marrin, A., *The Last Crusade: The Church of England in the First World War* (Durham, NC, 1974).

Marshall, C. J., *Warfare in the Latin East, 1191–1291* (Cambridge, 1992).

Marvin, L. W., *The Occitan War: A Military and Political History of the Albigensian Crusade, 1209–1218* (Cambridge, 2008).

Mayer, H. E., 'Studies in the History of Queen Melisende of Jerusalem', in *Dumbarton Oaks Papers* 26 (1972), pp. 95–182; 'Angevins *versus* Normans: The New Men of King Fulk of Jerusalem', in *Proceedings of the American Philosophical Society* 133 (1989), pp. 1–25; *Varia Antiochena: Studien zum Kreuzfahrerfürstentum Antiochia im 12. und frühen 13. Jahrhundert* (Hanover, 1993).

Melville, C. P. and Lyons, M. C., 'Saladin's Hattin Letter', in *The Horns of Hattin*, ed. B. Z. Kedar (Jerusalem, 1992), pp. 208–12.

Menache, S., *Clement V* (Cambridge, 1998); 'The Last Master of the Temple: James of Molay', in *Knighthoods of Christ: Essays on the History of the Crusades and the Knights Templar, Presented to Malcolm Barber*, ed. N. Housley (Aldershot, 2007), pp. 229–40.

Metcalf, D. M., *Coinage of the Crusades and the Latin East*, second edition (London, 1995).

Michaud, F., *Histoire des croisades*, fourth edition, 6 vols. (Paris, 1825–9).

Mitchell, P. D., 'An Evaluation of the Leprosy of King Baldwin IV of Jerusalem in the Context of the Medieval World', in B. Hamilton, *The Leper King and his Heirs: Baldwin IV and the Crusader Kingdom of Jerusalem*, pp. 245–58; *Medicine in the Crusades: Warfare, Wounds and the Medieval Surgeon* (Cambridge, 2004).

Möhring, H., *Saladin: The Sultan and His Times*, tr. D. S. Bachrach (Baltimore, MD, 2008).

Moore, J. C., *Pope Innocent III (1160/61–1216): To Root up and to Plant* (Leiden, 2003).

Moore, R. I., *The Birth of Popular Heresy* (London, 1975); *The Formation of a Persecuting Society*, second edition (Oxford, 2007).

Morgan, D. O., *The Mongols*, second edition (Oxford, 2007).

Mortimer, I., *The Fears of Henry IV: The Life of England's Self-Made King* (London, 2007).

Morton, N. E., *Teutonic Knights in the Holy Land* (Woodbridge, 2009).

Mourad, S. A. and Lindsay, J. E., 'Rescuing Syria from the Infidels: The

Contribution of Ibn Asakir of Damascus to the Jihad Campaign of Sultan Nur ad-Din', in *Crusades* 6 (2007), pp. 37–56.

Munholland, K., 'Michaud's *History of the Crusades* and the French Crusade in Algeria under Louis-Philippe', in *The Popularisation of Images: Visual Culture under the July Monarchy*, eds. P. ten-Doesschate Chu and G. P. Weisberg (Princeton, 1994), pp. 144–65.

Murray, A. V., *The Crusader Kingdom of Jerusalem: A Dynastic History, 1099–1125* (Oxford, 2000); 'Money and Logistics in the Forces of the First Crusade: Coinage, Bullion, Service, and Supply, 1096–1099', in *Logistics of Warfare in the Age of the Crusades*, ed. J. H. Pryor (Aldershot, 2006), pp. 229–50.

Netton, I. R., 'Ibn Jubayr: Penitent Pilgrim and Observant Traveller', in *Seek Knowledge: Thought and Travel in the House of Islam* (Richmond, 1996), pp. 95–102.

Nicolle, D., *Constantinople 1453* (Oxford, 2000).

O'Callaghan, J. F., *Reconquest and Crusade in Medieval Spain* (Philadelphia, PA, 2003).

O'Meara, C. F., *The Iconography of the Façade of Saint-Gilles-du-Gard* (New York, 1977).

Özcan, A., *Pan-Islamism: Indian Muslims, the Ottomans and Britain (1877–1924)* (Leiden, 1997).

Payne, S. G.,*The Franco Regime, 1936–1975* (London, 2000).

Pegg, M. G., *A Most Holy War: The Albigensian Crusade and the Battle for Christendom* (Oxford, 2008).

Perry, M., *The Jarrow Crusade: Protest and Legend* (Sunderland, 2005).

Peters, R., *Jihad in Classical and Modern Islam* (Princeton, NJ, 1996).

Phillips, J. P., *Defenders of the Holy Land: Relations between the Latin East and the West, 1119–1187* (Oxford, 1996); 'Ideas of Crusade and Holy War in *De expugnatione Lyxbonensi (The Conquest of Lisbon)*', in *The Holy Land, Holy Lands and Christian History*, ed. R. N. Swanson, *Studies in Church History* 36 (2000), pp. 123–41; 'Why a Crusade will lead to a Jihad', *Independent* (18 September 2001); *The Fourth Crusade and the Sack of Constantinople* (London, 2004); *The Second Crusade: Extending the Frontiers of Christendom* (London, 2007).

Piana, M., *Burgen und Städte der Kreuzzugszeit* (Petersberg, 2008).

Pic, P., *Syrie et Palestine* (Paris, 1924).

Powell, J. M., *Anatomy of a Crusade, 1213–1221* (Philadelphia, PA, 1986).

Prawer, J., *The Latin Kingdom of Jerusalem: European Colonialism in the Middle Ages* (London, 1972).

Preston, P., *Franco: A Biography* (London, 1993).

Pryor, J. H., *Geography, Technology and War: Studies in the Maritime History of the Mediterranean, 649–1571* (Cambridge, 1988); 'The Crusade of Emperor Frederick II, 1220–1229: The Implications of the Maritime Evidence', in *The American Neptune* 52 (1992), pp. 113–32.

Purkis, W. J., *Crusading Spirituality in the Holy Land and Iberia, c.1095–c.1187* (Woodbridge, 2008).

Queller, D. E. and Madden, T. F., 'Some Further Arguments in Defence of the Venetians on the Fourth Crusade', in *Byzantion* 62 (1992), pp. 433–73; *The Fourth Crusade: The Conquest of Constantinople*, second edition (Philadelphia, PA, 1997).

Reeve, M., 'The Painted Chamber at Westminster, Edward I, and the Crusade', in *Viator* 37 (2006), pp. 189–221.

Reilly, B. F., *The Kingdom of León-Castilla under Queen Urraca, 1109–1126* (Princeton, NJ, 1982).

Rejwan, N., *Nasserist Ideology: Its Exponents and Critics* (Jerusalem, 1974).

Reuter, T., 'The non-crusade of 1149–50', in *The Second Crusade: Scope and Consequences*, eds. J. P. Phillips and M. Hoch (Manchester, 2001), pp. 150–63.

Richard, J., 'Aux origines d'un grand lignage: des Paladii Renaud de Châtillon', in *Media in Francia: Recueil de mélanges offerts à Karl F. Werner* (Paris, 1989), pp. 409–18; *Saint Louis: Crusader King of France*, ed. S. Lloyd, tr. J. Birell (Cambridge, 1992).

Richards, D. S., 'The Early Life of Saladin', *Islamic Quarterly* 17 (1973), pp. 140–59; 'Imad al-Din al-Isfahani: Administrator, Litterateur and Historian', in *Crusaders and Muslims in Twelfth-Century Syria*, ed. M. Shatzmiller (Leiden, 1993), pp. 133–46.

Riley-Smith, J. S. C., *The First Crusade and the Idea of Crusading* (London, 1986); 'King Fulk of Jerusalem and "the Sultan of Babylon"', in *Montjoie: Studies in Crusade History in Honour of Hans Eberhard Mayer*, eds. B. Z. Kedar, J. S. C. Riley-Smith and R. Hiestand (Aldershot, 1997), pp. 55–66; *The First Crusaders, 1095–1131* (Cambridge, 1999); *What were the Crusades?*, third edition (Basingstoke, 2002); 'Islam and the Crusades in History', in *Crusades* 2 (2003), pp. 151–67; 'Were the Templars Guilty?', in *The Medieval Crusade*, ed. S. Ridyard (Woodbridge, 2004), pp. 107–24; 'The Structures of the Orders of the Temple and the Hospital in *c.*1291', in *The Medieval Crusade*, ed. S. Ridyard (Woodbridge, 2004), pp. 125–44; *The Crusades, Christianity and Islam* (New York, 2008).

Roach, A. P., *The Devil's World: Heresy and Society 1100–1300* (Harlow, 2005).

Robinson, F. C. R., 'Other-Worldly and This-Worldly Islam and the Islamic Revival. A Memorial Lecture for Wilfred Cantwell Smith', in *Journal of the Royal Asiatic Society, Series 3* (2004), pp. 47–58.

Roche, J., 'Conrad III and the Second Crusade: Retreat from Dorylaion?', in *Crusades* 5 (2006), pp. 85–94.

Röhl, J. C. G., *Wilhelm II: The Kaiser's Personal Monarchy, 1888–1900* (Cambridge, 2004).

Roskell, J. S., 'Sir Richard de Waldegrave of Bures Saint Mary, Speaker in the Parliament of 1381–82', in *Proceedings of the Suffolk Institute of Archaeology* 27 (1957), pp. 154–75.

Runciman, S., *A History of the Crusades*, 3 vols. (Cambridge, 1951–4); *The Fall of Constantinople, 1453* (Cambridge, 1965).

Russell, F. H., *The Just War in the Middle Ages* (Cambridge, 1975).

Sanchez, J. M., *The Spanish Civil War as a Religious Tragedy* (Notre Dame, IN, 1987).

Segal, J. B., *Edessa: The Blessed City* (Oxford, 1970).

Schein, S., '*Gesta Dei per Mongolos* 1300. The Genesis of a Non-Event', in *English Historical Review* 94 (1979), pp. 805–19; *Fideles Crucis: The Papacy, the West, and the Recovery of the Holy Land, 1274–1314* (Oxford, 1991).

Shannon, R. T., *Gladstone and the Bulgarian Agitation 1876*, second edition (Hassocks, 1975).

Shepard, J., 'Cross-Purposes: Alexius Comnenus and the First Crusade', in *The First Crusade: Origins and Impact*, ed. J. P. Phillips (Manchester, 1997), pp. 107–29.

Siberry, E., 'Images of the Crusades in the Nineteenth and Twentieth Centuries', in *The Oxford Illustrated History of the Crusades*, ed. J. S. C. Riley-Smith (Oxford, 1995), pp. 385–9; *The New Crusaders: Images of the Crusades in the Nineteenth and Early Twentieth Centuries* (Aldershot, 2000).

Singer, L. (ed.), *The Minbar of Saladin* (London, 2008).

Sivan, E., 'La génèse de la contre-croisade: un traité damasquin du début du XIIe siècle', in *Journal Asiatique* 254 (1966), pp. 197–224; 'The Crusades Described by Modern Arab Historiography', in *Asian and African Studies* 8 (1972), pp. 109–49.

Smith, C., *Crusading in the Age of Joinville* (Aldershot, 2006).

Smith, D. J., '"Soli Hispani?" Innocent III and Las Navas de Tolosa', in *Hispania Sacra* 51 (1999), pp. 487–513.

Sturtevant, P. B., 'SaladiNasser: Nasser's Political Crusade in *El Naser Salah Ad-Din*', in *Hollywood in the Holy Land: Essays on Film Depictions of the Crusades and Christian–Muslim Clashes*, eds. N. Haydock and E. L. Risden (Jefferson, NC, 2009), pp. 123–46.

Sumption, J., *The Albigensian Crusade* (London, 1978).

Tabbaa, Y., 'Propagation of Jihad under Nur al-Din (1146–1174)', in *The Meeting of Two Worlds: Cultural Exchange between East and West during the Period of the Crusades*, ed. V. P. Goss (Kalamazoo, MI, 1986), pp. 223–40.

Talmon-Heller, D., *Islamic Piety in Medieval Syria: Mosques, Cemeteries and Sermons under the Zangids and Ayyubids (1146–1260)* (Leiden, 2007).

Thorau, P., *The Lion of Egypt: Sultan Baybars I and the Near East in the Thirteenth Century* (Harlow, 1992).

Throop, P., *Criticism of the Crusade: A Study of Public Opinion and Crusade Propaganda* (Amsterdam, 1940).

Tolan, J. V., *Saint Francis and the Sultan: The Curious History of a Christian–Muslim Encounter* (Oxford, 2009).

Turner, R. V. and Heiser, R. R., *The Reign of Richard the Lionheart: Ruler of the Angevin Empire, 1189–99* (Harlow, 2000).

Tyerman, C. J., *England and the Crusades, 1095–1588* (Chicago, 1988); *God's War: A New History of the Crusades* (London, 2006).

Urban, W., *The Baltic Crusade*, second edition (Chicago, IL, 1994).

Van Cleve, T. C., *The Emperor Frederick II of Hohenstaufen: Immutator Mundi* (Oxford, 1972).

Vaughan, R., *Philip the Good: The Apogee of Burgundy* (London, 1970).

Vincent, M., *Catholicism in the Second Spanish Republic: Religion and Politics in Salamanca, 1930–1936* (Oxford, 1996); 'The Martyrs and the Saints: Masculinity and the Construction of the Francoist Crusade', in *History Workshop Journal* 47 (1999), pp. 69–98.

Vincent, N., *The Holy Blood: King Henry III and the Westminster Blood Relic* (Cambridge, 2001).

Wakefield, W. L., *Heresy, Crusade and Inquisition in Southern France, 1100–1250* (London, 1974).

Ward, B., *Miracles and the Medieval Mind*, second edition (Aldershot, 1987).

Weiler, B., 'Gregory IX, Frederick II and the Liberation of the Holy Land', in *Holy Land and Holy Lands*, ed. R. L. Swanson, *Studies in Church History* 36 (2000), pp. 192–206.

Weiss, D., *Art and Crusade in the Age of St Louis* (Cambridge, 1998).

Williams, J. B., 'The Making of a Crusade: The Genoese anti-Muslim Attacks in Spain, 1146–1148', in *Journal of Medieval History* 23 (1997), pp. 29–53.

Yewdale, R. B., *Bohemond I, Prince of Antioch* (Princeton, NJ, 1924).

Index